THEY GAVE ME A SEAFIRE

DEDICATION

At all costs we must draw the flower of our youth into piloting of aeroplanes.
Winston Churchill, House of Commons, 28 July, 1936.

This book is dedicated to the flower of our youth who did not return, in World War II.

THEY GAVE ME A
SEAFIRE

Commander
R. 'MIKE' CROSLEY,
DSC, RN.

An Airlife
CLASSIC

First published in the UK in 1986
by Airlife Publishing Ltd
This edition published 2001

British Library Cataloguing in Publication Data
  A catalogue record for this book
  is available from the British Library

ISBN 1 84037 245 1

Printed in England by St Edmundsbury Press Ltd, Bury St Edmunds, Suffolk

Airlife Publishing Ltd

101 Longden Road, Shrewsbury, SY3 9EB, England
E-mail: airlife@airlifebooks.com
Website: www.airlifebooks.com

Contents

Appendices

Bibliography

Churchill as Warlord, Ronald Lewin, (B. T. Batsford).
Air Power at Sea, John Winton, (Peter Davies).
Aircraft and Sea Power, V/A Sir Arthur Hezlet, (Peter Davies).
The Battle of the Atlantic, Donald Macintyre, (Severn House).
Strikes from the Sea, Robert Jackson, (Arthur Barker).
Pictorial History of FAA, John Rawlings, (Ian Allan).
Carrier Operations of WW II, J. D. Brown, (Ian Allan).
The FAA History, Lt/Cdr J. Waterman RD, RNR, (Art Press Ltd.).
A Sailor's Odyssey, Viscount Cunningham of Hyndhope, (Hutchinson).
Action this Day, Admiral of the Fleet, Sir Philip Vian GCB, KBE, DSO,
    (Frederick Muller Ltd.).
Wings on my Sleeve, Captain Eric Brown OBE, DSC, AFC, RN Rtd, (Airlife).
A Most Secret Place, Brian Johnson, (Janes).
Second World War, Winston Churchill, (Cassells).
Seafire, David Brown, (Ian Allan).
World Crisis, Winston Churchill, (New English).
'Pedestal', Peter Smith, (William Kimber).
The Arctic Convoys, A. B. B. Schofield, (MacDonald James).
Menace – Life and Death of Tirpitz, Ludovic Kennedy, (Sidgwick and Jackson).
Operation 'Torch', Vincent Jones, (Pan/Ballantyne).
Find, Fix and Strike, John Winton, (Batsford Books).
Battleship, Middlebrook and Mahoney, (Allen Lane).
Fly Navy, Brian Johnson, (David & Charles).
Carrier Fighters, David Brown, (MacDonald, Newton Abbot).
The Forgotten Fleet, John Winton, (Michael Joseph).
The Art of Leadership, Captain S. W. Roskill, (Collins).
Victory at Sea, Lt/Cdr P. K. Kemp, (Muller).
Doenitz, Peter Padfield, (Gollancz).
Air Defence of Great Britain, John R. Bushby, (Ian Allan).
The Strike Wing, Roy Conyers Nesbit, (William Kimber).
Churchill at War, Patrick Cosgrave, (Collins).
Fighter Pilot, Chaz Bowyer, (Dent).
Monty, Nigel Hamilton, (Coronet, Hodder and Stoughton).

Acknowledgments

The book is intended to be a personal narrative of a Fleet Air Arm fighter pilot in World War II, with enough technical and strategic background to place the various incidents in perspective and to explain them more fully.

The book would neither have been written nor published without the help and advice of many people. Amongst them I would like to thank: Mr. Stuart Jewers, DSC, FSMC; Mr. Peter Arkell, Mr. Dennis Kirby, MVO, MBE; Mr. John Joly; Lt/Cdr Jack Sisley; Lt/Cdr George Willcocks, DSC, VRD; Mr. Norman Goodfellow, DSC; Lt/Cdr Arthur Keepe; Sir Edward Singleton; Lt/Cdr Geoffrey Russell-Jones, DSC; Mr. Mike Banyard; Mr. Sam Mearns, DSC; Mr. Kenneth Percival; Mr. Ivan Henson; Mr. David Brown; and, in particular, Captain Nigel Hallett, DSC; Lt/Cdr Jack Waterman, RD of the Fleet Air Arm Officers' Association and those at the Fleet Air Arm Museum, Yeovilton: the Director, Cdr Dennis White, OBE, the kind advice of Mr. Vernon Hillier, FRSA, and the Curator, Mr. Graham Mottram, MA, C Eng, whose Secretary, Mrs. Barbara Broadwater did much of the typing, and Mrs. Denese Adams who helped so much.

A Fleet Air Arm Song

They say in the RAF that a landing's OK
If the pilot gets out and can still walk away.
But in the Fleet Air Arm the prospect is grim,
The landing's piss poor if the pilot can't swim.
Chorus:
Cracking show. I'm alive!
But I've still got to render my A25*.

They gave me a Seafire to beat up the Fleet,
I polished off *Nelson* and *Rodney* a treat,
But forgot the high masts that stick out from *Formid*
And a seat in the Goofers was worth fifty quid.
Chorus, etc.

*Form A25 is rendered in quadruplicate to higher authorities, by the Squadron concerned, to establish the cause of the accident.

Chapter 1
Mediterranean Incident – August 1942

My soup plate flew up and hit me in the face — and all the lights went out. A second later the reason burst upon my senses in three or four shattering explosions.

Every one of us in the wardroom of *Eagle* was lifted off our seats and thrown onto the floor.

There was a small, grey, shaft of light coming from one of the scuttles. By its light I could see shadows leaping over the tables and making for the door.

Perhaps it was only some idiot Stringbag (Swordfish) pilot dropping his depthcharges too near the ship. But the ship was already taking on a list and no depthcharge from a Stringbag could do that. We had obviously been hit by something big. Anyway, lunch was off for the moment and I joined the crush outside the wardroom in the darkness of the wardroom flat. By the light of the emergency lanterns which had switched on automatically when the power had failed, I searched amongst the lifejackets and Mae Wests hanging up, trying to remember where I had left mine. The slope of the deck was increasing by the second so I gave up looking and joined the surge aft towards the quarterdeck.

Smoke was coming up from the open hatchways as we passed them. The smoke smelt strongly of cordite and it was as black as hell. We must have had two or three torpedoes in the ship's engine rooms. The old girl was obviously not going to last long.

As we shuffled along in silence we could hear dreadful sounds coming from below, crashes and shouts as the ship leaned over more and more. Out onto the quarterdeck and into the blessed daylight, I had time to think. I remembered where I had put my Mae West. It was in the pilots' crewroom, a small caboose on the top deck of the Island between the funnels — six or seven decks up and miles away. I looked up to the forward ladders leading from the quarterdeck. They were jammed solid with men coming down and were totally impassable. How on earth was I going to get there in time?

On Board the German U-boat U73.

Kapitän Leutnant Rosenbaum had not had much luck in the Mediterranean — or anywhere else — so far, in the war. He had commanded *U73* for over a year and his patrols had ranged from Greenland in the north to Freetown in the south, but nothing large had come his way.

Four months previously he had been chosen with 15 others to go across the Atlantic to the American coast and join in the fun there. He was just beginning to enjoy the thought of easy pickings and the chance to raise the spirits of his crew, when he was told to reverse course and make for the Mediterranean. He and his crew had always considered that the Med belonged to the Italians. It was Mare Nostrum, so they kept saying. They had 70 boats there, somewhere; but he had yet to hear of anything that they had done. Now, he supposed, the German Navy would have to help, just as Rommel had had to help their ridiculous army in North Africa. No sooner had he arrived with his boat at La Spezia on the north-west coast of Italy than he was ordered to run some urgent tank spares to Tobruk for Rommel. He duly unloaded these, and while he was feeling his way out of the harbour the following early morning, in very shallow water, he happened to look up just in time to see what looked like an old-fashioned biplane flying straight towards him. He could not dive in the shallow water, and in spite of his two machine gunners opening fire on it, it came steadily on and dropped a bomb or a depth charge right alongside the stern. It then flew off out to sea, leaving Rosenbaum to assess the damage. The diving gear aft had been bent out of all recognition. So he would have to run on the surface for the entire thousand mile journey back to La Spezia. This was something which no submarine had ever done before without being spotted, for the sky was relatively crowded with British aircraft in the Mediterranean, compared with what it was like anywhere else.

Mercifully, he made the five-day voyage without sighting any — a minor miracle — and entered La Spezia without further mishap. The boat took three months to repair. The crew had to eat more Italian food and, more disappointing still, were not allowed any leave back to Germany. By August, *U73* was back at sea again. Rosenbaum was assigned to a patrol area about 80 miles north of Algiers. This was a fruitful area as it was smack in the middle of the British convoy route from Gibraltar to Malta. Last year, in November, the largest and best British carrier, *Ark Royal,* had gone down with just a single torpedo from *U81* in the same area. The new, silent and wakeless electric torpedo had also surprised *Galatea* — a large cruiser — and she had turned over and sunk in two minutes, with a single hit as well. Apparently, none of these boats had been detected by the screen of British destroyers, either before or after the attack. He told his crew in *U73* that they had every chance of glory. All they needed was a small share of good luck.

Every night, *U73* surfaced to receive any special orders from La Spezia, by radio. On the night of 10 August Rosenbaum was told that the British were going to try to run a large convoy through the Gibraltar Straits to Malta. It was vital that this convoy should not get through with its 14 merchant ships, but, Admiral Kreish said, *U73*'s priority targets must be the aircraft carriers. Until they were out of the way, the German Air Force could not get at the merchant ships. He must not waste torpedoes on merchant ships at the start of the convoy, but hit the carriers.

Next morning, it all seemed too good to be true, for the hydrophone crew heard ships propeller noises approaching from the west. Fifteen minutes later and with *U73* making her best speed submerged towards the noise, Rosenbaum raised the periscope as high as he dared. He could make out the masts of a destroyer about three miles to the north-west. Almost at the same time a carrier appeared, almost bow-on, a thrilling sight for the U-boat commander.

At her full eight knots under water, U73 came closer to the path of the two ships. Her skipper could now see six or seven destroyers ahead of the carrier in some sort of formation. The whole lot seemed to be in a continual alteration of course — a zigzag with at least 40 degrees change of course each time.

Rosenbaum swung the periscope lens round in a complete circle, using the wide-angle lens. He saw a forest of masts, some of which were tripod masts and must surely belong to battleships. So this must be the convoy. There were smiles amongst the officers and men in the control room that morning. Rosenbaum slowed to three knots — *U73*'s best silent speed. This was only just in time, for he had to duck quickly as two destroyers passed right overhead, their propeller noises deafening in his earphones.

Raising the periscope once more, he could now see a cruiser with a large radar aerial leading the nearest line of merchant ships. They were all within easy firing range and a spread salvo from all tubes would sink the lot. They would not even see them coming.

Sixty more seconds and the carrier — which Rosenbaum had identified as *Eagle* — came so close that it filled the viewfinder of the periscope camera. He could see fighters — and one old biplane — on her deck. One of the fighters had its engine running, but he could not see a single aircraft in the air.

He ordered 20 feet as the depth setting for the bow torpedoes, and a point aim, so that all four would hit where they hurt most — in the engine rooms. With the tip of the periscope just breaking surface occasionally, he hoped that the sailors he could see on *Eagle*'s deck would not look his way and spot the telltale bow wave. *Eagle* made a fine sight, he thought. He could even hear the rumble of her bow wave as she divided the water in a high, white curve, only a few hundred yards away.

U73 fired all four bow tubes together at a range of less than 300 yards. With *Eagle* beam-on and at this point-blank range, *U73* could not miss. The time was 1315.

Aboard *Eagle*, at 1317, no one had yet thought of jumping over the side from the quarterdeck. Even with dead engines, *Eagle*'s 21,000 tons momentum still took her through the water at about four knots, two minutes after being hit. If anyone dived over now, they would fall astern and not be rescued. In any case I had no Mae West yet.

It was hopeless trying to get to the Island by the normal route. There was only one way. I had used it once before. This was the batsman's escape route from the flight deck to the main deck, a vertical distance of about 50 feet. It was a pipeshaft, about three feet in diameter, with a rusty ladder fixed inside. It was entirely dark inside and as its lower level on the port side was by now under water and at about 40 degrees from the vertical, once I had started up the ladder, there would be no turning back. Just as I bent down to get into the tube, with my feet already in the water on the low side of the heeling ship, I looked above me. I could see an officer trying to organise the launching of the ship's whaler. As the edge of the flight deck, above the whaler's davits, was just about to touch the water, I thought that he would have to be fairly quick. Still, it was none of my business and I started going up.

At the top of the tube and in the sunlight once more I spoke to 'Boris' Morris, one of the Swordfish pilots. He warned me not to go onto the flight deck as he had just been missed by a passing Hurricane as it slid off the deck into the nets, just alongside. There it was, a lovely Hurricane, caught in the deck-edge netting like some huge fly and about to crash on the bodies in the sea below. But, of course, Boris was a wise virgin and already had his Mae West on and inflated. I could not stop, and continued onto the flight deck, regardless of the other four or five Hurricanes perched precariously above me. I pulled myself up the 45-degree heeling deck by the arrester wires, hand over hand.

The next ladder to climb was from the flight deck level to the first deck in the Island itself. I could get into the aft doorway all right, but the ladder was, of course, jammed with bods coming down. The only way to get up was to climb up their backs faster than they were coming down.

I found my Mae West exactly where I had so stupidly left it, hanging up alongside my flying gear in the Ready Room. What an honest lot the crew of *Eagle* are, I thought.

The next thing to think about was how to get into the water. Many already seemed to be taking flying leaps, and some were landing on hard objects in the water — including their messmates — and were getting hurt. The best way seemed to be by climbing down the ship's side.

I took off my watch and put it above highwater mark in a pocket in my Mae West and climbed up the 45 degree sloping deck towards the door of the Ready Room. As I stood up by the doorway, I saw my HMV portable clockwork gramophone lying upside-down on the deck, surrounded with broken records. Outside again, I helped myself to some huge Admiralty Pattern gunnery-spotting binoculars by way of compensation, and placed the strap around my neck. I climbed over the rail opposite one of the funnels — the guys of which were bar-taut and obviously taking a strain for which they had not been designed — and studied the scene some 70 feet below. I could feel, as I waited, that the old ship was still slowly laying down on her port side exposing more and more of her weedy bottom. The angle of descent down her starboard topside was about the same as a barn roof. As I had often climbed down barn roofs at home, I thought I could manage *Eagle's*

I had just stopped with my feet on the huge anti-torpedo blister, making up my mind to jump in, when there was a slithering sound from above and a bod hurtled past, taking me with him. The binoculars hit me in the face as I hit the water and they disappeared. I couldn't have swum with them anyway.

There were about 50 sailors in the water round me. Many were singing, perhaps with relief at getting away and into the pleasantly warm Mediterranean water. But I could still hear the screams and the pitiful shouts of men's voices echoing up the engine room ventilators as they lay trapped below in darkness. I thanked God, as all aviators did on that day in *Eagle*, that we could do our job in the sunlight and the fresh air and not in the bowels of the ship, 30 feet below the waterline.

Next the Commander came by. He had his brass hat straight and firmly on his head. He made a fine bow-wave. He had time to advise us to stop singing, as we "would need our breath later". We hoped we wouldn't need it all that badly as we expected to get rescued fairly soon. The destroyers, however, all seemed to be busy doing something else and some were dropping depth charges far too near for comfort.

Just before I fell in I had caught sight of the Captain's motor boat — the pride of the Ship's Boats Officer — with only a few feet of bow above water. 'Spike' King-Joyce, my flight leader, was balanced on top. He had shouted to me to come on board and do a bit of fishing — or something like that. Feeling a bit lonely, I had a look around for him and set off in the last direction that I had seen him.

I could hardly make any progress at all in my bulky Mae West — they were obviously not designed for swimmers — and I soon gave up the idea. In any case, the ship was, even now, still moving and he would have been miles astern.

As *Eagle* passed me in the water, she slowly turned completely upside-down, impaling the whaler on her port outer screw as she did so and tipping those in her into the boiling white foam as if they had been rag dolls. About 20 or 30 men walked round her bilges as she turned bottom up. I wondered why they stayed with her. She had 500 tons of high explosives somewhere inside her, only a few feet under them as they walked up and down her long straight keel.

The next time I looked in her direction all I could see was a cloud of white water vapour shooting skywards and, above it all, those four, huge, bronze propellers rising higher and higher as she took the final plunge. She went carefully. She never meant to hurt a soul.

At about this time I began to feel a terrible pain in the groin as if I had stopped a cricket ball. As the ship had now taken the noise with her below the surface, I could make out, in the comparative silence, the rumblings of underwater explosions. Perhaps these were the depth charges which may have slid off her deck or those of the destroyers looking for the U-boat which had sunk us. I hoped they would have the sense not to drop them too close to the hundreds of us in the water. Every time an underwater explosion concussed our vitals I could hear the most dreadful oaths coming from the bobbing heads, new words which I had never heard before. Then I came across two or three bods in the water who were not swearing at all —just afloat in their lifejackets. One had white foam around his mouth and I realised that he was drowning.

As I had so much excess buoyancy, I was the obvious person to try to help. Luckily there was a Carley float nearby. I dragged three of them, one by one, to the float and the good swimmers on board jumped off the float and made room for their drowning shipmates. Those left on the raft must have carried out life-saving drill and saved their lives, for, some years later, a Petty Officer came up to me and thanked me for getting him to the Carley float and saving his and his pal's life that day.

I spent the next two hours swimming about trying to get near enough to one of the two or three destroyers around to be picked up. Directly I seemed to be getting near one, she would suddenly let in the clutch and steam off somewhere else. I was, by now, camouflaged with oil and I was beginning to look like any other piece of flotsam and not like a human being at all. Then, HM Tug *Jaunty* hove into view. She brought up right alongside — for I was incapable of swimming by now — and I hung on to the rescue netting draped over her side.

On deck at last I took a swig out of a rum bottle going the rounds on her tiny foc's'le, and dried off in the sun.

There was a feeling of relief and sadness aboard *Jaunty*. Those of us who were able, tried to do something useful to help the injured and to encourage those who were pale and motionless. Others of us were scanning the oily water looking for and pointing at floating objects, asking the crew of *Jaunty*, who had binoculars, whether they were human. This fine little vessel picked up 198 men from *Eagle* and she left no one behind. She was so overloaded that the skipper told us to get down from her rigging in case she capsized. He slowly edged his little tug alongside the destroyer *Malcolm* and thankfully discharged us aboard her. In all, 962 men and 67 officers from *Eagle* were picked out of the Mediterranean.

Aboard *U73*, after the torpedoes had left the tubes, Rosenbaum sent all available men forward to compensate for their weight and to prevent the submarine from breaking surface. She had thus been able to dive deep immediately after firing, disappearing below the Mediterranean's protective layers of water which, because of their sudden density changes, confused and often stopped altogether the response that the hunting destroyers got from their Asdics. (See Appendix 1 for a brief technical description of Asdics.)

Then as the dials on the depth indicators in *U73* showed the first few metres, the crew heard four explosions. The German account states: "Two minutes later, the crew heard the strange, cracking sound — a drawn-out rending groan — of the ship going down. Twelve minutes after that, the hull of the U-boat was shaken by a deep-throated, rolling explosion; the unmistakable sound of *Eagle's* boilers blowing up under water. Only then did the crew hear the pip and hiss of Asdics as the destroyers looked for them. This went on for four or five hours."

Rosenbaum obviously knew all about the Mediterranean. He knew that the 'ping' of the Asdics from the British destroyers would be refracted, reflected or blurred by the sudden change in water density, and that once he could dive below the warm layer and into the cold, he was relatively safe from discovery.

The Mediterranean probably saved *U73* from the angry destroyers and Rosenbaum and his crew lived to return in glory to La Spezia. There, he was decorated for his skill and bravery — and that of his crew — with the Knight's Cross of the Iron Cross. He lived for two more years, dying in a plane crash on his way to the Black Sea to take command of a new Pocket U-boat flotilla.

Eagle sank in six minutes. She took four minutes to turn over, allowing all but 231 of her 1142 crew to escape. The four torpedoes hit her engine rooms and boiler rooms. Although she had started life as a battlecruiser for the Chilean Navy in 1912, the hardhitting torpedoes of 1942 were more than a match for her protective blisters and they pierced her vitals with ease.

When we had climbed over the rail of *Jaunty* onto the foredeck of the destroyer *Malcolm*, the tug immediately opened up her powerful engines and careered eastwards after the vanishing fleet. She would be wanted in Valetta Harbour in Malta, for towing in damaged merchant ships without delay before they could be sunk by further bombing.

As we turned westwards, it seemed from the sound coming from the direction of the convoy that it had already struck trouble from the German and Italian Air Forces. We hoped that they would have enough fighters now that 12 out of the 16 Hurricanes of 813F and 801 Squadrons were lying, with *Eagle*, at the bottom of the sea.

Our day was over. We sat around *Malcolm's* quarterdeck, her huge, creamy, stern-wave piling up behind, the whole ship shaking with her efforts to catch up with *Furious* and the rest, haring back to Gibraltar.

That night, 12 August, we tried to get some sleep on deck, but we were so excited at the day's events few of us did. Suddenly, at about 0100 we felt the ship heel over with an alteration of course under full helm. Then we could see small blue lights passing down either side, low in the water. We could hear voices. They seemed to be shouting something as they swept by.

We resumed our course almost immediately and without slowing. Sub-Lieutenant Godfrey Parrish of 801 Squadron went up to the bridge to ask the skipper, Commander Campbell, what it was all about. Apparently the destroyer *Wolverine* ahead of us and also crowded with *Eagle* survivors, had surprised the Italian submarine *Dagabur* on the surface and had rammed her at full speed, cutting her in two. We had just steamed through her wreckage and survivors. Parrish was a trifle angry that we had not stopped to pick them up. However, it was near the Balearics, and the Spanish eventually reported their rescue.

So ended my first six months of operations in *Eagle*. Operation 'Pedestal' as this convoy was called, was only the second occasion on which the Navy had used any of its carriers with an adequate fighter defence. Even the United States Navy took note of this and learned something from it for their own war in the Pacific.

'Pedestal' succeeded in spite of the loss of *Eagle*'s fighters and her spare deck. Only one merchant ship was sunk while the carriers were still able to provide their fighter protection. Our only consolation in *Malcolm* and *Wolverine* was that, at least, it was better to be sunk in the warm waters of the Mediterranean in summer, than the icy waters of the Arctic whence our rescuers had just come and where they were about to return for PQ18.

Chapter 2
Little Acorns Grow

I was born on 24 February, 1920, at Rockferry, near Liverpool. My father was a Principal Tenor in the Carl Rosa Opera Company and was on tour, at the time, from Covent Garden. My mother, like so many stage wives, moved from lodging to lodging, hoping one day to have a home of her own. I, and Peggy my sister, must have travelled around with our parents for most of the time, but I remember nothing about that.

Eventually it must have been altogether too much for my poor mother, because by 1925 — when I was five and my sister eight — my mother had left my father and faded out of our lives for ever. She probably realised that looking for a new husband would be a full-time job, because she farmed us out to one set of strange foster parents after another — and to separate ones at that. The only time we saw her was when she moved us from one set to another.

But when I had just had my eighth birthday, life unexpectedly took on an entirely new look. My father's mother took us both under her loving wing and we went to live with her in Croydon.

My father had by this time married one of his leading ladies — a protégée called Rose Hignell. He later gave up the stage because of asthma and started a nursery, overlooking the river Hamble. He was therefore permanently within sight of boats — his main joy — and usually within the sound and sight of aircraft, his other hobby.

While living with Granny in Croydon in her big Victorian house, she taught me to sing. So, on moving south when grandfather died, she had the brilliant idea of sending me, when I was ten, to a voice trial for Winchester Cathedral choir. I was lucky to get into the choir at that age. However, Doctor Prendergast — organist and choirmaster — had a poorish lot to choose from that year, for I was accepted and given a scholarship to the Cathedral School in the Close. Granny listened outside the vestry door during the voice trial and she said that I had been a credit to my father even though I had sung the words of the hymn in the wrong order. So the summer of 1930 marked the beginning of my education at a proper school.

Following some serious trouble involving the Headmaster, no less, the school was immediately closed and refounded from top to bottom in an entirely new building at the opposite end of the Close. It was renamed the Pilgrims' School. This was because the 'new' building, designed by Wren, was attached to the Canterbury Pilgrims' Barn. It was all set in the most beautiful grounds stretching down to the river at the bottom of the garden and surrounded by ancient buildings and some trees which had been planted by Charles II.

I was, of course, junior boy in the choir to start with and this meant that I had to pump the practice organ for a good deal of the time during choir practice. Our choir practice was held twice a day except Sundays. It took place in the vestry in the Cathedral. Dr. Prendergast and his assistant organist, Miss Hilda Bird, sat at the organ keyboard in the vestry. Opposite stood the twenty choirboys, more or less held upright by six large and ancient wooden lecterns on which they balanced their music and carved their initials.

By the side, in a dark corner, stood us probationers, two fingers stuck in the side of our mouths to keep them wide open when we sang. Behind the choir rose the practice organ itself, a majestic edifice — perhaps by Grindling Gibbons — of polished and carved woodwork, pipes of brass, large square ones of wood, swell boxes, louvres and levers — and all covered with the dust of ages. It reached to the vaulted stone roof and it made a terrific noise at full throttle.

Towards the end of, I believe, Handel's Halleluja Chorus, Doctor Prendergast shouted "Blow" to the copy boy. Unknown to me, this was the standard way of asking the copy boy to distribute the next bit of music to be practised — by the composer's name. I naturally thought it was a demand for more wind and I redoubled my efforts. After a few more "Blows" (William Blow, King's Musician and Cathedral Organist 1669-1702), the copy boy — Rooke by name and Captain of Soccer — finally heard the order and went to look for the music. The last shout from the Doctor coincided with the top A and 'Full Organ' of the closing bars of Handel's Oratorio. Something happened up aloft amongst the organ pipes and a paper aeroplane, dislodged from its ancient hangar by the unaccustomed rush of wind, began a circuit of the vestry. It slowly lost height in a series of graceful fugoids, finally making a perfectly judged approach and touchdown at about middle C on the top manual of Doctor Prendergast's organ. Could this fine example of man-made airmanship, to such inspiring accompaniment, have kindled in my boyish mind the first appreciation of the art of aviation?

I was beginning to understand, from sailing, how air can lift things and, although it may be soft and invisible, it can yet exert frightening forces when it likes. Sometimes it seemed to me that air took pleasure, almost, in flowing round the natural sweet curves of a seagull, to cradle it gently in its arms. I wondered what it might be whispering as it passed, say, an albatross — a bird so sweetly designed that it scarcely needs to flap its wings once to stay aloft, day after day, in the South Atlantic, and its instinctive knowledge and beneficial use of natural phenomena such as ground effect, thermals, cliff-edge effect and wind shear, which no glider pilot could hope to match. Then, those fighter pilots, the darting swallows, as they plucked their food with superb judgement from the air, insects too small for me to see and flying too quickly for me to follow with my eyes. How rudely must nature's love affair be broken at Heathrow each morning when man takes to the air in his own creations. Who can blame it if it sometimes plucks them angrily aside and hurls them in pieces to the ground.

One Christmas, at the Pilgrims' School, one of the masters decided to invite parents from far and near to see us do a few scenes from *Macbeth*. I started off at rehearsals as Lady Macbeth in the sleepwalking scene. However, as we were very busy choirboys, most of us had little spare time and the master asked for rehearsals at awkward times. One of his sudden requests coincided with my determination to get steam-up in my steam engine. It had just been repaired by the school gardener for 1/6d (7½p) and I was looking forward to seeing it working again. Steam engines included many of the things that I liked doing, such as striking matches, messing about with meths and seeing the blue flame spread everywhere. Then there was filling the boiler with water and the pleasure of hearing it splutter and hiss just before it suddenly blew off steam from its purposely over-pressurised safety valve. The master in charge of *Macbeth* did not appreciate this scientific cliff-hanging at all, and would pick just such a moment to say, "Come on, Crosley, I hope you've remembered your lines".

As a result, on such occasions, I made a particularly emotional and vicious Lady Macbeth and actually got congratulated sometimes. However, the part itself was so far removed from even the furthest flight of my imagination that I made no real effort to learn the lines or remember the meticulous exhortations of the master as he strove for perfection.

So, after forgetting my lines for the umpteenth time and laughing when I dropped the candle, I was taken off the part of Lady Macbeth and was offered the lesser part of Macbeth himself, in the second witches' scene. Having been bequeathed a sword, a shield and some armour from Jack Graham — the outgoing Macbeth — I would have been an idiot not to accept. As this part seemed to need no acting ability —·being conducted in almost pitch darkness — and the lines seemed to be less illogical and easier to remember than Lady Macbeth's, I managed to stay the course. Graham, as Lady Macbeth, brought the house down. But I was not cut out for the stage, I would have to think about joining the Navy or something.

At about this time, as a belated birthday present, I was taken up in a DH (Cirrus) Moth by my father. He was a member of the Hampshire Aeroplane Club at Eastleigh. He did the slowest slow roll, with me clutching the sides of the front cockpit, that had ever been attempted. The engine stopped, I hung on to my straps listening to the sound of wind in the rigging wires and wondering whether I would ever like flying again. But by the time I had landed a quarter of an hour later, I could hardly wait to have a go myself. I longed to be able to frighten my own passengers. However I would have to learn how to drive a car first. This I did by practising on my father's 1925 'Bullnose' Morris, used for carting manure around the nursery. As it only had back wheel brakes, it was marvellous for practising ground loops in the mud.

Living so near Calshot and right opposite Hamble airfield, the sky buzzed with aircraft all day long. Some were flying boats. In the summer I could watch them from our boat in the Solent. They came over and landed a few yards away, showing off to the 'J.' Class racing yachts, sometimes with the King at the helm of *Britannia*. It looked terrific fun, and the fact that they were being paid for doing it completed the heavenly picture. They splashed around throughout the summer months, their crews waving at us as they passed, the hulls of their Saro Clouds glistening with the water running off them as they rose with a roar from the white-flecked water. They looked so masterful, skilful, and brave in their leather flying jackets and helmets. and obviously officers. The Training Ship *Mercury* in the Hamble, run by C. B. Fry and his famous wife, lay near our moorings and such was the Spartan life the boy sailors led, I determined, if I ever joined the Navy, that I would be an officer, for the life of a rating seemed too hard.

The Schneider Trophy races then took place in the Solent. The last two series of races were based at Calshot. We naturally took a ringside seat in our boat. The red, blue and green seaplanes thrashed off in a cloud of spray and disappeared in the direction of Ryde, to reappear from the Portsmouth direction in one or two minutes at speeds of up to 350 miles an hour, and in vertical banked turns only a few feet from the sea.

Of course, the British won the Schneider Trophy. We took such things for granted. No one could beat the British at anything in those days — or so we thought. However, by 1931, government money for such semi-military things was scarce. So we were all delighted — and so was the RAF and the race committee — when we heard one morning that a Lady Houston, OBE, would 'defray the cost of Britain competing' from the vast wealth left her by her third husband, Sir Robert Houston, when he died in 1924. Far more important than the eventual winning of the trophy and the world's speed record was the fact that the Rolls-Royce and Supermarine teams — the latter under a genius called R. J. Mitchell CBE, — were kept in being. So that, when war seemed inevitable in 1938/9 we had the Merlin engine (its supercharger design being a direct 'production' model of that in the Buzzard) and, of course, Mitchell's Spitfire, which used much of the experience gained in the further development of the 1931 winner — the S6B.

When my voice broke at the age of 14, it was decided that all my father could afford was to send me to a day school, King Edward VI at Southampton. I lived at our new house, 'Broomhill', at Sarisbury Green and caught the Bursledon Flyer to school each day.

The train dated from about 1910 and it took an hour to accomplish about five miles as the crow flies. It included in its journey every hamlet and village for miles around as it wound its wheezy way, like a damp catherine wheel, out of Bursledon and in the general direction of Southampton.

My hobby was, of course, boats and boatbuilding. I added to my stock of brass screws for the boat that I happened to be building at the time by unscrewing these from the carriages. Brass screws were both expensive and essential, and the Southern Railway used hundreds of them.

I came back a few years after leaving school and I sat in the same carriages. The same screws were still missing. I mentioned this to the stationmaster — by this time employed by British Rail. He was very reassuring and told me that the carriages had been going since he was a boy and would last for ever, with or without screws.

As I walked home each night from Bursledon station up to Sarisbury Green, Moody's boatyard was on the way. I was naturally unable to resist the temptation of a sail in my boat during the summer, particularly when the tide was high and the wind blew softly. Moody's also allowed me to watch their shipwright apprentices in the boatbuilding sheds. They used beautiful woods — oak, Burmese teak, silver spruce, American elm, pitchpine from Norway and mahogany from the Philippines. They were building yachts to last 100 years.

With all these attractions to take me away from schoolwork it was surprising that I passed the School Certificate with a 'possible' of six distinctions. My father was sufficiently impressed to allow me to take the examination for 'Special Entry' to the Royal Navy, at the age of $17\frac{1}{2}$.

About two years later I sat the exam at Burlington House in Bond Street, a very frightening experience for a country boy. I was told by nearly everyone who had had anything to do with the Navy that the interview was by far the most important part of the exam. A quarter of the marks were given for it and as boys failed to get in by as little as a single mark sometimes, I would do well to find out what the questions at the interview might be, and what the correct answers were. As these answers were based on custom rather than logic, I was advised to find a Naval Officer who had had the experience.

One said he failed probably because he didn't know the number of the taxi that brought him to the Admiralty. Another said that I must be prepared for, and not be afraid of, a line of about 20 Admirals staring at me across the interview table at a range of a few inches, all with earwhiskers and all with gimlet eyes. One or the other of these fearsome creatures could then open fire with questions such as; "What's wrong with me, young man?" One of my advisers said that he had passed because he had cleverly noticed that one of the Admiral's shirt buttons was undone, below his stiff, winged collar. He said he got a verbal pat on the back from the Admiral for this fine piece of observation.

I felt thoroughly inadequate as I knocked on the high mahogany door of the interview room in the Old Admiralty Building. It was 5th November 1937.

I looked up. I could see opposite a huge oil painting of what looked like Admiral Byng just before he was shot for 'failing to do his utmost' to capture Minorca. I certainly did my utmost, but I tended to be too honest in my answers and I forgot all the trick replies that I had learned. But I was glad when the subject turned to sailing, for it was obvious they knew little about it and were pleased to find someone who did. Then we talked about cricket, another subject I was interested in. I was beginning to think that I was doing quite well. Then I ruined it all by two answers that must have given them the impression that I was, at the very least, a Fletcher Christian, if not a red-hot Communist. They asked me with whom I sided in the Spanish Civil War that was going on at the time. Instead of answering as I was advised to do: "I'm glad you asked me that question sir, for it was worrying me," I said: "I stick up for the Government side of course, Sir." As this was in the hands of the Communists, and they were fighting the Fascists, my answer was bound to be wrong whichever way I answered.

I made a complete porridge of the next question as well. One Admiral, who had been silently weighing me up from short range throughout the inquisition, now asked: "And what books have you read on the Royal Navy, young man?"

This was another loaded question. At first I could only remember such schoolboy authors as Percy F. Westerman. In his books, a Sub-Lieutenant hero straight from Dartmouth did very dashing things indeed — usually in destroyers — and the RN always won — even the Battle of Jutland. So I skilfully chose another author. The only one I could remember was Admiral Sir Barry Domville, Bart. How was I to know he was the Naval equivalent of the Red Dean of Canterbury?

Later, when I mentioned that I had chosen him as my Naval author, my friends in the Service shook their heads. So did Their Lordships. I failed to get in by 13 marks out of 1600 — or seven places in the order. Forty-five were accepted into the Navy from about 1000 who took the exam that November.

So I joined the Metropolitan Police instead.

Chapter 3
Eighty-Two Charing Cross Road

Life in the 'Met' started off with the usual short-arm inspection and about six months of training at Peel House. This training school was in Rochester Row off Vauxhall Bridge Road in London. After having our hair removed — except for an eighth of an inch on top — we settled down to learn 'Primary Objects'. "The Primary Objects of an efficient Police are the prevention of crime. The next, the detection and punishment if crime is committed. To these ends, all efforts of Police must be directed . . ." We were each given a copy. We were told that if we wanted to do well on the course we must learn the whole thing off by heart. It was packed with vital information, legal definitions, Acts of Parliament, affrays, riots, nasty crimes of which I had never heard, and powers of arrest and detention. The 1930 Road Traffic Act was particularly interesting for it seemed that after reading it, every car on the road was committing at least half-a-dozen offences before it even moved.

There were 20 Acting, Temporary, Probationary Constables on my course. We were given instruction by Sergeants and Inspectors. This was mostly on real-life situations, enacted in the classrooms or in the yard.

During my training, the threat of war became very real. This added to our training syllabus. It included instruction on gas precautions — phosgene and mustard gas — and we were issued with tin hats, gas capes and gas masks, in addition to whistles, notebooks, truncheons and a book on first aid. The Country had been misled by pacifists into believing that war could be avoided by non-involvement, by disarmament and by appeasement. So that, when preparations were at last begun in London, late in 1939, they showed all the signs of panic.

After completing the training course, I and a fellow-embryo named Ralph Kirker, were posted to 'C' Division. Our Sub-Division was based at Vine Street police station off Piccadilly, covering the central part of the West End of London. We lived at a police section-house — number 82 Charing Cross Road — a Victorian workhouse of a place, still there, by Cambridge Circus.

Being a country boy, I consulted Ralph Kirker about girls. He said that only a very small outlay was required if you chose the right kind of girl; a suit, perhaps, and at the very most, a car. To start me off on the right foot, he agreed to take me on a fact-finding sortie, providing I paid for the beer and he could choose the girls.

A few evenings later, after loading up with the remains of my £3.19s pay, we went to the Palais de Dance up Charing Cross Road. Dancing was the quickest way, Ralph said. A quick whip round the floor and you could assess the chances of further delights without any complication or expensive outlay.

I admired the confidence of the man. I was more worried about whether the girl would like me rather than whether I would like her. They all looked absolutely delicious to me, anyway.

"Now remember," said Ralph, "I'll do the choosing."

We paid our shilling and walked on to the dance floor. After five minutes, I had chosen mine, so Ralph had to have her friend. With our partners we made a few circuits. Presently, Ralph overtook me on the inside track and said: "Mine's a bloody 'pro' you idiot!" He then went back to the bar alone, finished his beer — and mine, and left.

So I had to force on alone. Mine looked a sweet girl to me and could not possibly have been a 'pro'.

After a few more dances we walked out into Shaftesbury Avenue. As by now I only had a quid left I wondered what we could do at about midnight in the blackout. However, she said she knew a nightclub where you didn't have to be members. So we went there. I knocked on the door and was allowed in.

The man brought me a bottle of White Horse whisky — very scarce indeed at that time — and he only charged ten bob (50p) for it, too. About half an hour later we were both sitting down at a table and I looked across at my partner. Whatever I did and however hard I tried, I could not get both of her to form a single image. I had met this optical effect in the physics labs at school but this was the first time I had met it outside. I must be drunk, I thought. So this was what it was like. I asked the girl how she felt — as she was getting a bit quiet. She didn't reply and soon afterwards fell off her chair in a heap on the floor.

The doorman helped me to carry her to the outside air and after a half-crown (12½) tip he got us into a taxi. As I could not get my partner to tell me anything of interest, let alone where she lived, apart from something that sounded like Brewer Street, I got the cab driver to drop us off there. We shambled onto the pavement and made for a doorway. Here we stayed, sitting down in the pitch darkness. If we could remain unseen for a bit, I thought, then the mists would drift away and the girl would once again become intelligible, and perhaps say where she lived in Brewer Street.

It was no good. Things got worse, if anything, and she went to sleep. While I was looking down at the pavement with half-closed, crossed, eyes, I noticed four polished boots no more than a few inches from my nose. I followed up the trousers and my eyes came to the unmistakable black belt of a night-duty policeman. A voice from above said: "Hallo Maisie. What are you doing here? This isn't your regular, is it?"

Things would still have been alright had Maisie not lost control at the appearance of the policeman. Her whole attitude changed and the effects of the wood alcohol that we had doubtless been given took charge. There was only one thing for it, the Black Maria. I was dropped off at 'Number 82' and, if Maisie had given someone the chance, she would have been delivered to her flat in Brewer Street. However I afterwards found out that she had tried to fill-in the constable in the Black Maria and was put in the cells at Marlborough Street police station. Here she spent most of the night shouting for PC 447, my number, to come and let her out. It took me some time to live this down at Vine Street, and Ralph would not lend me his suit again for months afterwards.

On 3 September 1939 I was having some eggs and sausage before going on 'late turn' at 1400. We had just heard Neville Chamberlain, the Prime Minister, regretfully tell us that we were at war with the Germans. Suddenly, the siren went off directly above us. Trust the ruddy Germans, we all thought.

We immediately put on our blue enamelled tin hats labelled 'Police' and went out. None of us had any clear idea of what to do, so we just watched.

I saw people running up one side of Charing Cross Road and down the other side. Most of them had tin hats on with various initials, saying what they were. As the skies were expected to open at any moment and rain down bombs, the officials were telling people to take cover.

As nothing happened after an hour or so, the public started to come out of the shelters and ask what was going on. We told them there had been a short-circuit in the local siren. Several people believed my story of an electrician finding a fused caterpillar. The warning was, in fact, caused by the unscheduled return of a diplomat from Europe in a small, light, plane — a fine test for the new radar defences.

Our duties, for the first 11 months of the war, were remarkably boring compared with what was going on over our heads. Night duty had its moments, however. Our main task in the 'phoney' war was to preserve the blackout. When the bombs started, the strictness of its observance tended to be in proportion to the tonnage of bombs dropped. The more bombs, the more summonses.

We were warned against accepting invitations into flats and houses to check on blackouts, particularly if these belonged to a lady. The Sergeant urged 'perspicacity' in all our dealings. The expensive flats and houses in Mayfair were often on my night-duty beat and some of the occupants were beautiful, lonely and rich. The minimum number of officers allowed to investigate such flats was two, one to check on the lady's blackouts, the other to see that there was no hanky panky.

It was often both frustrating and dangerous for coppers in London during the summer and autumn of 1940. Furthermore, we and the whole country expected to hear each day that Hitler had at last landed on the south or east coast at the head of his troops, and was heading for London. There were no plans on what we should do when this happened and it was worrying.

One night I was, as usual, at Vine Street Police Station on standby, when I was told to go to Piccadilly tube station to deal with a 'disturbance'. A few fire bombs had fallen on the roof of the Criterion restaurant and had set a part of it alight. As the flames could act as a target for more bombs, the Londoners revelling in the vicinity, queued to get down the underground to use it as an air raid shelter for the night. The 'regulars' resented having to move up a bit along the platforms, and blows were exchanged. By the time I got there, it had of course subsided and everyone was all smiles and co-operation, or fast asleep. I enjoyed an hour talking to them, everyone in high good humour, before returning to the Station. Some were sailors. I wondered how long it would be before I too, was in the Navy.

On the way back, having once more become accustomed to the blackout, I noticed a shaft of bright light shining skywards and a few flashing torches. This was at the junction of Swallow Street with Piccadilly. I could hardly ignore such serious offences, so I advanced, black notebook at the ready.

A 1930 Austin Seven Saloon had been demolished by hitting one of the bollards on the pedestrian refuge islands in the middle of Piccadilly, one headlight sending a shaft skywards. A crowd of people around were watching four or five Army officers emerging, with difficulty, from the remains.

"Who is the driver of this vehicle?" I said.

This had absolutely no effect at all, and the occupants propped themselves up, one by one, against the bollard and tried to light each other's cigarettes. This process took some time — as either the fag would not stay in, or the match would go out. It could have gone on for hours until one or two of the onlookers took a helping hand.

As it was Friday on the morrow and my long weekend, I had no wish to run any of them in for being drunk-in-charge of a motor vehicle — which they all were — for I would have to appear at Bow Street Court on my day off. However I had to do something, as the Sergeant would be coming round shortly.

As most of the occupants seemed to have tried to pass through the windscreen when the car hit the bollard, there was a good deal of blood about. So I settled for an ambulance rather than a Black Maria. While I was waiting for this to turn up, I had another go at trying to get some particulars, but their replies were unintelligible. They sounded like strange Celtic incantations — Urquart, Farquhart and Colquohoun — names which neither I nor even they could spell at that time of night.

Next morning I visited the soldiers in hospital at Charing Cross for 'further particulars'. They told me that they had been going back to their hotel after a party to celebrate their safe return from France. The driver told me that the accident happened when the red light he was following suddenly stopped. I told him that it was a red light marking a bollard. He said that that would account for it.

During August and September it was very hot in a copper's uniform. Ralph and I watched the sky, envious of the RAF above us in the summer sunshine. One day — 15 September — we saw two or three Hurricanes making quarter attacks on a German Dornier bomber over Shaftesbury Avenue. We could see and hear everything, the roar of the Hurricane's fire and the bright sun flashing on the shattered perspex of the bomber's cabin as the bullets hit it. We were both sure that we could drive an aircraft, for we could drive cars quite dangerously at times. We applied to join the RAF at the nearest recruiting station at Putney, passed the medical and then waited impatiently for our call-up papers.

After two or three weeks, these had not arrived. On telephoning the aircrew recruiting office at Berkeley Square, we found out that the RAF already had enough pilot volunteers to last them for the next six months, but "would we like to be rear gunners on Halifax night bombers?" We dropped the receiver with a clang. We heard even worse news at about this time. The Police was now a 'Reserved Occupation'; that was to say that we could not leave the Force even if we wanted to.

Both of us submitted requests to resign from time to time on Form 728, to see if the rules had altered. One month later — it seemed an age — we were told we could see the Chief Constable. He told us that as we were still Probationary Constables we could now volunteer for the armed forces. Better still, we could have our pay made up to copper's pay while we were being trained*.

So I gave up asking the RAF and changed to the Fleet Air Arm. I was immediately accepted. I returned my 'accoutrements' to the stores at the new West End Central police station and the same day I drove down to Gosport in my father's spare car, a 1934 Morris Minor two-seater. Within two days I had started my training as a Naval Airman Second Class. It was the 11th of November, 1940, the night of the Fleet Air Arm's first major success, Taranto night!

---

*Police records show that 501 Met. Policemen lost their lives, and 202 gained honours or awards, while serving in HM forces during World War II. One hundred and five were killed, 11 of these from 'C' Division.

Author — Hyde Park, 1939.

Sea Hurricane Ib's lining up for take-off from *Indomitable*, Operation 'Pedestal', August 1942. *(FAA Museum)*

Hawker Hart. *(FAA Museum)*

Chapter 4
Naval Airman, Second Class

The entrance gateway to HMS *St. Vincent* in Gosport looked exactly like a smaller version of Holloway prison. I knocked on the gate and a sailor with a bo'sun's whistle around his neck emerged and said: "Yes sir?"

Definitely the correct approach I thought, so far. "Well, I've come to join Number 21 Course. Can I take my car inside?" Having established that I was not an officer, his wary deference gave way to kindly co-operation. He replied: "Park your car over there, mate — by the air raid shelter. Come back and sign in."

As I walked back from the car across the five acre parade-ground, I glanced back over my shoulder at the four great barrack blocks with their regular line of windows. They looked more like Holloway than ever, and seeing sailors running hither and thither, reminded me of the training ship *Mercury*, in the river Hamble. Placed centrally in front of the buildings I saw a huge mast from some 18th century battleship, complete with ratlines and crow's nest. I assumed the catch-net all round its base was for us when we fell off. Looking aloft, I saw the clouds scudding past its shining gold truck, and the largest and whitest White Ensign blowing out proudly above all. I hoped that Number 21 Pilots Course would not be required to 'man the yards' or anything silly. Flying was one thing, but that sort of thing was asking for trouble.

I signed a large book in the Quartermaster's office. The Petty Officer told me to report to the Officer of the Watch. "Hut five," he said. "Take your gear to Block D, first deck. You'll draw blankets at 1800 after supper. Shore leave tonight's from 1830 to 2230." He continued with the *Southern Daily Echo*.

Seeing that I was still there he said: "Carry on, son. That's all."

"Yes sir," I said. I had nearly said "Aye Aye sir," but thought that might only be for officers.

"Not 'Sir' at all. It's PO. That's what these cross-anchors mean."

So far, so good. The PO sounded quite human too. Nothing like a parade-ground Sergeant at all.

As there was a queue outside hut number five, I took my gear up to the 'dormitory' in D Block. It was a high, bare room about 70 feet long. The floor was covered with highly polished lino of a uniform brown colour. It had green glazed tiles halfway up the walls and 'hospital' lights hanging at regular intervals from the ceiling, their dim light shining through the cigarette smoke of the 20 or so new arrivals. I selected an empty bed near the far end. The windows were half shuttered with blackout screens. The window glass was covered with thick, varnished tape like 82 Charing Cross Road, as a guard against bomb blast.

Men were either stretched out on their beds taking stock of the situation or standing around talking, smiling and laughing. I joined the nearest lot and listened. Apparently a chap called Bruce Dunfield and another called 'Clunk' Watson (later of 880 Squadron, CFB Summerside, Prince Edward Island) were telling the others that they had, that very morning, come off a merchant ship at Liverpool. These two Canadians had stowed away at Halifax, Nova Scotia and made their passage free. They had been caught after a few hours on board and had been put to work cleaning out oil tanks and doing other dirty jobs. But directly the British crew had seen that they were genuine volunteers — and for the Fleet Air Arm at that — they had taken them to the captain. He 'signed them on' as temporary crew and paid them the going rate for Able Seamen in the Merchant Service. This was slightly more than a Lieutenant in the Royal Navy.

When I eventually saw the Officer of the Watch in hut five, he told me that I was required for interview at the Commander's Office at 1800 the next day. Gawd! Not another interview. The main anxiety was that I should convice them that I was not only pilot material, but fighter-pilot material. I had to make it quite clear that I would be no use whatever as an Observer. As I had heard that they tended to choose the intelligent-looking ones for that job, I would have to try to be fairly useless, not too knowledgeable or wise. A bit "Whizzo chaps — whattabout a car race round the parade-ground". That sort of thing. The very prospect of having to cope with compasses and dividers in the freezing back of a Swordfish and unable to see where you were going, reduced me to a frightened wreck in no time. Fancy not being master of your own destiny and with only a single Lewis gun pointing the wrong way to beat off the Hun coming up your jacksie at a high rate of knots.

Kit issue was scheduled for 0830 next day, so we had another 12 hours of civilian life, after which the Commander would be addressing us. It seemed we would have about five minutes to get used to being sailors before he arrived. Pretty swift organisation so far and no haircuts either.

After blanket issue, I and John DuCane, my next door neighbour in the dormitory, got into the Morris Minor and went to see my father at Sarisbury Green. The main reason for the visit was to load up with a bit more petrol. After this we all had a couple of beers at the 'Swan' at Bursledon and another couple at the 'Bugle' at Hamble. We eventually repaired back on board our stone frigate at Gosport at 2230 — just in time.

We awoke to a frightful noise. Bells, loudspeakers, bugles, lights, whistles and a man shouting: "Wakey-wakey-wakey. Rise-and-shine. The-morning's-fine, you've-had-your time. C'mon, on-socks, you-lot. Show-a-leg-show-a-leg-show-a-leg!" Then, in a voice of patient exasperation: "Cummon, son. Mother's brought you a cuppa, darling."

The man took a brief gasp for breath and started off again, even louder. This time he ended up with: "I-don't-want-to-see-hanynone-'ere-by-ho-seven-double-ho. All-bunks-made-up. Tables-clear-and-boots-in-order-of-size-underbeds. . ." The rest trailed off, as he went to the dormitory next along the passage, and repeated the whole thing twice.

After we had had our porridge, kippers, doorsteps-of-bread, marmalade-out-of-a-tin and a mug of bubbly NAAFI 'bromide' tea, it was cleared away in 30 seconds by the 'Duty Part' of the Watch. We 'new boys' watched spellbound as the Duty Part from the Course ahead of ours performed.

"D'you mean to say we'll be doing that shortly?" said a chap called Brian Madden. "I was just about to ask for more, like O. Twist," he said. "They whipped it away when I wasn't looking!"

We were now looking forward to seeing ourselves dressed-up as sailors. J. B. Madden, who was called 'Tich', was telling us stories of life in Liverpool. He was wondering whether the Navy would have a uniform small enough to fit him. So were we. Then, with a mound of brown paper parcels, green suitcases, kitbags and black tin hatboxes, gas masks, oilskins, boots and 'HMS' hat ribbons, we went to the dormitory to try to put them on. In addition, we had two sets of Number 3s, spare sailors' collars, lanyards, penknives, tooth brushes, clothes brushes, boot brushes, nailbrushes, soap and a 'hussif'. The latter was a clothes mending kit, a 'housewife', which I still use to this day. All the gear, especially the towels and sheets, could be guaranteed to wear out any modern-day washing machine before showing signs of wear itself. It was top quality at a time of severe wartime rationing, and without coupons too.

We strained and heaved at the jumpers. We straightened each other's collars as we had been shown in the store issue room and went down to the mess-deck for the Commander's address. A Petty Officer formed us up into lines.

At 1030, all eyes were on the doorway. We could hear important footsteps. "Rodney . . . Rodney-HOW!" demanded the loudest voice I have ever heard. This order was followed by the shuffling of 232 feet for a few seconds. Then by giggles. Then by dead silence.

Chief Petty Officer Willmot — for it was he — raised his eye in supplication to God to give him strength, and marched up to the Commander and reported: "Rodney, Number 21 Course, mustered and correct, sir".

The Commander, in brass hat and telescope, muttered something back. CPO Willmot turned round to us, fixed us with a sceptical eye and ordered: "RODney . . . STANNAT . . . HIZE!"

We did our best, but moving 232 feet apart does take a considerable time. The dim light from the Scutari-type lighting system fell upon the Commander's face. It was weatherbeaten, grim-jawed, a chip off the Earl St. Vincent block. It would be no good asking the time of day from him. Just "Yessir, no sir, three bags full, sir".

"You there," said the Commander, opening his speech of welcome. "Yes, *you*. Near the window," pointing down at Tich Madden who was looking out of it at a time. "Read out what it says over Hut Four."

Tich read it out to us: ". . . something, something, something", he mumbled, then, suddenly getting the gist, he shouted out loud and clear ". . . but be a sailor *first*". He could barely keep a straight face when he turned back to resume his normal place in the room. We could not meet his eye, for to do so would ruin everything. Once he started to giggle, he lost all control.

The Commander obviously detected a certain irreverence and he swivelled a gimlet eye momentarily in Tich's direction as if to say: "Watch it, sailor!" The inscription was, after all, the text for the Commander's peroration for those about to die, and heaven help anyone who found it a laughing matter.

We were told that we had now joined the Royal Navy and *not* the Fleet Air Arm. "It doesn't matter a fish's tit", shouted the Commander, "whether you can fly like Alan Cobham if you are not, first, a bloody good seaman and fit material to become a bloody good officer. I can see that some of you have a long way to go," he added, looking in Tich's direction. That night we asked each other: "What's good officer material?" The matter obviously needed further study.

The interview turned out to be a great deal easier than I had expected. It was nowhere near as high-powered as the one at the Admiralty in 1939. There wasn't a picture of an Admiral to be seen anywhere, just the odd cruiser with two or three long, thin funnels in a sepia-coloured photograph, and a few signatures underneath.

Lt/Cdr Sykes was on the Board at the interview. I had already had an interview with him when I first came to see the recruiting board at Gosport. He must have told them that I was keen, for he knew that I had taken the 'Spec-En' exam. I had no difficult questions and I seemed to have judged everything about right. There was no talk of Observers. If I kept my nose clean I could be flying fighters in a few months time.

That same afternoon we had our first go at the parade ground. I had been one of those detailed for the 'First Part of Port Watch'. There were about 25 of us. We shuffled out onto the parade ground, holding our backs towards the piercing wind. Petty Officer Oliver lined us up in order of size and told us to watch him. We were told that he was a 'Gunner's Mate' from Whale Island, a 'Prussian-army' type of Naval gunnery rating, all of whom were noted for their guardsmanlike approach. His: "'ats will be 'ung on the 'ooks provided, leavin' no 'olidays," still sticks in my memory.

He gave us one or two incredible demonstrations of how to march, how to stan-at-HIZE and how to HOW! He put some sort of suppressed vigour into all his movements, so much so that you could hear sinews crack and muscles twang. Yet, in the Navy, there was no sign of needless stamping or crashing around and none of the facial contortions of the Army Sergeant Major.

We tried to do likewise, but our brains and our muscles fought with each other, each pulling different ways like a short-circuiting robot. All was not lost, however. Some had already done a little time in the Navy, so we tried to follow them, sheltering in their shadow whenever possible and not daring to do anything off our own bat unless it was absolutely essential. It was a fine test of quick reactions; so essential, we thought, for fighter pilots.

The one man at *St. Vincent* whose personality and presence ruled out Michael-taking altogether was Chief Petty Officer Willmot. He was a unique example of the *human* Naval Gunnery Petty Officer. He probably did more than Cunningham's tradition, Earl St. Vincent's disciplinary code, Kempenfelt's divisional system and Nelson's example to turn us towards the Navy. "Gosh," we thought, "if they can spare men like him for training, what must they be like in actual ships?" In addition to Willmot and Oliver, there was Chief Yeoman Saxby, our Signals Instructor, and Gunner's Mate Crowley whose favourite expression was "For Christ's sake if not mine".

Next day at 'stand easy' in the canteen, as if to set us a standard of heroism to which we should now aspire, we read in the papers that the Italian Fleet had been attacked at night in Taranto harbour by Swordfish aircraft flying from 'one of our aircraft-carriers in the Mediterranean'.

We thought flying at night was clever stuff in itself, but flying at night from carriers was beyond anything that we had ever imagined. I spoke to John DuCane about it. (His brother, Peter, had 'done' Dartmouth, retired in 1931 as a Commander, and was now Managing Director of Vospers in Portsmouth.) "John," I said, "Surely the Navy won't expect us to do that sort of thing straight off, will it?"

"No one's going to ask us to do the impossible 'straight off'," he replied. "They'll give us a bit of time in the squadron first, I'd reckon."

Next day we saw photographs taken by our aircraft of Taranto harbour. They showed two battleships sunk and a third half-submerged with oil seeping out. There was another picture of the inner harbour at Taranto, showing two destroyers wrecked, oil tanks gutted and a wrecked seaplane base. If just a few Swordfish could do this, what a marvellous job to be in. It was twice as much as we had done to the Germans at Jutland and for the loss of only Swordfish.

One night a little later, when I was 'Duty Part' once more and watching some cockroaches walking round the galley stove where I and they were keeping warm, we heard a bos'un's pipe: "Duty Part o' the Watch muster outside D Block. Rig — oilskins."

We all rushed out into the blackness. There was a glow in the sky by Portsmouth, but that wasn't anything new. The Germans had turned their main attention away from London and had recently struck Portsmouth, Southampton and Coventry. We wondered what was up.

The Duty PO checked his list of names to see that we were all there. He told us that we were going on 'Damage Control' duty at the Royal Naval Victualling Yard, Gosport, as it was on fire. It sounded fraught with interest.

"Damage Control party HOW," said the PO quietly so as not to attract the Commander. "Right turn, quick march," and we all shambled off with our oilskins like cold, clammy, straightjackets, hanging down to our ankles.

As we made our way down the road towards the ferry at Gosport, we were overtaken by an empty Army lorry. We thumbed a lift as it went by, and it took us to the gates of the Victualling Yard. We marched as smartly as we could down the cobbled road between the tall lines of warehouses. Many of these had been built in Pepys's time and were 'listed buildings'. We kept going downhill towards the glow. Coming round a corner at the bottom, we saw a brilliant bonfire. It turned out to be the rum store. Rum was pouring down the walls and windows, and, being already mixed with the right amount of water from the fire hoses, made a nice drink. So we settled down to a few grogs, our Petty Officer having gone off to find us some damage to control. We enjoyed ourselves, warmed by the friendly fire, and watching the sparks fly skywards as the grog slid smoothly down our throats.

After about six doubles and when the Gosport fire brigade had put out the fire, we wound our way back to *St. Vincent,* the happiest bunch of neo-sailors that had ever been on Damage Control and only just in control of ourselves, too, as we came through the gates under the suspicious eye of the Duty Chief Petty Officer.

It is, of course, impossible to make sailors in two or three months, but *St. Vincent* had a very good try. It certainly gave us some idea of life aboard ship and a few wrinkles on Navy customs. But there was no time to learn the black arts of mooring a battleship, fixing a position by sextant, launching a ship's cutter or firing a gun. All we could manage was eight-words-a-minute morse, some semaphore and a few flags — although how it could be done in the back of a Swordfish we could not imagine. The Petty Officer TAG, Tubby Credland, told us that it could. Everything except playing a grand piano could be done there, he said.

The Course just senior to us was composed entirely of New Zealanders. They had not travelled across the world to be told how to behave by a lot of 'pommies'. So they preserved their Kiwi way of life with 'Haka's' in the canteen each night and some exceptionally comprehensive 'runs ashore' in Pompey. The early morning muster, where we all lined up in our separate courses for 'Colours', was always enlivened by some Kiwi sky-larking. CPO Willmot was the only man in Gosport who could get their attention for more than two minutes at a time.

One of the more memorable 'japes' by the Kiwis occurred at Colours on Christmas Day. The Duty Part was, as usual, required to provide the Guard, fallen-in with rifles, bayonets, gaiters, webbing, caps square on heads, and chin-stays down. Luckily, CPO Willmot was not on duty, otherwise the Kiwi's ploy for ruining the ceremony on this day would have been rumbled.

However, when the Colours were bent-on to the halyard ready for hoisting, a pair of WRNS (Women's Royal Naval Service or 'Wrens') blackouts (knickers) flying at the masthead on the same halyard and unobserved in the grey morning light, changed places with the White Ensign as it was hauled up. They crossed by the Crow's Nest and made a pretty picture to anyone watching at the time. Of course the Kiwis were watching in marked contrast to everyone else.

As the last notes of the bugle squeezed out, the blackouts descended into the view of the Officer of the Watch. the Kiwis' bayonets wavered in the cold air. What would the Officer of the Watch do? Would he, in the prescribed manner, preserve monentous calm with masterly inactivity and pretend the whole thing hadn't happened, or what?

True to his training, he carried on as if the WRNS' blackouts, now being reverently unhitched from the halyard, formed part of the ceremony. After the 'Carry On' had sounded, they were carefully folded and handed by the the rating in charge of the flags to the section leader in charge of the Kiwi guard, as if they were some priceless battle honour — which indeed they were.

This parting gesture was voted a 'fair cracker' and a 'beaut' both in its planning and execution.

There was never a chance that it would be punished. 'Collingwood' Term, the Kiwis', was due to leave immediately for Elementary Flying Training School and the Commander did nothing to retard this process. Like Nelson, he turned a blind eye.

After passing the simple examinations, the 116 men on our Course also left for flying training. Most went to the United States. The remainder were shared between two Elementary Flying Training Schools for Fleet Air Arm pilots, at Birmingham and Luton. The Birmingham (Elmdon) lot, used Tiger Moths. I was sent to Luton, Number 24 EFTS, and we flew monoplanes — Miles Magisters. I hoped that flying monoplanes was a sign that I had been considered for fighters rather than Swordfish. My thoughts kept returning to that morning in the summer of the Battle of Britain when I had watched the RAF Hurricanes shoot down the Dornier over Shaftesbury Avenue. I could hardly wait to do battle with the Hun myself.

My father and Granny, however, gave me a good talking-to at about this time. Although my father was more resigned to the dangers of my chosen wartime job, my Granny was not. She told me, bless her, to: "Always fly low and slow and not take risks by going too high and too fast." I told her that 'it' couldn't happen to me. It always happened to the other chap who did silly things. My father knew only too well that it depended upon luck as well as a fair amount of skill. He and I kept our fingers crossed, but Granny prayed each night.

Chapter 5
24 EFTS, Luton

Twenty-five of us were told to report to 'Luton Hoo'. At least, that was the address on our draft chits. I arrived at Luton station with my kitbag. Cars were not allowed, and I asked a taxi-driver to take me there. He seemed to be a bit surprised, but we set off into the blackout, through the deserted streets and out into the country. I asked him why everything was shrouded in mist in the built-up area of Luton. He told me that it was a new secret device for hiding the factories from German bombers. They would then bomb all the wrong places and not the car factories or Napiers — who had a secret aircraft engine on test — or the 'shadow' aircraft factories so much. "They would then concentrate on the private houses instead," he said with a certain sharpness. I asked him where Luton airfield was, and he said: "By Vauxhall's car factory."

We swept up the gravel drive to the magnificent Luton Hoo — back entrance — and I got out. Even the back entrance looked like a Greek palace and I wondered how the Navy managed to afford such a place.

After a while I heard a drawing of bolts, the sliding of locks and a huge door opened — not the one on which I had been knocking — and a man appeared. I said that I had come to join Number 24 EFTS. Seeing my sailor's uniform, "Oh", he said, "you're round at the stables. Straight down the road, you can't miss it," and closed the doors again.

My bed space was in the hayloft above the horses. The Petty Officers and the RAF had the grooms' quarters. Down the wooden ladder from the hayloft was another 'dormitory'. The stable partitions and mangers were still in place, although the horses and the hay had been removed to make way for the beds. The bottom ends of the beds lay in the gutter and looked a bit down by the stern. Of heating there was no sign. There was as much fog inside the stables as outside.

With my shaded torch and half-a-crown, I groped my way outside towards some noise that I could hear coming from a separate building in the stable yard. I pushed my way in through the heavy blackout curtain and emerged into the brilliant light of a canteen. There were tables and chairs everywhere, with soldiers and a few sailors and ATS (fore-runners of the Women's Royal Army Corps) seated with them. A couple of stewards were at a long bar at one end of the hut. They were dispensing baked beans on toast — without butter — and beer in tall glasses.

In the far corner, near a pillar stove, I could just make out David Ogle, 'Clunk' Watson and Dennis Holmes. So I was, indeed, at the right place. Everyone was still in greatcoats with collars turned up. Dennis was warming his beer by dipping a red hot poker in it. "Otherwise," he said, "it's impossible to taste." Dennis could best be described as "Every thinking-woman's dreamcrumpet". He was soft-hearted, brave and resourceful as well as being marvellous company. Two more of Rodney Course came in — Tich Madden and Phil Broad — and they joined us. We soon fell into the scheme of things, continuing the conversations we had been having at *St. Vincent* almost without interruption, and, of course, looking forward to flying, in new leather helmets and flying boots, perhaps on the morrow.

The Course at Luton lasted about three months. Ours took a little longer because the weather was so bad. The Elementary Flying Training was the first of three parts of our flying training which would take about nine months in all. At the end of this time we would, in theory, be ready to join a squadron. We were supposed to do a minimum of 50 hours flying at each school. In fact I only did about 35 at each, about a third of the hours attained by trainee pilots by the end of the war. At this stage they must have been very hard-up for pilots in the Fleet Air Arm.

My instructor was Pilot Officer Jack, an ex-civil flying instructor of immense experience and much respected by the others, it seemed. I was extremely lucky to have him as my instructor, as his wise counsels, which I still remember, saved my life on many future occasions.

We turned out of our 'pits' each morning at 0630. The NCOs at Luton Hoo stables were the most inconsiderate crowd of RAF Sergeants and Corporals. They would brook no sky-larking at any time. There were no washing facilities at the stables and we had to pile into open lorries. These took us to the airfield canteen and washrooms, come snow, rain or fine. Each morning there was usually a fair amount of hoar frost or dew on the oilskins we had put over our bedding, as well as condensation on the inside. There was therefore no point in getting up until the last moment before rushing for the transport, for fear of shivering to death.

It was only the blessed thought of daylight, the warm crewroom, breakfast, and the yellow Magisters lined up outside, that kept us going. How I longed to hear: "Crosley, you're next. We'll do a few steep turns and side-slips this morning."

What utter joy this flying was. It all seemed so logical and easy. Strapping in, with Pilot Officer Jack's breath misting in the cold morning air as he reminded me not to put my boots through the wing as I climbed up to the front cockpit. Then starting up, the chocks in position, brakes on, petrol on, throttle half an inch open, 'suck in' with the two magneto switches off, then 'contact', and she might, or might not fire with the first pull of the propeller blade. 'Chocks away', and the tentative opening of the throttle to get moving over the hard, frosty ground; arriving cross-wind at the down-wind end of the airfield, my instructor passing reminders to me through the 'Gosport' tubes leading into my flying helmet.

When I got a 'green' Aldis light from the Duty Pilot's hut, I turned into wind, opened the throttle gradually and got moving. I kept straight with rudder, easing the stick forward to get the tail off the ground, so that I could see over the nose and where I was going. Then, with about 50 knots on the clock, I eased back on the stick until she left the ground with a final bump on the rough grass. The earth melted away, the ground became a blur, rushing backwards and downwards as we soared into the air. This was the life.

The Miles Magister was one of the first monoplane training aeroplanes. A requirement for all trainers was, and is, that they should give good stall warning and be easy to get out of a spin. The Magister was exceptionally good at getting itself into spins, as it had a vicious wing-drop at the power-on stall. Thereupon, it entered a spin automatically without the pilot having to do a thing. It would then frighten its pilot even more by not coming out of the spin for a turn or two when 'anti-spin' action was taken — ie stick eased forward and 'opposite' rudder applied. Consequently it had a bad name in some flying schools. Pilot Officer Jack had just taken me on a spinning trip. During the hectic manoeuvres, the Gosport tubes had become disconnected and I was no longer getting any help from the back cockpit. I glanced over my shoulder and I saw Jack point to the ground and I knew he wanted me to land. In spite of a windy day with about 20 knots of wind shear in the last quarter mile of the approach, I made a reasonable 'power-on' landing, more or less on three points, where I thought I should have done. It was quite nice doing it all in silence — without the usual comments: "And how many landings do you think that one was?" — and so on. As we came to a stop across-wind, at the up-wind end of the airfield, I glanced back to see if everything was alright. I just had time to catch sight of Jack heaving himself over the side and onto the ground, then running like a hare in the direction of another Magister taxying round in circles nearby. Gawd, I thought, what on earth did I do wrong that time?

Jack came up with the Magister as it was still moving and ran to try to get into the cockpit. As it swerved a bit nearer, I could see that there was no one in it at all. However, there was a muddy figure of a pupil-pilot, in bell-bottoms, being dragged round and round, hanging on to its port wing. Jack threw himself head first into the rear cockpit, grabbed the throttle back and the whole lot came to a halt. What he said to the pupil pilot — Naval Airman Second Class Smith — was later translated to all of us by 'Smithy' himself. Smithy was on his second solo and, having got himself bogged down in the middle of the airfield and with no-one noticing in the control tower, he had used his initiative. This was a bad thing for anyone to use at this time in our training. He had climbed out and tried to get the aircraft clear by himself. He had not tightened up the throttle-lever friction control sufficiently and the Maggie's throttle had slowly wound itself open until it was going at full chat. He was made Duty Pilot for a week.

Spring eventually came to Luton and the sun came out. One day, full of fine, white cumulus clouds which towered up to 10,000 feet and more, Phil Broad and I managed to get our solo trips to coincide. We made an assignation over the cooling towers at Dunstable at 3000 feet, intent on having a dog fight. We went in and out of the clouds, flicking off steep turns, doing home-made versions of Immelmann turns, loops, rolls, dives and stalls and chasing each other in line-astern, terrific fun.

After about half an hour or so, we signalled each other that we had had enough. Phil went off one way and I went off in the other. Then it suddenly occurred to me that I was lost. I looked down for the cooling towers, but they weren't there. Then I looked at the fuel gauge and that was showing a hairsbreadth from zero. We had used it all up while we were at full throttle doing our dogfight — at three times the normal rate.

There was only one thing to do; as Pilot Officer Jack had said: "Land early before the fuel situation gets desperate, then you can pick a good field. Otherwise, you'll end up in someone's back garden and do yourself a mischief." So I made my first forced-landing approach to the first large field that I could find which was into wind. I came in far too fast, as the fuel gauge was reading zero by then and I didn't want to land short. Unfortunately, I floated over most of the field I had chosen without getting anywhere near a touchdown. As the far hedge came nearer and nearer, I thought: "Crosley, this is getting dangerous". I had to avoid the hedge, so I hopefully opened the throttle, hauled back on the stick, and, seeing a perfectly good second field in front, stuffed the stick forward again and managed to land in that. It was a bit too short for comfort and I had to avoid the iron fence at the far end by putting on full port brake and sideslipping the Maggie to a standstill as I had practised in the Morris at home. She just nicked the leading edge of her starboard mainplane on the iron fence. There was an 80 foot road-cutting below the fence so I was glad that I'd made it, for lorries were whizzing up and down it at a high rate of knots.

I got out of the cockpit, trembling a bit, and, with my parachute climbed over the fence and thumbed a lift. They all swept by like Pharisees. Perhaps they thought I was a German who had been shot down. Eventually one stopped. He gave me tuppence for a phone call and I spoke to Pilot Officer Jack. This was lucky, for he did not make a fuss at all. If the Wing Commander had found out, he would have been bound to punish us — *pour encourager les autres*, and we might have been 'dipped' off the course. Pilot Officer Jack forgot about it, especially as Phil Broad had landed correctly at a proper airfield — Abingdon.

It was War Weapons Week in Luton, and three of the most daring of the instructors took their pupils up to do a formation 'beat up' of the Mayor and Corporation. Unfortunately, 'Clunk' Watson's instructor stalled his Magister in a steep turn and spun in, in full view of everyone in the town square. They lifted the wreckage but the instructor who was underneath was dead. Then someone who was smoking set the whole lot on fire. The minor explosion of the leaking petrol dislodged one of the wrecked pieces of the starboard wing, and there, with its arm through the side of one of the petrol tanks in the wing, was a sailor's body. The crowd bravely dragged it free, just in time before the flames seized upon it.

'Clunk' was alive. He spent almost a year in hospital and, through sheer determination to fly again, recovered fully. He eventually made Admiral in the Canadian Navy, and retired in 1973.

We finished the Course at Luton in May 1941. Five or six failed the Course, mostly due to airsickness. We concluded that pilots were made, not born, but some were made easier than others. In wartime, time is short, so we had to learn quickly. Slow learners were at risk. The difficulty was knowing who was suffering from nerves and who was not, for we were all so keen that we tried to hide our anxiety. It required a very experienced instructor to recognise 'twitch' before it became dangerous.

On the last day at Luton, we put up our 'hooks' — single 'foul-anchor' on the left arm, denoting (Temporary Acting) Leading Naval Airmen. Naval pay was about seven shillings (35p) a day, enough for about two and a half gallons of petrol — if you had any coupons — and a gallon of beer. I was very lucky indeed, for I got my pay made up to £4 per week by the Metropolitan Police, and I was rich.

During our 10 days leave, we received our draft chits. Mine was to the Service Flying Training School at RAF Netheravon in Wiltshire. As we were allowed to have cars there, I drove down in style in the Morris Minor. Spring was in the air. Things were improving.

Chapter 6
RAF Netheravon

Netheravon is on the A345, about 12 miles north of Salisbury, between Amesbury and Upavon. In those days it consisted of two grass airfields, one alongside the other. As with Upavon, the RAF's Central Flying School a few miles to the north, it dated from the days of the Royal Flying Corps in the First World War.

I arrived late. This was because the car's petrol pump — one of the early electrically-driven types and nearly as large as the engine itself — was not working properly. It had to be helped by a blow with a hammer, administered over the windscreen by the driver, and with the engine bonnet removed for easy access. The clutch was also slipping, the brakes were fairly useless, the generator was oiled up and the battery kept falling out. Luckily there was nothing much on the road.

Our Course of about 20 joined the two other Courses already at Netheravon. We lived in the same buildings, wooden huts built to World War I standards and far superior to the Nissen huts of our war — as did the 'real' officers, who were mostly our RAF instructors. There were also two genuine, straight-striped Naval officers learning to fly. They were, however, rather superior and understandably had very little to do with us rabble next door.

Life was serene compared with the existence in the stables at Luton Hoo. Civilian stewards made our bunks and, in theory felt the bath water. They also advised us on the RAF's funny habits. 'Colours' parades were particularly difficult to understand, with everyone marching about in different directions, apparently for no reason at all. Tich Madden was having trouble keeping a straight face — again.

I was moved in with a chap from a senior Course. He was a son of a famous chocolate manufacturer. I felt a bit awkward busting in on him so late in the evening, but he was quite nice about it. I asked him why an RAF Corporal was standing outside his cabin door with a rifle and everything. He said that there had been some sort of misunderstanding about some aviation petrol which had found its way into his MG Magna, but as he was engaging a QC (a famous and very expensive criminal lawyer of the time) at the Court Martial, he would probably get off.

Apparently the RAF authorities were worried about the misuse of petrol. They had observed the chocolate king's MG Magna, with its row of hissing carburettors and a full load of Leading Naval Airmen and blondes, on the road to London and elsewhere, nearly every weekend. They had 'dipped' the MG's tank. The petrol was bright green, the colour of 100 Octane aviation fuel as used by the Merlins in the Fairey Battles we were going to fly.

I sympathised with him entirely as everyone else did. "There but for the Grace of God," we said to ourselves, for we had all used His Majesty's petrol from time to time. However, in my case, I was very lucky, for my father had still managed to retain some of the 400 gallons of pre-war petrol in his tank at the nursery, and he gave me some whenever I visited him.

I asked my temporary cabin mate about the flying. He said the Hawker Hart and Audax were particularly nice aeroplanes to fly, and we flew Fairey Battles as well. They had 900 horse power R-R Merlins. The Harts and Audaxes used a sort of scaled-down version of the Merlin, the R-R Kestrel of about 510 hp. The Battles had three-bladed propellers with a 'two-speed' gear. This gave 3000 rpm for take-off in fine pitch and about 2200 rpm in coarse pitch. Two chaps had, so far, been slung off the Course. One for landing with his wheels up — the Battle had a retractable undercarriage — and the other for trying to go round again after a missed landing in coarse pitch.

On this 'go round again' he had disappeared into the dip in the airfield and reappeared over the top, still only doing about 30 knots. He had piled in through the hedge by 'A' Flight. "Naturally", said Coco, "we all rushed out with our Jerry cans and filled up. Everyone hates to see waste, don't they?"

RAF Netheravon was the 'halfway house' in our flying courses. Luton had taught us the basic principles — landing being by far the most difficult — but Netheravon taught us how to do these basic skills in much more powerful and sophisticated aircraft. We did some navigation, dive-bombing, formation flying, and night flying as well.

Before attempting night flying, we practised flying 'on instruments' in daylight — cloud flying. We also practised instrument flying ('I/F') in the 'Link Trainer'. This was a small box-shaped device with vestigial wings — the forerunner of the multi-million pound simulator of today. It was equipped with a set of blind-flying instruments, engine instruments and controls. Shut up in darkness, the pilot was given various courses and speeds to fly at various heights and for set times, by the instructor. Everything the pupil did was repeated by a row of instruments in front of the instructor. He acted like a back-seat-driver, nagging away until the pupil got it right or went into a spin in desperation. A small pen would trace out the course that the pilot steered on a large piece of squared paper. The instructor would then show the pupil what he had done, together with his various rude remarks alongside. The final passing out test was the 'T'. We had to steer a set of courses and speeds such that we came back to the same place that we had started from, mapping out a 'T' the while. The results were then pinned up, for all to see. Some disappeared clean off the paper, others were interspersed by accidental spins, stalls and various other interruptions. The perfect 'T' was a matter of practice — just as 'Space Invaders' can be vanquished once the operator has got used to the machine's habits. The 'Link' was so crude that it could never teach anyone to fly safely in real conditions, but it was a help and saved flying hours and doubtless many lives.

Compared with the 'Maggie's' 90 mph top speed and the Hart's 170 mph, the Battle did about 210 mph at about 4000 feet. The Battle was a dangerous flop in France in its role as an Army recce-bomber, but the Hart series were very popular with the Naval and RAF pilots who flew them in their many peacetime variants. Unlike the early Magister, both types of aircraft at Netheravon were so easy and safe to fly, that it was entirely your own fault if you crashed one.

The forward view from the Hart's front seat was restricted, though not seriously, by the upper mainplane and by the longish nose of the Kestrel in-line engine. The view downwards and backwards was, however, excellent. It was great fun listening to the screech of the wind through the struts and wires. It even had a 'blow-back' airspeed indicator — a sort of early head-up display. The faster the aircraft flew, the more this spring-loaded piece of metal blew back, ticking off the mph on a crudely painted scale.

I was detailed to join nine others in 'A' Flight. The Flight buildings consisted of a shed or two for the ground crew, instructors, and the CO. He was Squadron Leader The Hon. David Douglas-Hamilton, DFC and Bar, and like some others at Netheravon, was an ex-Battle of Britain fighter pilot. In the warm sunshine and surrounded by the Wiltshire chalk Downs with the skylarks and the white clouds overhead, flying was a marvellous pleasure compared with the gloom of the midlands in winter. Butterflies — the Small Copper warming its wings, the Chalkhill Blue; birds — the curlew, cornbunting and the kestrel quartering the hillside or perched on any convenient pole, watching.

The first solo take-offs and landings were a great responsibility, for there were no spare aircraft at Netheravon and if we ground-looped, and broke a lower mainplane we were not only very unpopular with the instructors, but even more so with the pupils.

One day, the instructors, led by the Wing Commander, carried out a flying demonstration for OC Flying Training Command. They made a formation landing. The two outer Harts swung outwards on their landing runs in a beautiful Prince of Wales' feather, and each ended up on its nose, with perfect timing. The OC was not impressed, but we thought that it put the whole thing into its proper perspective and relieved some of our tension.

David Douglas-Hamilton was a keen sportsman as well as a popular Flight Commander, and he organised an inter-station boxing contest. The future British Light-Heavyweight Champion — a milk roundsman from Bournemouth and one of the bravest boxers there has ever been — Freddie Mills — was our 'Springer'. He was particularly keen that RAF Netheravon should win. Geoffrey Russell-Jones, on the Course ahead of ours, was also a good boxer and he gave me one or two practice bouts, which I lost rather painfully. At the contest itself, held in the gym with a thousand watching, I was drawn against a pale, mean, wiry individual, a little shorter than me. Geoffrey, who had already won his bout, advised me to use my longer reach and not get too close to him. I began to wish I had taken Naval advice — not to volunteer for anything. My chap's face was so narrow I couldn't hit it once with the straight jab that Mr. Geary of Winchester College had taught me at the Pilgrims' School, and I stupidly tried to mix it, throwing the clever stuff to the winds. He immediately realised that he had nothing to fear and swooped upon me and by the third round I found myself on the floor, knocked out for the first time, ever. I stupidly got up and another blow came from somewhere else and that was that. Next morning Douglas-Hamilton told me that I could not fly for a day after a knock-out, "just in case".

Night flying was the most difficult hurdle to jump at Netheravon. Although the Link Trainer was supposed to give a sprog pilot an insight into the business, it had an artificial horizon amongst its array of flying instruments. This told you immediately whether you were diving, climbing or banking to the left or right and was about the best invention since the bicycle. However, the Harts and Audaxes did not have this vital link with reality — only a 'turn-and-bank' indicator. Thus, the only way of finding out whether you were diving, climbing or turning in the Hart at night was to study the turn-and-bank. If its two needles were wobbling all over the place, recourse had to be made to the 'rate of climb/dive' instrument and the compass. As this instrument only told you what you *had* been doing, but never what you actually *were* doing, you spent much time and energy chasing its exhortations up and down, never finding touch at all. The final pair of instruments in this search for knowledge was a very large air speed indicator and a very small altimeter. If the airspeed was winding itself down and the altimeter was winding itself up and the noise in the rigging got less, it was safe to say you were climbing — and *vice versa*. Night flying in Harts was therefore interesting and dangerous, particularly on dark nights with no stars, no horizon, and, in wartime, no lights on the ground. As the nights which were chosen for night flying practice were always the darkest possible — because the Germans came over on moonlight nights to see what they could find — and as we also had to operate well away from Netheravon at a small grass field near Shrewton, the whole thing was asking for trouble.

As we waited our turn to fly at Shrewton, we crept around aimlessly in darkness on the ground, not knowing what phenomenon to expect next. When our time came, we searched the blasted heath with care, looking for our aircraft and our instructor in all directions. Then, just as Macbeth might have stumbled upon the three witches, we, too, suddenly came across our instructor and some ground staff and followed them into the darkness towards a distant, silent aircraft.

Once we got into the air, our wanderings were not over, for we then had to try to find the airfield again, which had disappeared astern somewhere. There were only two or three 'goose-neck' flares visible from the air and once we had lost sight of them — perhaps while looking for a few intelligible instruments in the dimly lit cockpit — life became very lonely.

One of the pupils on an earlier course had been airborne at the same time that a Ju 88 had come over. It had dropped a bomb near the goose-neck flares. These were immediately extinguished by the ground crew and the pupil became lost. He suddenly thought of his yachting days and flew south to Portland Bill, identified Portland Light, still operating in wartime, and flew back on a compass course to Shrewton. By that time they had turned on the 'Chance Light', a sort of searchlight at ground level, to give him an emergency landing direction. We had heard of these tales, told with such sang-froid by the people concerned, and we wondered if we could hope to live up to such heroism and skill ourselves. Night flying was, therefore, not just a test of our flying but a character test as well.

After passing our night flying test, we were transferred to Battles, flying from the northern airfield. At about this time, an officer, Midshipman Williams RNR, distinguished himself by achieving the 'blue note' in a Battle. This immense propeller noise, the blade tips going round through the air so fast they were supersonic, could be achieved by selecting fixed fine pitch on the Battle's airscrew and then pointing it earthwards from a great height and at full throttle. We heard the screaming noise at lunch-time one day, and we left our soup plates to watch.

As it is not possible to hear much of the noise in the cockpit of an aircraft making a blue note, Midshipman Williams was unaware of his success when he landed. However, as his aircraft was covered from stem to stern in black oil and smelled awful, he had to say something about it on Form 700. He put the aircraft U/S (unserviceable) due to a "slight oil leak".

When the fitter came to check the oil, there was none left, only white metal and black sludge in the filters. The engine was a write-off, and questions were asked. A farmer rang up complaining that a Battle had just whipped over the top of his barn and frightened his cattle; and even more questions were asked. The Wing Commander had to act and Williams was posted to a target-towing squadron in Gibraltar on Skuas. As this was a fate worse than death, we decided we would never be caught out like that.

The Battle, had, of course, been designed to dive-bomb as well as level-bomb its targets. The RAF at Netheravon reckoned that its dive-bombing capabilities should be used in the training role. Before being allowed to drop the 25 lb. 'smoke' practice bombs and use up valuable ranges, we all had to do practice dives without bombs, using painted circles as our aiming point on the nearby Army firing range. Some of the Battles were dual two-seaters and two pupils often went up together, doing their dive-bombing sorties and then carrying out instrument flying practice. The spare pilot had to keep watch for mid-air collisions, while the other pilot had his head stuck 'in the office', with the blind flying hood pulled over so that he could not cheat.

Phil Broad and I were detailed for such a trip one day, and we thought we would do a bit of unauthorised low flying. I sat in the front of the Battle and Phil sat in the rear seat, some 20 feet down towards the tail. We polished off our bombing very quickly and started our instrument flying practice. As Phil and I were so far apart, it was too far to expect the 'intercom' to work so that on changing control from one pilot to another, we decided to use a stick-waggling drill. One waggle — "you take her". Second waggle — "I've got her", sort of thing. Of course, even this method of transfer of control was chancy so Phil and I determined to use this characteristic to excuse us in case we were caught low flying. If caught, we would plead that the transfer hadn't worked, and neither of us had "got her".

Phil 'did' a couple of Army pubs at Downton and then it was my turn. I chose a patch between two poplar trees — the local dare — and just as I was pulling up from my second dive, I glanced to the port side and saw, as clear as daylight, a Hawker Fury II, right alongside us. As this could only have been flown by an instructor — as these beautiful fighter versions of the Hart series were in short supply — I knew we were in trouble. Mistake number two and with Phil Broad, too. But perhaps the excuse would work?

So Phil and I flew carefully back to Netheravon, obeying all the rules that we could think of. We climbed furtively into our cars at dispersal and drove to the mess for lunch. Five minutes after sitting down we heard the Tannoy tell us to report to Wing Commander Flying.

We told him our "you've got her, no you've got her" story, separately and without putting a word wrong. The Wing Commander then asked us both back into his office — to give us, we hoped, a combined "Now be more careful next time" talking to. Instead he said: "That accounts for one dive, now what about the other five?"

We were extremely lucky that we were not thrown off the course. Instead, all we had to do was a week's extra Duty Pilot — shining lights at aircraft and counting them out and counting them all back. We also had our leave stopped, but as we had no money left it hardly mattered.

The last fortnight of the Netheravon Course was spent at RAF Stormy Down, an airfield at Porthcawl in South Wales. We did some dive-bombing at a mark in the Bristol Channel. Four Battles were taken down, three by instructors with terrified passengers in the back — and the fourth by a pupil, chosen for his sang-froid, reliability and various other qualities. No one volunteered to fly in the back with him, so he had to go alone with our baggage.

Someone also brought a huge Austin 14 tourer down as well, with the remaining half dozen or so of us. It was summer and we all looked forward to a holiday by the seaside at His Majesty's expense, with a little flying on the side.

The target was a 40 foot yellow triangle of wood, with a flag on top, floating in the sea. As we dived at it using the front gunsight to aim with, a team of four WAAFs plotted our dive direction and angle with theodolites. We were supposed to hurtle down from 6000 feet to the release height of 3000 feet. The WAAFs aimed their theodolites at the smoke, and, where the bearings crossed, the hit was marked on the target chart. The results were telephoned to the airfield and we were told how well we had done by our instructor. There was a complicated system of Aldis signals as well. These told us to stop or to start our dives when everything was ready. There were no radio transmitters in any of the aircraft.

My results on the first day gave me an average error of about 80 feet. On the second day I determined to do better. It was flat calm and, with no wind, I thought it would be easy to get good results. I had worked it out that by releasing the bomb a good deal lower then the 3000 feet prescribed, I could confound the critics and actually hit the target. I might even qualify for flying the fourth Battle home instead of risking it in the Austin. The first dive was normal, the second dive was a bit lower and the third, I thought, was about 50 feet lower still. However, I misjudged the height for the pull-out in the glassy sea conditions and I remember seeing floating debris go by the same level as me, and very fast. I had to pull-out very sharply indeed.

This had far reaching consequences. In order to relieve the pilot's 'out-of-trim' control loads, each flying control surface — aileron, elevator, or rudder — has a trimming tab which pre-sets the main control in the desired direction. It is usually operated by a graduated wheel in the cockpit. I had therefore set the elevator slightly 'nose-up' to assist with the pull-out. When I added my pull to the stick — and a sharp one at that, having misjudged my height so badly — the poor old Battle whipped up out of the dive very sharply and I blacked-out. When I came too, having become unconscious, I remember looking down at the red throttle knob in my left hand and wondering what it was. The noise had come back to my brain a bit after my vision, and touch sensation also returned, but all at slightly different times. The brain was therefore hopelessly confused at all these weird, mistimed inputs, and I must have spent several seconds in a condition of 'masterly inactivity'. Luckily, this was exactly the course of action which Pilot Officer Jack would have recommended: "Do nothing, Crosley. Leave the bloody thing alone. It'll get out of trouble better than you."

This is what the faithful old Battle did. When I came to, I worked out eventually that the aircraft must have been on its tail, slightly inverted, still going upwards and with one wing low. It must have fallen out of the ensuing stall, on its own, just like a child's paper aeroplane. I came back shaken and stirred. This was booboo number three, and with only about 60 hours in my log book, too.

After I had signed in and put 'DCO' (Duty Carried Out) in the Flight Authorisation Book, my instructor came over with my results. He said that the WAAF Sergeant plotter had said that I had pulled out of the last dive too low. The surface had been ruffled by the aircraft's slipstream as it pulled out, missing the water by about two feet, she said. Luckily it was the last bomb, so that I had appeared to have obeyed her Aldis red light — which I never saw, and, "after a few aerobatics" she said, I had gone home immediately. She wasn't annoyed as a result and I managed to get away without the matter being referred to higher authority. The results were fantastic, the average error being about 10 feet. However, I was extremely lucky not to have pulled the wings off the aircraft. The Battle was stressed to take fighter-type wing loadings, as it was a dive-bomber. In this case it must have withstood over seven 'g'. The basic reason for the overcontrol was because it was being flown with its CG well forward of the position allowed for dive-bombing. This encouraged pilots to use the trimming wheel to give extra pull-out of the dive with the unfortunate results which I have described. Yet, had I pulled the wings off, it would probably have been classed 100 per cent 'pilot error'. There was general ignorance of such things.

Back at Netheravon for the last week, there was time to consider the Morris Minor. It had not reacted well to 100 octane poured down its clutch housing to prevent the clutch from slipping, and the Flight electricians had not been able to understand the fuel pump. The brake shoes were down to the rivets and the steering wheel seemed to have less and less effect on where the car was going. Furthermore, the general tone of the car was not in keeping with a dashing fighter-pilot image.

Close by the George Hotel at Amesbury there is a garage. It was then run by a certain Wally Scott, who exhibited in the front of his garage courtyard a beautiful blue M2-type MG, featuring two P100 chrome headlamps. It also had an overhead camshaft — a very good thing to have — cycle-type mudguards, knock-on hubs, a noisy exhaust and a benchtype seat for easy poodle-faking. Furthermore, the air in the seat could be adjusted to any pressure to suit any female bum which happened to be there. The MG was decorated in a tri-colour, a blue/black and silver motif. On the radiator cap was a chrome flagstaff with a large Union Jack. Wally wanted £75 for it. I sold him the Morris Minor for £45 and cashed £30 Post Office savings.

The snag was, as my father, the owner of the Morris pointed out, that I had lost his 1934 car and gained a worn-out 1931 model and, had had to pay £30 for the privilege, adding that the Morris's and MG's engines were identical except for the overhead cams. But I told him he had gained a very marketable car if anything happened to me before anything happened to it, instead of the dreadful Morris. He kindly forgot to ask for the MG back as the war progressed and it became my unofficial property.

The final two joys in my life at Netheravon were first, to be measured by Gieves for a Sub-Lieutenant's uniform complete with wings. The next was to drive down to Yeovilton in the MG to begin training on a real single-seat fighter, the Hawker Hurricane Ib. (Appendix 2 — Naval Air Power — describes the Fleet Air Arm and some of its 'props and scenery' at this period in the War.)

Chapter 7
RNAS Yeovilton

The premier Naval Air Station Yeovilton, HMS *Heron*, is off the A303, north of Ilchester. Twelve of us arrived at the end of July 1941, for a three or four month course. The object of the course was to learn to fly, fight and deckland an operational fighter aircraft. At that time there were only a few Sea Hurricanes with deck landing hooks in the FAA. Four were in *Furious* in 880A Flight and just about to take part, though we did not know it, in the tragically costly and totally unproductive strike on Petsamo/Kirkenes. A few more had been sent out to Gibraltar in packing cases intended for *Ark Royal* They hardly became operational before she was sunk. (I was allowed to filch two of these left-overs for *Eagle* in May 1942.)

When we arrived at Yeovilton, we saw several Fulmars Is parked out on the airfield besides the couple of dozen Hurricanes. The Fulmars were two-seat Naval escort fighters, not interceptors, and were little faster or lighter than the Fairey Battle, from which their design had been derived.

Our first lesson at Yeovilton was, therefore, that Hurricanes were extremely valuable and in very short supply. One act of carelessness or a second genuine accident, and we would find ourselves towing targets in Skuas or Boulton-Paul Defiants.

I shared a cabin with Geoffrey Russell-Jones of the Course ahead of me. Our simultaneous arrival must have been a mistake because half of us were given ground duties for three weeks and had to wait patiently while sufficient Hurricanes became available. We occupied our time doing 'duty boy' in the Air Watch tower.

After about three weeks of this, we joined 'C' Flight. Our CO was Lt/Cdr Rodney Carver, DSO, DSC, RN. My instructor was Lt (A) 'Wiggy' Wiggington, DSC, RN recently rescued from Crete. Two others were Lt (A) 'Jimmy' R. E. Gardner, DFC, RNVR, and later in the year, Lt (A) 'Dicky' Cork, DFC, RN. These two DFCs — changed to DSCs later — were awarded by the RAF for their work in Hurricanes in No. 242 Squadron in the Battle of Britain.

One morning we were taken for a walk round the airfield where we saw our first Skua. It was 'resting', Wiggy said. We were all impressed with its size, its dive brakes, its anti-spin parachute and its lethal appearance. However, Paddy Brownlee did question the size of the 'glasshouse' along the top of its fuselage and suggested, not for the first time, that it would be good for growing tomatoes if only they would take the aircraft outside in the sunshine and not keep it in the darkest corner of the hangar.

There were still two Gladiators at Yeovilton. There was also a captured Italian CR 42. Wiggy and our CO, Rodney Carver, had a dogfight over the airfield and the CR 42 won. This was rather glossed over later, and no one would admit it; but it was true.

The Hurricanes we flew were ex-Battle of Britain and had no hooks. They seemed very ancient. They were always running out of brakes, leaking oil all over the windscreen, oiling up the plugs — a sure sign of worn engines — and having coolant leaks. Some had fabric wings. However, the Sea Hurricane Ib had already been decklanded by a Naval pilot called Bromwich, who had pronounced it "easy". But we also heard that it was very "tricky". We were going to find out for ourselves at the end of the Course, aboard *Argus*.

One day a beautiful American single-seat radial-engined fighter arrived. It was dark blue and, as it had an arrester hook, we were interested to find out what it was. It was a Martlet — the Royal Navy's name for a Wildcat — the Grumman F4F -1. Forty of them were leftovers from a French Naval order and we now had them for our own use. However, this early version had Wright Cyclone engines which were always overheating, seizing up or just stopping if hard pressed, for they were designed for civil aircraft. So only experienced pilots were allowed to fly them. They seemed to chuff around the circuit very fast indeed and the squadron pilots thought they were wonderful and far faster than a Hurricane. They were proud that they had been chosen to fly such a difficult aircraft, with its mass of mixture-control levers, its two-speed supercharger, its throttle which, someone said, opened the wrong way, its narrow, manually-raised undercarriage and its impressively large cockpit covered in dials, levers and switches.

My first flight at Yeovilton, my first ever in a high performance single-seater, was an unforgettable experience. The Hurricane Mark Ib had been through the Battle of Britain and was, therefore, a highly developed machine. Everything in it was made as easy as possible for the pilot so that he could concentrate on finding, fixing and killing his opponent. It had automatic boost control and mixture control, a fully constant-speed propeller and, best of all, a modern blind-flying instrument panel with an artificial horizon and a 'geared' altimeter. (The altimeter had two hands, the 'minute' hand going round once for each 1000 feet.) The only control the pilot had to make a conscious effort to remember — besides the radiator flap — was to change-over the fuel cock from the small 'gravity' feed tank of 15 gallons, to the main tank. This had to be done after take-off otherwise the engine would stop 20 minutes later.

We practised steep turns without letting the nose drop or allowing the aircraft to flick over on its back with a 'G' stall. We did formation flying in cloud, mock interception exercises, camera-gun attacks, 'oxygen climbs' to about 25,000 feet, and dogfights and aerobatics.

While I was Duty Officer in the Air Watch tower, I saw several prangs. These were mainly due to brake failure, swinging on landing, heavy landings or taxying accidents. A typical accident was one which happened to my cabin mate, Geoffrey Russell-Jones. He describes it 40 years on: "I adored the Hurricane Is, with the 'gate-change' hydraulics, but one day, in my anxiety to keep up with my flight leader, I came in to land a bit quick. I have a vivid recollection of heading for the gate to the (A37) roadway at the end of the runway and seeing a Naval Policeman deserting his post and diving for cover. At that point my starboard tyre burst (brakes overheating) and I spun round — and there was yourself, flashing rude messages from the Control Tower. I wrote my report for the Wren secretary to type, including a little humour for her eyes only — and she showed it to the CO." (On his A25 the secretary had unfortunately typed it verbatim, and it had referred to the tyre bursting sequence as: "I popped the starboard tyre and swung off, nearly collecting the police box" — words to which Their Lordships took exception.) "I was sent down to St. Merryn (another Naval Air Station near Padstow in Cornwall), where an engineer officer was madly screwing Hurricanes together from bits sent to him in crates. I used to test fly them, thus continuing to distribute some of the unsecured bits round Cornwall."

My first take-off in a Hurricane was like a first ride on a high-powered speed boat, noisy, shaky and out of control and, with the same colossal acceleration which almost dragged my hand off the throttle and jerked my head back against the headrest, it was so unexpected. The aircraft took charge. It shook with power as the 900 horses, only a few feet in front, wrenched round the propeller and dug it into the air. It was frightening too, for the whole thing leapt into the sky well before I was ready for it and having used only a quarter of the runway. It was so different from the Battle, where there was always sufficient time between one occurrence and the next to keep ahead of the game.

The first landing was just as exciting, for none of us were used to an aircraft having such a high power/weight ratio and which would respond so crisply to the smallest throttle adjustments or stick movements and forces on the approach. The view over the nose was excellent and allowed the runway to be seen straight ahead, even in the tail-down attitude. Sydney Camm had designed the Hurricane for use on grass airfields. It had fat, low-pressure tyres and a wide-track undercarriage, easy enough to cope with bumpy grass surfaces. The only problem with having to land on concrete runways was the rolling resistance was far less than on soft grass surfaces. The aircraft had therefore to be pulled up entirely by the harsh use of the brakes, something for which they were not designed and in which they consistently overheated when the touchdown speeds were high. High touchdown speeds always occurred in calm wind conditions and sooner or later we might have the bad luck to fly an aircraft where the brakes were weak. One or the other of the brakes would then overheat, depending perhaps on any crosswind conditions, and the Hurricane would swing off onto the grass. It was then a matter of luck whether we could avoid a ground-loop — an uncontrollable backwheel-skid-type manoeuvre — and 'writing off' the undercarriage due to side loads. ('Write off' was a stores procedure for taking something off-charge when it was no long any use.) With the CG behind the wheels — as in all tail-wheel aircraft — this 'back wheel skid' could only be prevented by having a lockable tailwheel held firmly on the ground to prevent the swing from starting, or, by doing a 'wheeler'. This latter was what the RAF usually did anyway, for it was by far the most sensible method of landing. In the case of the Navy, 'wheelers' were discouraged because they could get us into bad habits for decklanding.

It is marvellous to watch a swan, or even an old cormorant taking off from the water. They always take off into the wind, even if this is into danger. Likewise, all bird-landings on water are made without the slightest drift, dead into wind. But mere humans seem incapable of judging skid or drift with such marvellous accuracy and often make the dreadful error of coming in to land across-wind, or even downwind on some occasions, with disastrous results. There is no excuse for landing out-of-wind on a grass airfield, but where there are only a few runway directions from which to choose, it is sometimes necessary. If the direction of crosswind were from the port, or left side, this was very awkward in the Hurricane. It would often start to 'weathercock' uncontrollably. The pilot might then say, "Gawd, I've made a cock-up here!" and suddenly decide to go round again for another try. This could easily increase the swing tendency, for the propeller torque (rotation, being clockwise, from aft), would tend to stall the port wing and swing the tail further to port (due to the twist in the upper half of the propeller wash striking the fin) and the whole thing could end up like "a can of worms". With thoughts of Skua-dom flashing through the mind on more than one occasion, I can thank my lucky stars that I was not one of the ground-loopers.

The Commander (Flying) at Yeovilton in 1941 was one of the very few surviving 'vintage' Naval aviators. He lent dignity to an otherwise somewhat light-hearted activity. He was large, rubicund, frightening, and without humour. He could, nevertheless, very nearly understand the average RNVR sprog pilot. As we found it difficult to understand ourselves, this was no mean achievement. He flew the Station Gladiator each morning at 0730 as a strict routine. After the beautiful little biplane fighter had been brought out of its hangar, it was suitably arranged into wind and near Air Traffic Control, ready for the Commander.

He would drive up, answer the smart salute from the rigger and climb up some short steps, specially placed in position, to the cockpit, his brass hat glistening in the morning sun. After having each strap handed carefully to him from each side of the cockpit by the fitter and rigger, he would adjust various controls in the cockpit, ready for the 'off'. Then he would lower his hand over the cockpit side for his gloves to be handed up to him. This was the routine.

One morning, I was Duty Boy in the Control Tower and I saw that the routine proceeded normally, noting that the brass trimming on the steps could do with a polish. This time, there was a new rigger on duty and when the Commander lowered his hand for his gloves, the rating, believing the Commander was offering his hand in a last farewell before he rose into the air to fight the Hun to the death at dawn, shook his hand warmly, instead.

The Duty Boy had other things besides the Commander's Gladiator to try to organise before breakfast. He had to collect the Fulmars and Hurricanes parked out on the airfield. They were dispersed as a precaution against losing too many at once if a Ju 88 or Me 110 came over on a strafing run. There happened to be a stray Swordfish in a far-off corner of the airfield. This was naturally a challenge to any Hurricane pilot, bored with being Duty Boy and not having much fun. It therefore had to be rounded-up whether it wanted to be or not.

There was a routine for starting Swordfish which called for advanced standards of airmanship, split-second timing and a nearby fire-engine. If none of these conditions applied, there was usually trouble, especially if fighter pilots, used to easy, electrical starting, had a go. The routine was written down somewhere in 'Pilot's Notes' for the Swordfish. After the removal of the covers, I climbed into the cockpit and failing to find the Notes, I made one or two inquiries of the riggers and fitters who accompanied me. Apparently, the routine worked something like this:

"Magneto switches — off. Turn prop by hand to check no hydraulic locks. Prime engine cylinders with fuel. Check brakes 'on' and pressure OK. Chocks in position. Select the strongest volunteer to insert the starting handle and commence turning. If no one volunteers, detail someone."

"The volunteer inserts handle into any suitable-looking hole he can find in the engine cowling and winds it round, getting faster and faster. There should be a grinding, whining sound. If there isn't, select another hole for the starter handle and try again."

"When there is no further chance of the winder increasing the revs from what must obviously be a sort of flywheel buzzing round inside, he should signal the pilot in the cockpit to 'engage'. This links the grinding sound with the crankshaft of the engine in some way, and the grinding then gets slower as the engine gets faster. Both then come to a halt, and the whole thing has to start again. If, in the unlikely event, the engine fires, the propeller starts to go round. The man with the handle should then remove it from its hole and run away quickly, before he gets covered in oil, flames or smoke, or gets hit by the propeller or loses his hat down the air intake."

I did not see the rigger's frantic signals that he had reached the end of his energy in turning the flywheel. However, I had enough sense to realise that the revs were not getting any higher, so I pulled the tit to 'engage'. The thing gave a slight chuffing noise for about half a revolution, and there was silence once more; silence, that is to say, except for panting sounds and expletives coming from the rigger. Reinforcements arrived and two men then started turning, one either side. (Another handle had been found in the observer's cockpit behind me.) This took the engine by surprise as the revs obtained were much higher than before. It began to fire on two of its nine cylinders. If it had been a Merlin, I would have kept the starter button pressed and the priming pump going during this 'will she — won't she' period, and the other cylinders would have had to have joined in, through sheer embarrassment. But with the Swordfish, only the waning revs from the flywheel arrangement could continue to give power. With but two cylinders out of nine, it is not enough on a cold morning for the engine to wake itself up unless something urgent is done. I was now told what this was by a crowd of interested onlookers.

"More dope, pilot." "No, you've given to much already. There are flames coming out of the air intake, sir." "Try again with more throttle." Then, aside: "Put your hat over the air intake and put the flames out, you idiot." "No, you'll have to blow out now, she's too rich."

Eventually, with me priming as hard as I could the other cylinders gradually joined in with the two that hadn't let me down, and the whole aircraft disappeared from sight in a cloud of blue smoke, visible from Queen Camel four miles away. The birds flew up in alarm, the fire tender crew fingered their nozzles, others ran after their hats, but all was well. Having recovered a little of my confidence, I waved the chocks away and trundled the Swordfish towards the 'Duty Flight' hangar.

The Swordfish was a rare bird in Somerset. It was not often seen in the south, even in summer. However, when it came in small numbers, it always tended to merge with the countryside more than the flying machines of a later age. Had I left it there in peace that morning, it could easily have become overgrown by long grass in a month or two and become, like any other picturesque farmyard machinery, a home for rabbits and birds. But this was not to be, for one morning a strange pilot came along, dressed in a fur-lined leather flying jacket. His name was 'Boris' Morris, a Sub/Lt (A) RN, my wardroom snooker opponent. He placed some golf clubs in the back, started it up first time and flew it back to Scotland, to Crail, to Wick or somewhere, where Swordfish lived. It was six months before I saw another Swordfish so far south.

One Monday morning, I came back from a weekend at home and found a whole lot of Wall's Ice Cream tricycles — 'Stop-me-and-buy-one's — on the grass outside Air Traffic Control. While everyone else was taxying past them in clouds of dust, various officers in flying helmets were pedalling them all over the airfield. They were apparently listening-in to radio signals. This, I was told, was the new, Fighter Interception School in action.

Although ADR (Air Direction Radar) and all the skills of interceptor-fighter operations had been in marvellous and vital use for two years in the RAF — and in the Battle of Britain in particular — the art had not spread to the Royal Navy.

It still preferred to rely on AA guns rather than interceptors. It also abhorred 'chatter' over the r/t and had refused to use radar or r/t much at sea for the past two vital years, thinking it might give away the position of the Fleet. However, sanity began to prevail, as one ship after another was disabled in the Mediterranean by the Stuka dive-bomber and enemy torpedo aircraft. Lt E. Lewin, DSO, DSC, RN, a fighter pilot from *Ark Royal*, had come to Yeovilton to get ADR operators trained for interception duties in carriers and in 'air defence' cruisers.

A 'Schooly', Lt/Cdr Coke, RN, who organised the daily work of the school itself, managed to do this on 'a shoestring' and without fuss.

The Wall's ice cream tricycles were the 'aircraft'. The 'pilots' pedalled them under radio directions from a small transmitter in the Control Tower, which was the 'aircraft-carrier'. Some tricycles were enemy 'bombers'. They pedalled slowly. Others were 'fighters'. They pedalled faster — but only a *little* faster, we noticed.

The pilots of the bombers and fighters carried their wireless sets where ice cream should have been. The bombers steered a course for the carrier, and the fighters were sent to intercept them. They steered whatever course and speed that Lt/Cdr Coke ordained, using a compass below the handlebars to give them the required direction and a metronome on top of the ice cream compartment to give them their pedalling airspeed.

Neither bomber nor fighter could see where they were going, so we watched each collision as it occurred. We would then listen to the polite comments of the fighter pilot towards the bomber as they unseated each other in mock combat. Sometimes there were r/t failures. The Tower then lost contact, and aircraft would get lost on the airfield and sometimes be seen pedalling slowly down the roads between the hangars or by the Captain's office. We suspected that they had purposely switched off and were making a beeline for the wardroom bar. There was no let-up, come-rain-come-shine. They even worked during the lunch hour. Some would take sandwiches and beer with them. They kept them in the ice cream compartment, munching them while they pedalled. It was odd to see, at times, a fighter making about 1000 knots equivalent speed. When we asked him why, he said that he had had to 'land' to have a 'strain off' and was making up for lost time.

Some of the cyclists were Wrens. We thought that a particularly large one should have had 'Buy me and stop one' written on her tricycle. It was in the days of Lisle stockings. A few could look quite formidable at times, particularly those wearing 'St. Trinian' Naval hats over their eyes on dark nights. Fortunately, these were scarce. Most were beautiful and all were kind. They were the delight of our lives at Yeovilton.

By September 1941 there were only two more flying hurdles to climb for my Course. One was the art of making camera-gun attacks on other aircraft. The other was trying to hit a target towed at the regulation 160 knots by a frightened Skua or Defiant pilot, with real live bullets. All fighters naturally had their guns aligned to the mean line-of-flight of the fighter itself. The gunsight was aligned to the same spot. In theory, all the pilot had to do was to fly his aircraft at the target, press the button, and the whole thing would disappear in a thousand smoking pieces. As this seldom happened even in theory in our camera gun attacks, we soon came to the conclusion that air-to-air firing was a very difficult business.

Attacks from dead astern, were, of course, asking for trouble. First, you gave the rear-gunner of the bomber an easy no-deflection shot at you. Secondly, he might have 0.5 inch guns to your 0.303 inch and so he could easily out-range you. He could then start shooting at you 150 yards before you could hope to hit him with your much less powerful Brownings. Thirdly, by spending any time right behind him, you would find that your fighter aircraft would become uncontrollable in his slipstream. Accurate aiming then became impossible.

The answer was to do a quarter attack, starting from about 30 degrees to one side or the other of his stern, or from above or below. This avoided the slipstream effects and provided the bomber's rear gunner with a difficult target. (See Appendix 3 — Air-to-Air firing from a fighter in World War II.)

Difficult as it was, some pilots took to it almost immediately. They were those who could judge speeds of approach, angles-off and 'curves of pursuit', by using eyesight and the equally marvellous computer in their brains to arrive at 250 yards from the target, with an overtaking speed of about 50 miles per hour and at an angle-off of about 30 degrees. They would then have about three seconds of firing time as they closed the range from 250 to 100 yards. During this time, their eight front guns would shoot off about 500 bullets, 10 per cent of which should, if correctly aimed, hit something vital.

When we were learning to judge distances, ranges, angles, heights and approach speeds at Yeovilton, we only had about 10 hours of Hurricane flying in which to master these skills. We then had to try them out on our poor instructors. As many of them had already spent part of the war flying unmanoeuvrable and underpowered fighters such as Skuas and Fulmars, and had probably lost half their fellow pilots and observers in doing so, they did not take kindly to pupils putting them to further unnecessary risks when they were again the targets.

Wiggy, my instructor, a skilled fighter pilot himself who was reputed to have shot down an Me 109 with a Skua, took me aside one day. "Crosley", he said, while walking on the airfield, "you have a certain amount of flying ability, but you are going to kill yourself and me as well, if you go on with your quarter attacks as you are doing at the moment. You silly idiot, you broke off at about 10 foot range this afternoon and I could hear your engine noise, it was so close, as you passed underneath me. It's all very well for you. You think you know what you're doing and you don't worry. I know you don't know what you are doing and I'm frightened fartless. So don't do it again, otherwise I'll chuck you off the course. Got it? Good."

I'm glad to say I was sensible enough to do what he told me. However, it was impossible to receive any sort of detailed instruction while in the air, as the TR9D radio sets in the aircraft seldom worked. However, they occasionally served some purpose, for if there was a sudden crackling noise — like a thousand Donald Ducks — you naturally inferred that it was your instructor getting angry at what you were doing, so you did something else.

Yeovilton has always had an aura of fun, competition, Wrens and fast cars. In 1941, the phenomenon of the 'immobile' Wren was new to us. The thatched country houses in the surrounding villages all seemed to have one, each more beautiful, rich and well educated than the last. Some had even been to Roedean.

The 'immobile' part of their title was intended to remind the Naval Appointment authorities at Lee-on-Solent — the Fleet Air Arm headquarters for ratings — that these particular Wrens were not volunteers for any job but only there for the one which was near their home. They therefore lived at home in splendour, knowing they could not be posted to Singapore, Colombo or Scapa Flow. Their mums were naturally keen that they should meet a good cross-section of Fleet Air Arm officers. There were therefore plenty of party invitations for us. We played tennis and croquet outdoors and various other games indoors.

Many of the pupils were extraordinarily gifted in the Arts. Sub/Lt (A) Barry Lyster on Course 20 was able to play and sing as well as Noel Coward or 'Hutch' and would keep us round the piano until the small hours. Some of the Sub-Lieutenants were extremely rich, including one with an orange Rolls-Royce. Local mums tended to be a trifle more protective than usual when they were around.

Then there were barn dances at North Cadbury. Wardroom dances were organised off the Station because KR and AI (King's Regulations and Admiralty Instructions) forbade us to dance in public with Wrens in uniform as they were ratings and we were (perhaps) officers. Neither could the Wren ratings be invited into the Wardroom. To get round this, the Wrens dressed in their party dresses and danced with us at a suitable distance from Yeovilton. The dance was better and safer than those at the Café de Paris when Barry Lyster organised it, and cost us nothing but the beer.

At one of the parties, the time had come to leave. I and my immobile Wren were seated on the MG's bench-type, air-cushion seat, ready for the off. Along came Geoffrey Russell-Jones, and I offered him a lift back to base. He climbed on to the bonnet and we set off. As the huge P100 headlamps on the MG still had their peacetime 65 watt bulbs, they soon ran the battery down unless peak revs were sustained. Since only a dim light emerged from the blackout masks, we had to follow the car in front and use his illumination.

A hill leads down from North Cadbury village and it suddenly turns left at the bottom, over the bridge. The red light of the car in front — another MG — had set off at a furious rate, and I couldn't keep up. We just about managed to keep him in view down the hill when his light suddenly turned left over the bridge, leaving us in total darkness.

After coming to a standstill with a crash against the stone wall of the bridge, I had a look round for Geoff. I climbed out over the windscreen and peered over the bridge and listened. His description, as he remembers it, is as follows:

"One evening we went to a party somewhere, and coming back we all piled into your little MG. You had a bird beside you and I sat outboard on the nearside wing facing aft. You never quite managed a small bridge. The bird went through the windscreen and I carried on with a lamp under my arm doing a graceful somersault and landing on the bank of a stream 20 feet below. After you had sorted yourselves out, you could not find me, and there was a suggestion that I was simply a myth of someone's imagination. Fortunately, after a square search, I was recovered."

I asked him as politely as possible whether he had broken anything important. Having been reassured that all he was missing was his hat, we thumbed a lift home in a Station lorry. I went to the sickbay to have an arm stitched up and Geoff kindly ran my immobile Wren home in a proper car — his Hillman coupé — painted bright yellow and with a good lighting system.

Next morning I collected the MG from where I had left it. All that it needed was the light refixing and the track-rod straightened. I looked down into the reeds either side of the river and rescued Geoff's hat. Fashioned by Gieves, it was still afloat. The accident showed that Wiggy was right. I was still following too close astern of my targets.

The Great Reaper took his usual five per cent per month at Yeovilton, as anywhere else in the wartime flying business. Lt K. V. Spurway, DSC, RN (who had helped to sink the *Königsberg* in Skuas) was driving his motorbike along the

Sparkford to Ilchester Road and had a fatal head-on collision in a sudden fog patch. Two Fulmar squadron pilots, working-up at Yeovilton and practising night landings, piled in at almost the same place in their down-wind circuits on the same night. The Fulmar was not then fitted with an artifical horizon. Without it, the pilot had to keep his eyes outside the cockpit, looking for clues on the ground, rather than rely on the 'turn-and-bank' instrument. With only very few, dim, runway flares and with everything else in total darkness, the eyes could be misled. The spiral into the ground could start at the time the pilot selected undercarriage and flaps down. There was a gentle nose-down trim change as the flaps extended which required re-trimming. With his head in the office for a moment, the pilot could easily become disorientated. The whole lot might then spiral gently into the ground — a mere 250 feet below.

Of course this is only conjecture, but it seems a probable cause. The reason for the shortage of artificial horizons was the bombing of the Fleet Air Arm stores in the Midlands and a shortage from RAF sources owing to the sudden decision to increase the size of Bomber Command. In the first three years of the war, a combination of blackout, poor night flying illumination, pilot inexperience and a shortage of proper cockpit instrumentation, was responsible for many Fleet Air Arm crashes.

The last part of the Yeovilton course was drogue-shooting. It took place over the sea off Portland and we flew from a small clearing in the gorse on a hilltop airfield near Exmouth. It had been a flying club in peacetime, using Tiger Moths. It was far too small for inexperienced Hurricane pilots.

The social arrangements were, however, quite good. We were put up at a local hotel. While waiting to fly, we sat in the rustic clubhouse in comfortable armchairs, warming ourselves by a log fire. When fog descended in Lyme Bay, we ordered drinks from the bar from the club's steward, and imagined ourselves to be pioneer aviators, like Amy Johnson (we had learned that as an ATA ferry pilot, she had recently disappeared over the Thames flying an Oxford) and other flying heroes. Their pictures, together with a few animals' heads, festooned the walls. The drogue shooting results were not very good. Some did not manage to get a single bullet on the target.

We were allowed.to use two of the eight guns on the drogue, 100 rounds per gun. This was enough for about five attacks on each of five sorties. The target-towing aircraft was a Boulton-Paul Defiant, not a Skua. Incidentally, we heard that the Defiant had had a brief moment of daylight fighter success during the withdrawal from Dunkirk. Its success was entirely because the Germans thought it was a Hurricane and, of course, came straight up its jacksie to shoot it down. As it had a revolving turret which could point most ways, the gunner in the rear of the Defiant had a nice shot with his four guns at the unsuspecting Me 109, — which hardly ever got back to base to tell its friends. However, one German pilot had baled out and survived. He told the other German pilots to beware of the 'Hurricane that shoots backwards'. They then carried out head-on attacks and that was the end of the Defiant.

When we returned from our flying club holiday in Devon, we learned that we were going to do some decklandings in Fulmars, but first we would have to learn to fly it and do ADDLs (Aerodrome Dummy Deck Landings) on the airfield.

The runway which was chosen for ADDLs had white lines painted across it as make-believe arrester wires. The batsman told us that he was in charge and that if we did exactly what he signalled with his bats we would not be blamed for any crashes. This was the policy. The Form for any accident was the A25. The policy giving the batsman the power to fly us into the deck, over the side, or perhaps straight into the barrier, and then if we did not follow his orders to blame it on us, was a tenuous one. Batsmen were therefore carefully chosen: for their strength of character and their ability to charm, juggle with facts, conjure with strange devices, influence with weird signs, confuse with science and sway by emotion the decisions of others more senior, as to who was to blame for the thousands of accidents they presided over, and to equally influence Their Lordships that it could not have been their fault, when filling in Form A25.

    "The batsman says: 'Lower'. I always go high. I drift off to starboard
and prang my Seafire. The blokes in the 'goofers' all think I am green, but
I get my commission from Supermarine. Cracking show, I'm alive, but
I've still got to render my A25."

Generally speaking, a pilot of any ability at all was allowed two accidents. The theory probably worked on the principle that one could be misfortune but two must be carelessness. If there were to be a third — within, say, a year or so — he was classed as 'accident prone'. This was a sign that the pilot might then be trained to become a batsman. Eventually this policy was discontinued and batsmen were chosen for their flying knowledge and skill. There was much wringing of hands in the policy change-over period, for until the new brand of batsman could be seen to be a radical improvement, they all tended to be tarred with the same brush. The better batsmen eventually became key appointments in a carrier and wielded as much power on the flight deck as Lt/Cdr (Flying) himself. A ship which could trust her batsman was a happy ship with a low accident rate.

However, our batsman at Yeovilton was one of the originals. He used the early signalling system — which always seemed to be telling you to do something elese. This mandatory approach encouraged paranoid behaviour and was the opposite to that of the American batsmen. The American system informed you politely that you were doing something wrong — such as: "I think you are too low, too fast, or too high". It was then up to you to do something about it. You took the responsibility, not the batsman.

We found that the Fulmar, compared with the Hurricane, was a very staid old thing on the approach to land. Once trimmed into the approach, it would sometimes stay there. The visibility over the nose was not as good as in the Hurricane and for this reason, and because we could not get the same number of visual cues when landing it as in a Hurricane, we tended to obey the batsman more. There were therefore several broken undercarriages and burst tyres on our Course. This further reduced the numbers of Fulmars available at Yeovilton. In the event we were not required to go up to Scotland, as *Argus* was needed as a Hurricane ferry to Russia. Consequently, we left Yeovilton without any decklanding experience.

Most of the instructors had already had 18 months — some two years — of continuous operations and were usually glad to be allowed a comparative rest at Yeovilton. They still retained their sense of humour and their joy of life still burned bright. Each one of them could have made Admiral, had they lived. One of the most outstanding of our 'heroes' was Lt (A) R. J. (Dicky) Cork, DFC, RN. He was perhaps the smoothest aviator of them all. He was, moreover, irresistible to every Wren on the Station. He left a wake of wistful-eyed beauties wherever he went. He was entirely unaware of this effect and the emotional havoc he caused. He remained, it seemed, unselfish, impeccably mannered, a marvellous example to us less experienced youngsters.

Dicky left Yeovilton in October to join 880 Squadron as Senior Pilot to take part in the Petsamo operation. He it was who later had his own 'private'

Hurricane in *Indomitable*. This was a hybrid, with the cannon-fitted Mark IIC wings but with the older, original Sea Hurricane I fuselage and engine.

When we said goodbye to our immobile Wrens at the end of the course at Yeovilton, none of us had been given any idea where we might be appointed. First we had to attend a 'knife-and-fork' course at the Royal Naval (Staff) College at Greenwich where Their Lordships had allowed us a month off flying to teach us how to behave. They failed to do so. However, we were impressed with the beautiful surroundings at Greenwich, especially the Painted Hall. We all thought that the Navy had organised itself very well to have such a beautiful palace as an Officers' Mess in wartime. There were even white-coated, be-gloved stewards padding about, distastefully, yet deferentially sliding plates of rubber-egg, baked-beans-on-toast and watery porridge under our noses as we sat down at the lines of beautiful oak tables. However, the snooker tables were of high quality and so was the wine to those who had police pay to augment that of an Acting Temporary Sub-Lieutenant. There was also a sort of rumpus room — the Gunroom — where there was a strongly constructed piano of fine English kicked oak, and a vaulted stone roof which made singing such a pleasure — for the singers. As it was Christmas, several of us including Wrens, made up a choir. We sang carols and songs such as *Early One Morning* and *Lyndon Lea*. None of us had any idea what the technical aim of the course might have been. At the end of it we were still none the wiser about new weapons, new aircraft, new carriers or who was winning the war at sea.

In fact the Navy might as well not have had a single carrier at Christmas time 1941, for all the use that was being made of them in their proper task. *Courageous, Ark Royal* and *Glorious* had been sunk by November 1941 and the two large armoured carriers, *Illustrious* and *Formidable*, were in America under repair for a further six months. Both had been caught by Stukas while lacking fighter defence. *Furious* and *Argus* were ferrying RAF aircraft as usual. *Eagle* was on refit in Liverpool. *Hermes* was on 'trade protection' duties in the Indian Ocean. This was a totally useless task in the so-called 'hunter-killer' role — and, without a single fighter on board, she was shortly to be sunk by the Japs' carrier aircraft in what was about to become a Japanese-owned carrier-fighter-patrolled lake. The new *Indomitable* was working-up in the Caribbean just before she ran aground at Kingston. (As a result she missed the *Prince of Wales* and *Repulse* episode.) This only left *Victorious*. She was at Scapa, but once again she had left her strike squadrons to fend for themselves in Coastal Command while she went on yet another ferrying trip — RAF Blenheims for Takoradi. Her fighter complement of 12 Fulmars and two Wildcats was meanwhile at RNAS Hatston in the Orkneys.

As we watched the postman each morning, hoping to find out from Their Lordships which fighter squadron wanted us, we had no knowledge whatever of this extraordinary and sorry tale. There were no slots for Sea Hurricane pilots — and no Sea Hurricanes either — except two pilots for 800 Squadron in *Indomitable* and one for 813F in *Eagle*, when she came off refit in December. I was the lucky pilot picked out of the bag for *Eagle*. Paddy Brownlee went to *Indomitable*. I have no idea about the others although Barry Lyster did not survive long. He was killed in a collision while flying Wildcats in the USA.

My appointment arrived two days before New Year's Day. It told me in similar language to that used to appoint Admiral Byng: "Repair on board *Eagle* by 2400, 28 December, 1941". I was to be spare fighter pilot.

Chapter 8
HMS Eagle

Where on earth was *Eagle?* I enquired at Yeovilton and was told she was on the China Station, flying Swordfish only. I wondered how many Hurricanes she would have now that there was a war on — 20 or so?

The Captain's Secretary at Yeovilton gave me a travel warrant to visit Their Lordships in London suggesting that they would know where she was. So I said goodbye to my immobile Wren, my dad and my MG and went up to London with kitbag and gramophone to ask Their Lordships. They told me she was in dock in Liverpool. They had no idea where her squadrons were, probably somewhere in Scotland. This was indeed a Silent Service.

I met my copper friend Ralph Kirker in London. He said that the Service was silent because it didn't know anything, not because it had anything to keep secret. The RAF was not like that, he said. He suggested I should go straight to *Eagle*. At least she would have duty-free on board.

I arrived at Liverpool Station at about midnight. A taxi took me straight to *Eagle*. The driver told me she had just come out of dry dock, was loading ammunition and taking on aviation petrol. She would be off on trials soon, he said. He also said that he hadn't seen any of her aircraft but "it was difficult to see her flight deck from the dockside".

Eagle towered up into the black sky alongside the quay wall. She was in total darkness, emitting muffled sounds of high-speed machinery and cascades of cooling water from her condensers at intervals down her port side, a very impressive sound and sight.

I was shown to the wardroom. I opened the polished mahogany door. The sole occupant was sitting in an old black leather chair, his back to me and warming his feet on the surrounding high fender of a small electric fire in the centre. I crept around to one side, keeping quiet in case he was asleep. I saw that he had red stripes between the three bands of gold braid on his sleeves, so that he must be the PMO. (Principal Medical Officer). He glanced across at me, peering under bushy black eyebrows.

"Evening, sir," I said by way of conversation. "You got anywhere to sleep — what's y' name?" "Crosley, sir, and no sir," I said. "I'm O'Rourke," he said. "Ring that bell and a steward may know of a cabin, or something. I've closed the bar, so that's that." Commander O'Rourke of O'Rourke dozed off again.

When a steward miraculously appeared from somewhere I asked him where I could sleep for the night. He suggested a camp bed in the Captain's Secretary's office opposite the wardroom. He explained that 'Scratch' was on leave, but he wouldn't mind my dossing down there for a night or two, if I could get it cleared up by daytime.

I was desperate to know what aircraft *Eagle* had and what I should be flying and where. I asked the steward. He said that there were a couple of monoplane fighters in the hangar, brought back from Crete, but he had no idea where the rest were.

I could not spend another night wondering what aircraft I would have to fly, so I groped my way along the main deck until I came to a steel door labelled 'Hangar Access'. I went in through the double doors into a dimly lit, steel-sided, empty cathedral of a place. There, in a far corner, I could see two Brewster Buffaloes, painted in light grey paint. My heart missed a beat, particularly as I saw that they were fitted with arrester hooks. I had heard terrible stories about the Buffalo — and that it had the unreliable Cyclone engine and very poor flying characteristics which made it particularly unsuitable as a deck-landing fighter. Still, I thought, Their Lordships wouldn't ask anyone to do the impossible straight off, and if we had to fly them they would give us time to learn. At least they weren't biplanes. But I hardly slept that night. It must have been the thought of doing battle with the Hun in a Buffalo!

Next morning, I heard the Captain's Writer come in. He soon started to type and I gave up the idea of trying to sleep. I suddenly realised that he of all men on board would know exactly where 813F was and what type of aircraft they would be flying.

"Ah," he said, "you must be Sub-Lieutenant Crosley. I think you should be at Arbroath, I'll give you a travel warrant, sir," and, in answer to my inquiry: "They fly Hurricanes."

Music to my ears. I could withstand any privation, climb any mountain, ford any stream, so long as there was a Sea Hurricane to fly at the end of it.

Two days later, after many vicissitudes, I arrived at Arbroath on the east coast of Scotland. There, the wardroom secretary told me that 813 Squadron's mail was being redirected to Macrihanish. This was another RN Air Station north of Campbeltown at the southern end of the Mull of Kintyre — on the other side of Scotland.

The Naval bus ride took all day and most of the night. I piled out in darkness with kitbag and gramophone and knocked at the door of the only hotel in Campbeltown, now being used as an Officers' Mess.

After the usual: "We haven't got any bunks made up, there aren't any cabins and there isn't any food," I was eventually allowed to sleep in a cabin whose occupant had just been killed night flying in a Swordfish and therefore wouldn't be back.

A Wren officer woke me up next morning, but as it was too late for breakfast — she had only come into the cabin to make a list of the poor chap's possessions — I spent my time asking anyone I could find where 813F Squadron was as I was their spare fighter pilot. No one knew for certain.

I went outside and listened. Like a good soldier, I determined to 'follow the sound of engines' which I had heard flogging around. Eventually I came to a small grass airfield. I could see a couple of Swordfish parked out by some lop-sided, wind-blown trees in the corner. I was just about to give up hope when a Sub-Lieutenant came out of a tent and told me that 813F was back at Arbroath. It had left Macrihanish the day before and was now doing its ADDLs there.

Next day I caught the bus back to the other side of Scotland and 'signed-in' again at the wardroom.

Next morning I struck gold in the person of 'Spike' King-Joyce. He was 813F Flight Commander. He said: "You'd better fly with me as my Number Two. We've got two Hurries and they are both U/S. But tomorrow all four of us should be able to have a go at some ADDLs. The other two pilots in 813F are

Bob Spedding and Bernard Bullivant. We've only got two Hurricanes."

Spike had the brightest dark brown eyes, long shiny black hair and 'buggers grips' on each cheek. He was tall and well built, very good looking — in a typical Irish way. He wore his RN reefer jacket with the top button undone. Thenceforth I did also, like all other fighter pilots in first-line squadrons.

After lunch, Bernard and I walked over to the other side of the airfield and, as yet without leather flying jackets — for they were in short supply — nearly froze solid waiting for our turn to fly. We watched Bob and Spike showing us how it should be done.

The batsman said that he was wasting his time waving his bats about "at those two" and he told Bernard and I to be more respectful, particularly as Spike had just made his final landing making a 'V' sign as he flashed past. However, Bernard and I had already decided that we were no longer pupils but men of substance with minds of our own. Batsmen who had never flown Hurricanes should not be allowed to throw their weight about too much.

Spike's approach to flying was verging on the intrepid. He never delved too deeply into an accident's cause or apportioned blame. Provided no one was hurt, his only remark would be "Hard cheeze", addressed kindly to the aviator concerned. He would sign Form A25 without commenting how a future accident of that sort might be avoided. He was to be my Section Leader for the next year and I could not have been more fortunate.

After a few more ADDLs — where Spike did the batting and so avoided any unpleasantness — we declared ourselves fully worked-up and capable of forming the entire fighter defence of HMS *Eagle*, as indeed we were. Spike and Bob flew our two Hurricanes back to Machrihanish. 'Bully' and I took the bus again with the ground crew. We spent hours peering through the streaming glass windows at blackened sheep, with one leg longer than the other as they struggled for a footing on the steep, barren hillsides lining the mountain roads.

It was New Year's day, 1942 when we arrived for the second time at Macrihanish. The same day, *Eagle* appeared in the misty Clyde to the south, demanding her Swordfish back.

Spike and Bob flew on board the same day with our two Hurricanes and Bully and I followed in the back of a Swordfish, freezing cold and struggling for a footing against the slipstream and the tendency for a blackboard and easel, lodged in the gunner's seat, to fly over the side. When we came to a sudden halt on the flight deck arrester wires, we and our kitbags and the blackboard and easel slid forward against a long-range fuel tank and everything smelled of petrol for the next few days. No one wanted us to share their cabins as a result and Bully and I were both told to bivouac in the Captain's Secretary's office again, this time tastefully partitioned off with a white enamelled canvas screen. It remained our cabin for seven months until *Eagle* was sunk. We each had a camp bed on the floor and the use of a small desk and two chairs for our clothes. Otherwise we lived out of our kitbags. There were no chests of drawers, wash basins, fans, wardrobes mirrors or such luxuries. However, I could see no sign of the Buffaloes — and this offset many a privation in our domestic arrangements. Had we have heard that the Gloster E.28/39 — an experimental jet single-seater, powered by a Whittle gas turbine, had made its first flight in England, we would have been further encouraged.

Eagle still had most of her original peacetime complement on board. The aircrew in her two squadrons — 813 and 824 — were ex-China Station, well established, and sure of their position in the wardroom. The fighter task, entirely limited to the chance shooting down of snoopers and not in any way intended to be a fighter defence against raiding aircraft, had hitherto been carried out by two Gladiators. The Gladiator pilots were now elsewhere, and we new boys who had replaced them, were therefore low down in the pecking order. *Eagle* had not yet heard of Churchill's "Action this day" message demanding more interceptor fighters aboard our carriers, or of Cunningham's "The Fleet must take its own air defence with it". Neither, apparently, had anyone else. *Eagle's* main purpose was still to supply the Mediterranean Fleet with long-range hitting power through her Swordfish. The fighters were but a small consideration. The only difference was that *Eagle* now had two Hurricanes instead of two Gladiators. As they were to be the very first in the Mediterranean, whither we were bound, we hoped that we would be able to use them well and put *Eagle* on the map. We had no doubt that the Sea Hurricane (albeit the Mark Ib instead of the Hurricane IIc) was the master of any Italian aircraft and we hoped that when we had to meet a Ju 88 snooper, that we should have the height advantage and be able to catch it up by diving on it. Once the fighting started, we expected the ship would take a little more notice of her four fighter pilots.

I could hardly wait for my first decklanding. It was all very well watching the Stringbags flop down, their undercarriage legs splaying out as they chuffed slowly into position over the wires. They had an easy task. Thus Bully and I felt conspicuous on the day chosen for our debut. The fire-party was much in evidence and the 'goofers', usually a platform abreast the funnels where aviators watched others doing decklandings, was packed to overflowing.

As Bully was a Midshipman, I had the privilege of going first. Apart from an instinctive tendency to keep high when coming over the round-down and consistently disobeying the batsman, I managed to do about six landings before the ship had to turn round to avoid Ailsa Craig. When Bully's turn came, 'goofers' was empty and most of the interest had gone. It must have looked easy. It certainly seemed easy to us. The Hurricane was a lovely decklanding aircraft and we wondered what all the fuss was about.

Bully and I discussed the day's flying in our 'cabin' afterwards. "The thing that got me," said Bully, "was how small the ship looked when I had a look round after take-off. They must be mad, I thought, if they expect me to get down on that."

"Did you hear that a Naval chap called Scruffy Bromwich had decklanded a hooked Spitfire?" I said.

"God, I'd hate to do that," replied Bully, "I can't imagine that they'd ever use them in carriers. You couldn't see a thing over the nose." "Yes, but it wouldn't half surprise the 'Eye-ties', wouldn't it?" "And the Japs too, it looks like," said Bully.

I went down into the hangar afterwards and talked to the riggers and fitters who were looking after our two Hurricanes. They told me, in answer to my question about oil on the windscreen, that they were going to fit a 'mod' which pumped cleaning fluid onto it and this would keep it clear. They told me that the engines in our two Hurricanes had done about 200 hours each in sandy conditions — according to their log books — and were beginning to use a lot of oil.

The west coast of Scotland in a winter depression is hardly the place for seagulls let alone Fleet Air Arm sprog pilots. We were operating entirely without homing aids and as for the TR9D radio, if it worked, the ship's did not, and *vice versa*. The cloudbase was usually down to the tops of the hills on the coast and visibility could vary from the length of the flight deck to one or two miles almost in the time it took to range the aircraft on deck and start them up.

One morning about eight Swordfish took off. The weather this time was anti-cyclonic and they had set off in bright sunlight. Spike and I were 'standing by' in our cockpits on deck to intercept two of them which were going to pretend to be snoopers. The Swordfish 'strike' went away about a hundred miles or so. By the time they came back they were flying over fog. We were still on deck in fog ourselves, with the ship vainly trying to find a clear patch in which to land the eight Swordfish. No word had been heard because their r/t was not working. The Captain — L. D. Mackintosh of Mackintosh, himself an observer and the first RN officer with wings to command a carrier (the only other one in World War II was Captain Bulteel, HMS *Argus*) sent a man up the mast with a Very pistol to see if he could see them above the fog. Apparently this worked for we could soon hear their engines flogging about overhead. However, the ship could not find a clear patch and the Stringbags, running short of fuel, made for the mainland. Miraculously they found a clear patch by Glasgow and landed at a small 'matting' airfield called Renfrew.

So far, we in the Hurricanes had not been frightened in this way. We badly needed an FDO — a product of the 'stop-me-and-buy-one' school — and I learned from Doc Whaley, the wardroom secretary and ship's senior Surgeon, that a chap called Lt Tricky, RNVR, was due to arrive.

Lt J. Tricky arrived and immediately made a point of getting to know the four of us flying Hurricanes. He told us to go to the Supply Officer and get an Omega 'beacon' watch put on our flying clothing list. He would immediately get the ship's beacon working and have some exercises with it on the next flying day. He obviously knew his onions. He was a Public School science master in civilian life and could therefore understand science and the young mind. We fighter pilots soon built up a superb rapport with him, and gained confidence in the radio, in the ship and in ourselves.

We were looking forward to being told our destination. There was a party of Royal Marines on board. They worked 'X' turret — two of the eight, 1912, six-inch guns which we hoped they would not fire while our Hurricanes were parked nearby. We watched closely in case the Marines embarked a fresh supply of tropical pith helmets, a sure sign we would be bound for the Arctic. Bully, who knew something about geography, said that running convoys round the northern route would be impossible in winter. There was total darkness and ice everywhere. So I wrote to my immobile Wren and told her that we hoped to go to warmer climates, but I found our later that this vital bit of information had been torn out by the ship's censor. So she never knew that we had left the UK until we were 2000 miles away.

On 17 February we went to sea again. Something was up because we spent the following four nights at Lamlash Bay in the Isle of Aran, well away from possible foreign ears in the pubs of Gourock on the mainland. On the fifth morning out, we met *Malaya* and, later that day, four merchant ships. We knew we were off somewhere.

We had just read in the papers that *Scharnhorst, Gneisenau* and the cruiser *Prince Eugen* had escaped from Brest and had run up the Channel in broad daylight without our ships or the RAF being able to do anything to stop them. This was the crack of doom. It had not happened thus since the days of Van Tromp. Much later, we heard of 825 Squadron's attack with six Swordfish, led by the gallant Eugene Esmonde. Why, we thought, had they taken off — from an RAF airfield too — without the RAF doing anything to help. We saw 'artists' impressions' of the Swordfish meeting a 'curtain of AA fire' which shot them all down before they could deliver their torpedoes. However, we eventually got to hear that this was untrue for it was the standing patrol of about 40 Me 109s which shot down the six Swordfish, un-intercepted by a single one of the ten Spitfires which eventually turned up too late to protect them. The latter were unaccustomed to the task and lacked any support from their search aircraft, whose radar had been purposely and skilfully jammed from the outset. The German fighters, on the other hand, had a slow, compact target to intercept and which came to them, and for which they had no need to search. The strategic result of this action was that Their Lordships were heartened that a battleship — even a German battleship — could still protect itself from air attack and they continued to plan for another Jutland as before. The Germans, on the other hand, had already largely written-off the battleship as a waste of time and effort and they consequently made only low priority repairs to *Scharnhorst* and did not bother with *Gneisenau* at all. Both had been mined by the RAF on the last leg of their voyage to Germany.

Passing round the north of Ireland, we steered west for two days. After that we turned south for Gibraltar. We made this immense circuit out into the Atlantic to clear the U-boats in the Biscay area and to pass outside the radius of action of the Focke-Wulf armed recce aircraft which were beginning to organise U-boat 'wolf-packs' on a large scale.

The Swordfish took off in twos and threes and disappeared into the Atlantic murk on their A/S patrols. They carried small depth charges under each wing and they also had ASV radar aerials which could detect a surfaced submarine from a distance of several miles, giving by night or day its range and bearing on a small, shielded, display for the observer in the back of each Swordfish.

The Captain told us over the Tannoy that we were to become the carrier force in Force 'H', based at Gibraltar. Our new Admiral was Syfret, who had relieved Admiral Somerville. He, in turn, was taking over the Far Eastern Fleet to beat the Japanese. We wished him luck — having just heard what the enemy had done to our two battleships out there already.

We arrived 100 miles off the Rock on the evening of 24 February, my 22nd birthday. All except three of the Swordfish and ourselves, flew off to North Front airfield, leaving us to enter harbour in darkness that night.

After we had tied up at the quay under a huge crane, 15 huge packing cases were brought up by lighter and were lifted onto our flight deck by the crane. In darkness, a host of RAF men descended upon them, ripping off their sides and rolling out Spitfire aircraft in desert camouflage. Other cases had wings which were also quickly stowed down below in the hangars. By dawn, we had 15 Spitfires in the hangar and not a sign of anything on the flight deck.

I asked Tricky what was going on. He usually knew most things as his job was near the wireless office and he saw most of the signals. He told us that the Spitfires were for Malta. We could see that they had 'Vokes' airfilters on their air intakes and because they had desert camouflage, we thought that they were bound for the Desert Air Force. But how on earth were they to get to Malta? They only had about 250 miles range and if we flew them off the deck as near as that to Malta we would be right under the German and Italian fighter cover from Sicily.

After breakfast we went into the hangar to have another look at the Spitfires. Amongst the piles of ammunition, wireless sets, pilot's seats, propeller spinners, tail steering arms, wing mats, sweating bodies and noise, we could see several huge slipper-shaped petrol tanks. Some of these were being offered up to the underside of the Spitfire's fuselage — where a bomb might ordinarily be — and the fuel lines were being connected by an invisible, sliding fit. There was only a half-inch gap between the underside of the fuselage and the top surface of the tank, which was all of six feet long by two feet wide. We found that it could hold 90 gallons of 100 octane fuel. This was more than the Spitfire carried in its internal tanks. A closer study of the jettison arrangements showed that a Bowden cable release in the cockpit let go the lifting ring — stressed to three tons breaking strain — in the top surface of the tank. The tank then slid backwards onto two lugs sticking out two inches from the fuselage underside. The nose of the tank then dropped and the airflow forced it downwards and clear of the fuselage underside. The slightest skid, we thought, and the whole thing would come clear of the two lugs, slide back and hit the tail. However, the Spits would now have a range of 400 miles and would allow a fly-off to Malta well before we got to 'bomb alley'.

Bully and I awoke in our camp beds next morning to the pipe: "Special sea-dutymen to your stations". Soon, the ship started to shake and the paint started to fall from the deckhead as the ship's main engines began to take over, and we set a course east-north-east for Malta. After breakfast we went on deck. There were the 15 Spitfires, glistening in the early morning sun. The Rock was still in sight astern. We could see *Malaya* and *Cleopatra* (the latter, a brand new Dido class cruiser, going through to become Admiral Vian's Flagship at Alexandria to replace the torpedoed *Naiad*) and a few destroyers ahead. At breakfast I had found out from 'guns' that the reason why the Spitfires had been assembled in the hangar at night was because of the Germans with binoculars in Algeciras opposite the Rock. They reported everything that went on in Gibraltar harbour to their ambassador in Vigo, and from there to the German submarine base at La Spezia in Italy.

We saw that several of the Spits, with their noses pointed outboard and their wheels chocked up, were having cannon magazines loaded in their wing bays. The two 20 mm cannon and four .303 inch Brownings were then fired, with the whole aircraft jumping backwards and upwards with the recoil like a startled hare, with clouds of black cordite smoke drifting past us, the empty brass cartridge cases flying everywhere. We spoke to several of the RAF pilots. Some were Australians in their distinctive dark blue uniforms. One was a famous Sergeant called 'Screwball' Beurling. Many had DFCs. When they found out that we flew Hurricanes, they asked what it was like taking off from the flight deck. We said that all you needed was about 20 knots of wind over the deck, a little left rudder and you were unstuck by the Island from a start position about opposite the aft gun turrets. This did not reassure them very much for, they pointed out, they would have an extra half ton of fuel on board, and not one of them had taken off in a Spit like that yet. We reckoned, we told them, that if their engines were the same power as ours, that they would be able to do a loop and a roll off the top once they were over the bow. There would be at least 30 knots of wind for them, as the Captain and Commander Coke, our 'Wings', knew their stuff.

During that afternoon and for some of the night, the Spitfires' engines were run to check the functioning of the long-range tanks. By morning it was learned that very few of them worked reliably. They would neither suck fuel nor jettison satisfactorily. The Squadron-Leader in command said: "We've got no confidence in them whatever, at the moment. If they fail after take-off it means baling out or ditching, and that's fatal either way, with a full tank hung up".

So we returned to Gibraltar with the Spits pushed down below again and with the ship trying to pretend to the German spies in Algeciras that nothing had really happened.

A week later, on 9 March, we tried again. The pilots were much happier, as the tube feeding the fuel from the tank was now made of better material and could be checked visually by shining a torch up through a gap cut between the tank and the underside of the fuselage. After each fitter had checked it, the pilot ran up the aircraft to full power to recheck it before the aircraft was signed 'S' for serviceable in Form 700.

We arrived at the flying-off position two mornings later. With a natural wind over the sea of about 10 knots, the Captain gave the RAF pilots about 32 knots over the deck.

There were only two dramas. One was when one of the Spits swung badly on take-off and the pilot only just managed to pull up his nose in time before hitting the sea on the port side. The second drama was the sight of a Spitfire returning, after the rest had set off eastwards, with steam coming out of its engine cowlings. This was boiling coolant. The cause of overheating was that the starboard undercarriage had not retracted properly. This obstructed the airflow through the radiator under the starboard wing.

After circling the Fleet for about 10 minutes, the pilot eventually plucked up courage to bale out, as the lesser of two evils, and we all cheered as we saw his parachute. He baled out by turning the aircraft on its back at about 2000 feet and dropping out. The little Spitfire then stalled inverted and plunged into the Mediterranean, its short life snuffed out. The pilot was soon picked up by the whaler from a destroyer and we all turned back west and made for Gibraltar before the Italian snoopers could find us. Our Hurricanes had done nothing and we felt a little browned off. What on earth were the Italians doing? We were only a hundred miles from their Sardinian airfields at the time of the fly-off, yet they and the Germans in Sicily had not found us. They would certainly regret the day, for this would be the very first time that they would have to face Spitfires over Malta, a very different proposition to the Hurricane Ib in fighter v fighter combat.

We repeated the whole business on 23 March. This time there was no elaborate attempt at secrecy as the RAF insisted on proper assembly and testing in daylight and with plenty of time to cure the faults. Apparently, when the pilots had arrived on 9 March with the 14 Spits over Hal Far in Malta, the Germans were waiting for them. When they came to use their guns, none of them appeared to be properly harmonised. They only had three Spits left by the end of the third day.

Their second arrival over Malta on the 23rd coincided with the 'Second Battle of Sirte'. This 'battle' was surprisingly claimed by C-in-C Med, Admiral Cunningham, as a 'brilliant victory' — even after the war — for which its leader, Rear Admiral Vian was knighted. (See Appendix 2 — Naval Air Power.)

After returning from this trip, Commander Coke allowed our two Hurricanes to fly ashore to North Front before entering harbour so that we could keep in flying practice. Next morning, Bob discovered an old Skua on the airfield and he thought he would fly it. He was an experienced Skua pilot. It was pushed out of the hangar one morning and we watched as he climbed up to the cockpit and disappeared inside.

He chuffed gradually down the runway on his take-off run and finished up, minus his undercarriage and in the flying position, neatly balanced on some oildrums at the far end of the runway. He had taken off in coarse pitch, forgetting that the fine pitch position of the lever was aft, not forward. Apart from a smear or two of oil, he seemed entirely unmarked by the incident.

There was always something amusing going on at North Front. It was the first stop for RAF replacements, flying out from the UK. They had flown 1000 miles over the sea and sometimes arrived at the end of their tether, in Beaufighters, Wellingtons, Blenheims, and Coastal Command's Beauforts and Hudsons. The runway at North Front lay between the huge rock to the south and the Spanish border to the north. It had orginally been a horseracing track and, at the time it was converted, the runway length was sufficient for aircraft then in service. Today the runway stretches out into Algeciras Bay. In 1942 it was half the length and only sufficient for a safe arrival if the wind was blowing straight down it. A 'Levanter', a strong, sandy wind from the desert, would sometimes arrive very unexpectedly. It put the runway into the lee of the rock. Airflow was therefore extremely turbulent and came from all directions, including upwards and downwards. There were many accidents, because ferry pilots had no diversion and had to approach through the intense turbulence at either end of the runway whether they liked it or not.

To make matters worse, the twin-engined strike fighter, the Beaufighter I, was very much under-finned, and if the poor pilot then had to make a single-engined landing, either in turbulence or, for that matter, in the short distance available, it always resulted in a write-off, even if he was lucky enough to touch down. Often the pilot was caught in the turbulence and never made the end of the runway at all.

The surfaced length of the runway was about 1400 yards. This was about 400 yards longer than the longest runway at Yeovilton and we considered, with our lack of knowledge of the cross-wind situation, that it was more than adequate for a Hurricane. I had watched other aircraft approach from the east at a time when the windsock at the far end was showing a westerly wind of 10 knots and, at the near end, an easterly wind of 10 knots. In between, a third windsock was showing no wind at all. As we had had no flying for about six weeks, Bully and I were impatient to get started. All we had to do, I reckoned, was to approach to land a little faster than usual to cope with the down-wind eddy, and then trust in the brakes to stop us going off the far end into Algeciras Bay.

All went according to the Crosley plan until just before I crossed the threshold of the runway where it met the Mediterranean. Here there was a huge increase in the aircraft's airspeed as I hit the 'fanning out' of a down draught. The Hurricane went sailing aloft a 100 feet or more, miles over its proper approach height. I hadn't touched a thing. I wondered what Pilot Officer Jack would do. It flashed through my mind that I could now expect a sudden reversal in the wind gradient or speed. Sure enough it happened! The down draught itself then hit the aircraft. The airspeed dropped from 100 knots to about 50 in the space of about a second. Dirt came up from the floor, the engine cut from the zero 'G' (which mercifully kept the aircraft from stalling) and I lost height rapidly. I selected full throttle and right rudder and waited. By some miracle, the engine came on at full power just as the airspeed needle wavered above the 70 knot mark again. I avoided hitting the sea by about five feet or less. This was booboo number four, I reckoned, and I was lucky once more to get away with it. I did not tell anyone, but put the aircraft U/S for brakes when I landed, so that Bully could not fly it and have the same experience. "You came in a bit fast, didn't you?" said Bully.

That was the end of it, thank goodness. No one else took much notice of anything that the Navy did at North Front. It was usually so odd that the RAF in Air Traffic Control had given up trying.

Midshipman Williams — of Netheravon Battle fame — was at North Front. As Bob had pranged his only target-towing Skua he was wandering about with nothing to do. He had appointed himself 'Naval Air Armaments Officer', an odd appointment for a Midshipman. This entitled him to a key of the Naval Armoury which consisted of one Army revolver. He wore this in a Tom Mix-type holster, low on his starboard hip. He was practising the quick draw one day and had shot himself through the foot, luckily not very seriously. One afternoon he was asleep on his bed in the Nissen hut 'dormitory' and a large piece of the Rock came through the roof, just missing his bed. The Sappers (Army Engineers) had overdone the explosive while making some more gun positions in the Rock. They were also increasing the 25 miles of tunnel to accommodate a complete Brigade Group of the Rock's garrison. Williams dived under his bed and hit his head on his Gieves tin trunk, requiring several stitches. He was a lovely chap, but he must have been a great trial to the Senior Naval Officer at North Front who had no sense of humour and took life far too seriously.

The SNO was a Lieutenant Commander, RNVR. There was no duty-free, there were no indigenous Wrens, no proper offices — the SNO's office was one of the Spitfire packing cases with a soapbox as a desk — and no transport. He could not understand why Bully and I wanted to live ashore in such conditions and bother him, when life on board must be so luxurious. However, he did not realise that we eschewed the comforts in *Eagle* to avoid having to do 'Assistant Officer of the Watch in Harbour'. In this duty we had found out that we did all the work and took the blame for everything but had none of the perks to go with it — such as 'Up Spirits', the issue of the daily rum ration. Typical of this low grade task was the Assistant's telescope. It consisted of a piece of canvas-covered copper tubing with two bits of glass stuck in each end.

Our first stay ashore at North Front lasted about ten days. This was because *Eagle*'s steering gear had packed up at the end of our last 'club run' and she was having it repaired. During this period in the war the Royal Gibraltar Yacht Club had a most obliging Army Secretary and he allowed me to borrow the club Sharpies. It was important to keep clear of the RAF's Sunderlands in the harbour. They ran up their engines, while taxying, to take-off power and endeavoured to catch us with their slipstream to capsize us when we weren't looking. After a sail, I also had to clean off all the fuel-oil leaking from some limpet-mined ships in the harbour.

The best hotel in Gib was The Rock. This was halfway up the 'Rock' itself and commanded an excellent view. Most of it was taken over as the Wrens' quarters. The hotel reckoned that if its charges were cheap to the Admiralty, they would recoup any losses from the resultant stream of Naval and Army types visiting the Wrens. However, it had not reckoned with the Queen Wren who guarded her young ones with the greatest care. All she allowed was a little harmless bathing at Sandy Bay, or tennis at the Pavilion, and 'back on board the Rock by 2230'. Nevertheless, Force H's 'runs ashore' were well catered for. There were several bars with orchestras which played Spanish music. Competition for thirsty sailors was intense. One bar had an orchestra composed entirely of Spanish ladies. Towards the end of the evening when things were really warming up, one or two of the ladies would accidentally allow a bosom to pop out while they were playing. The cheers could be heard across the border in La Linea.

The Rock Apes — recently reinforced at Churchill's request — had inhabited the Rock through many wars. Nothing was new to them. Likewise the Gibraltarians were hospitable and their police were friendly. They sometimes gave us the benefit of the doubt. They and the ageless apes seemed to realise that we were young, fearful and far from home.

During this time, in the first three weeks of April 1942, Malta's need for more fighter aircraft became even more desperate. Churchill, with the help of President Roosevelt, persuaded Admiral King, the Chief of the United States Navy, to lend the RN the carrier *Wasp* for ferrying purposes. While we were stuck in Gib for repairs, she delivered 47 more Spitfires on 22 April — in one go. When our repairs were completed we made a third trip with *Wasp*, on 9 May. This gave Malta a further 64 Spitfires. (*Wasp* then returned to the Pacific War. She lasted until 5 September 1942, when she was sunk by a Japanese submarine while operating alone.)

By 9 May 1942, Malta had received 150 Spitfires since our first 'run' in late February. However, in spite of them the Island remained almost entirely under the heel of the German Air Force until the following March 1943. Then, at last, the Germans had to leave Sicily for good, allowing Malta to recover. During most of this time, the George Cross Island was bombed and strafed by an Air Force a third of the size of the RAF — some 250 Ju 88s, Ju 87s and Me 109s, and about 150 bombers and fighters of the Italian Air Force. Betweeen 9 April and 9 May 1942, the average tonnage of bombs dropped on Malta during 17 of these days and nights was equal to the highest rate dropped on London during the Blitz. The RAF was again towards the end of May down to 20 or so Spitfires so that another series of ferrying trips was planned.

After the 9 May 'Club Run', while I was getting a new eight-day clock from the stores at North Front for one of our Hurricanes (I had attached it with two easily-removed screws, so that I could rescue the clock if it became necessary to throw the aircraft over the side), I had happened to notice a couple of aircraft crates in the store. These turned out to be two Sea Hurricanes which had been intended for *Ark Royal* before she was torpedoed seven months previously. I soon convinced Spike that they were just what we wanted for they would double *Eagle's* fighter force overnight. They were therefore assembled and Bully and I flew them aboard in time for the next 'Club Run'.

At last Bully and I had an aircraft of our own, with our 'own' fitter and rigger. But they were terrible old things really, their engines so worn that they used most of their three and a half gallons of oil in an hour's flying and had to be fitted with an extra oil tank. Their propellers even 'windmilled' on deck if the wind was over 40 knots. The main result of our having four aircraft instead of two was that the Captain felt free to 'take risks' with us and he allowed us to fly at the slightest whiff of a 'bogey' on radar. Tricky was also delighted as he could now practice fighter interceptions. He soon became very proficient. We seldom ever missed and Tricky could somehow manage to bring us up-sun and above our practice bogey nearly every time. He made use of a quirk of the type of radar that we had, as it had 'null' spots at certain heights and distances. This allowed him to assess the height of any approaching raid without having the more modern height-finding radar in the ship at all. Being a practical scientist he had worked this out for himself.

Also at this time, we had to fit a new 'black box' in the back of our Hurricanes. This was the IFF (Identification Friend or Foe), to help identify us so that we should not be mistaken for a German or an Italian. In addition, we had a new, four-channel, crystal-tuned r/t set — TR1196 — to replace the single channel manually-tuned TR9D. The new set had a lever which selected any of four HF channels. The old wire aerial was removed from between the tail and fuselage and a short 'whip' aerial substituted. The improved performance of the radio transformed the fighter situation. We knew now that we could intercept any raid provided it approached above radar height, and that we could trust Tricky completely to bring us in at exactly the most advantageous position each time.

The ice cream tricycles and improved radar ` `had achieved an immense breakthrough. All we needed now was a few Ju 88s or SV79s to come flogging over above 2000-3000 feet, and we could have a good chance of an interception.

One day, early in June, we noticed a newcomer in the harbour. She had the body of a liner but with the funnels, cabins and bridges sheared off and a flight deck substituted. We heard that the smoke came out through a hole in the flight deck — except when she was landing or taking off aircraft. Then, it came out somewhere else and blackened her beautiful teak quarterdeck. The *Argus*, for it was she, was called 'The Flat Iron'. She looked exactly like one. We wondered what could have brought her to Gibraltar this time.

On the day she arrived and on the way to the airfield, Bully and I asked the driver of our taxi why she was in Gibraltar. He said that a complete squadron of Hurricanes had already landed that morning at North Front and, having hooks, they could only have come from *Argus*.

We were dropped off at the 'frontier' end of the runway and found that it was 801 Squadron, with 12 Sea Hurricane Ib's. They looked a very force-on crowd, especially Pete Hutton, one of the Flight Commanders. He told us that Rupert Brabner, their CO, was a Member of Parliament — a good thing to have in the Fleet Air Arm. He had escaped with Alan Black from Crete just before the Germans had arrived — in a Sunderland of all things.

Soon the buzz started that we would be going on another trip to Malta, this time with *Argus* and with some merchant ships as well. *Argus* was to be loaded with Spitfires, and a few Fulmars as 'dusk fighters' and 801 would reinforce us, making 16 Hurricanes in all.

This fighter force, albeit only 25 — with spares — and with six anti-submarine Swordfish, was the very first occasion in Naval history when British carriers were put to their proper use in a defensive war, running convoys under enemy-occupied airspace. It had taken nearly three years of war for the Royal Navy to find out how to use aircraft carriers.

Chapter 9
Operation 'Harpoon'

By June 1942, Rommel was again master of the North African coast and airfields between Alexandria and Tunis. General Auchinleck, through no fault of his own, was back at Gazala. The Luftwaffe resumed control of the skies over Malta and the RAF Chief in Cairo — Air Vice-Marshal Tedder — had given up hope altogether. He said that with only three months food left, Malta was not worth defending.

Following a further 20 U-boat reinforcements, the Mediterranean under-sea battle was also hotting up. These few German submarines — taken from their 'happy time' off America by Doenitz's orders — did more damage in six months in 1942 than the 70 Italian submarines did in the whole year.

By June, substantial help to Malta was at last on the way. It came from our western end. Despite Russian demands — now that the ice had melted — for more Murmansk convoys and in spite of the desperate state of affairs created by the Japanese in the Indian Ocean, five large, fast freighters were loaded and sent out from the UK bound for Malta through the Straits of Gibraltar. Escorted by *Cairo* — a new Air Defence cruiser — they passed through the Straits on the night of 11 June. In support were the cruisers *Kenya*, *Charybdis* and *Liverpool* with nine destroyers. The Flagship, with Vice-Admiral Curteis in command of this operation 'Harpoon' — was the battleship *Malaya*. *Eagle* and *Argus* joined up next morning.

We had already embarked six Swordfish of 813 Squadron for A/S duties and the 12 Hurricanes of 801. These all went down in the hangar — apart from our usual four Hurricanes on deck — to give the spies in Algeciras the impression that we were merely doing another 'Club Run'.

At a general briefing session in the wardroom, aircrew were given a packet of Italian money, escape maps (if we landed in Africa), French money to bribe the French politicians to let us go and not turn us over to the Germans, and some sea-dye marker. This turned yellow in the water and made it possible for a search aircraft to see where we were if we got shot down.

We all realised that we were bound to meet opposition this time. Of course in 813F we would pretend to be old hands at the game, for we had had four Club Runs already. We had the advantage over the newcomers for we had been broken-in gently. What was more, we knew the ship, the ADR set-up and the possible dangers far better.

I told any member of 801 who asked me that I thought that we would not be spotted until at least the evening of the next day. The enemy air force would have to make a special effort even then, for our distance from Sardinia would be greater than the effective snooper range of the Ju 88 and only just within the effective range of the other recce aircraft used, the Italian Cant 1007Z.

Maps were produced of the 'narrows', giving the position of five or six airfields crowded with all manner of German and Italian aircraft. A colossal list of aircraft was produced. We had only seen pictures of some of them, their silhouettes, pinned up on the Heads doors so that we could study them while we sat on the thunderbox. *Malaya's* Walrus was acting as our private air/sea rescue aircraft and if anyone went in the drink from a decklanding accident the usual destroyer would lend a hand. There would be on-deck stand-bys, pairs only, until Force H was discovered. Then there would be two Hurricanes airborne and another four on deck ready to scramble. The CO stressed the importance of getting in close when firing and he would shake the hand of anyone who managed to shoot down a Ju 88. Brabner also told us that the carriers and *Malaya,* plus a cruiser or two, would be turning back at the Narrows. *Cairo* and a few of the destroyers would, however, be carrying on through the night, hoping that the Italian fleet would not venture out and try to force a night action. Come next morning they would then be very nearly within sight of Malta, and under the RAF's umbrella of Spitfires. The only question was, of course, whether *Cairo's* ADR would work properly and whether, in consequence, effective use could be made of the Spits. Brabner also said that it had been decided to fly a squadron of Beaufighters to Malta from the east to give fighter cover at long range. The Beaufighters would be relieving 807 Squadron's Fulmars at dusk, just as we turned back at the Narrows.

That afternoon, 12 June, Spike and I sat in our cockpits on stand-by. The fitters plugged the starter lines in and went to sit in the shade. We sat and waited under the hot sun, looking from time to time at Tricky's radar aerial to see where it was searching. Expecting, perhaps hoping, to see 'Wings' on the bridge give us the start-up signal as we got nearer and nearer enemy-held air territory. It was one of the most thrilling and anxious days of my life.

Then, while there were only ten minutes left of our two hour stand-by, the Klaxons sounded and we were given the start-up signal. Tricky must have spotted something. I hoped it was the real thing this time. We rushed off the flight deck and, for the first time, I knew from Tricky's urgent voice on the radio that we should at last find something to shoot at. I was determined to get in close and make every bullet count from all eight guns. I gave the guns a short burst — just to make sure they worked.

I followed Spike up to about 3000 feet. Tricky gave us a course to steer: "Bogey for you at 15 miles. Steer one-five-zero. Buster, over." Spike's voice answered, "Roger," and we opened our throttles to maximum climb power.

I flew about 400 yards to one side or the other of Spike's aircraft. This allowed sufficient freedom, so that I could use my eyes to search the sky but still be near enough to allow me to keep up with him in case he altered course suddenly.

I looked through the side panels of my beautifully polished perspex hood and tried to imagine what I would do if I were a German snooper flying in search of a British Fleet, 200 miles from my base and with only two-tenths cloud cover available at 3000 — 5000 feet to hide in. Besides feeling very frightened, I reckoned I would, if I were a snooper, fly at cloud height, about 3500 feet, and use what cover there was and stay just outside visibility distance once I had spotted the Fleet, only moving in from time to time to spot any changes of course. I would certainly keep an eye open for fighters and if I spotted one I would 'open the taps' and make a beeline for the nearest cloud in a direction away from the fleet.

As I strained my eyes, willing myself to see something, the unbelievable happened. I could see a black spot moving slowly eastwards, about five miles to the south on our starboard beam and below us. I immediately piped up on the radio and turned towards it, opening up to maximum revs and take-off power. "Bogey three o'clock below, five miles, turning now, over."

"OK, boy," said Spike.

His aircraft shot ahead of mine as he turned under me and I, too, selected the boost control cut-out, giving maximum emergency power of 12 pounds per square inch boost — the first time ever.

The next time I glanced towards Spike, my eyes otherwise glued on the enemy aircraft, I saw Spike's aircraft streaming black smoke and dropping back.

"I'm not going well, boy. My engine's packing up. I'm throttling back." This is what I think he said, although it sounded confused to me at the time. I went on ahead.

Perhaps I could surprise the enemy aircraft. It had got nearly abeam as I closed in to five miles, and I hoped that the pilots and observer in the cockpit of the snooper would have their eyes forward and not over their shoulders. As the range decreased, I could clearly see that it was a three-engined aircraft, with three lines of exhaust smoke coming from the engines. This could only mean that they had seen me and had opened their throttles fully, thus the rich mixture and the smoke from the exhausts. It was now a chase. A Hurricane *versus* a Cant 10007Z making for cloud, for that was what it was. I knew I would win.

I remembered the silhouette on the Heads door, and that it had some guns pointing out of its backside. I was determined, therefore, not to come straight up its jacksie, but to do a proper quarter-attack, so giving the rear gunner a deflection shot, not an easy shot at me.

From a position abeam and above him I entered the prescribed and much practised quarter-attack from his port side. I was shattered to see that I was still miles out of range by the time I was at about 30 degrees off his quarter, and that I should be in line-astern, and an easy, no deflection, shot for his rear gunner if I continued to come in from there. Still there was nothing I could do about it now, except perhaps come in from below and astern and keep clear of his slipstream that way.

I had an overtaking speed of at least 40 knots and I had to push the stick forward quickly to get this plan into operation before I got too close and within range of his four rear guns.

I found myself over-correcting on the controls. I was already breathing hard. I remember telling myself not to over-correct and take time over things. Take easy, slow, aim and don't jerk everything about.

I could now see the dark exhaust smoke from his three engines passing over the top of my hood as I closed in. I was determined to get his wing span to fill the entire gunsight ring before I pulled up and made my attack, for I would lose speed on the pull up and perhaps I would not be able to close on him as fast as I would like.

With cloud cover for the enemy now only a short distance ahead I could not contain myself any longer and pulled back on the stick, got his underside flying into the centre of the ringsight and pressed the firing button. As I did so I could see sparks, either from his guns or from mine, coming from the Cant's tail. Then I could see smoke coming from his port side. I continued firing through the smoke, hopelessly in his slipstream by now, until I caught sight of a wing tip so near that I pulled away and downwards, having got too close for safety.

I overshot him as I turned away into the clear and could see that his port wing and engine had flames coming from them as well as smoke. He was already turning slowly to port and losing height. I thought that I might have to have another go and was just making up my mind how to do this, when I realised that he could not possibly survive and that all he was trying to do was to turn into wind and to make a landing in the sea. He had given up.

When his aircraft touched the sea it left a trail of yellow pieces of fuselage behind in its wake. It soon came to a stop, floating on the water. Perhaps I should have another go at it. My blood was up, and I was frightened at what I had done. I dived on them. But just as I took aim, I saw that there was a yellow inflated dinghy alongside the aircraft in the water. At the moment I touched the button I realised that I was doing something wrong. Mercifully for my conscience in after-years, only one or two bullets left the guns, for I had already finished my ammunition. I like to think that I could have made some friends of those Italians, albeit quite by accident. If they are still alive, perhaps they might contact me if they read this. Fortune certainly smiled on them for the crew were picked up later by one of our returning destroyers. None of the seven crew were lost or injured.

I told Tricky over the radio what I had done and heard that Spike had already landed-on with a duff engine. After I came to a halt and the arrester wire was reset behind me on the flight deck, I taxied forward and was struck down into the hangar. It was evening and the setting sun was shining down on the batsman so clearly, and making it so easy to land accurately and gently. Decklanding worries receded during combat flying. The excitement of shooting down an enemy aircraft obliterated all other anxieties.

I went up on the flight deck again and saw Spike. He told me that when he had pulled the tit, it had been too much for his engine. It had put a con rod through the crank case. Luckily this had happened only in the last few seconds of flight. He had returned to the ship with his oil temperature off the clock one way and his oil pressure off the dial the other. The engine was making a noise like an Irish harvester, he said. The filters were entirely full of white metal from the melted bearings, and the whole thing was smoking hot. When he touched down, it all came to a grinding halt without him touching a thing. Spike said that our Captain, Mackintosh, had turned *Eagle* into wind to land him on without waiting for permission from the Flagship, otherwise he would never have made it. How lucky to have a Captain like that.

Next morning, Spike and I were on the second morning patrol at 0730. I could still only just believe my luck in getting the Cant, yet here we were airborne again, and with no one yet having seen a solitary thing. Once again I had a feeling that we might strike lucky. We were right in the middle of Italian and German airspace and it would only be a question of time before we were again spotted and reported. Perhaps the Cant's failure to return would spark off a maximum search effort.

The weather was, once again, bright and clear and visibility was extremely good. Just as we had raised our wheels, what should happen but Tricky gave us another vector to steer.

"Possible bogey, low, 20 miles. Steer one-five-oh." Then, later: "Buster, over".

Once again we complied and this time we flew low, looking upwards to the clouds to try to see the bogey before it could see us. This time Spike did not dare pull his emergency tit. and we stayed at take-off power.

Once again I saw it. This time, as we were flying low, I saw it at about six miles range, silhouetted against the underface of a white cumulus cloud. It was flying at about 2000 feet above us. It was moving away from the Fleet, towards Africa. We remained low, using our grey camouflage to hide us from his eyes against the sea. The target looked dark and menacing. It was a Ju 88 and going very fast. I had no idea whether it had seen us or not, but, to try to remain unseen for as long as possible, Spike and I kept low.

Spike was my leader and I was perhaps a trifle relieved that it would be his job this time to go in first. I was determined to make sure I had enough speed and enough distance ahead before I turned in. This was so that I could make a proper quarter attack within a range of 250 yards, as I had been taught. I climbed up on the Ju 88's port beam, well ahead and at a distance of 1000 yards. Spike was still closing astern of him on a firing run and I could see his aircraft getting closer and closer to the Ju 88. Then I could see his gun smoke as he opened fire in a long burst, perhaps eight seconds. Not a thing happened to the Ju 88. My heart beat faster as I realised that it was now my turn to do something brave.

As I turned in on his port bow 1000 feet higher than him, I could hardly believe my eyes. The damned Ju 88 turned about 30 degrees away and leapt ahead of me as I tried to position myself once more for a quarter attack. It was moving at twice the speed of our practice targets at fighter school and I was moving at three times the speed. By the time I was at the correct angle-off of about 30 degrees, I was still too far away from him to stand a chance of doing him any damage.

All I could do was to carry out the same sort of attack that I had done on the Cant. I pulled the tit to get a bit more speed and, thank God, I could see that I was gaining on him. There was nothing I could do until the range decreased, and I spent the time, a few seconds only perhaps, jinking around in case he might have long-range 20 mm guns and be firing at me.

I clenched my teeth and, no doubt, half shut my eyes in a grimace, as I forced on, closer and closer. It was terrifying, but I was determined to close in and make sure of him. It would be awful, after all this, to have to return to the ship without having hacked him down.

"What the hell," I thought, "I've got to do it." I pressed the firing button. It was now or never. The shape was wandering in my sight, huge and black, first one side and then the other. His two propellers appearing stroboscopic in turn through my windscreen as I weaved about, in and out of his slipstream. I finished the entire 12 seconds of ammunition and must have been closer than a hundred yards at the end. I saw the deWild ammunition hitting his port wing, sparking like firecrackers. Bits of aircraft flew past me, or so it seemed — or they might have been the rear gunner's empty shell cases. I was sure I had hit him and mortally wounded him. I saw a burst of smoke from his port wing root again, this time after I had finished firing all my ammunition and had pulled away to his port side and out of range of his rear-gunner and out of the smoke of his exhausts.

The Ju 88 flew on in a shallow dive and I found myself easily overtaking him. He had slowed right down to about 160 knots. I was sure he was a 'gonner'. I didn't wait this time to see him splash and short of fuel after the chase I joined up with Spike once more, who was watching it all.

When we landed on, we claimed one Ju 88 probably shot down. Tricky said that he had lost sight of our enemy on the radar soon after Spike had announced he was opening fire, so that there was every chance that he had eventually ditched, as we were certain that he was going to.

Spike and I spent the rest of the morning in the pilots' small crewroom. This was on the top deck of the island between the funnels. It was near 'Guns'. He moved from side to side, looking through a huge pair of binoculars for enemy snoopers and speaking to his gun crews through a telephone headset from time to time. We had the gramophone going. One of the tunes was *The Captain sat in the Captain's chair as he played his ukelele as the ship went down.* Guns did not join in.

At about 1000, the Tannoy announced an approaching raid and the ship came to full Action Stations for the first time. I had my father's 9.5 mm Pathé movie camera and I was determined to get pictures of bombs falling, preferably onto other ships of course. I used up a few feet from the goofers, taking pictures of four Hurricanes scrambling to do battle. They climbed up and disappeared to the north. Almost immediately they had left, one or two guns opened up from *Malaya.* She had obviously seen something.

About two minutes after that, our 1912 six inch guns started to fire as well and several bombs hit the water on our port bow. I rushed out to get a photo and was just too late to get a picture of the splash of a bomb falling in the sea about 200 feet from our port bow. It was so near that the spray wet us as we came out to watch.

Then, about two or three minutes after the bomb spray had dispersed, I saw Guns pointing at an aircraft approaching from the north-east, low on the water. Every gun in the Fleet seemed to be firing at it, but it came on and on and flew across our bow, disappearing into the distance without making the slightest attempt to evade the splashes all around it. It had dropped a fish (torpedo) at someone in the screen, for we all turned to port amidst much sounding of ships' sirens as we did so. This was exciting stuff and more or less what we had seen on British Movietone News.

No ships had been hit by this combined torpedo and high-level bombing attack, and the four Hurricanes landed on, claiming only a couple of Italian torpedo aircraft as 'probables'. They had not had time to climb through 20,000 feet to reach the bombers. At least there had not yet been any Ju 87s.

After lunch I was 'duty stand-by' on deck, with Bully as my Number Two. We knew perfectly well that we would be required, for the plot was full of bogies. It was only a matter of time before they came in again. When we were told to scramble, I climbed up at full power, not waiting for Bully — who in the event didn't get off at all — and was told to steer 090 degrees and climb "Buster" to 5000 feet. Tricky said: "Many bogies on this bearing, about 20 miles".

So I flogged on, keeping my eyes open. I could hear other voices chiming in from time to time, including some excited Italian voices shouting something like "a la deresta, a la deresta", which I was told afterwards might have been "Look right, look right".

After about five minutes, I was just about to ask for a few more directions from Tricky, when I saw below me and on my starboard side a light-brown camouflaged fighter aircraft. It looked something like a long-nosed Hurricane, but the colour intrigued me and I dived down on it. It hadn't yet seen me, for it kept on its heading of west and seemed to be going very fast indeed. I had about 2000 feet excess altitude and this was sufficient to build up a nice overtaking speed as I dived down on him. He still didn't seem to see me and I opened fire at about 300 yards, rather too far I feared. He immediately pulled up in a steep right hand turn. I tried to follow him, but, going much faster, I blacked out hopelessly and he must have flown right through my sights. I have no idea what happened after I 'came to' for he was nowhere to be seen. I continued the turn to starboard, fearing that I was about to be attacked myself. I couldn't believe it possible for an enemy fighter to be flogging around on his own without several others, and I was damned if I was going to be hacked down myself. Eventually I gave up the steep turn and continued on my normal course. He was, it would seem, a Reggione 2001, armed with fragmentation bombs. About eight of these fighter/bombers had apparently been detailed to drop their fragmentation bombs on our flight decks and so ruin all our aircraft on deck and the aircrew as well, before we could get airborne. As no one saw more than a couple of attacks made by these aircraft, perhaps my appearance some 20 miles away from their target and before they had got there, discouraged one or two from going further.

So I continued on my original vector, 090 degrees, still watching out for what I assumed would be more Reggione fighters.

Then I saw them. These must be what Tricky was getting all steamed up about. They were flying in tight formation, coming towards me, slightly to port and down-sun and about 1000 feet below me. If Tricky was , in fact, vectoring me alone, and not a lot of other Hurricanes, then he had done a superb job, having positioned me up sun and with a good height advantage. There were at least four flights of four or five SV 79s, each flight in a typical 'Balbo' line astern. They were so close to each other that it was only possible to attack the single 'arse-end Charlie' in the formation, and the rear one at that. The only chance was a classic quarter attack, coming in from the south, positioning up sun with my shadow superimposed over the target at the start of the turn-in, breaking-off before reaching the line astern position. My attack would still have to be on the rear of the four flights, for fear of colliding with the others coming on behind.

All these thoughts were adding to the chaos already going in and out of my brain as I again pulled the red knob of the emergency boost override. Everything started to shake and vibrate once more. This time I was more than ever determined not to allow the quarter attack to develop into a line astern attack. I built up a massive overtaking speed, carefully trimming out the rudder forces as I did so. I turned in, feeling naked behind me and wishing that Bully was there, and started my firing run while still at about 40 degrees off. I rapidly closed the range so that I was pulling far too much 'g' for accurate sighting. However, I was so close by the time I broke away, that the cockpit was dark with the shadows of surrounding Italian aircraft and the air bumpy with their slipstreams. I had no idea whether they were all firing at me or not, but I felt that they were and it was very frightening. I had expended all my ammunition in the two attacks apart from a very few rounds, and I certainly wasn't going into the deathtrap again. I pulled up, up sun of the formation and I could see that the rear formation now only consisted of two aircraft instead of four. I couldn't see the others in the formations ahead at all.

Just then, someone from 801 Squadron piped up "Tally Ho" on the radio, and I had a grandstand view of their four going into attack, óne after the other. They hacked down one of the remaining two while I was watching, and the formation ahead completely broke ranks and fell all over the sky. The separated aircraft still made ground towards the Fleet. However, all thoughts they might have had of making a combined and effective torpedo attack must have gone.

Almost immediately after the 801's attack, I found myself being fired on by our own guns so that I knew that I was nearing home. I, and a few others out of ammunition, then went into the waiting position to the west of the Fleet. From here, we landed-on safely about 20 minutes later, very short of fuel.

I claimed a 'possible' Reggione and one 'probable' SV 79, but do not know what happened to them. Regardless of confirmation our five plane attack on the torpedo bombing formation had succeeded, for they achieved no hits whatever. They dropped their torpedoes miles out of range of the destroyers and got nowhere near the carriers.

I have since read that there were two further main attacks on the convoy, making four in all that day. The first was directed mainly on poor old *Argus*, which because of her low speed had to operate her aircraft separately from us. The final attack, in the early evening, was against the cruiser *Liverpool* and the destroyer *Antelope*. *Liverpool* had been hit on the third raid by a bomb from a Stuka attack flown by Italians, and had had to retire early towards Gibraltar with her attendant destroyer.

Next day, while *Liverpool* was making her slow and painful way back, her lookouts saw a cloud of yellow smoke about ten miles away. They made towards it and found three German airmen in a dinghy. They had been attacked by four Hurricanes, they said, and had had to ditch. As this was in the position of our early morning snooper, Spike and I claimed half a 'confirmed' Ju 88 each, instead of a 'probable'.

The lonely *Liverpool* was responsible for drawing off the afternoon's strikes from the convoy. I could appreciate the Germans' point of view. *Liverpool* had no fighter escort and only one destroyer's close range AA fire. Similarly, when *Argus* was separated from the main Fleet, she too made a much more attractive target. However, 807 Fulmar Squadron did well, intercepting and destroying two Stukas before they could make their attack, and breaking up the remainder. *Argus* was then able to make herself a very difficult bombing target to the less skilful Italians and escaped with one near miss. Only one or two bombers came near *Eagle* again after the main SM 79 raid. They were, however, mostly 'empties' returning to Sicily who accidentally flew over us on their way home after bombing *Liverpool* or *Argus*. Number Four in Red Flight in 801 was Sub-Lieutenant Fisher. He was from a famous Naval family and thus under close scrutiny. He had been rather put out by *Eagle's* pom-poms which had fired at him as he flew by to make his first landing circuit. He was also rather short of fuel. He had already made three almost perfect approaches, but had held off about two feet high and had floated over all the arrester wires each time. On the fifth approach, Wings leaned over and, in his most restrained voice on the loud hailer said.

"Bats, get him on this time. Offer him money, jewellery or a month's leave, but for God's sake, get him on."

Luckily Fisher made it. That same evening, the dusk patrol — Lieutenant Frazer-Harris and Sub-Lieutenant Peter Twiss (who later became Chief Test Pilot of the Fairey Aviation Company) — came on board in their Fairey Fulmars. They were the CO and senior pilot of 807 Squadron in *Argus*. Pete's aircraft had a cannon shell hole in its airscrew spinner and the whole of the oil in the constant-speed unit had blown back and covered his windscreen. He managed to see the deck by hanging his head out to one side. Even then, his goggles were covered in the stuff and were almost impossible to see through. Yet, when he landed, he did not even bother to tell any of us about it.

As we turned back west at 1900 that evening, Spike and I were stand-by on deck. I happened to look up and glance astern into the darkening sky to the east. I could see sparks climbing skywards and I could hear the muffled crump of AA shells. But nothing seemed to happen our end of the Mediterranean and we continued on our way westwards.

In the wardroom afterwards I asked about the gunfire. I was told the Beaufighters were having trouble finding the convoy. When they eventually found it they had made the incorrect recognition signal and had been fired on. "Typical RAF," I thought unkindly, and got on with my supper. The eight Beaufighters had in fact arrived over the convoy at the proper time, at dusk but, being fired upon, they thought they had arrived over the Italians, particularly as they could not get them to stop and could not get a word out of them over the r/t. Their leader had then searched round in the growing dusk for a short period, calling the cruiser *Cairo* on the briefed frequency continuously. Just then, he saw below him other white wakes in the water. The ships had dark grey topsides, but as they, too fired at him "slightly harder" — he told us in the bar at Gibraltar, afterwards — he wondered if they were the Italians after all. Meanwhile, he heard what may have been *Cairo* saying that she was under air attack. It was all very confusing.

While the Beaufighter leader was flogging about the Mediterranean, he realised that he was wasting his time, for there was no chance, in the poor visibility and the failing light that he would see any enemy aircraft. He would have needed the ADR from *Cairo* for any successful interceptions. So he and his seven other Beaufighters pushed off back to Malta. There, the RAF telephoned Flag Officer Malta and told him the news — that there was probably an Italian Fleet at sea as well as our own.

Next day, *Cairo's* r/t was still useless, and with no ADR, the Spitfires and the Beaufighters from Malta could make no impression on the enemy aircraft. Because of this, three ships out of the four merchant ships in Operation 'Harpoon' were sunk, together with the destroyer *Bedouin*.

This time, the Naval public relations did not claim a victory as it had after the Battle of Sirte. 'Harpoon' was hardly mentioned in the Press. However, it was important because it was the first convoy with sufficient naval fighter aircraft in the carriers in company to effect a proper air defence. The Navy was no longer relying on AA gunfire. It was beginning to see the light. The ADR-controlled fighters were very effective in breaking up, disorganising and scaring off the enemy aircraft before they arrived over the Fleet, so that in 300 sorties they missed with their bombs and could make no determined and co-ordinated torpedo attacks. They had failed to score, apart from a lucky bomb hit on *Liverpool* and one merchantman.

'Harpoon' unloaded 20,000 tons of vital stores in Malta. 'Pedestal', the famous August convoy, five times the size, would manage 35,000 tons and at a cost of five times the number of ship casualties and five times the aircraft casualties. 801 Squadron was to lose two pilots and 807 Squadron one. We would claim eight enemy aircraft destroyed.

While this had been taking place, Admiral Harwood at Alexandria had put Admiral Vian in charge of the 15th Cruiser Squadron and another westbound convoy. Without the benefit of air cover from the North African airfields, they ran into continuous air attacks. Several of the merchant ships could not keep up and two were sunk. Eventually the whole Fleet turned back short of AA ammunition. This was at the order of Admiral Harwood who had listened to Vian's troubles on the r/t, back in Alexandria. The cruiser *Newcastle* and the destroyer *Hasty* were torpedoed. *Nestor* was sunk and *Centurion* and *Arethusa* disabled by air attack on the second day. *Hermioné* was then torpedoed on the return journey. With no carrier and no fighter protection the results were predictable.

Meanwhile, back on the Rock, morale was high as we flew ashore with eight Hurricanes of 801 Squadron and two of 813F. A Swordfish of 813 taking off ahead of us from *Eagle* had kindly agreed to carry our quarter-ton trolley-accumulator which we used for starting our Hurricanes. He also had a couple of bicycles as well as a full crew, so there was not enough room for all the crew's suitcases. He had therefore stowed these on the *top* surface of the lower wing —

"the only remaining place", he said. They had burst open when he applied lift, and their contents had had to be swept up by the 'Duty Part' before we could continue flying. However, all was not lost for he found on landing that he still had some pyjama trousers and a dressing gown wrapped round his tailplane. Ashore at North Front that night, we continued on the La Ina and Tio Pepe until the Senior Naval Officer appeared with his telescope at 0200 and told us to go to bed. He said we were waking up the soldiers inside the Rock.

While we had been away, Midshipman Williams had found yet another vocation at North Front. Every two days he was told to fly a terrified observer in a Fulmar to Casablanca and back. The observer was told to photograph the contents of the harbour. The French Dewoitine 520s objected and kept discharging their guns a few feet away — alongside the Fulmar. The observer was in a terrible state when he landed, not only because the redoubtable Williams wanted to mix it with the fiery French pilots, but also because he had dived on La Linea when he came back from Casablanca, drawing the Spaniards' fire, just to show them who owned North Front.

During the remainder of June and July 1942, *Eagle* and *Argus*, plus a small escort, continued with the Club Runs. *Eagle's* faithful four continued to supply stand-bys on deck, occasionally being scrambled for false alarms, completing each sortie without mishap and adding some 70 more Spitfires to Malta's fighter squadrons; keeping pace, almost, with the Island's frightening losses. In all, *Eagle* with *Argus*, and twice with *Wasp*, flew off 300 Spitfires to Malta in the first six months of 1942.

But this was not enough and by the first week in August we knew that once more, something special was in the wind. Our ground crew were recalled to the ship on the evening of 4 August. We, at North Front with 801 were then told to rendezvous with *Eagle* off Cape Trafalgar at 0530 next morning. Through the murk of the early morning we could see from our cockpits, not only *Eagle*, but the dim outlines of two or three more aircraft carriers, four cruisers and about 16 destroyers, heading out towards the west.

Soon, *Eagle's* masthead light flashed out an 'F' and we closed on her in formation and landed on, one by one, without mishap. Bringing up the rear was Boris Morris. He was leading the first of six Swordfish for A/S duties.

Operation 'Pedestal' was under way.

Chapter 10
Operation 'Pedestal'

Four carriers, seven cruisers, 24 destroyers, 14 fast merchant ships the size of liners, tugs, minesweepers, two battleships, four Admirals, 86 fighter aircraft — 60 of them Sea Hurricanes — and with 16 A/S Swordfish and Albacores, re-entered the Straits through fog on the night of 9 August 1942. Five days earlier some of this huge fleet had left the Clyde, ostensibly for West Africa. *Indomitable* (R/A Boyd) and four cruisers had then joined from the Indian Ocean. *Victorious* (Captain Bovell) had just returned from covering PQ17 — the 'scattered' convoy — and had driven *Tirpitz* back into harbour without her firing a shot. But none of these ships had worked together in the radar direction of fighter aircraft and none had operated a quarter that number. They had therefore been ordered to meet 300 miles west of the Rock to operate their aircraft and to learn the elaborate plan which Vice-Admiral Sir Neville Syfret in *Nelson,* had worked out for them. In spite of having the good fortune to pass the Straits in fog, the enemy soon learned of their re-entry into the Mediterranean, because the fleet was overflown by a French civil airliner. *Victorious,* lacking Mediterranean experience but possessing the best radar, was Fighter Direction Ship. She scrambled her fighters to intercept it. This annoyed the French pilot. He announced over the radio that he was being attacked whilst overflying a huge force of aircraft carriers. The French in North Africa informed the Germans and the German commander put his long-formed plans for air and sea attack into operation. We were sorry in *Eagle* that Tricky would not be directing us over the radio.

Rupert Brabner briefed us. He said the air opposition had increased even more since 'Harpoon' to some 400 Axis aircraft. We could expect raids of 60 at a time instead of the usual 30. The Germans were now using He 111s armed with two trackless torpedoes each. We could expect them to be in company with twin-engined Me 110-4s armed with eight cannon. The Italian Fleet had already left La Spezia, Taranto and Augusta and it looked as if Admiral Burroughs, who had just returned from the Arctic convoy, would have to fight a night action against them in the Narrows. His flagship *Nigeria* and *Cairo* were the two ADR/AA cruisers and would be directing the RAF Beaufighters and Spitfires from Malta to provide the convoy with air cover when we and the rest of the carriers turned back at the narrows.

"Furybox" (*Furious*), said Brabner, "is flying off 40 more RAF Spits to Malta. They were worried about her short flight deck — 100 feet shorter than *Eagle* — so they have had all their props changed to ones with finer pitch."

Brabner told us that *Indomitable* had 24 Hurricanes, in 800 and 880 Squadrons, and that *Argus* had 12 more in 807 Squadron. *Victorious* could only take six as a deck park, as her lifts were not large enough to take them down into the hangar. He told us who the COs were. Names like 'Buster' Hallett (884), Rodney Carver (885), Bill Bruen (800), Butch Judd (880), Frazer-Harris (807), Captain Alan Marsh RM (804) and so on. It seemed that much of the fighter Fleet Air Arm was there.

During the first sunny morning of the journey westwards, the Fleet practised AA fire. *Nelson* and *Rodney* fired their main armament, newly fitted with high-angle mountings on the 16 inch guns. The half-ton shells made a colossal bang when they went off at about 10,000 feet, but how on earth the turret could be traversed quickly enough if a raid came over at that height none of us could work out. Perhaps they were intending to put up a barrage, hoping that the Stukas would fly through it. Whatever the plan was, we made a mental note to give the Fleet a wide berth whenever possible.

Rupert Brabner's interesting briefing was interrupted on several occasions by the ship's siren. This denoted emergency turns to avoid torpedoes. We went on deck as we could not bear to miss anything. We saw several of the screen of 24 destroyers dropping depth charges — as we had before on the 'Club Runs' — but we had never seen them dropped so far west before. Perhaps the Swordfish had found something on the surface.

The air battle that evening and the next day, and the night action in the 'narrows' which followed have often been described elsewhere, but several incidents in it relate particularly to this narrative and are worth including. On the late evening of the day *Eagle* was torpedoed and three or four hundred of us were speeding back to Gibraltar in *Malcolm*, we could see from her deck a mass of AA fire and tracer rising in the eastern sky. The mighty battle started just as we left. However, we knew that 801 Squadron was represented, because four of her Hurricanes had been airborne at the time our ship was sunk and they had landed on *Victorious*.

Towards the end of the first night's air battle, six Hurricanes of 880 from *Indomitable* led by Dicky Cork their Senior Pilot — and a couple from *Victorious'* 885 Squadron from Buster Hallett's Squadron, were airborne. The Fleet was under attack, they were short of fuel and it was impossible to find which was their own carrier in the darkness. They were being fired on whenever they came near and it seemed as if they would have to ditch. *Indomitable's* Captain, Tommy Troubridge, was, however, giving his fighters all the help he could to find his ship in the darkness, ignoring signals from *Nelson* that he must tell them to ditch. He took his great ship out of line, steaming her into wind on his own with his masthead and deck landing lights full on. He again ignored Syfret's order to douse his lights and to "rejoin immediately", just as Nelson would have done. He said later. "What is the good of a carrier without her fighters?"

Quite apart from Troubridge's brave action — later backed up by his Admiral Sir Dennis Boyd also on board *Indomitable* — the incident had been equally unpleasant for the Hurricanes. They were consistently fired upon by each ship in turn as they tried to regain *Indomitable*. In desperation, Tommy Troubridge put on a searchlight and shone it at the clouds above his ship. Even then, when the Hurricanes came right past the ship with their hooks down and nav-lights full on to join the landing circuit, they were still fired on by their own carrier's pom-poms, 300 yards away.

Next day the air battles started again. The remaining 60 fighters made 200 sorties, four times the flying intensity per pilot of a peak day in the Battle of Britain. It could not have been sustained. But only one of the 14 merchant ships was hit, leaving the others and the 45-ship escort to continue.

Then, on this second evening, after the air battle seemed to have subsided, and just before the Fleet divided, the Germans made yet another determined attack on *Indomitable*. She was hit by two bombs in the soft part of her flight deck by the lifts and she had to retire westwards early. Her fighters, then airborne, had to crowd into *Victorious*. As *Vic* had no room, she had to pitch them over the side. Later *Indomitable* was hit again, with a near miss by her wardroom. Because wardrooms were always used for briefing and debriefing aircrew in RN carriers during action stations, the carnage was awful.

Meanwhile Admiral Burroughs continued through the early part of the night towards Malta. From the experience in 'Harpoon', Burroughs had realised he needed to double-up on his cruisers fitted with ADR to ensure that at least one would be available for directing the RAF fighters. The remainder of the cruisers and nine destroyers, tugs, minesweepers and other vessels were also considered essential for the last lap, to fight off the Italians during the dark night that followed and to clear the mine fields near Valetta and tow damaged ships to the docksides. Burroughs' air cover was to be provided by parts of eight Malta-based fighter squadrons, half Spitfire Vbs and the other half Beaufighters. Provided that the 24 Beaufighters arrived smack on time, Admiral Burroughs considered that he would have a well balanced force to meet anything he might find in the Narrows that night or next morning, whether they were enemy U-boats, MTBs, surface fleet or air.

However, during the confusion of a second MTB raid against Burroughs that night, an Italian submarine fired four torpedoes, almost at random, in the direction of the tightly packed convoy. It managed to sink his Flagship, *Cairo,* and disable *Nigeria*. So Burroughs quickly lost his entire ADR capability, for no other ships were fitted with 'stop-me-and-buy-one' radar or r/t.

Having lost his Flagship and thus communication with his Fleet, Burroughs was unable to control its subsequent movements. The 20 or 30 German and Italian MTBs (Motor Torpedo Boats) raced about inside the remains of the destroyer screen, firing torpedoes in all directions. Several of the merchant ships fired at each other. The MTBs sank four merchant ships in the first 45 minutes of the action and later torpedoed the cruiser *Manchester*. She was scuttled and her 700 crew were barbarously imprisoned by the French in the desert until North Africa was liberated in 1943. A second Italian submarine disabled the cruiser *Kenya,* the submarine's skipper saying in his report that he could hardly miss as she was silhouetted against the burning merchantman.

Next morning with no ADR and no Flagship, and with the convoy spread over 2000 square miles of Mediterranean without a leader, the Beaufighters and Spitfires were set an impossible task to intercept enemy raids in the poor visibility. Many of the RAF fighter pilots returned to Malta without sighting a single ship or enemy aircraft. From 400 sorties the RAF claimed 13 enemy destroyed. The Fleet Air Arm's claim (which the Admiralty did not bother to announce) was 39 enemy destroyed from 250 sorties. Even if both claims were to be halved — which they should be — the effectiveness of operating fighters with and without ADR can easily be judged. With ADR and when operating from carriers with the Fleet, the fighters were five times as effective per sortie and ten times as effective per flying hour. This was exactly the figure established in the Biggin Hill experiment before the war. (See Appendix 2 — Naval Air Power.)

Back at Gibraltar, we watched the entrance of the harbour for the returning ships. We were seated round a table at the Yacht Club, sipping John Collins. I had just returned from the GPO post office where I had sent a telegram to my immobile Wren and to my father saying "Woe is us for we are sunk. What a corpuscular nuisance". I looked up and saw *Indomitable* slowly entering harbour and turning to starboard to come alongside the southern mole. She had her glistening Royal Marine Band sounding forth on the sunlit flight deck.

"Christ!" said Bully. "The band's on top of her lift and that's 20 feet off the flight deck. And look at those scars on her side."

We walked round to the mole and went aboard. There I found Paddy Brownlee and we went round the ship together. Butch Judd, Mike Hankey and six other Hurricane pilots were missing from air operations. Three Albacore aircrew had also been killed by the near miss in her wardroom and 70 more injured. The dockyard men had begun to pick off human remains stuck to the underside of the shattered lift.

"What's that awful smell, Paddy?" I asked.

"That's 'Junior' Young's rhino horns and hooves. The bomb spread them around the lift well," replied Paddy.

Apparently 'Junior' Young, Sub-Lieutenant John Young, DSC, RNVR, 800 Squadron, had shot a black rhino while at Mombasa. This was nothing unusual in those days, of course, but he had done it one morning on his own, using a soft-nosed bullet. He shot it as it had charged at him, bringing it down ten feet short of where he was standing. He was lucky to have hit it in the mouth, the only place that a soft Army rifle bullet could have pierced the skull.

"How was Butch killed?"

"He went in too close to a Ju 88 in a straight-in stern attack. Funny thing was, he had lectured us not to do the same thing the day before."

I met Dicky Cork and also Bill Bruen, now the COs of 880 and 800. They both seemed entirely unconcerned at the chaos all around them, the shattered wardroom and the smell of entrails everywhere.

Indomitable went back to the repair yards of Norfolk, Virginia. We, from *Eagle,* went aboard *Argus* for our voyage home. I sat in the ancient leather armchairs in *Argus's* wardroom and read the paper. All it said was that the Fleet had fought its way through with the convoy, and the RAF had shot down 13 enemy aircraft. Churchill later upbraided Admiral Pound the First Sea Lord: "Where is the mention of the Fleet Air Arm's 39 victories?" he demanded. "This would put a very different complexion on the air fighting."

Back in the Clyde we all went on three weeks leave. After a trip to London's Grosvenor Hotel — where I managed to get a new Naval uniform free that had belonged to another sunken sailor who had not returned — I spent the remaining two weeks with my immobile Wren at her mother's house in Queen Camel. It was heaven.

Searching through some letters the other day, I came across this written by Granny to my father: "Thank you dear for your letter which came this morning. I was so very pleased to hear about Michael; as his ship has been sunk, he will I expect have a good rest and it will be fine it he goes to America; the time he has gone through must be a very great strain on him, but he is young and keen; he always has been a dear, good boy; I do hope he will be spared to be a great help and blessing to others." Wasn't that sweet of her.

It was true that I was glad of the rest that *Eagle* had given me. There was no scheme at that time in the Fleet Air Arm to limit operational flying as in the RAF. Fleet Air Arm aircrew just went on until they were killed or until they were no more use because of 'twitch', sometimes call 'lack of moral fibre'. The average appointment to a ship was two and a half years in peacetime and in war. This also applied to Royal Naval aircrew. So that, working on this basis, I should not qualify for a rest until I had done another two years in a first line fighter squadron. As the average life of a first line pilot or observer or TAG was about five months of operations, the chance of anyone surviving in the Fleet Air Arm was entirely due to luck, or his ship being sunk, or his 'lack of moral fibre'. When I saw Bill Bruen on board *Indomitable* in Gibraltar, he already had a DSC and a DSO. When I asked Paddy what he had got these for, he replied that they were for the Norway raid and Petsamo and "a whole lot of other ops". He had spent all the war in 800 or 803 Squadrons and he was about the only one left.

So I was lucky to have this three week break. I used it well. As the letter that my Granny had written shows, I seemed to have needed a secure home and a family more than most young people of my age, doubtless because of my upbringing. Therefore, it seemed inevitable that I should want to get married. I was determined to marry my immobile Wren. I asked for her hand one night on the sitting room sofa. She surprisingly agreed and so did her mother next morning.

We got married because we both felt that life hung on a thread and the thread might part before we had tasted life's goodness. Life was for living while it was still possible. Our thoughts went no deeper. Our eyes saw no further. The long future was a hazy vision, nothing discernible. We lived only for the present.

So we were married in the church at Queen Camel. Her family and her friends looked on amazed and indeed happy for us both. We spent a three day honeymoon in a small hotel in the middle of Dartmoor; after which I reported to Bill Bruen, my new Squadron Commander — 800 Squadron — at Lee-on-Solent.

Chapter 11
800 Naval Air Squadron

Having lost *Indomitable*, 800 Squadron now found time to re-equip with the new Mark IIb and IIc Hurricane. It was a famous squadron and Spike King-Joyce and I were lucky to have been appointed to it. Bill Bruen was well known and much respected. This allowed him to get his own way with higher authority, and he was always a firm ally to help us when we had our brushes with the upholders of 'Good Order and Naval Discipline'. The Senior Pilot, Hamish Muir-Mackenzie, was one of the few ex-Dartmouth Lieutenants flying at that time. He played the piano furiously, mostly ominous-sounding stuff like Rachmaninoff's C Sharp Minor Prelude. Like Barry Lyster and a few others he flew fighters more or less as a pleasurable pastime, although his first love was music. He usually got lost when he led us round England, but when he flew with us round Scotland he knew every inch of the ground. Indeed, so well, that if he suddenly recognised a crag or a mountain a few hundred feet away while flying in and out of the clouds with us, he would suddenly alter course without warning and leave us to catch up as best we could. Seldom did we arrive at our destination at the same time. Sometimes we were days apart. However, since only four out of the 13 in 800 Squadron were not already experienced pilots, we seldom came to grief. There were many old hands: John Hastings, 'Junior' Young of rhino fame, Andrew (A. J.) Thomson, Maurice Bannister, Dougy Yate, Ron Outwin, Bill Roberts, Roy Hooker (RNZNVR) and 'Sammy' Hoare. There was also Midshipman 'Roncers' Roncoroni (RNR). 'Greyhound' Thompson was my Number Two, and, or course, there was Spike King-Joyce as the third Flight Leader, besides Hamish and Bill.

Exceptionally, I was given permission to live ashore with my wife in a hotel. Its cost was borne out of my normal pay and hers, as there was no marriage allowance under twenty-five.

Our new Hurricanes were armed with 12 x .303 inch Brownings or four 20 mm Hispano cannon. They had ex-bomber Mark XX Merlin engines, with a nominal 1460 hp take-off power. This was 300 more horsepower than the Mark Ib Hurricane. The Mark II was also fitted with a new two speed super-charger. The two speed gear changed automatically at about 10,000 feet to higher gear whenever the maximum boost fell below about eight pounds per square inch. However, as the gearing took an extra two hundred horsepower out of the engine to drive the turbine — although the final power output was much greater than the Mark I Hurricane — it used fuel at a frightening rate. As the Pilot's Notes of those days contained only the most rudimentary 'do's and don'ts', many of us had to find these things out for ourselves.

The four cannon were by far the best improvement to this new Mark. They were what we had been waiting for. The 20mm guns fired at 700 rounds per minute, very fast for a cannon, and could do lethal damage to an aircraft at 400 yards range. They could be armed with ball, armour piercing or incendiary/explosive shells. They had a muzzle velocity of about 2000 feet per second, or about twice the speed of sound.

Greyhound and I managed to get to 35,000 feet in our Hurricane IIcs one day. We were frozen stiff and could only manage an indicated airspeed of 85 knots, flat out. Of course we also did other, more useful exercises, including cross-country navigation, shooting off our new cannon at a wreck off Selsey, formation flying in cloud and quarter attacks using the camera gun. Much to the annoyance of Ventnor radar we also managed the odd shoot-up down the river Hamble and over my father's nursery.

We had only been in civilisation for three weeks when Bill called us into his office and regretfully had to tell us that once more we had to face the rigours of the north.

It was difficult to climb out of a beautiful warm bed, unwind the soft arms of my exquisite blond immobile Wren and tear myself away for the next seven months.

'Press tit' time was 0630 on 17th September 1942. We all got away in good order, not forgetting to shoot up the sleeping officers' mess. We set course for Hatston in the Orkneys, via Finningley, Drem and Lossiemouth. We had fine weather over the Scottish mountains and the Senior Pilot behaved quite well. We were able to follow his every move.

On the 1st of October, four of us flew south again to Henlow. There we had our wings modified to allow us to carry two 45-gallon long range fuel tanks under each wing. Thereafter we could almost make the 700 mile journey from Lee-on-Solent to Hatston in one go. On the way back we hit some fog and were forced down at RAF Crosbie-on-Eden in Lancashire. Next morning dawned 'loud and clear', so we started up and taxied out. We did a formation take-off in pairs and then, at the request of air traffic control, we did a gentle shoot up.

This annoyed the Group Captain in Command who reported us to Bill Bruen. "Crosley, you'd better bring your three chaps in to me. The Group Captain is very angry. He said he had to duck as you came past and his hat came off, so that's how near it was."

"Well, sir, the air traffic people asked us specially to do it. They said that they had no thrills at all at Crosbie. I would never think of doing such a thing unless they had asked me."

I heard nothing more of it. It was becoming so common at that time and so many cows were giving birth to premature calves and so many retired Colonels were spilling their sherry that something had to be done. Otherwise, perhaps, the Group Captain might have welcomed the idea and waved his hat at us as well. But you never knew with Group Captains.

Hatston airfield in the Orkneys had happened. It had never been designed. It had grown up from a landing ground often used in peacetime by RN officers and others who had their own aircraft in which to fly south during the mating season. When war came and it needed a runway for Skuas and such, the main road was closed permanently to cars and opened for aeroplanes. Hangars and Nissen huts were added, blast bays were dug, an air traffic control tower was built and it became the premier Royal Naval Air Station in the north. The Captain had been carefully chosen for his strict husbandry of Naval Stores and the First Lieutenant for his immaculate conception of all things disciplinary. So it happened that when I was Duty Air Officer one night, I fell foul of Number One.

The routine was that the Duty Air Officer was responsible for the safety of the aircraft parked out in the open in the blast bays or in the hangars. He had to do 'rounds' from time to time with a torch and a Petty Officer, to count them and make sure they were still there. He would then sign as having done so in the Log Book in the Air Watch Tower. This was normal procedure at any Naval Air Station. However, those at other Naval Air Stations, the ones in the south, had some reasonable types as the Station non-flying officers. They were human. But some of those at Hatston must have been sent there for some special reason, perhaps they were so efficient, so observant, and such a pain in the neck that no ship would have them. So they were given shore jobs which did not matter much. Whatever the reason, we seemed to have a right bunch at Hatston.

I had just turned-in after doing my rounds at 0200. Directly my head had touched the mattress — there were no pillows or sheets — the phone went and I was summoned to Air Traffic Control. It was the voice of the First Lieutenant and could not be denied. I groped and slanted my way through a 60 knot gale to the Tower, found the Log and read: "Hurricane 261 — a gaping hole in the fuselage through which ice and snow could enter".

I pushed my way out into the black screaming night, heading towards the blast bay where I knew Hurricane 261 was. It was one of 800 Squadron's aircraft and its crew had left it well covered up and lashed down. I searched the aircraft for the gaping hole. All I could find was the hand-hold for climbing up onto the wing, designed by Sydney Camm for that purpose.

When I got back to the Tower, I signed the Log with the remarks: "Hole inspected. It was designed thus by Sydney Camm, Esq."

The First Lieutenant had not heard of Sydney Camm and thought I was trying to be funny, which of course I was. I had to go and see the Captain. He told me that it was lucky that we were going aboard *Biter* next day, otherwise he would have 'Logged' me for impertinence.

Accordingly, next morning, I and eight others in the squadron fell into the back of three Swordfish and landed on *Biter*. The rest of the squadron followed behind in four Hurricanes. We then carried out decklanding practice. As a 50 knot wind was still blowing, *Biter* steamed round into the lee of the headland and turned into wind. We did our arrivals with her making bare steerage way and pitching ten feet or more, with rain squalls included. Pilot Officer Jack would not have allowed such a thing. We had to make very large and 'ham' corrections to try to keep steady on the approach. The turbulence and wind shear astern of the ship was frightening and reminded me of my experience at North Front. There was only one accident, however, a skid into the island by Ivan Scanes.

When we got back to Hatston that night, Muir-MacKenzie was hard at the Rachmaninoff again. Watching the decklandings had done his nerves no good. However, Greyhound told us five more stories about a racing greyhound — that was always getting its owner into trouble. Junior Young also recounted his rhino adventures in darkest Africa and Tich Madden, flying F4F four Wildcats of 882 Squadron in *Victorious* was also on hand. (I had seen a Wildcat coming in to land without a pilot, so I knew that Tich must have been around.) Twelve of us flew on board *Biter* on the 14th of October. This time we stayed, for we were going to the Mediterranean again. We were glad to see the last of the mighty aurora borealis and the First Lieutenant each night at Hatston. Morale was high.

Chapter 12
Operation 'Torch'

Biter was one of four 'Woolworth' carriers known as the Archer Class. They had started life as freighters, but were converted under lease-lend by the Americans to escort/assault carriers, building on a hangar and a flight deck from the main deck upwards. The work was done at the Hoboken Shipyard in New York in the space of a few months.

When we landed on board, and had seen our aircraft safely lashed down, we went round the ship. We found that we were each given a cabin with running hot and cold water, a desk, wardrobe and chest of drawers, and a very comfortable bunk. There were spacious briefing rooms, 'Ready Rooms', Met Offices, ADR plotting rooms, Ops rooms, huge sickbays, air conditioning, showers galore and many other luxuries. There were also proper bunks and comfortable messes for the ratings, instead of hammocks slung in any corridor they could find, and they had buffet eating arrangements with a choice of food served in separate dining spaces. So this was the life in an American carrier or in an American merchant ship.

Biter was always an efficient and happy ship. Our Captain, 'Wings' in the *Courageous* when she sank, was Connolly Abel-Smith. We were lucky with our Captain and crew. Others were not; notably *Dasher*.

We had arrived in *Biter* on 14th October 1942. We sailed from the Clyde for Operation *Torch* — the invasion of North Africa — on 25th October. We were in company with a huge convoy of 42 liners, merchant ships and escorts. *Dasher, Furious, Victorious* and ourselves made up the carrier force. Our morale was high. It was fun firing our four cannon into 'splash' targets towed astern. It was an impressive sight from the cockpit and from the flight deck, seeing about 50 shells-a-second exploding as they hit the sea and feeling the whole aircraft take a step backwards with the recoil of these powerful guns.

We ploughed and plunged our way 1000 miles into the Atlantic and were at last told of our new task — to provide fighter cover for an Allied invasion of North Africa.

Several of us had time to think about the progress of the war and how long it might last. We knew that things were not going well. The first months of 1942 had brought one disaster after another. Rommel had outmanoeuvred and out-fought Auchinleck's Eighth Army and was now at El Alamein, 250 miles inside the borders of Egypt. In February, *Scharnhorst* and *Gneisenau* had escaped from Brest, Singapore and Hong Kong had been lost with scarcely a fight and Ceylon was threatened. The great carrier *Indomitable* was again being used as a ferry carrier in an attempt to reinforce the Far East with RAF fighter aircraft, but soon to be destroyed on the ground, by the Japanese Admiral Nagumo's carrier aircraft within hours of their arrival. Churchill had also reinforced the east with the entirely useless 'R' class battleships in addition to the now repaired *Formidable* and *Illustrious* in an attempt to discourage the Japanese and encourage Australia and New Zealand.

Had Admiral Somerville dared to use these 'R' class ships as Churchill intended, they would have disappeared without trace. As it was, he wisely withdrew them into the open wastes of the Southern Indian Ocean, and waited for Nagumo to go away. Had he risked a battle, his three carriers had but 39 fighters between them, only 12 of them Hurricanes. They would have had to compete with Admiral Nagumo's four carriers with 120 Zero fighters and another 120 torpedo bombers. As for the British battleships, they remained at anchor in Addu Attol lagoon, growing weed and discontent, immobilising 3000 highly trained officers and men of their crews until they were ordered home. Even then it was as much by good luck as by judgement that Admiral Somerville's fleet survived. All he lost was the carrier *Hermes*, with but five Swordfish on board at the time and no fighters, and the cruisers *Dorsetshire* and *Cornwall*. Nagumo then retired eastwards where his presence was more urgently required in the Pacific and where the angry Americans were growing in strength and numbers by the hour.

The Naval position in the Mediterranean was still very serious. Although Malta had been reprieved by the last two convoys — until October at the latest — the immense losses suffered per ton of stores delivered made it imperative that some other method, other than surface reinforcement, be adopted to relieve the strain on this vital Mediterranean stronghold. Submarines were used. Also the fast minelayer *Welshman* was used, anything to get through the Narrows with the vital stores and men needed to keep Malta's fighter and reconnaissance aircraft in the air.

Many alternative relief operations were discussed between our new Allies in Washington and Churchill and the Army Chiefs in London. By July 1942, the Americans were at last convinced by Churchill and Cunningham that the solution to the Malta problem and to the land battle in North Africa should be a further landing in North Africa, to the west of the Malta Narrows. The aim of the landings would be to squeeze Rommel between Montgomery's newly inspired, reinforced and retrained Eighth Army which would advance westwards from El Alamein and a newly landed army under the US General Eisenhower advancing eastwards from Casablanca. Two other landings would also be made, one at Oran and another further east still, at Algiers. Not only would such landings silence Russia, now demanding a Second Front (as well as more Hurricanes) but it would act as a final dress rehearsal for the final Allied landings in Europe.

French reaction to operation *Torch* would be difficult to judge. The French Generals, Admirals and politicians shifted their position as the weather in April. The various French governments in Northern France, in Vichy France and in the colonies in Algeria and Morocco, distrusted each other as well as everyone else. Likewise there was no telling what de Gaulle, the Free French leader in Britain, would do. As for the French Navy, none of them had forgiven the British for their 24 June 1940 sequestration of the French Fleets at Dakar, Casablanca, Algiers, Alexandria and Oran or for our take-over of Syria. Overall, lay a jealous Gallic pride which was close to hatred in the French Navy, planted by the French ignominy of 1940 and fed while Britain herself went on fighting afterwards.

However, the Americans had high hopes that the C-in-C of all French landforces in Africa, General Giraud, would unite the French Navy and Army once the landing had taken place, such that all would fight the common foe. Frantic diplomatic efforts were made to bring this about during the four days immediately before the landings took place.

Unfortunately, the French Admiral Darlan — the French equivalent of Sir Dudley Pound — happened to be in north Africa. He had heard of the Allies' intentions. He was a pro-Fascist Vichyite and had an intense hatred of the Royal Navy. He was the last to give way to the American requests for help in their landings, and was mainly responsible for the French resistance at Oran, Algiers and Casablanca.

Because of the known French anti-British feeling, the landings were given all the appearance of being 100 per cent American. Our planes were painted with stars instead of British roundels. The first troops to land were to be American. All Allied airmen would carry with them the assurance that the US President, not the King, would reward handsomely any French or Arab soldier who handed over an airman unharmed to the Allies if he were shot down or captured.

We had slightly different ideas. We considered that our planes had been painted with white stars so that the American GIs would not mistake them for French aircraft which also used tri-colour roundels.

As the GIs had travelled all the way across the Atlantic and had never seen a Hurricane or a Seafire — Seafires were to be used from *Furious* and *Victorious* for the first time — and had yet to fire a shot in anger, our reason was probably the better of the two.

The three armies approaching Africa had travelled between 2000 and 4000 miles to get there. They were in 327 ships. They had 9000 vehicles and 400 carrier-borne aircraft. They were put ashore in 100 landings ships and protected by fighters from 12 aircraft carriers. Two hundred RAF aircraft from North Front at Gibraltar and Britain and another 250 US Navy aircraft from carriers would then arrive and take over the ex-French landing grounds.

By a series of ruses, the 20 German U-boats in the Mediterranean were encouraged to concentrate to the east of the landings. Those in the Atlantic were encouraged to go south to Freetown and not hang about the Bay of Biscay or the entrance to the Straits. As a result, and with our now instant ability to crack the German *Enigma* coding machine, not a single ship of the huge, converging, convoy was sunk by a U-boat.

Biter and the rest of our particular convoy took ten days to reach the Mediterranean. Only on the first and on the last two days was the weather any good for practice flying. Even then, only *Victorious* performed, perhaps because she was even more out of practice than *Biter* or *Dasher*. As we steamed in her wake, we could see Albacores of 832 and 817 Squadrons making practice landings on her pitching flight deck. Already we had seen two of her 17 Albacores float past us as they fell over her side. Their crews sat in their heaving dinghies, waving as they passed us and grinning all over their faces. As the third lot went by, our batsman said that he had seen the same crew twice, that of Sub-Lieutenant 'Mat' Wotherspoon. By the end of the day, there was a queue of destroyers waiting near *Victorious* to return the various aircrews to her, by jackstay transfer.

It was now 7 November. Bill Bruen summoned us to the wardroom to tell us some further details of our task. Our squadron was to provide the close escort for the first strike on Oran, against the French airfields. 804 and 891 Squadrons, each with eight Hurricane Mark IIs in *Dasher*, were to provide the top cover for this strike. The Albacores of 882 Squadron from *Furious* were to be loaded with 500 pound bombs. Their target was to be the French fighter and strike aircraft at

La Senia, the main French military airfield. It was to be a dawn attack and we could expect French fighter opposition — up to 30 Dewoitine 520s. The other French airfield, Tafaroui civil airport, was to be covered by the newly embarked Seafires flying from *Furious* in 801 and 807 Squadrons. Their main job was to prevent DW 520 reinforcements reaching La Senia during our strike. The two Fleet carriers, *Victorious* and *Formidable,* would be providing the general air defence of the Fleet further off shore. This surface force, including *Nelson* and *Rodney,* would remain ready to provide shore bombardment or defence against any Italian or French Naval attempt from Taranto or Toulon to hinder the landings. In the event, the French scuttled most of their Toulon fleet to prevent the Germans from seizing it and the Italians did not appear at all.

We asked Bill Bruen what the chances were of the French fighters coming up against us. He replied that the French Navy was determined on revenge and their Air Force would back them up.

We were pleased to hear that each carrier would be controlling its own aircraft. There was also an HQ ship — a small liner bristling with aerials, radar, 20 mm flak, Admirals, Generals and Air Vice-Marshals — ready to take charge of the land fighting in its early stages.

Bill Bruen was particularly experienced in escorting strikes of Albacores against shore targets, for he had flown with 800 Squadron Fulmars on the Petsamo/Kirkenes raid in July 1941. He had not talked about the raid. One did not shoot a line in the Fleet Air Arm. We assumed that it had been a great success and knew nothing of its stark tragedy. As we got up from the meeting, Bill called out six names, mine and Greyhound's among them, to report to the briefing room after supper. Greyhound and I exchanged winks for we had been chosen with four others to do the pre-dawn strike escort on the morrow.

After supper we went up to the Ops room and met the very down-to-earth and experienced Ops Officer, Lt/Cdr 'Rab' Phillimore, DSC, RN. First the Met man told us that the weather would be cloudy over the sea but clear over the land. Ops gave us our call signs, the layout of the French AA defences at La Senia and along the coast, and information that there were 200 French strike, torpedo and fighter aircraft at their two main airfields and at their seaplane base at Arzeu. We were also handed American automatic pistols and ammunition, about £800 (today's value) in French money, and maps and escape gear. The six of us, Bill Bruen and Jock Ritchie, Bill Roberts and Outwin, myself and Greyhound, then went down to the hangar to have a last look at our aircraft and tell our crew that they would have to get up at 'o-crack of sparrow fart' the next morning. Greyhound and I slid a couple of empty wine bottles into our Hurricanes' flare chutes to frighten the citizens of Oran as we passed overhead next morning. It had been an excellent briefing and we felt confident.

La Senia airfield was at the eastern end of a 25-mile-long, dried-up salt lake. It was about five miles from the coast and south of the town of Oran. The dawn raid was intended to make it impossible for French aircraft to attack our fleet or invasion barges. If we struck before dawn they would be caught on the ground. If we did enough damage, they would be discouraged from taking any part in offensive fighting at all. They might then show us white flags. We were told to look out for them. The fighting might all be over in a day.

Although our task had been made crystal clear to us, I was not at all confident on my and Greyhound's night flying ability. I had only done six hours night flying in my life and only two of those on Hurricanes. Here we were, escorting slow old biplanes from some other carrier, in darkness, never having seen an Albacore at close quarters before and flying into a possible hornet's nest of DW

520s. Howevers we put our trust in Bill. Furthermore, we had faith in our 'Admiral', Commodore Tommy Troubridge. He had come to visit us in the wardroom informally to get to know us. He was a great character, with his opera glasses round his neck, and his forthright manner that we could trust. We had heard of his extremely brave action in shining *Indomitable*'s searchlight in operation 'Pedestal' to give his Hurricanes a chance of finding his ship. We knew that he would not now be sending us on some sort of Balaclava.

Lt J. McNares was leading the Albacores. Bill had said at the briefing that he knew him well as an excellent strike leader with vast experience. He had told McNares that he would position our six Hurricanes in the dark part of the sky during the approach to the target so that he could silhouette the enemy fighters against the dawn sky if they came in to attack the Albacores. This, we all thought, was fabulous stuff. Not only had Bill taken the trouble to brief us on what he was doing, but he had also told the Albacore leader of his outline plan before we had even sailed from Greenock.

My diary, dated 10th November reads:

"On the morning of 'D' day, Sunday 8 November, we got up at 0430 and were given a few last minute orders and climbed into our aircraft. As usual we flew our own aircraft."

"It was pitch black when we got up on the flight deck to man our aircraft and we thought it would be a matter of luck whether or not we managed to find the Albacores taking off from *Furious* that we were supposed to be escorting — close escort. Six Hurricanes from *Dasher* (all from 804) were doing the top cover."

"We had to take off in any order, as our aircraft were not arranged properly except that the CO had had his aircraft moved to the front. I was doing 'dots' on my upward recognition light with Nav lights on. Bill did 'dashes' to attract Outwin. The CO did a 'steady'."

"We climbed up through a thin layer of cloud, still not seeing a thing except, down below, the wakes of a few ships here and there. Greyhound saw me all right. I looked out to the right and there he was, about 20 yards away, his exhausts shining red hot. I found the CO with Jock Ritchie and joined him. But Outwin didn't find Bill Roberts and didn't come at all."

"The CO got the Albacores silhouetted against the lightening sky in the east and we went after them. The CO weaving above and behind, me and Greyhound a bit lower, and Bill underneath somewhere. We had about 200 feet difference in altitude between us as we weaved, trying not to overtake the Albacores which seemed to flying at about 75 knots to our slowest safe speed of 160."

"The top cover (804 Squadron from *Dasher*) then arrived, very ropey indeed. One of them saw Bill on his own and tried to form up on him. He broke r/t silence to tell him to bugger off. The 'applecores' went so slowly I thought we should never get there at all. Some idiot — in 804 — had left his transmitter on and we had to listen to heavy breathing for most of the way in. The only way of finding out who it was, was to ask for a 'tell off' of all those present. The chap who doesn't answer is the culprit. We had to try to keep quiet so we never found out who it was."

"After the first 45 minutes, there was still no land in sight so we started to economise on the juice a bit. It was getting a bit lighter now and we switched off our lights. Greyhound said afterwards that he switched off his mag switches by mistake."

"We arrived over the target after an hour's flying, without any opposition, when I looked up and on the port bow, and beginning a dive down on the Albacores ahead — who were just turning right into the hangar area of the target — I saw what might have been Seafires from *Furious*. I called on the radio and slammed the throttle and fine pitch lever forward just in case they weren't Seafires. I looked out at Greyhound. He had seen the puff of black smoke from my exhausts and had followed. (He is a super Number Two)."

"There were about ten of them and they were easy to see against the light sky. Then one or two of the leaders started to fire yellow tracer at something. I pushed the nose down to get a better look and saw another light-coloured fighter getting in behind an Albacore, already in its bombing dive. So I turned sharp right and followed him down. Before I could get in range I saw another yellow-looking aircraft on my port quarter above me. He fired and I could easily see the (20 mm) tracers, little yellow blobs chasing each other, as they passed me by to my left. I turned left steeply so that they passed me harmlessly behind."

"By pulling hard on the stick I was able to out-turn the chap shooting at me and after two more complete turns I was beautifully on his tail, closing in on him all the while. After no more that a touch on the button I saw yellow flames coming from his exhausts and almost immediately I saw the pilot climb out of the cockpit and fall away. The DW 520 dived straight in and that was that."

"I had not been able to watch my tail while I was chasing the 520 and there were aircraft all over the place. I took such violent avoiding action in case any Froggies were on my tail that I did a few turns of a flick roll by accident, before realising it. The nose had dropped and in pulling up out of the dive I blacked out, coming to in the usual steep climb and feeling very lonely."

"No one could possibly have followed me in such manoeuvres for I was out of control myself, so I began to feel a little safer. I had a look below (I was at about 8000 feet by then) for a bit more game. I could see masses of flames from the airfield now in the distance to the south west, so I turned towards them. I next saw a yellow-painted job following a Hurricane and got him more or less in my sights, closing in under and behind, to get a good shot at him before he saw me. He turned too late and nowhere near steeply enough. I turned well inside him and I could not miss. He stupidly reversed his turn during the fight and made it even easier to get on his tail. This one only took another half second burst, if that, and he too disappeared in a yellow flash of flames as his whole aircraft blew up, 100 yards in front of me. The pilot didn't seem to get out this time and he crashed like the first, just north of the airfield."

"I felt thoroughly frightened by now expecting to be set on by furious Frenchmen who could not have failed to see what I had just done. I called up Greyhound on the r/t. He at last answered. I told him to start back to base and he agreed, but he said he was having a difficult time getting away from the Froggies. I told him to make for the town of Oran at 5000 feet, where I would wait for him. A few minutes later he told me that he was now clear and was going back on his own. So I did likewise. He sounded very excited, his voice reaching top C."

"In the half-light of dawn I felt naked. I asked the ship for a homing vector. I sighted *Furious* and circled her for a bit, not sure where *Biter* was and short of fuel by now. I saw *Rodney* or *Nelson* in the distance and did

not go near for they always fire at you. As *Furious* didn't answer my r/t
call and *Biter* did, I steered the course they gave, 060, hoping she wasn't
far away."

"When I arrived over her I was down to 1600 revs and minus two boost,
just enough power to stay airborne, and with the fuel down to five
gallons. She then told me to land on *Dasher* instead."

"When I landed on *Dasher* I found that the gun patches on the three
outboard guns on the starboard side were still intact, ie three out of the 12
Brownings in the IIb that I was flying had not fired at all. No one could
possibly believe me now, that I had got two DWs with only 60 rounds
gone from the other nine guns and with 90 per cent of the ammo left. (I
needn't have bothered, however, as Greyhound, the CO and Ritchie all
got one and all five were confirmed by the Army next day."

"I asked the Ops Officer in *Dasher* why I could not land on my own ship
and he told me that they had had a prang on deck and as I was short of
fuel, *Dasher* had accepted me."

"After this I thought that I ought to tell the Ops Officer in *Dasher* that I
had seen several other Hurricanes orbiting *Furious*. One of 804 had had its
flaps down and looked about to ditch. I also told him about 804's
attempts to join up with our close escort and that no one had seen
anything of them the whole way in or afterwards in the air battle. He then
told me the news that not one of the six Hurricanes of 804 Squadron had
returned and that they were by now well overdue."

Later that day, amid chaos in *Dasher*, we found that most of 804 had got lost.
The ship had been miles out of position so they had failed to find her. They had
then returned to the salt lake where several had made 'wheels down' landings.
There was a chance that some would get back to the ship if they could get their
aircraft refuelled by the Army. One of the six, Sub-Lieutenant K. A. 'Piggy'
McClennan, a New Zealander, had baled out over a destroyer which had picked
him up. Later, he told us that when he pulled the ripcord and his parachute
opened with a jerk, his flying boots had come off and he watched them fall into
the sea far below him. He was still going round the ship in his socks at the time,
as his cabin was out of bounds because of a bad petrol leak nearby.

Outwin's aircraft had gone U/S after take-off and he had landed straight back
aboard *Biter*. Bill Roberts had not yet returned. He had landed on the salt lake
too. When he got back next day his story was that he had borrowed fuel from
some American Dakotas which had landed on the salt lake as well. Apparently
these Dakotas had come from UK with paratroops and had also got lost. We
wondered what tales 804 Squadron pilots would have to tell and why they had
all missed the show.

I was, apparently, the only pilot from 800 Squadron in *Dasher* that day. There
were a few pilots of 891 around. They didn't seem to know what was going on
either. Then, when I was beginning to think about breakfast, the Tannoy told
me to report to the Ops room. I was told to take off alone, then join up with
another five from *Biter* who were taking-off at the same time. I asked *Dasher*'s
Ops what they had in mind, and was told that *Biter*'s aircraft would probably
know but no one aboard *Dasher* had a clue. I was just to join up with them.

So, at 0930 I took off and joined up with what I soon realised was the Senior
Pilot's Flight of four, plus my number two, Greyhound. We flew round and
round the beach at Arzeu and saw nothing apart from some dust and a little
friendly flak. I noted:

"When we got back to the ship after nearly two hours of wandering about, I heard *Biter* tell us to land aboard *Dasher*. So we all went over to join her circuit, except Muir-Mackenzie, who landed aboard *Biter.*"

"When the five of us landed on *Dasher*, 'Blinkers' Paterson, the batsman, told us we were now in place of 804 Squadron who had all got lost. We took a poor view of this and told him so."

"Soon we got to hear that there was a 'flap' on. Some French destroyers had come out of harbour from Oran and were about to make some sort of dirty dive at the nearest landing craft, or something. We asked anyone we saw who looked as if he might know, where they were. I and Andrew Thomson went up to the bridge to ask someone there, but they didn't know either. Time was getting short, the aircraft were by now nearly all refuelled and the ship was turning into wind. Andrew and I rushed back down on deck and climbed into our aircraft with not a single clue on what, how, why or when, we should be required to attack the Froggie destroyers."

"As Greyhound and I only had .303 guns in our particular Hurricanes, we should be a fat lot of good making strafing attacks on destroyers. Still, we were ready for take-off and I hoped that Andrew and I could make a go of it."

"Luckily the *Aurora* (a cruiser) took care of the French destroyers and we didn't have to go on this mad scheme at all. We just continued to sit in our cockpits, waiting for the next cock-up that this ridiculous ship would think up for us."

"Just as we were allowed to climb out of the cockpits and go down to have some food for the first time since 0430, we were told that we would have to fly at 1300. As it was five minutes to one at the time, we duly got back on deck to try to find out what we might have to do. The choice, we though, was almost infinite. Yet not a soul appeared to know, not even 'Blinkers' Paterson, the only sane member of the ship's company that we had met so far."

"When we got airborne and were orbiting the ship asking *Biter* what we might have to do, *Dasher* at last came up on the r/t, for the first time ever, and said: 'Patrol map reference position . . .' (La Senia airfield apparently, after much juggling with maps in the cockpit), 'and watch out for bogeys coming in from . . .' (another impossible map reference position. Tafaroui?)."

"I was just about to set course when my engine stopped stone dead. I was in formation at about 2000 feet. I pushed under the formation and called *Dasher* for an emergency landing as my engine had stopped. They answered; 'Wait. Over.' I explained that I couldn't wait. They answered something or other, but as I couldn't make out what it was I put the hook down and selected coarse pitch to prolong the windmilling glide. I remembered what Pilot Officer Jack had said about allowing plenty of height on the turn in and the final approach, and miraculously arrived over the rundown with flaps and wheels down in time for a proper glide decklanding. I waited for the pull of the arrester wires. It didn't happen and I continued on into the barrier. They had forgotten to put the wires up. The flight deck engineer had gone to lunch and couldn't be found in time. So my beautiful Hurricane was wrecked in the barrier."

"I suspected a fuel leak or something. But the very clued up Air Engineer Officer of 804 Squadron (Lieutenant 'Spike' Tracey) told me it was water in the petrol, so all *Dasher's* flying was cancelled until the offending ship's tank was found and the fuel lines purged."

"They found the fault, so they said, by tea time. All refuelling after that was done through chamois leather filters and took three times as long as a result."

The Archer Class of 'Woolworth' carrier had a water displacement system instead of the inert nitrogen gas used in RN ships to guard against aviation fuel vapour explosions in half empty fuel tanks. The American system caused continual trouble and made the use of chamois filters mandatory, until the Royal Naval system eventually replaced it. The diary continues:

"The morning's alarms and excursions, orders, counter-orders and half-baked ideas all seemingly coming from the ship's Ops room but with no one really owning up to them, made it the most twitch-making day I have spent in the war so far. All of us were browned off by tea time and we had nothing to show for it."

"Next day, after sleeping in the Captain's day cabin on camp beds in our flying overalls and feeling a bit unshaven, we sort-of stood by, sort-of took off, sort-of planned to shoot up some Froggie staff cars at some road junction or other. Actually we did none of these things and got more and more frustated."

"*Dasher* could only make about 12 knots because of her engine trouble. There was a terrible smell of petrol everywhere down below and no one was allowed to smoke on board. We asked one of the junior engineers, who came down to the wardroom for lunch — complete with sweat rags, cotton waste in his overall belt and a dirty, anxious face — what was going on. He said that the 'Bloody diesels had blown another pot' and one engine was only giving half power. This explained why the ship was jumping a foot in the air at about 100 times a minute." (See Appendix 4, HMS *Dasher* and 804 Squadron's failure at Oran.) I noted:

"That evening after much palaver and entreaty, we were allowed to fly back aboard our ship, *Biter*. I was allowed to take one of 804's spares. This was rather nice of their AEO who, I think, sympathised with us in 800 Squadron. It was so nice to see my own crew again and they quickly repainted the Squadron crest on 804's spare aircraft."

"No wonder I could not land on after the DW battle. This was because Greyhound had pranged his Hurricane, coming in on a semi-glide through lack of fuel, and making a full toss into the barrier. He said — in his priceless way — that he hadn't even noticed the prang when he landed, he was so excited at having shot down a 520. He only remembered that 'it seemed a bit lower than usual' when he climbed off the wing."

"Three Albacores had failed to return, but two of the crews were safe. The leader had, however, gone down in flames in his first dive. They had set the hangars on fire and there were a lot of extra explosions."

The operation was as good as over for us. Twenty Spitfires from Gibraltar had now arrived and had taken over Tafaroui, and finally La Senia airfields, for their own use.

We eventually read in our history books that two RN sloops, *Walney* and *Hartland*, full of infantry and technicians, were sunk in Oran harbour. They had been wrongly informed that the French would allow them in but were cruelly and revengefully ambushed and fired on at 50 yards range by the French destroyers there, suffering murderous casualties.

As junior Subs in the RNVR we were, of course, impressed with the sight of *Rodney,* the bombardment ship. We assumed that she had done a good job. It was not until after the war we learned that because of the inaccuracy of her 16 inch armament, she was asked to stop by the HQ ship who could see what she was doing, as she was "preventing the Americans from getting ashore". Future naval shore bombardments were done using spotter aircraft where possible.

Another point of interest was that on capturing the airfield at La Senia on 'D' plus one, and the seaplane base at Arzeu, the troops found that all of the 46 French aircraft destroyed had been fully armed with torpedoes or bombs. Had not our raid against La Senia succeeded so well, our two assault carriers would have presented them with a fairly easy target if they had been found in the poor weather, for the Seafire defence was mostly providing CAP over Tafaroui in the early morning. We had only 40 fighters at Oran. Although this was a huge number by RN standards, it was only a quarter of the number used by the Americans in their similar landing at Casablanca.

The Oran landing was the only one of the three which was decided by force of arms, and not by early capitulation by the French. Lt Barry Nation landed at Blida airfield near Algiers and accepted its written surrender. The document is on view at the FAA Museum at RNAS Yeovilton, Somerset. He flew back with it to his carrier — *Formidable* — and handed it to his Captain. Besides the seven DW 520s shot down, only one German aircraft was shot down — a Ju 88 from France. This was by Seafires of 880 Squadron from *Argus*, off Algiers.

On our journey back to Gibraltar, we sat down to a semi-formal dinner in *Biter's* wardroom. We were feeling happy that night for we had just heard the news of Rommel's first defeat — Monty's breakout from El Alamein on 2 November. It was also the night of the second anniversary of the Battle of Taranto, already enshrined in FAA history. The Commander, the Mess President, made a speech. He voted 800 Squadron the best in the RN in spite of Taranto, and Bill Bruen modestly agreed.

Chapter 13
804 Naval Air Squadron

We stopped at Gibraltar in *Biter* to refuel on 12 November and sailed for the UK next day. We had about 20 'empty' liners in company with *Avenger* and *Argus,* and we took it in turns to do standby on deck, hoping for a Fw Condor to shoot down.

On the morning of the first day out of Gibraltar we heard the ship's siren sound off. We rushed on deck into brilliant sunlight to see the 20,000 ton *Warwick Castle* down by the stern and rapidly dropping behind the convoy. She sank in about an hour with heavy loss of life, the sea conditions making rescue difficult. *Avenger* was operating her A/S Swordfish at the time but the U-boat *(U-155)* which torpedoed the liner was not found.

One of *Avenger*'s Sea Hurricane pilots — Sub-Lieutenant Gavin Torrence — landed on our carrier. *Avenger* was another of the dreaded Archer Class and was having trouble with her arrester gear again. He told us how her diesels had packed up — just like *Dasher*'s — on the last day of the Algiers landing and she had had to go into Algiers harbour to make repairs.

Gavin slept on board that night. When he awoke next morning he came into the ante room. "I'm not looking forward to going back to that ship. She's got a jinx."

His hand shook as he lit a cigarette and he looked pale and tired. One of the ship's officers was nearby. "You from *Avenger*? . . . Well, you aren't now. She went down last night. Torpedoed. Exploded. Only about half a dozen picked out of the water."

His squadron, with 883, with six Sea Hurricane Is each — had fought PQ18 — the September Russian Convoy — through to Archangel in *Avenger* against some 90 Ju 88s and torpedo-carrying He 111s, but he still could not understand why we told him how lucky he was.

There were 17 survivors from *Avenger*. One of the lucky ones from 'tween decks was said to have slung his hammock just where the ship split in two. None of the others in bunks could get out in time.

We flew off on 21 November, after a nine day voyage which we were thankful to complete without further drama. We landed at Macrihanish in Kintyre and went on a week's leave. A week was not long enough to get to Somerset and back by train and bus even if I'd had the money for the fare. Gavin was the only one who could afford it as he had 'survivor's leave' and a free travel warrant home. So I had a look round the Swordfish squadrons at Macrihanish. I came across a Lieutenant Horn who was flying a Swordfish down to Lee-on-Solent for some reason. I got into the back seat — and froze solid in spite of a leather, fur-lined flying jacket I had just acquired.

However, we got stuck at Blackpool with 'weather down to the deck' and all I could do was to telephone my immobile Wren twice each evening for the regulation three minutes. Two days later I returned from Blackpool via Arbroath and Donibristle, where I picked up a replacement Hurricane to help me on my way back to Macrihanish. For the next three weeks I spent hours by the phone each night hoping that I could get through to my wife or that she could get through to me.

Macrihanish was like a prison. There was nothing whatever to do in the long winter evenings apart from drinking watery beer, playing snooker in our flying clothing for warmth, and watching the wind lift the linoleum off the floor as it howled past our Nissen hut wardroom at 60 mph two nights out of four.

However, S/Lt Maurice Bannister provided us with some entertainment one night. He had organised a squadron dance. As he was our armament officer, he had naturally included a few explosions in the evening's entertainment. The Wrens had put on their best stockings and we were all gathered round the fire between dances. There was a blinding flash and coal leapt all over the chairs and tables. Maurice had put a 20 mm cannon shell in the fire. Although he had refilled the cartridge case with Very Light powder — for a nice coloured effect as a Roman Candle — he had forgotten to remove the detonator at the far end. This ignited first and blew the rest all over the room, taking various articles of clothing with it. That was the end of the dance and Maurice was hauled up in front of the Captain and the Queen Wren next morning, with a 'logging' as the result.

On 23 December, Bill Bruen announced a week's Christmas leave. This time I was determined not to be caught napping. I had already earmarked a Swordfish which I knew wanted to migrate south at this time. I had never flown a Swordfish, only started one up. But this made no difference. In two hours of flying I managed to get as far south as RAF Valley in Anglesey. The weather had got worse and worse on the way and by the time I landed I was having to follow every single indentation of the coast at nought feet in 500 yards visibility and with the cliff tops disappearing into the cloud. I had no r/t of course. Pilots of Swordfish were not allowed things like that. I therefore considered it unwise to go on.

The RAF put me up at their country house Officers' Mess. There was plenty of room as it was Christmas Day and everyone was at home with their families or sweethearts.

So I spent Boxing Day struggling south again. The RAF said that even the seagulls were flying on instruments, but after I had explained that this sort of weather was nothing to the average Swordfish aviator, they let me start up and taxi out into the mist and disappear. The Stringbag was perhaps the only aircraft that was able to fly in such weather. I picked my way south, round every bay — hoping I could find the entrance again — as far as RAF Angle, in Pembrokeshire. It was so wet, cold and frightening by then that I landed there.

Next day I crossed the Severn estuary and followed the railway line to Exeter from the direction of Ilfracombe. The cloudbase was still about 200 feet and visibility about 500 yards. The railway line suddenly disappeared into a tunnel after a few miles. I had worked it out that when this happened I would climb up straight ahead into cloud. Then, after a bit of cloud flying — and if the map said that it looked safe — I would push the nose down and hope to pick up the railway line again as it came out of the tunnel at the far end. Pilot Officer Jack would have said that no immobile Wren, however warm, soft and beautiful, was worth taking risks like that and would have thrown me off the course. However, it worked well enough and I landed at Exeter to ask the way to Yeovilton. Once more the Swordfish reputation worked and they let me take off in the direction of Yeovilton, They forgot to warn me about the balloon barrage round Westland's airfield at Yeovil, and the Observer Corps rang Yeovilton after I had landed there to ask whether a slow flying aircraft which they had heard fly straight through the barrage had arrived yet, or whether they should report the strange occurrence to Fighter Command.

My reward was to spend a glorious 18 hours at home until the early hours of 28 December. I discovered there was a Spitfire Vb at Lee-on-Solent, so I pretended I was an experienced Spitfire pilot — although I had never even sat in one — and they let me fly it back as far as Arbroath. The journey back took just over one and a half hours, above 'the weather' at 20,000 feet, instead of six hours of fog and rain at zero feet in a Swordfish. Lt Denham then flew me back to Macrihanish in a Percival Proctor, a wooden aircraft and quite the most frightening part of the trip.

When I got back to the squadron offices, everyone was gloomy. I soon found out why. The squadron was being broken up to re-form 804 and 891 Squadrons after their unhappy performance at Oran. The remains of 800 were going as instructors, or to reform on Hellcats in America, or to second-line duties for a rest. Bill was going to Yeovilton as Chief Flying Instructor, Bannister and Hastings to 891, I and Dougy Yate to 804. The only compensation was, first, that Bill had recommended me for Senior Pilot, perhaps of 804 eventually, he said. The second compensation was that I had been awarded the Distinguished Service Cross for my part in the squadron's success at Oran.

The new 804 Squadron formed at Macrihanish on 3 January. We flew to RAF Ouston two days later with our CO, Lt (A) Jackie Sewell, DSC, RNVR. We nearly missed it entirely as it was covered in snow and was indistinguishable from the local countryside. It was just west of Newcastle. RAF Ouston had a beautiful brick-built mess, heated hangars, wide runways and a good 'homer'. In other words, it was a run-o'-the-mill RAF 'peacetime' station. Reading 804's line book, I found it had a war record equal to that of 800 Squadron. Jimmy Hancock was the Senior Pilot. He and Norman Goodfellow, 'Piggy' McClennan, 'Spike' Tracy (the Air Engineer Officer), and Jimmy Crossman, had been in the squadron for 18 months already. They were all very experienced, their flying dating from about Number 10 Course, a whole year before I had started to fly.

At Ouston, Dougy Yate and I were intrigued to come across several extremely smart Royal Marines. They tore us off the most shattering 'beavers' whenever we passed them and we wondered what we had done to deserve them. At lunch we found that the Marines came with the squadron as our own stewards. Such luxuries were a forgotten relic of the peacetime 804th. The CO, naturally, had kept quiet about them and Their Marine Lordships had therefore mislaid them. As the squadron had spent most of the war at such places as Sydenham and Eglinton in Northern Ireland, no one had spotted this anomaly. Our bathwater was felt, our uniforms pressed with knife-edge creases, our socks darned and these shattering salutes were received for another six months before our good fortune was discovered. Even the RAF was impressed. Life took on a new meaning. The squadron was born anew and we christened Ouston 'Jolly, Jolly Ouston' in our flying log books.

While at Ouston, we discussed Oran, and why our CO now had to attend a Board of Enquiry. Neither Dougy nor I had any idea of the basic reason why 804 and 891 in *Dasher* had lost nine out of their 14 aircraft at Oran. (See Appendix 4, HMS *Dasher* and 804 Squadron's failure at Oran.) Norman Goodfellow and Sub-Lieutenant Jimmy Hancock told us that they had landed out of fuel on the salt lake at Oran. Norman described how he was fired at by the gunner of a Walrus on spotting duties. He writes: "By chance I met a chap from *Rodney*, the Walrus' parent ship, ages later in Scotland. He said that the gunner had so riddled the Walrus hull with bullets while shooting at me that it almost sank before they could hoist it on board again."

Life went on peaceably at Ouston. We sat in our warm, brick built dispersals when we were not flying, listening to the Ink Spots or Tommy Dorsey on a radiogram which some old ladies had presented and which had become part of the 'Squadron Mobile Equipment'.

In February 1943, Jacky Sewell called us into his office and asked for volunteers for an operation. We all volunteered, but only six were needed. So the CO, Dougy, Norman Goodfellow, Murdoch Tait, Jimmy Crossman and I flew aboard the dreaded *Dasher*. The date was 13 February and it was probably a Friday.

Once we had landed on board we learned that we, and some of 891 Squadron who were already on board, were *en route* for Iceland. We were to be the fighter cover for JW 53 Russian convoy. The Ops Officer on board *Dasher* pointed out that, sadly, *Avenger* could not be with us. As if we didn't know.

Things had not improved on board since we had left her at Oran. Still the greasy overalls in the Wardroom, the terrible smell of aviation fuel, no water in the cabins. The weather, too was awful and allowed no flying.

There were seven hours of semi-daylight in the Arctic at that time of year. Several of us remembered having spoken to members of 802 and 883 Squadrons from *Avenger* when she had returned to Scapa from PQ 18, the convoy before this one. They had had a very rough time indeed in their Hurricane Is, not only because of their lack of gunfire power against the 20mm guns of the German aircraft, but from their own AA which had shot down three of them. They warned us that the sea was so cold that if you ditched, you had three minutes before you passed out. They spoke about the Admiral's insistence upon wireless silence for most of the time and, unlike the Germans operating from Norway, a relative lack of air/sea rescue arrangements for the British aviators. We six in 804 and the other six in 891 were not feeling too confident on the way to Iceland, but at least we would have cannon-armed Sea Hurricanes this time.

We sailed with 28 freighters. Then we ran into the worst storm for ages — a Force 11 'Severe Storm'. By the time we had reached half way to Iceland, six freighters had turned back, the cruiser *Sheffield* had had a complete gun turret roof removed by the seas breaking over her and we in *Dasher* were shipping it green over the flight deck and into the hangar and had lost two men overboard. The six Hurricanes lashed down on the flight deck were dripping salt water and I, for one, was prepared to be clapped in irons before I flew them.

Down in the hangar all chaos reigned. There were four Hurricanes in the roof of the hangar, as spares. They were slung on wires, without wings. They had worked loose and were butting each other, propeller spline against propeller spline, burring the spindles over as they crashed together. Below them on the hangar deck, the lashings on our Hurricanes had had to be tightened to such an extend that they had collapsed the oleos. Oil from them was leaking out onto the hangar making it like a skating rink. A complete 18-inch American torpedo had broken adrift and was washing to and fro in the water in the forward lift well. A five gallon tin of aircraft dope with its lid off was leaving a trail as it rolled in time with the torpedo. Although all aircraft had drained tanks, a strong smell of AVGAS as well as dope pervaded. I suppose a single spark could have set the whole thing off.

Barely maintaining steerageway and head to wind, the ship would occasionally fall off into the hollow of a huge wave. She would then roll through ninety degrees, broadside on. Down below, it was no more difficult to walk up the fore-and-aft passageway walls than it was to walk up the passageway deck itself. Sleeping and eating were impossible. There was nothing for it but to hang on to something solid and, like Jonah, wish for the day.

That evening the storm had eased somewhat so I thought I would make my immobile Wren a Hurricane 'penny'. This was a copper penny, cut, bent and polished to the shape of a Hurricane. I had just found a workshop with a vice and had started sawing out the penny with a hacksaw when the ship gave an immense heave. The huge steel workbench came off the side of the bulkhead and smashed me back against an engine packing case behind me. I escaped only because I happened to be pushed back into a hip-sized indentation in the engine itself. I decided against anymore workshop do-it-yourself and retired to my bunk where I wedged myself in for an hour or two.

Later, I lurched, wide-legged and aching, to the wardroom. There, not to be beaten by the elements, were some other good sailors, Norman and the CO. They told me, with their glasses at 45 degrees and without spilling a drop, that the ship was coming to bits. There was a half inch gap between wind and water for 30 feet along the ship's port side. It opened and closed everytime the ship rolled or heaved, and let in about a ton of water everytime. The ship's galley fires were already out and the ship's company were on cold rations. We were retiring to Seydisfiord on the west coast of Iceland to assess the situation. Few of the ship's company realised this because the Tannoy system was also out of action. Later that evening, the RN ship's Senior Engineer came into the wardroom and described the crack still further, saying that you could see the entire convoy through it when it opened. He also announced that because two men had fallen off ladders which had become unwelded as they climbed down them, and had drowned, the Captain had ordered the Duty Part to assemble in the welldeck with 14 pound ballpeen hammers to knock off any of the hand holds or ladders which remained. The welldeck had been filled with rusty iron in no time at all.

Next morning, with the storm abated, we dropped our pick in Seydisfiord in about 40 fathoms, using all the ship's cable end to end. We then brought up some of the better-looking Hurricanes onto the frosty deck and changed their fuel, checked r/t, oleos and engines and sprayed them with fresh water inside and out to get rid of the salt. As this immediately turned to ice, they were taken down below again to melt. Jacky Sewell and some others of us had fun on the deck tractors, towing them about and sliding in ice-rinks of frozen green 100 Octane, spilled from our tanks. We looked ashore at the black and white misty mountains and the cold, ice-strewn sea between, and we hoped that we would not have to fly or force land or bale out.

As *Dasher* was once again quite useless, we managed to retrieve our 80 fathoms of cable after two hours of heaving in, and set course back to Scotland. Four days later Jacky, Norman, Bannister and I flew ashore in the only four flyable Hurricanes, determined at all costs to get airborne even if our engines were only firing on half their cylinders. I was flying a Hurricane from the hangar roof reserve, now with wings of course, so I made a special check that the aileron rigging wires had not been reversed accidentally by the rigger. All I noticed was that they were very stiff to move. The rigger said that he knew that, but it was only to be expected.

Once airborne, I thought I would do a turn to port in the normal way. I found I could only move the stick an inch either side of central and only by hammering it with the side of my hand at that. This process continued all the way to Arbroath. I did not complain over the radio. First, it was not working, second, I might be told to bale out or something stupid like that.

When we had all landed and were having a nervous drag, the Petty Officer rigger of Station Flight handed me my parachute bag out of the gunbay and told me that the aileron control lines were twisted. The CO heard my reply and looked at me in silence for a moment. But when I told him that taking the aircraft was the lesser of two evils and that *Dasher* was the other one, he agreed to take no further action.

We did not return to Ouston and the rest of the squadron was brought up north to join us at Hatston. Hatston was crowded with fighters including some new Seafire squadrons working-up for *Illustrious* and *Formidable*. We watched them taxying round the narrow perimeter track, unable to see ahead without swinging their long noses from side to side. Sometimes they overdid it, running onto the grass and up-ending in a drainage hole. They were doing their decklanding practice somewhere out in the North Sea. They were very impatient when we, on the runway, kept them waiting. They suffered badly from overheating particularly when taxying downwind — and they would start waving frantically from their cockpits at air traffic control to let them take off before they boiled. We had already seen one of them take off in a cloud of steam.

On 5 March we were at Hatston sitting in our Nissen hut crewroom with the radiogram full on and thick snow on the airfield and runways outside. Norman came in and told us that David Wilkinson had just landed his Seafire with a chap on his tail. The man was his fitter from *Furious* and he was so cold that he had to be kept in the same shape without bending him, all the way to the sickbay. The story was told in the Press next day. Lt (A) David Wilkinson, RNVR was a former Lord Mayor of London's son, and therefore pressworthy. The papers of the day gave a remarkably truthful account of the drama and I will quote from it.

"For 15 minutes, Leading Air Mechanic James Edward Overed, 35, FAA technician, who had been swept off the deck of an aircraft carrier, clung to the tail of a Seafire."

Here is his own story:

"The aircraft carrier was operating in home waters on a cold windy day with a snowstorm likely to break at any moment. We had headed out to sea at about 1100. The snowstorm had already begun and, with a hurricane blowing, we could hardly stand on the flight deck. When the order came over the loudspeaker the aircraft were duly ranged and placed into flying position, with the air mechanics standing by their respective kites. I was responsible for Lt Wilkinson's and he was first off. The planes were all being 'run-up' as the ship turned into wind, and a terrible wind it was, too. Lt Wilkinson's plane was running at a fast tick-over, warming up before the full-power check. He gave the signal for two men to lie on his tail, while he revved up to full power."

"This task was done by another rating and myself. We both lay prone on the tailplane, he on the port side and me on the starboard, and we waited for the pilot to open up. After a while, the other rating got off to remind the pilot that we were waiting for him to open up. Then the fun began. The pilot opened up his throttle to full boost and up came the tail. I knew this had happened but still thought he was doing the full-power check. Then, the aircraft started to move forward but I had no feeling of forward motion. The terrific slipstream plus the hurricane was doing its utmost to remove me from the tail. The only grip I had was at the elevator hinge, so with this and my legs swinging in mid-air, I held on."

"I had a feeling that the tail had come down on the deck again and I got ready to get off at any second. I had my eyes closed, but on opening them I saw to my horror that the carrier was below and astern and that we were just passing over the top of a cruiser underneath.I hung on like glue. . . I thought of my wife and daughter. . . I thought my number was up. I was tempted to let go when I saw the cruiser, for he might rescue me if he was watching, but decided to hang on. After about 15 minutes or so, I heard a reduction in engine revs and I prepared for a crash landing, not knowing where I was. The runway (at Hatston) was white with snow so I thought he was crashing in a field so I pulled my legs up in order not to have them trapped under the fuselage. After landing I did not remember anything more until I 'came to' inside the ambulance."

"I was told afterwards that the pilot removed me and placed me upon the snow and covered me with his flying coat and put his Mae West under my head for a pillow . . . Next morning the pilot visited me in hospital, and though I was too full of admiration for his skill to speak, he said: 'Good show, jolly good show'."

If anyone wanted a better description than this of flight deck conditions before take-off, it would be hard to find. During the engine 'run-up', the two crew on the tail would have been in Wilkinson's blind spot. When the man on the left hand tailplane got off, the pilot, already watching to the left to keep his eye on the flight deck officer for taxying instructions, would have seen him and assumed that both men were now off the tail. L. A. M. Overed's continued presence on the right tailplane would, however, have been noticed by everyone on the starboard side of the flight deck and to those on *Furious*'s small bridge. However, there was no means whatever in *Furious* for wireless or loudspeaker communication between members of the deck party, and the noise of the 50 knot wind would have drowned their shouts. So, when the green flag went down, Wilkinson took off. The bump reported by Overed was probably the Seafire's tail striking the raised portion of *Furious'* deck just before reaching her bow. Although the Seafire, with full slipstream over the tail plane would have had more than enough lift from fully forward elevator to hold the tail in the normal flying position with one man's weight on it, it was nevertheless, a resourceful piece of aviation, particularly, when coming over the 'hedge', with the airfield covered in snow and at reduced power.

During the last days in March 1943, we and our 'chummy' Squadron 891, were ordered to carry out some decklanding practice. This was for the benefit of the new boys who had just joined. The only ship available for decklandings was the dreaded *Dasher*. She was back at Scott-Lithgow's in the Clyde where she had just completed further engine and flight deck machinery repairs. When we returned to Hatston we had to leave Maurice Bannister behind in *Dasher's* sick bay with 'flu as he was too sick to fly. Shortly afterwards we heard he had been killed, learning later that *Dasher* had been torpedoed off the Clyde. Then we heard that she had 'blown up' of her own accord without any assistance from the Germans. We believed the last news. We could easily guess why. Much later, I met Lt/Cdr (A) Brian 'Blinkers' Paterson, MBE, DFC, RN, the batsman aboard *Dasher* when she blew up. He said that someone smoking had touched off the petrol vapour in one of her compartments below. He was batting an aircraft in to land at the time, when a great flame shot into the air all round him. He immediately dived 60 feet over the side. As he always wore a Mae West —

even in the shower — he floated high out of the water and was picked up.

He told us that when he had 'come to' in the water astern of the flaming *Dasher* he could see hundreds of her crew jumping over the side straight into the black smoke and red flames of the burning petrol, where they were swallowed up and burned alive, unable to swim faster than the spread of burning petrol on the water.

Very few of her 600 crew survived the horror of 27 March 1943. Maurice Bannister was trapped in his cot in the sickbay. Of course we did not hear the truth straight off. We merely thanked our lucky stars that we had cleared off the ship the day before. Much later, we heard that we in 804 had been selected to embark again in this frightful ship to attack Tovey's nightmare — *Tirpitz*. The idea was that we should attack her at her moorings in Altenfiord with a dozen Swordfish in the Arctic summer midnight. As she was surrounded with two layers of anti-torpedo nets and positioned alongside the vertical face of a 1000 foot mountain, a torpedo attack would have been impossible. It was particularly lucky for us that *Dasher* blew up when she did. This was just one of the insane ideas that Tovey's Staff thought up against *Tirpitz*. She was now a hulk, but Admiral Pound still described her as 'the ship on which the whole strategy of the war depends' and which must be removed.

Of course, we wondered how our Russian convoy, JW 53, had fared without us in *Dasher*. We learned after the war that it had reached a position 250 miles north of Altenfiord before first being reported by a Ju 88. Only one ship was damaged by air attack on 25 February and, having relinquished the convoy to the protection of the Russian Navy and their Hurricane IIc CAP for the remainder of their voyage to the Kola Inlet, the British escort had returned to Scotland by 15 March 1943, unscathed. It is interesting to note that there was a Squadron Leader 'Nat' Gould, DFC, RAAF, at Murmansk at that time, teaching the Russians how to fly these Hurricanes. He and twenty other 'Aussies' later joined us in 880 Squadron at the end of the Pacific war, as 'reinforcements' for the intended Operation 'Olympic II'.

A week after our arrival at Hatston we were ordered to remove ourselves to RNAS Twatt. If Hatston was primitive, Twatt was Neanderthal. We slept in the usual unheated Nissen huts, but these were dispersed over several fields, half a mile from the wardroom and totally unlit. The intervening fields were only partly drained by deep ditches covered in thin ice and camouflaged with snow. Aviators returning to their pits in the Nissen hut at night from the bar in the wardroom would arrive like despondent Christians, having lost themselves and fallen into the frozen slough of one of these ditches.

During the preceding summer the drains at Twatt had given the Captain much trouble. His neighbours at Skeabrae operated Spitfire XIIIs. When Skeabrae was down-wind, the telephone would ring in his office with a Group Captain at the other end complaining that his boys couldn't fly at 40,000 feet because they were suffering from Twatt's disease. After many unhelpful conferences with the Ministry of Works, the Captain had decided to use his own initiative. He emptied 50 gallons of neat Lysol into the station's sewage works and that cured the smell. However, the smell got infinitely worse after a few weeks and even Hatston, ten miles away started to complain. The Captain's efforts had killed all the bugs, both the good and the bad. Life being what it is, the bad ones then reappeared first, overcame the good ones and they now ruled again. The new brand of bug was quite beyond the experience of any drainage expert. Finally, the frosts came again and all the bugs hibernated. We were hoping that we would have moved on by the time summer came again and the bugs emerged once more.

I then caught chicken pox and was carted off to an isolation sickbay on the side of a hill overlooking Scapa Flow. After 14 days of this I talked my way into some sick leave, arriving home in Queen Camel unexpectedly. I was not a great success. I was spotty and pale and not the dashing fighter pilot image at all. However, all was not lost, as Jacky wrote to tell me that the 804th was coming south and I was to stay on leave until this happened. The reason why we came south was because the Navy had run out of Archer Class carriers and Sea Hurricanes, the former mostly having gone to the bottom and the latter having gone to Russia or to the Far East. We were going to be put out to grass, at the small grass airfield of Charlton Horethorne, a few miles from Sherborne. Furthermore, Jacky told me he had appointed me Senior Pilot. With this news, a beard to hide my spots and a visit to Buckingham Palace with my wife to collect my DSC, I was once again popular at home.

The difference between Twatt in midwinter and Charlton Horethorne in early spring was so extreme that several of us in 804 became delirious. Within days we changed from tense, introspective, disgruntled, under-confident grey shadows, into relaxed, outgoing and very gruntled fighter pilots. Jacky saw to it that, on this small 'private' airfield, I organised our flying mainly for pleasure, like a flying club. Our polished, becrested Sea Hurricanes — mine had a green knock-kneed camel painted on it — were spread out in lines. We stretched out on the beautiful green grass beneath them and listened to the skylarks. Occasionally one of us would take the squadron 12-bore and go down to the rabbit warren on the hill side and shoot some supper. Others would organise squadron parties, bathe or tinker with their cars. We called it 'Jacky's Holiday Camp', having our own film shows, our own piano and radiogram in the airfield 'clubhouse', our crewroom. The Station Officer was a mere Sub-Lieutenant RNVR and he always warned us when 'royalty' was about to descend upon us from Yeovilton nearby. We would put on our uniforms and hats, begin to study Admiralty Fleet Orders and salute anyone we had not met before.

New flying techniques flourish in such surroundings. We became very proficient at the new fighter formation known as 'finger four'. This was first used in Spain by the Condor Legion and later by the Luftwaffe in the Battle of Britain. It allowed free movement and the use of everyone's eyes to guard each other's tails, unlike the close 'vic' formation as heretofore. Eventually, we could turn, dive, climb, strafe, re-form afterwards and then join the landing circuit, almost without altering our throttle positions and without the use of r/t. We could make a co-ordinated strafing attack — 16 aircraft 'firing' at once from three or four different directions — the first time this had been part of a squadron's repertoire.

Four of us were then required to attend a week's course in Ayrshire, funded by Lease Lend, to gear us up for our new aircraft — the Hellcat. We shared a famous golfcourse hotel with about 20 old ladies and 40 Pekinese. The ladies had paid heavily to get away from the war in the south and it seemed as if they resented our sudden appearance. They switched off the radio when we wished to hear of each new disaster as it happened and further encouraged their Pekinese to misbehave with each other and to occupy all the chairs and settees. The course turned out to be a waste of resources, for half of it dealt with the Double Cyclone Engine which was not used in the Hellcat.

Back at Charlie-H and with our wives and sweethearts once more, we heard that 'Titus' Oaks — our 'flying water-pongo' — had had his rudder removed by Snottie Bullen's prop while in close formation practice for a war weapons week at Balbo over Devon. Both landed safely. Then, S/Lt Barker overshot his landing one day on the wet grass of Charlie-H and finished up with his spinner in the Sub-Lieutenant's In-Tray, removing part of the Nissen hut *en route*. He was suffering from anoxia at the time after carrying out an oxygen climb with a defective oxygen mask valve.

A few days later a signal arrived at dispersal by cleft-stick messenger hotfoot from Yeovilton, to say that Dougy Yate, Norman Goodfellow, Murdoch Tait and I, instead of joining a Hellcat squadron in the States, had been appointed as instructors to the new fighter school at Henstridge, flying Seafires. Jacky Sewell and most of the others were appointed to the USA on Corsairs. Sam Mearns, much to his grief, was appointed to a Sea Hurricane A/S outfit in the Atlantic, on escort carriers.

It was inevitable that the FAA had to have the Seafire. It was the only fighter available that would fit into the new, low-hangar-roofed *Implacable* and *Indefatigable*. There were no other British aircraft. Hawker's Hurricane replacement — the Typhoon — was too large, the Martin-Baker MB5 was not being built and the Blackburn Firebrand had yet to fly properly. The Hurricane itself was not available in sufficient quantity and it was unlikely to be fitted with the Griffon engine or be modified to allow wing folding. Nevertheless, we had heard much about the beautiful Spitfire and we looked forward to our new task at Henstridge, although we were sorry that the 804th, raring to go and with its very high morale, had been broken up — on the First of June, too.

Sadly, we heard later that Jacky had been killed soon afterwards in a collison in a Corsair with his new Senior Pilot — Lt David Watson — of 1837 Squadron in the States. I also heard that Lt/Cdr (A) Rupert Brabner, DSC, MP, RNVR, had been killed in a flying accident.

Walrus. *(FAA Museum)*

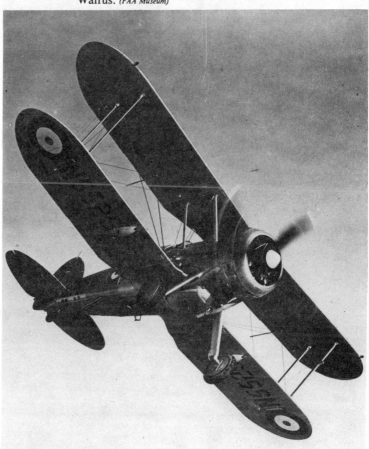

Sea Gladiator.
(FAA Museum)

Hellcat F6F. *(FAA Museum)*

804 Squadron at Charlton, Horethorne, 1943, Sea Hurricane IIb and IIc.
Left to right: 'Bob Cranwell, 'Titus' Oakes, 'Dougy' Yate, 'Sam' Mearns, Author, 'Bob'
Tracy, Jacky Sewell, 'Piggy' McLennan, Jimmy Crossman, Norman Goodfellow, 'Snotty'
Bullen, John Barker, Murdoch Tait, 'Al' Burgham.

Chapter 14
RNAS Henstridge or HMS Dipper

When the Henstridge farmers heard that the low-lying land to the south of their village on the A30 was to be turned into a Naval flying station they thought that the river would be allowed to flood the valley for Naval seaplanes to take-off and land. Instead, they were surprised to see the immense drainage scheme that was undertaken — the first since the days of King Alfred — which made it possible to lay asphalt runways in four directions, plant Nissen huts and hangars round its winding perimeter track and build more Nissen huts in the undergrowth for accommodation. After this, they watched their pubs gradually fill up with sailors, then pupil aviators and finally, instructors. Then the Seafires arrived.

The aircraft were secondhand Spitfire Is. Some had hooks fitted and were called Seafires. The older Spitfires still had their bullet-proof attachments to the front of their windscreens where they had been added as an afterthought in 1939 at the insistence of AVM Dowding.

Norman Goodfellow, Snottie and I were detailed for 'B' flight; Tait and Yate for 'A' Flight. Our Flight Commander was Lt (A) 'Ben' Lyon, DSC, RNVR and 'A' Flight Commander was Lt (A) David Carlisle, RN. The Chief Flying Instructor was none other than Lt/Cdr (A) Dicky Cork, DSO, DFC, RN. Other instructors were S/Lt (A) Gavin Torrance, RNVR, Lt (A) 'Blinkers' Paterson, MBE, DSC, RN — the Air Gunnery Officer — S/Lt (A) Tim Singleton, RNVR (the son of a Lord Chief Justice who had given the Pilgrims' School an extra half holiday for our singing one year) and the 'orrible 'otchkiss — S/Lt (A) Sam Hotchkiss, RNVR. Beside the Captain and the Commander there were only five straight-stripers on the Station and of these, three were RN (A) 'Short Service' Officers.

The day I arrived, Dicky Cork saw me in the wardroom at lunchtime. He said: "Hallo Crosley. You've flown Spits before I suppose. Get hold of one and meet me over the airfield at 1600 for a bit of formation flying. OK?"

I re-read Pilot's Notes for the Spitfire Ib. I tried to cast my mind back to a Christmas, eight months ago. I had flown it in a careful straight line and had learned nothing about it. 'Ben' (John) Lyon showed me the 'taps' and I strapped in, started up and, pretending to know what I was doing, taxied out and took off.

After a few private loops and rolls and a bit of slow flying, I came over Henstridge to meet Dicky. He flashed by me out of the sun and I spent the next five minutes catching up and trying to formate on his port wing. I could not have been making a very good impression for I found the stick forces so light in the pitching plane that I was continually over-correcting. My Spitfire was prancing up and down alongside him like a mustang.

I found that the aircraft I was flying was not a Spitfire Ib, but a hooked Seafire Ib. The latter had almost zero stick forces on the elevator control, a phenomenon that I had not expected and which was totally different from the Hurricane. I described the flight in the 'Duty' column of my flying log as: "Trying to formate with the CFI".

I had heard that the Seafire, like the Spitfire was a delight to fly. I would have to get used to the much lighter stick forces. I soon found out its other characteristics. Its thin wings and smaller frontal area increased its level speed over that of the Hurricane by 30 knots IAS at all heights, at identical power settings. In the dive, whereas the Hurricane more or less stopped at 330 knots, the Seafire got faster and faster until it had some 380 knots on the clock.

Ex-Hurricane pilots and those of our pupils who had been trained on the American Harvard must all have found the Seafire's light elevator forces very difficult to get used to. The American-trained pupils must also have found navigation difficult. Whereas they could fix their position easily in the US by a quick look over the side to spot the only river or only road for 100 miles around; when flying over southern England, the countryside looked like a patchwork quilt, every patch looking the same as its neighbour and full of identical rivers, railways or roads.

Flying training in the Seafire was a tricky occupation. It was a superb flying machine, but, like the Hurricane, it had been designed to operate from grass airfields. Grass gives freedom to taxi from side to side so that in a long-nosed aircraft like the Seafire, the pilot can easily see where he is going when on the ground. Likewise, when landing on grass, the soft ground has a far greater rolling resistance than hard runways. The Seafire's brakes, were, therefore, over-used at Henstridge and tended to fade due to overheating after a short runway landing. The Seafire, as opposed to the Spitfire, had the immense weight of an arrester hook added a long way aft of its centre of gravity, and the 28 pounds of solid lead added by the front engine bearers had not entirely corrected this tail heaviness. In the case of the Seafire III series, the aircraft was so unstable fore and aft that it should not have entered service in that condition. (See Appendix 11 (c) Stability Problems in the Seafire.)

I have already mentioned how the Seafire's progress round Hatston's narrow perimeter track was often interrupted by its running off onto the grass at either side. When this occurred at Henstridge, the wheels sank into soft clay and the aircraft became a write-off as it went up on its nose, shock-loading the engine and bending the engine bearers. Slow taxying to avoid this, or taxying downwind, led to engine overheating. Although this could sometimes be cured by turning across wind so that the prop slipstream went through the radiator under the starboard wing, this usually caused the oil cooler to overheat under the port wing and the aircraft had to be towed back to cool down and try again. After the anxiety of taxying — knowing that the eagle eye of your instructor followed you round — the pupil might at last be rewarded by the take-off. Once the tail was raised — by prop slipstream over the tail and a small push on the stick — and the pilot could see where he was going, the true enjoyment began. The acceleration was like a racing car. Once airborne, the Seafire responded with the sensitivity of a polo pony to nearly all our ignorant demands upon it. It behaved in its normal habitat with such unselfish grace and with such rapid response and power, that we knew we were being allowed to fly a thoroughbred. Once we were climbing away into the sky, all we had to do was keep our eyes open and the enemy could not touch us. (Appendix 11 (a) — Some Seafire flying characteristics.)

We instructors considered ourselves particularly lucky in having Dicky Cork as our CFI and 'Wings'. When 880 Squadron was landed ashore after *Indomitable's* retirement after sustaining her serious damage in 'Pedestal', Dicky spent a few months in the USA and then returned to UK to organise flying at Henstridge.

He was a valuable buffer between us 'branchmen' and the authorities. The Captain was a kind, almost benevolent man in his dealings with his RNVR aviators, but the Commander was not quite so patient. He was a destroyer man, and Dicky and he did not see eye to eye, "remarkable man though he is in many ways" the Commander was heard to say. The Commander himself was equally brave in his own way, verging on the intrepid. He was determined to learn to fly. He came past our Nissen hut at 'B' Flight one morning in a Tiger Moth with the 'orrible 'otchkiss in the back as his instructor. As the Commander was the senior officer on board, 'otchkiss had no power to alter things. There was a strong crosswind blowing, and two ratings, each grasping a wingtip, were having trouble keeping their hats on and the Tiger Moth on the perimeter track as it swept past. A flurry of yellow and blue, they zigzagged past us at about 20 mph and the Commander could be heard above the noise of his revving engine shouting "Handsomely, there. Handsomely", to each rating in turn.

The whole lot disappeared out of control past our hangar, in a series of groundloops. When we later asked one of the ratings on the wing tips what he thought 'handsomely' meant, he said: "Push like fuckinell, Sir, I expect".

We had no doubt that the Commander had seen our merriment as he went by. So next morning we expected and received one of his most meticulous inspections. He descended on us very early indeed and from a great height. There was a long list of matters to attend to in his report. The Commander told 'Ben' Lyon to make sure, next time, to have all ratings with hats on and chin stays down. They should be standing to attention by their aircraft. Drip trays were to be cleaned out, fire buckets were to be full of water or sand and not yesterday's half-eaten Tiddy Oggies (a Naval type of Cornish pastie) or fag ends. All aircraft were to have their cowlings on, even if they had no engines, and all pointed the same way. So far as the squadron offices were concerned, they came in for more criticism. There was to be "clean blotting paper on the desks and pens arranged in order of size". Ben then told Dicky that our flying would, henceforth, be nil on all inspection mornings, as the finding of clean blotting paper and pens in order of size would take time. We had no further trouble from inspections of this sort.

It was inevitable, however that one of us would eventually fall foul of the Commander. Norman Goodfellow was the unlucky man. In Dicky's absence, he had gone to the Captain to complain when one of his best pupils had been thrown off the Course for landing his Seafire in what was judged by authority to have been a carefree manner. Norman had reported that the cause of the accident had been because the pupil concerned was suffering from anoxia following an oxygen climb. When he landed, he, like Barker in 804 Squadron, could not remember a thing about it; but Norman's mistake of protocol in going over the Commander's head to plead for his pupil was frowned upon even more than the accident. The Captain sent Norman back to see the Commander and he rounded upon Norman and gave him a fortnight's Duty Boy.

Henstridge was an extraordinarily happy place otherwise and as time went on it was probable that the Commander realised that he should not try to apply the strictures of a peacetime battleship to a crowd of RNVR schoolboys enjoying themselves in the heart of the Dorset countryside. It was Gavin Torrance, assisted by the 'orrible 'otchkiss, who put aviators and administrators back on an even keel. Through some clever impersonations on the telephone they managed to arrange for a completely fictitious Course of new pupils to arrive ten days early. As these new pupils included some Indian or Moslem-type pilots, special eating and praying arrangements were laid on. The telephone was going all the time in 'B' Flight, with Gavin's arrangements falling into place, for days on end. When the transport sent to fetch them arrived back from Templecombe railway station at the appointed hour without a single pupil, an investigation was put in progress to find out where the Course had gone. This took until midnight, by which time the Commander's Officer realised that it was April the First.

During the autumn and winter of 1943, huge air and ground reinforcements came to England from the USA. These were some of the fruits of Churchill's and Roosevelt's Lease-Lend arrangements, made before Pearl Harbor and when British and Commonwealth blood was being shed for democracy for the rest of the world to enjoy. The Americans were generous. There were to be no cast-offs for the British. Wildcats, Hellcats, Corsairs and Avengers were in service in the Royal Navy simultaneously with those in the US Navy and Marines and at no immediate cost to the British taxpayers. (Appendix 6 — Inter-Service rivalry.)

Long range aircraft such as the Liberator, at last being made available from Bomber Command for their proper use as anti-submarine aircraft in the Atlantic 'gap', were also being delivered to England by air. They flew via Iceland straight from the USA. Sometimes they arrived over the UK and found it entirely covered by cloud up to 25,000 feet. The pilots had no idea where they were or whether it would be safe to come below the cloud. By the time that they had covered the British Isles from north to south without seeing the ground, they became desperate. Some used to break cloud a few hundred feet above the mountains and survive. Others would hit a 'stuffed cloud' and perish. Other luckier ones might break cloud and catch sight of an airfield. One of these airfields was sometimes Henstridge. These silent, white-painted monsters would suddenly appear off the end of the runway and screech to a smoking halt at the far end, propellers stopped. The crew would immediately come out of every hatchway, kiss the ground, throw the Dorset clay over their heads joyful in their deliverance. After they had collected their baggage we would take them to the wardroom in our various motor cars. There, with only short interruptions to send messages home, they would blunt the sharpness of their nerves in Strong's Best Bitter until carted off to bed in the small hours of next day.

We later found out the reason for their poor navigation. Lockheed used the metal fuselage for the 'negative return' to the aircraft batteries and variations in the electrical load and route taken, caused up to 15 degrees compass variation due to induced magnetism, which was unpredictable.

Next day, when the Liberator crew had sufficiently recovered, they would unload their huge aircraft of everything heavy, including its guns still wrapped in manufacturer's tape, and with three crew only, line up on the longest possible runway for a take-off. The four Double Wasp engines, their exhaust-driven turbo superchargers whining, would then flatten the hedges and trees behind them with their slipstream as they ran up to full emergency power on the brakes before take-off.

Although the Liberator sailed into the air with a few feet to spare, a Martin Marauder which tried the same thing a little later in the year nearly came to grief. Although the Marauder had a better power-weight ratio than the Liberator, its unstick speed was 35 knots higher. As any student of physics will know, the excess energy required for a take-off at this much higher speed was roughly in the ratio of 1:2. We therefore worked it out that the Marauder wouldn't have a chance of making it. So we all watched, with cameras at the ready.

A Wellington bomber had already overshot the far end of the longest runway a week before. It was still there, lying across the river, a useful pier from which to bathe or fish. Perhaps the river was now going to be bridged for a second time, this time with a Marauder full of even more exotic instruments, fan motors, and wireless sets for use in our cars.

At last a day arrived having a full 20 knots of wind blowing down the longest runway. The American pilot, superbly dressed in his highly polished boots, brown two-piece leather flying suit, studded with guns, goggles, badges, fasteners, knee pads, pencils and two stopwatches, smiled a dazzling smile as he climbed up into the cockpit of his lethal looking, anhedral, fighter-bomber. Getting a tractor to push him backwards against the hedge, so gaining a few more feet of take-off run, he started each 2000 hp engine in turn, warmed them up and then ran them separately at full power. In doing so, a man on his bicycle, passing astern of his aircraft on the road behind and all unsuspecting of the knife-edge blast of the slipstream across his path, was lifted with his bicycle into the far hedge as if he had been an autumn leaf.

It was exciting, watching the Marauder gather way slowly and begin its headlong dash for the far hedge, nosewheel held firmly on the ground. At the very last moment the pilot yanked back on the stick with full nose-up elevator. The nose reared up, the tail skid hit the runway in a shower of sparks and after an age, the roaring, smokey beast lifted off the ground a few feet, purely on the ground effect, and banged down again in a shower of turf and mud in the grass overshoot area. It continued like this until the wheels hit the far bank of the river which bounced it into the air again. This time it staggered along at hedge height, seemingly flying through several willow trees by the river, clawing its way skywards, its two airscrews thrashing white vortices into the damp Dorset air. Two minutes later, flaps, engine gills and wheels retracted, engines throttled back in polite deference, and in a beautifully judged shoot-up made in the best possible taste, the Marauder flew off to its Cambridgeshire airbase, there to work-up for the daylight raids shortly to begin over Germany and France, before the 'Second Front' landings took place in six months time.

In the winter of 1943 we often had to struggle to complete our flying programme in the short daylight hours and there was little time for relaxation with our wives or sweethearts. Even in the summer there was seldom time for cricket or some such relaxation unless the weather was *far* too bad for flying. One day, when we had waited all the morning for the weather to make up its mind one way or the other, Norman had an idea. This was to give the weather an artificial nudge. 'Seaweed' alone had the power to arrange matters. He worked at his Met charts in an adjoining Nissen hut. He seldom, if ever, looked through his small hut window to see what the weather actually was. He preferred to rely on his charts. However, Norman intended to give him an 'actual' from a watering can. He climbed stealthily onto the roof of the Met Office and poured the 'rain' onto the Met Officer's window with a watering can. While this was going on I telephoned Seaweed for his afternoon's forecast. It only needed for me to ask him to have a look outside at the 'rain' now falling and he cancelled flying for the afternoon, noting the onset of precipitation on his Met chart accordingly.

My immobile Wren and I now lived in a house in Long Street in Sherborne.

My wife's mum had died and it became necessary to move from 'Camel Farm' in Queen Camel. But when I had to sleep 'aboard' on duty I shared Hut 13 with the instructors. The beds were arranged as in a crowded and thoroughly septic 'Scutari'. Some had small wardrobes in between, others had small tables. In the centre of the hut was a small coal-burning, cast-iron stove. There were two ceiling lights, switched on and off by a switch at the door. There were no windows of any sort. The floor was of bitumen. The washing and other arrangements were in a separate hut about 100 yards away.

Each night, 'Seaweed' would rise from his bed in the darkness, shuffle his way towards the door and go outside for a walk to the Heads. We had long since decided that the Heads were too far away and preferred to pee out into the blackness of the night from the shelter of the hut doorway. This, as it happened, was all over Seaweed's radishes. When he produced a bowl of radishes from time to time at tea, he was surprised that none of us liked radishes. He offered his lettuces and none of us liked these either.

Porridge was another thing we seemed to dislike. It happened like this. Each night that we had both petrol and money, one or the other of us would tow a whole lot of instructors on their bicycles to the local pub, the Lion at Marnhull. On the way back, those who made it without crashing, repaired to Hut 13, there to await the cooked delicacy. This was usually heated-up leftovers from the wardroom galley. The 'duty cook' for the evening was Murdoch Tait. He found the galley had been locked and he had to get in through the pantry window.

He turned up late with our plates of food in Hut 13 and we were complaining. He told us that when he got in through the pantry window he had lowered his flying boot into tomorrow's still warm porridge. He said that he only noticed it after it had welled over the top and into his socks. It was getting all this cleaned off and back into the porridge tureen that had taken the time. None of us, including the Met Officer, had porridge next morning.

Then there was the case of Gavin's flying boots. He was one of the unlucky officers whose bed was by the door of Hut 13. He was slap in the path of the traffic to and from the radish beds. One night, in the total darkness, someone opened his wardrobe door instead of the Nissen hut door and filled his flying boots in his wardrobe. It was several days before he discovered this. It was no joke. Beds near the door were therefore allotted to newcomers who were not entitled to wardrobes anyway. Hut 13 was being used as a farmer's pigsty when I saw it in 1963 so that it had not changed much in 20 years.

At about this time, news started to filter through the grapevine that there had been a FAA disaster. Twelve squadrons had been operating more than 100 Seafire LIIcs as fighter cover from four or five escort carriers in the Mediterranean. Admiral Vian was in charge of the carriers supplying this fighter cover for the landings near Naples, Operation 'Avalanche' at Salerno. His report on their operational use and efficiency had been full of criticism, particularly of their short range, their lack of speed to catch the Fw 190s and their total unsuitability as decklanders. We heard that 70 had been lost in the first two days operations, in accidents. (For the proper reasons for the Seafire's failure see Appendix 5.)

In the summer months of 1943, an incident with the MG convinced my immobile Wren and I that it was time to get another car. Driving to Henstridge one morning, a lorry ahead slowed down as a cow walked across the road in front of it. With its inadequate brakes, the MG slid under the tailboard of the lorry and we stopped with it three inches from our windscreen. It bent the Union Jack flagstaff on the radiator, but did no further damage. The lorry driver got down out of his driving cab, looked down at our car and said; "Can't you see no Tri-bloody, angu-fucking-lation Mark?"* He then got into his driving cab and drove away, bending the flagstaff back the other way as he did so. Looking at the Union Jack, my wife said: "Let's get another car". So we did. The choice consisted of a 1934, red Hornet Special or a loan of my brother-in-law's 1939 BMW-Frazer-Nash 327. Both did about 90 mph and 20 miles to the gallon. Both were flashy cars, with open exhausts here and there and a good deal of chromium. The Hornet cost £75 and the brother-in-law's was free. However, he might return any moment from his job in the Army Legal Department in Beirut and I would have to hand it to him in the same pristine condition in which I had found it. That could be expensive. In the end we used the BMW for dignified occasions and the Hornet for mucking about.

During the trial runs of the Hornet, we had touched 80. There was nothing odd about this except it was in the blackout and in the winding country lanes round Henstridge. Dougy Yate was driving. Dicky Cork was on his left, pulling hard on the handbrake from time to time, and I was in the back, afraid. Dougy had been unaware of Dicky's braking precautions so that his opinion of the car's performance was not very good. Standing in the thin blue smoke of the red-hot Ferodo, he said that it lacked staying power in steep turns and would never make a good fighter. Apart from the Hornet's colossal oil consumption and its propensity for 'running' big ends in the resultant dearth of oil, it worked well until the end of the war. So much for social arrangements. How was work progressing?

So many FAA pilots — including Butch Judd — had been killed making stern attacks, we tried for much of the course to teach the pupils how to make quarter attacks. The Seafire was fast enough to make this a possibility — even against the Ju 88. (Those who are interested should read Appendix 11 (b) — Pilot Gunnery Instruction.)

While at Henstridge, Dicky Cork was visited by some of his ex-Battle of Britain friends. One was Wing Commander 'Splinters' Smallwood. He suggested that we should come and do a few 'sweeps' over northern France with his wing of Spitfire IXs, based at RAF Church Stanton in Devon. The idea was to give us some Douglas Bader-type 'Wing' experience. These huge RAF fighter sweeps were aimed at attracting the German fighters into the air and reducing their numbers before the invasion. Dicky Cork said that flying in formations of up to 50 fighters at a time was bound to be a feature in the Pacific war which we should all have to fight one day, and that it would stand me in good stead in case I ever had a squadron of my own. So I volunteered, although it meant more goodbyes to my immobile Wren wife.

I joined Number 10 Group where Splinters was the Wing Leader. It was interesting to be a part of a big organisation, entirely geared for flying and nothing else. The RAF were complete professionals. The two squadrons in the Wing were Numbers 165 and 131. The Spitfire Mark IX was a heavier and more powerful version of the Spitfire Vb and was about 20 knots faster with 20 per cent more internal fuel. First introduced into RAF service in July 1942 it became the replacement to the Spitfire V series. Later versions were the first to be fitted with a 'teardrop' hood, a beautiful transparent canopy which allowed marvellous air-to-air visibility from the pilot's seat. Some 6000 were introduced to equip 60 RAF squadrons.

---

*The Triangulation Mark was a red triangle painted on some vehicles built in the early thirties which had the new *four*-wheel brakes. The wording on the three sides of the triangle was "Danger — Four-wheel Brakes!"

Whenever we went over France the sky was often black with British or American aircraft, from zero to 30,000 feet. Although the Germans were now on their home ground it would have been the utmost folly for them to have tried to confront such air superiority and there was no serious opposition unless we attracted them into the air by combining with American Fortress raids as 'area support'.

I also had to do my stint of stand-by duties and did several 'Scrambles'. These were chases after unidentified low flying aircraft approaching from France. The last of these was on Christmas Eve 1943. We chased what looked like an RAF Typhoon — probably from Warmwell — to the coast of France, before turning round and coming back, unable to catch it up. It might possibly have been a 'tip-and-run' Fw 190 fighter/bomber, but I was doubtful. However, Fw 190 raids were quite a common occurrence at this time. They climbed to 25,000 feet over France, approached Plymouth at 400 knots in a steady dive, dropped their bomb and scurried off back home at nought feet, underneath radar. (This is exactly what they did at Salerno. No wonder our Seafire LIIcs could not catch them.)

The most impressive part of the RAF was not its flying, which was barely average by Fleet Air Arm standards, but its back-up organisation. Aircrew were briefed an hour before each flight, not a haphazard five or ten minutes as in *Dasher*. Every aspect of an operation was given in detail; r/t frequencies, call signs, air/sea rescue details, position of rescue aircraft and ships, likelihood of French agents to contact if shot down and weather in every detail. In addition we had extra 'airborne' rations; raisins, sweets, chewing gum for the nervous, soft drinks for those with dry mouths. Back at the Mess we would have extra eggs, fruit, nuts, orange juice and chocolate. There were special transport runs into the local town and to the local pubs. Entertainers visited the station regularly. Flying clothing was of a luxurious standard. We normally flew in battledress uniform at Henstridge as there was nothing else. The RAF flying clothing had pockets for everything and each pilot had a magnificent pair of black leather flying boots which, if we were shot down, would readily convert into tough, unobtrusive walking shoes. The Mae West was of a more recent pattern and had dye-marker, torch and whistle, and could be automatically inflated by pulling a toggle. Besides all this, the runways at Church Stanton were double the width and nearly half as long again as the longest Henstridge runway, making formation landings and take-offs safe and easy and with no strain on the aircraft brakes. Life was very easy and relaxed compared with the life aboard ship.

However, for some reason, we in the Fleet Air Arm, struggling with last year's facilities, were not in the least jealous of the RAF. We seemed to take it for granted that we should be the poor relation. In fact we thought ourselves rather special, being able to cope without it. (See Appendix 6 — Inter-Service rivalry.)

Dicky Cork was relieved by Rodney Carver as CFI at the end of 1943. Dicky was appointed as CO of 15 Wing, 28 F-4U Corsairs, working-up in America for operations in the Far East aboard *Illustrious*. Lt/Cdr Rodney Carver, DSO, DSC, was another fighter pilot of outstanding ability and a super replacement for the incomparable Dicky Cork.

At about this time the Fleet Air Arm was in urgent need of a sensible replacement for the Swordfish and Albacore torpedo/bombers. The Fairey replacement, the Barracuda, was showing all the usual signs of intractable obsolescence even before it was fully in service, and the Admiralty appointed as Assistant Air Attaché to Washington, Captain Casper John — to organise

Lease-Lend replacements. (See Appendix 6.) The latest American equivalent of the Barracuda was the Grumman Avenger. This was now replacing the Douglas Devastator in the Pacific US Fleet and forming new FAA Squadrons at home and in the States. It was a 45-foot wingspan, midwing monoplane in the Grumman style, with power-folding wings, a three man crew, a bomb bay stowage for a torpedo or 3000 pounds of bombs and a turning performance little short of a fighter after it had dropped its load. It could even out perform, out lift and out range the RAF's Wellington.

In January 1944 I was told to take part in a trial with two RN Avenger squadrons forming at Hatston. The Avenger squadrons wanted to know whether it was better to defend themselves with their rear turrets' 2 x 0.5 inch guns or to dispense with the guns, save weight and crew and protect themselves by evasive manoeuvres. The only thing wrong with their theory of using evasion in such a highly manoeuvrable aircraft was that they intended to remain in a close formation while they were evading. They had worked out that a sort of 'co-ordinated' corkscrew could be adopted. This would put the enemy fighters off their aim and still not cause collisions or separation among the Avengers while they plodded on to their targets.

Lt Alistair McAlpine arrived at Henstridge one day and we flew in his Stinson Reliant to West Wittering. There we collected two of the Naval Air Fighter Development Unit's Spitfire Vbs and flew them to Hatston for the trials.

It was so frightening watching the Avengers behaving in formation in such a dangerous and drunken fashion only 250 yards in front of us that we completed the trials as quickly as we decently could and flew home again. We had decided that it was far safer for them to rely on 'area support' or 'top cover' *à la* RAF than to rely on either guns or drunken corkscrews. While Alistair and I had been at Hatston, we had met many of the pilots who had just bombed the *Tirpitz* so successfully, on 3 April 1944. One of the pilots flying Barracudas on this operation was my Yeovilton cabin mate, Lt (A) Geoffrey Russell-Jones, DSC, RNVR. He told me what he had done so far in the war and I thanked God that I had stayed on fighters.

The New Year of 1944 saw several changes for us at Henstridge. We all became Lieutenants overnight. Their Lordships considered that those who instructed others should have the dignity of two stripes. COs of squadrons should all be Lt/Commanders. These qualifications just included J. F. ('Snottie') Bullen who had at last reached the age of 20. Our pay increased to 15 shillings a day which put me above that of a Constable in the Met, so their assistance ceased.

At Yeovilton, 887 and 809 Squadrons were working up on Seafires for the landings in southern France. As the school's Pilot Gunnery Instructor (See Appendix 11 (b) — Pilot Gunnery Instruction), I paid them a visit and met a couple of school friends, C. R. Prentice and Peter Meadway. Both had been in the choir at the Pilgrims' School and Meadway had been the solo boy before me. I also heard news of Fl/Lt Jack Graham, DFC who had been Lady Macbeth, and Andrew Fairbairn, one of the three witches. The former had been shot down over France and the latter made a POW as a Lieutenant in the Scots Guards.

Back at Henstridge once more in April, 1944, I found that I had been appointed as PGI to 3 Wing. The new Wing consisted of four squadrons and 50 pilots. Lt Manley-Cooper, DSC, RNVR was Wing Observer, We used an old farmhouse on the airfield as our offices. The Wing had 48 Seafire IIIs and my first job was to go down to the air-firing ranges over the sea at St Merryn in

Cornwall and take them up in the back of a Miles Master II to check out their air-to-air gunnery.

The tempo of the drogue firing programme at St. Merryn took the four squadron Commanders by surprise. In order to get enough firing done to make it worthwhile in the short time available, it was necessary to use each drogue, four times. It was then dropped, and the bullet holes counted. Each pilot's bullets were dipped in different coloured dye before they were loaded. The dye on the bullets marked the canvas of the drogue if they passed through it, and the pilots were credited with their score accordingly. The programme needed careful timing, each pilot taking off, arriving at the target towing area, waiting for his turn, finishing his shoot, landing, refuelling, reloading and taking off again with a new pilot, and so on, with six aircraft in the air at once. It also needed perfect r/t communications particularly from the pilots of the towing aircraft, who were responsible for safety.

Lt (A) M. W. 'Mat' Wotherspoon, DFC, RNVR was in command of the target towing squadron. His boys would sometimes take off with their drogues at 'short stay' on some misty morning and that was the last anyone saw of them until lunchtime. There were, therefore, mornings of chaos as well as mornings of success.

One of the COs, 'Willy' Simpson, complained that he was no longer in command of his squadron. However, the three others were only too glad for someone to do the donkey work for them. The shooting results averaged about seven per cent hits. This was fairly good, considering one in eight of the pilots could not hit the drogue at all.

In April 1944 our Wing Leader, Commander Shaw, RN was relieved by Commander 'Buster' N. Hallet. Although Buster was a straight-striper, a Dartmouth Cadet dating from 1926 and therefore 'suspect' to the average Branchman of that time, he soon set about changing our minds on that score. He must have been one of the very few people in the straight-stripe Navy who could understand the minds of us RNVR aviators. He could recognise our irreverent and lighthearted approach to traditional RN discipline as something which was necessary and which greatly increased morale and the joy of living for us in an otherwise unfriendly and dangerous world.

The second thing he did on taking over the Wing was to get us a better low-level version of the Seafire III. This had the Merlin 55M engine, which gave more output at low level and less at high altitude. This was because the 55M engine had a 'cropped' blower. It did not then absorb the engine power to no purpose at low altitudes. The energy saved was then available for going faster and farther on the same fuel. A third improvement then followed. This was the replacement of our fixed 100 mph GM Mk II gunsight with the new GGS Mk IID gunsight. (See Appendix 7 — The Gyro Gunsight Mk IID.) This sight had two 'rings'. One was a fixed, four-degree ring and merely substituted the GM Mk II ring for those who wanted to use it. The second ring altered its aiming point such that, if the pilot kept it on the target, it would automatically allow the correct deflection.

A fourth modification was then made to our Seafire LIIIs, as they were now called. This was to remove the last two feet of their elliptical wing tips. This allowed us a better rate of roll. The decreased area made no difference to our low level turning circle and the slightly reduced drag made a further small increase in indicated air speed (IAS).

The Seafire LIII now had 200 more horsepower at 3000 feet than the Spitfire IX. Its fuselage was lighter by about 200 pounds. It was further lightened in 3

Wing by removing half the gun ammunition and taking away the two outboard .303s altogether. In this condition it could out-turn, out-roll and out-climb the Spitfire IX at all altitudes up to 10,000 feet, a feature which would come into urgent use on several occasions in the forthcoming operations. At last the Fleet Air Arm had an aircraft which could out perform, in a narrow heightband, its contemporary in the RAF. All we needed was a certain amount of good luck, "excellent sight, very quick reactions and lots of self-confidence" (German ace Galland's opinion) — and we should succeed.

By May 1944 we were beginning to wonder what task Their Lordships might have in mind for us. All soon became clear, however. We were sent on a course of bombardment spotting to an airfield in Ayrshire. I journeyed northwards in the Master II. The Clyde was packed with ships bristling with guns. They pounded away at the Isle of Arran and we circled overhead, trying our best to give them directions by means of a complicated code over the r/t, so that their shells fell somewhere near the target. It all worked fairly well as long as there was good r/t contact between us and the ship doing the firing. This was, however, seldom the case and we wasted at least half our flying time trying to raise the Navy on the r/t.

During this time in Scotland we first met the 'C-Balls' or Carrier-borne Air Liaison Section, or Army language for half a dozen soldiers who told us, on maps, what they were doing ashore and how we could help. They taught us how to carry out the spotting routine in the safety of a cow barn on the airfield. The boss of C-Balls was Major Michael Scott, Royal Devons, assisted by Capt Bob Hudson, RA.

C-Balls rigged up a scale model of a typical enemy target. They used hessian canvas and models of farms, transport, cows, German soldiers, etc., camouflaged as we might expect them to appear from the air. The target area represented several square miles of territory. We sat around the target in the barn, staring down at it as if from our aircraft in real life.

Soldiers somewhere underneath then blew puffs of smoke from eye droppers through the hessian to simulate shell bursts. We then had to make corrections to the fall of shot to bring them onto the target. The soldiers would oblige with their eye droppers again.

There were two methods we could use. The first was 'Ship Control'. We could 'hang a clock' over the target, with 12 o'clock on north, using the clocktime as directional information. Distance information on the fall-of-shot was given in yards.

The second method, not as popular with the gunners as the first, was 'Air Control'. In this system of control we would tell the gunners what to do: "Up 400, right 600". The aim was to 'bracket the target' first of all, using just a few guns. Once the shot had been adjusted to fall over, then short, or right then left, of the centre of the target, to 'bracket' it, the pilot controlling the shoot would halve the distances between the two extremes and order "Fire for Effect". If he was correct and the ship's gunners had done what they were told, four or five broadsides would then fall on the target. If he was incorrect, or if the gunners had made a mistake, the four or five broadsides would fall in an adjoining field. Once the gunners started to 'Fire for Effect' they tended to get carried away. Nothing could stop them until they had completed their four or five broadsides.

When the battleships had completed these broadsides, a voice might then be heard over the r/t asking how they had got on. It was sometimes with poignance that we had to say that all their fifteen tons of shells had fallen a quarter of a mile away. It was natural under such circumstances that the airman got the blame.

Ships therefore tended to use 'Ship Control' and not 'air control'.

Before the Seafire became available for spotting, it was usual for the ship's own Walrus or Fairey Seafox to be catapulted for this purpose. When, early in the war, Lt E. G. Lewin, RN had spotted for the *Exeter's* guns in the Battle of the River Plate against the *Graf Spee,* he probably knew each gunner personally and they trusted each other. Success was therefore assured. This was seldom the case in large bombardment spotting operations. However those about to open fire over the Normandy 'D' Day beacheads were by far the most successful of any, for they carried out their shoots at close range with the ships at anchor and where the starting position of the shell and its hoped-for destination were known accurately.

After returning to Henstridge from our shooting practice we were shattered and sickened to hear of the death of Dicky Cork. Although it had happened 10,000 miles away, it hit us hard at Henstridge. It seemed he had scarcely left us. We heard that when he was about to take off from China Bay airfield in Ceylon, now Sri Lanka, another Corsair, driven by a sprog pilot, had landed on top of him. We did not ask for further details, for it sounded so typical an accident due to non-existent flying control, that we believed that it was the true story. After the war the history books told an entirely different story of this accident, blaming it on the dead pilots and absolving the airfield from all blame.

No one knows exactly what happened. However, it was beyond belief that the accident was due to Dicky Cork's disobedience of an air traffic control signal telling him not to land — as the report stated. He was far too experienced for that. It may therefore be interesting to sift the available evidence which I found for myself, when my squadron called at Ceylon in the following year. (See Appendix 8 — Dicky Cork's accident.) At the same time that we heard this news we were told to remove 3 Wing to Lee-on-Solent and we had to put the tragedy from our minds, for something more important was in the wind.

RNAS Hatston, near Kirkwall, Orkneys.

Sea Hurricane IIc of 804 Squadron, 20mm canon.

Seafire Ib to the scrapyard, RNAS Henstridge, 1943.

Chapter 15
Lee-on-Solent – June 1944

The four squadrons of Number 3 Wing had moved from Henstridge to Lee-on-Solent by 1 May 1944. We now had no doubt that the invasion area would be that part of the Normandy coast within range of our Seafires. After consulting the tide tables, and assuming a dawn landing at half tide, we could even forecast the date. The fact that the Germans were caught napping was not only because of the huge subterfuge plan by the Allies, and the shooting down — as it landed in France — of a photographic Me 109 on D-2, but because those at Lee-on-Solent and elsewhere did not give the game away by careless talk.

In order to make sure that I was not left out of any operations, I had asked Buster Hallett if I could be attached to one of the four squadrons, 886, with Lt/Cdr 'Val' Bailey, RN as CO and Lt Dicky Law, RNVR, as Senior Pilot. This was now arranged. The three other squadrons were — 885, Lt/Cdr (A) S. L. 'Tiny' Devonald, DFC, RN, 808 — Lt/Cdr (A) 'Jimmy' R. Rankin, DSC, RNVR, and 897, Lt/Cdr (A) W. Simpson, RNVR. In addition to our 48 Seafires, there were Numbers 26 and 63 RAF Squadrons, plus VCS-7, a US Navy outfit, all engaged in bombardment spotting or Army TAC/R. Finally, three Mustang squadrons would be using Lee for their spare airfield in case their own was bombed during the invasion. Our emergency landing ground was at Needs Oar Point by the mouth of the Beaulieu river and currently in use by Typhoons.

The most interesting of all the newcomers was VCS-7. The US Navy pilots flew Kingfisher OS2U amphibians, equivalent to our Walrus or the Fairey Seafox. Each US cruiser carried two of them for bombardment spotting and recce. The Americans arrived with their lovely little seaplanes one day, pushed them into a hangar and climbed into Spitfire Vbs. They had wisely decided to do this, rather than risk the Normandy beach-head in their floatplanes. Each of the spotting pilots in VCS-7 had a minimum of 500 hours in their Flying Logs and they seemed to have little difficulty in transferring to the Spitfire V, almost overnight.

A month before 'D' Day, the Lee-on-Solent air was thick with aircraft. The RAF did their usual wide circuits, disappearing towards Portsmouth or Southampton in the process. Number 3 Wing did the usual Naval circuits, met the RAF Spitfires on finals coming up faster from behind, with inevitable near-misses and arguments afterwards. The old-fashioned method of airfield control, as at China Bay where Dicky Cork lost his life, would not work and some sort of r/t-controlled discipline was essential. Lee Tower was therefore reinforced with two experienced pilots, Cdr (A) J. Keene-Miller, RNVR and Lt/Cdr Colin Campbell-Horsfall, RN, who set about organising an airfield control system using r/t for every movement; taxying, take-off, joining the circuit for landing, calling 'downwind' 'finals' and 'clear of runway,' after landing. It was unpopular to start with, but during the whole of the 33 days of operational flying from Lee and in 4400 movements, there was only one minor accident.

The wardroom and the Officers' Mess was like a five star, three storey hotel with 'hot and cold' and a view of the sea thrown in. It was a world apart from the pigsty arrangements at Henstridge, Hatston or Twatt. There were deferential, white-gloved stewards padding about again — anyway, to start with, and the whole was surrounded by tennis courts, sylvan walks for senior officers to salute each other, car parks, garages, impressive, sweeping entrances and Wrens. The Lee regulars were upset by the sudden arrival of 120 RNVR pilots demanding bed and board, and 1000 ground crew crowding into the Barracks. Notices were therefore pinned up in obvious places, telling us to dress properly, to keep to the Junior Officers' Anteroom (unless of Lieutenant rank or above) and to sit at various tables for meals at various times.

We were a noisy lot, and the 'knife and fork' course in the Painted Hall at Greenwich had obviously done us no good at all. There were only four RN officers amongst us, two of whom were RN (A) 'Short Service' Entries, and therefore didn't count. We tended to drink all the beer, eat all the rations, sing disgusting songs and cause delay in the eating arrangements. Furthermore, Buster Hallett had made sure that we were given our fair share of seafront cabins and refused to nag us for not saluting or not wearing our hats in the proper manner. Buster had also seen to it that we were given the same extra 'flying rations' as the RAF aircrew, much to the locals' disgust.

Although the Commander at Lee-on-Solent had obviously been chosen for his firm grip upon 'good order and Naval discipline', he was nevertheless a human man. We admitted to ourselves at least that he must have found it very difficult to ignore the oddly dressed RNVR Subs who lurched past as he marched smartly from the Wardroom Senior Officers' entrance to his office in the Administrative Headquarters. He did his best to look away, but there were some things he could not ignore. A young scion of a famous Russian family walked by one day. "You there, what's your name, Subby?"

On being told, the Commander declared: "I don't care if you're Peter the Great, but you're not going round the place wearing the DSO and those other medals which I know you haven't earned, and with hair all over your face. When you've shaved off those buggery grips and removed those pieces of coloured tape, come and see me in my office, in ten minutes."

The final improvement to 3 Wing's arrangements organised for us by Buster was the Franks Flying Suit. This was an anti-G suit. It was designed to prevent blacking-out in steep turns. As we should have to maintain high speed in case we were 'jumped' over the enemy-infested beach-head while spotting, and would also have to maintain an almost continuous steep turn to see the ground, the relief that the suit would give us would be welcome. (See Appendix 9 — The Franks Flying Suit.)

We continued flying at Lee in a relaxed manner, tuning up for the forthcoming battle which we knew could not be far off. On 3 June shore leave was cancelled. Next day came and went and still nothing happened. At 1800 we were told that we would be allowed ashore until 2230 that night, but not to go to any pubs.

Thereupon, eight of us, including Dicky Law, elected to visit my father and raid his supply of petrol and beer. We had enough petrol for one car, one way only. The Hornet could not take all eight of us, so we towed another car-full without petrol, for the five miles along the A27 to my father's house called

'Greenroof' in Bursledon, where he was now living.

It had been a year since I was in this part of the south coast. The A27 road between Portsmouth and Southampton was now almost unrecognisable. Mile after mile had been widened and laid waste by the passage of thousands of Army vehicles and tanks as they charged from one end to the other. They moved mostly by night. They seldom followed the exact contour of the road, taking in gardens, walls, lamp posts, petrol pumps and trees in their urgent progress. The road steadily extended into the fields on either side. Driving at night from Bursledon to Lee-on-Solent was therefore a difficult exercise.

My father was out when we drove up, so we got in through the larder window and consumed most of the barrel before he returned. He was not surprised to see us. He had worked it out that the Second Front, as he called it, could not possibly have started yet. The weather was too bad. He tapped the barometer to prove his point and the needle leapt a full five millibars towards 'Rain'. As he seemed certain that there would be no invasion on the morrow, we finished his beer, filled up the cars with his petrol and set off back to Lee with all engines going strong.

Next day, 5 June, we spent the time listening to the radiogram and tinkering with our cars at dispersal. That evening, with foreboding in our hearts, we looked for the appearance of next day's flying programme. It was pinned up at about 1900. It was the longest any of us had ever seen — 435 sorties. It started with the first take-off at 0430 and ended with the last landing at 2100. My first take-off, with Sub-Lieutenant Don Keene as my Number 2, was to be at the gentle hour of 0730.

"Time", so say the philosophers, "is nature's way of preventing everything from happening at once." But the flying programme for 'D' Day looked impossible. We slept fitfully, wasting the night in fruitless imaginings. The rain and wind was driving against the windows and we trusted that the morale of our soldiers in their landing craft would not suffer too much from seasickness. At least, we thought, we would not arrive over the beach, cold, wet, and with an empty stomach, and perhaps the Germans would not expect us after such a night as this.

Miles Master I.

Result of 'swinging off' the runway at Henstridge, 1943.

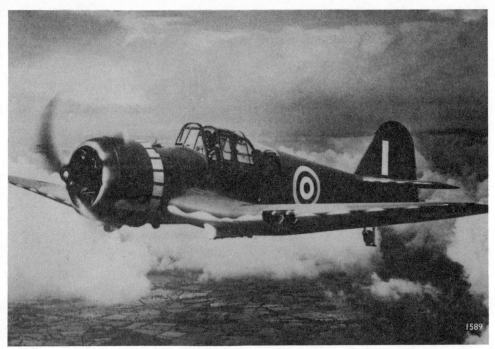

Miles Master II. *(Mike Banyard)*

The MG with Tim Singleton, Snotty Bullen and Dougy Yate, Henstridge, 1943.

Chapter 16
'D' Day – 6 June 1944

Next day, Don and I got up at 0500, had breakfast of fruit juice and went down to the briefing room in the blitzed hangar. There, we saw for the first time an impressive display of maps and photographs of the Normandy beach-head. One hundred and thirty thousand troops in 3000 landing craft escorted by 500 Naval ships would be crossing the Channel in the next 48 hours. Their five landing beaches stretched from Ouistreham in the east to St Mère-Eglise in the Cotentin peninsula in the west. Each German coast-defence gun position had an aerial photograph alongside it and the beaches were clearly defined and given names where American, Canadian and British landings — under the tactical command of General Montgomery — were to be made.

My diary records:

"Today, 'D' Day, we worked very hard indeed. Don and I flew three times over France, spotting for 'Spunyarn' (*Warspite*) flying a total of six hours fifty. Cloud was rather low and this meant we had to go down well below light flak height to do our spotting. Four blokes were consequently knocked down. Metcalf, of 'Tiny' Devonald's Squadron (885), managed to bale out over the Isle of Wight on the way back with only a broken arm as the damage. S/Lts Basset and Coghill were shot down and were killed. Lt Wallace was shot down and force-landed in France. My first flight took off at 0735, with Don Keen as my Number 2. We spend 45 minutes over France spotting on a heavy gun position near the coast at Trouville. The shoot was fairly accurate, by the clock method, but the broadsides had no effect as the guns could be seen still firing at the same time through the clouds of white concrete dust flung up by *Warspite*'s shells. Keene was a good Number 2 and let me know where the flak was."

"The second shoot was at an impromptu target, taking off at lunch time. *Warspite*'s r/t was better but she wasn't ready to start until it was time for us to go home. On the way home we shot up what could have been a German staff car. This overturned in a field off the road. One occupant got out and ran away. We also strafed and stopped a lorry about to enter a village. It was smoking badly when we left it. We were twenty minutes late getting back."

"The third time we took off my r/t was duff, so I landed and got into another aircraft and followed my Number 2, 25 minutes late. This aircraft was little better than the first. My jett tank wouldn't drop and the guns wouldn't fire. As I couldn't do a thing I came back and landed."

No one in 3 Wing knew what to expect. Only a few of the pilots had been on operations before. One unexpected worry was the extent of the danger from our own AA and fighter aircraft. We had been told, of course, that we would be well protected from the German Luftwaffe, not only by our own Number 2s guarding our tails, but by 150 fighters on CAP (Combat Air Patrol) overhead, stacked up to 30,000 feet. However, what we had not realised was how boring it must have been for all those RAF and USAAF fighters, without any effective ADR to tell them where to go for the first 72 hours, and not a sausage in sight. They naturally looked down to see what was happening. They could see us, in twos, circling over the beach-head and the countryside. Sometimes we were up to 20 miles inland. They could see we had square wing tips. They naturally thought, therefore, that we were 109s. In spite of huge white stripes on our wings and round our fuselages, they leapt on us in large numbers. Nothing we said or did for the first three days seemed to be able to stop them.

The other hazard, which some of us who had been near the Navy fully expected, was our own flak. We had seen some of the landing craft, now off Normandy, when they had been moored up the River Hamble. They bristled with 20 mm guns. Some even had 40 mm Bofors guns with gyro or 'Stag' computer gunsighting and with the new radio 'proximity fuzed' shells. The weather on 'D' Day had brought us down to about 1500 feet to do our spotting, well within the lethal range of these guns. The Army and the Navy shot off at anything that flew anywhere near them and this, not the Germans, accounted for the exceptionally high casualty rate on 'D' Day and the day after.

The fleet of invasion craft, spreading in zigzag lines across the misty and white-flecked Channel as we flew towards the south, and lined up in the shallows off the Normandy coast, made a very impressive sight. Lines of smoke blew inland from the clean line of the sand and surf on the shore. Clusters of shallow-draft landing ships were discharging their mobile cargo over lines of matting on the sand. Haphazard ribbons of transport and men stretched into the sand dunes beyond. Some ships were caught on sand bars offshore. The hazards were easily visible to us through the water from above, but not to their skippers as they steered through the shell splinters and explosions all around them. We could see the distant grey outlines of the fleet of bombardment ships at anchor about ten miles offshore, their guns flashing orange. Later, we could see the Mulberry harbours being towed into position and huge smoke screens intended to protect the sappers from air attack. We stayed at a respectful distance, hoping that our bombardment ships would reply at the appointed times to our radio calls.

After some minutes of calling, I might receive a reply. I managed, after a few tries, to note down on my knee pad the map reference of their chosen target. The next thing to do was to find the right Army ordnance map in the cockpit somewhere, fold it so that the target's six figure map reference was uppermost and then fly in that direction. Having identified it, to say: "Target ready," to 'Spunyarn'. While I was submerged in maps and with my eyes on the ground and trying to find the target, the engine might choose this moment to stop, because I had forgotten to transfer, and drop, the 25 gallon slipper tank and the engine pump was now sucking air. The next problem might be a warning from Don over the r/t that there were Spit IXs in the area and they were looking aggressive.

Eventually things might settle down: "Spunyarn, this is red one. Begin. Over."

"This is Spunyarn — shot. Ten" (seconds) "Over."

"This is red one — Roger. Out."

"This is Spunyarn," (eight seconds later) "Splash — Over."

Then after several more corrections which I would give to their ranging shots:

"This is Spunyarn — firing for effect — Over."

"Splash, Splash, Splash — Over."

"This is red one. Seen. Target obliterated. Smoke and corruption everywhere — good shooting — Over."

"This is Spunyarn. Thanks. Out."

The trip back would take 25 minutes. It was very pleasant not to have to make a decklanding at the end of it.

"'D' plus one. Wednesday 7 June. The weather dawned bright and clear over Lee-on-Solent. The good weather stretched right across the Channel up to ten miles inland into France. We had a look for a few targets east of Trouville. Nothing was moving along the road to Le Havre so Don and I went further inland. About 15 miles inland and south-east of Caen I saw what I thought was a Mustang or something stooging along above cloud, with not a care in the world. I could not believe it was a German for he was asking to be shot down as he stood out like a sore thumb, flying alone above the clouds. I flew by on an opposite course a bit up-sun. He could not have been a Spit or a Mustang. As I turned round after him, he disappeared into the cloud and I lost him. I followed along for a bit, came to the edge of the cloud and turned back inland again, hoping for a repeat performance. I climbed up to about 7000 feet to have a good look round to the south east from where he had come."

"Lo and behold I saw another one like the first, heading in a straight line for Deauville. This time I determined to have a good overtaking speed to make sure what he was, quickly. The top of the cloud was about 2000 feet below me and with 18 pounds of boost, everything shaking and clattering at about 360 knots on the way down, I was catching up fast. I still wasn't sure whether he was one of ours. I got in behind him very close indeed before I saw the Black Crosses on the side of his fuselage. I skidded in behind him again as best I could without wasting time. He still had not seen me, but there was not much time left as I was going too fast for comfort and was overtaking him. I pressed the gun button at about 150 yards range for about two seconds, seeing many hits with cannon on his wing and port fuselage. I pulled up to the left to avoid hitting him. I also felt as if he might have had a Number 2 up-sun of me, ready to pounce. I still could not understand how anyone could be so stupid as to fly alone in full view of everyone above him and towards a beach-head crowded with our own fighters, unless he was a decoy."

"I reversed the pull-up and had a look for him. I just caught sight of him, end on, before he hit the ground at the edge of the cloud cover, 3000 or 4000 feet below."

"I flew back, weaving all the way, expecting a furious German to come at me at any moment. I accidentally flew over the flak in and around Caen, but it did not seem as frightening as usual as I was so frightened already by what I had done. I stopped worrying once I was over the sea. I called up for Don, but could get no reply. So, I flew back to base."

On landing I found that I had only used 20 cannon rounds per gun. I noted in my diary that the two outer .303-inch guns had not fired at all. (I had not remembered that these had been removed at that time.) I asked the armourer to take care of the G45 film as it would make a very good picture at such close range. My diary account does not mention that I must have forgotten that any aircraft flying over Normandy without white stripes round its fuselage must have been a German, and that I had wasted precious time in making sure of the black crosses.

That evening, I telephoned the squadron to find out why the photographic section were saying that they had not got my film. I was told that the squadron photographic rating had seen that only a foot of film had gone and has assumed that it had not been used at all. He had thrown it in the gash bucket and fitted a new one. This was a bad advertisement for the PGI business. I should have run the whole film through before handing it in for processing.

The C-Balls told me that my Me 109 must have been a photo-recce German aircraft. Many had been sent over on the first two or three days to photograph the beach-head to try to find out whether the Normandy landings were the real thing. In the days after 'D' plus one, the RAF began to get the benefit from their own ADR set-up and we had less chance of discovering any odd Germans for ourselves before they pounced on them. However, more was to come . . .

"'**D' plus two, Thursday 8 June.** This was a most eventful day as the Germans were beginning to react in force. It started off early for Don and me. Our first take-off was at 0530, before sunrise. As the weather was bright and clear and the sun came up before we made the French coast, I told Don to fly above me down-sun and keep an eye open for Jerries in Fw 190s. The C-Balls had told us that they had some airfields in south-east France."

"We weaved our way south after passing the coast, keeping at about 6000 feet and above light flak height. We kept the airspeed indicator at about 275 knots, expecting to be jumped at any moment, for the r/t was full of excited voices telling us that there were some Jerries about. The ship wasn't ready for us, so we carried out a two-plane 'fighter sweep'."

Had we known it, the German Commanders in the field below us were already telling a worried Hitler: "The overpowering aerial superiority of the enemy and his Naval artillery, limit the possibilities of a large scale counter-attack on our part."

My diary continues:

"Don slowed down to drop his tank and at that critical moment I saw some Spitfires, so I thought, coming in from the north-east above him. I said, very relaxed like, 'There's a bloke on your tail,' and thank God he broke just at that moment as the 'Spit' started to fire tracer. Don broke well and truly, and the rest of them, about eight or so, came after me. I retired up-sun for a second or two in the steepest turn I've ever made, but not blacking-out, thanks to the G-suit, and came down again on what I hoped was their arse-end Charlie. However, in spite of going flat out from the word go I still wasn't going fast enough and I could not catch up. However, he wasn't the arse-end chap after all, because as I flogged after him, another Jerry 190 flew past my left side about 100 yards away, slowly rolling over on his back as he did so. He was upside down and seemed a possible target as he was nearest. Then others appeared from all over the place. Some might have been Spitfires of course who had now joined in from somewhere, and one Spit or Jerry pulled up vertically right in front of me going much faster than I was."

"However, I selected the bloke who was upside down and by now starting his dive, while he was still close enough for a burst at about 200 to 300 yards. He had been going a good 30 knots faster than me as he rolled over and having been diving for a few more seconds anyway, was getting away from me in the dive."

I had often followed others down in just such a dive and I knew that I would regain what I had lost at the bottom of the dive. For then I would still be diving while he was flying level, for a few seconds. But:

"I felt that there were several blokes following me down, either Spits (thinking I was a Jerry, as usual) or Fws. So I broke up in a tight loop rather than risk getting hacked myself. I did not see what happened to my target, on whom I have given about five seconds of fire between 250 and 500 yards."

"The Franks G suit again came to the rescue in the pull up and I was able to come down again on a bloke who must have been behind me, keeping 4-7 G on all the time. Unfortunately, I only had a few rounds left, for, by the time I had caught up with him right down on the deck and flat-out going south, the cannon stopped firing after about three rounds each. It was pointless going on. God knows what speed I had on the clock. My Number 2 had reported that he had been hit and was returning. As I had no ammo left I did so too."

My diary for this day goes on:

"I and Don were over France again at 1400. As we came over the beach I could see a rusty old battleship. We had heard that *Warspite* was u/s except for her guns (having been hit in the Med and not repaired) and here was an even older one, her foc'sle brown with rust. As I had been told to call *Ramillies*, it must have been her. Just as I was finding the target she had given us, we were jumped by Spits. We 'ducked' and showed our markings and shouted on the r/t to *Ramillies* to tell them to go away. She didn't seem to understand what we were talking about and kept on saying 'Wait one' and then silence. Meanwhile we were in steep turns with about 30 Spits, many of which seemed to be shooting at each other as well as at us, all in a huge great circle, flat out. It was very frightening, for they were better shots than the Germans and showed much more aggression. I wonder what the Krauts below us must have thought."

"After what seemed about 20 minutes, and us being able to outclimb the Spits while turning, they seemed to have been told who we were and they pushed off. However, we had used all our precious petrol and we could only place one or two shells on a road junction north of Caen on some guns and dug-in tanks, before we had to go home. We felt very browned off."

"Jerry certainly seems to be attaching a lot of importance to this spotting idea. All movement ceases when we come overhead and they dive into the nearest cover. Today some pilots reported that Jerry had joined in over the r/t and tried to give *Ramillies* and 'Sam' Lang (Lt H. Lang, RNZNVR) a lot of false reference numbers. They were told to pipe down, although we didn't use those worlds."

"Don and I got back to Lee with no further trouble after a two hour trip. Sam Lang had been shot down over Houlgate, apparently while he was looking for *Ramillies'* false target. His Number 2 had been hit and damaged by another lot of Jerries. Sam said that when he ran for cover — having bashed his head on the sight — he could only make 200 yards before running out of steam owing to the Franks suit. Sam is now in Leeds hospital (for a fortnight). Simpson made it back to Lee, so did my Number 2, Don, of course. S/Lt R. Chamen, was also bounced by the same tactic which got Sam. The Jerries were using some captured VHF sets (from our crashed aircraft I suppose) with our special frequencies still in them."

"The conversation between the Jerries and ourselves would go like

this, so said Tich Madden: 'Ello Red Sieben, your goot target at. . .'
Then followed a six figure map reference position in awful English, but in
a position on the map which was at an intersection of at least two maps, to
make it difficult to find in the cockpit. (This proved that it must have been
thought up by Jerry aviators who would have known how infuriating it
was.) "Zom Schpitfuss vill be zere to eskort you. Offer."

The gist of the various replies, which I heard over the r/t, might then
be: "F... off you b.....d krauts". And other statements to do with their
relatives and where they should be stuffed. The Germans, however,
persisted, and they eventually managed to spoof Chamen. Instead of the
'Schpitfuss' he found Fw 190s. He writes, from Vincentia in Australia, of
his experience, 40 years later:

"We were told to rendezvous with some Spitfires at a deserted airstrip
just south of Caen and upon investigation at about 500 feet, some
machine gun posts in the middle of this airfield suddenly opened up at us.
At about the same time a section of Fw 190s appeared and gave us an
anxious time. We returned their fire and I feel certain that we got one. . .
just before RAF help arrived. With odds now in our favour the 190s
departed. I was Tiny Devonald's Number 2 on this occasion. We had a
second confrontation at another r/v south-east of Bayeaux. The RAF
arrived in time on this occasion too, but on both occasions I returned
home with bullet holes in my Seafire."

Apart from Don, Simpson and Lang, there were a few more casualties. 'Tiny'
Devonald, the CO of 885, was the first pilot to be shot down from one of these
attacks by 190s. They had come down from out of the evening sun on 'D' plus
one. Tiny ditched his Seafire in the shallows through the 'friendly' flak and
balloons alongside the beach, as the beach was too crowded, and was picked up
by a landing craft. Keene-Miller and Campbell-Horsfall went on their own
'private' spotting trip. Both were bounced by Fw 190s. Keene-Miller
(Commander (A) Jack Keene-Miller, OBE RNVR, an ex-RAF and Imperial
Airways pilot) baled out and was captured, but made a marvellous escape. He
sawed through the planks of the cattle truck with his escape kit saw and returned
home, eventually, with several other evaders. Colin Campbell-Horsfall got shot
up but managed to get clear after being chased out to sea with no ammunition
left. He landed wheels-up at Lee-on-Solent.

Val Bailey, CO of 886, was also shot down, this time by our own AA fire. The
story in my diary is as follows:

"Val Bailey had a bad time today. He couldn't get out of his cockpit
when he tried to bale out, so he climbed back in again and had another go.
Eventually running out of height, he pulled the ripcord in the cockpit and
got dragged out. He landed, he doesn't remember how, on the beach and
got dragged badly. . . dislocating his shoulder."

S/Lt Foxley, F/O Wilcock of RAF Squadron Number 26 and Dicky Law,
Senior Pilot of 886, were also shot down, probably by German or British light
flak. Roy Foxley and Dicky Law made wheels-up arrivals in France. Dicky
called up his Number 2, S/Lt Taylor, who was circling overhead after the crash
landing, and said he was OK. Taylor then told him to walk about a mile to the
east where he would find a beach. Dicky loaded up with his r/t crystals (in case
the Jerries got them), his Gyro Gunsight (which was still secret) and his G45
Cinégun magazine, after destroying his IFF and burying his Franks suit, and
eventually got back to the squadron by 18 June, to continue flying.

" **'D' Day plus three. Friday 9 June.** Weather u/s. Blowing half a gale."

" 'D' Day plus four. Saturday 10 June. The weather was still marginal, but Don and I were told to have a go. We had an excellent shoot, this time with a new cruiser *Arethusa* whose r/t was the best I have ever heard and her shooting was to match. The target they gave us, or the HQ ship did, was a collection of tanks ten miles south east of Bayeux. In spite of it being near her maximum range with a shell flight time of 35 seconds, she plumped three broadsides of large bricks slap on top of them after only three ranging shots. The tanks that were left, started their engines and took off, dragging their camouflage netting behind them."

"The ridiculous thing about this camouflage stuff is that in the wet ground you could easily see their tank tracks leading into their camouflage netting, which gives the game away completely."

The diary goes on:

"Everywhere now our chaps are reporting that they are being attacked by Spits and 'T'-bolts. (American P47 Thunderbolts). Twin engined, twin tail-boomed Lightnings were also making passes, but not nearly as dangerously as the Spits, which were very good. Let's hope their aircraft recognition improves soon. The Jerries were also on the air again today, in better English too. 'Vat aircraft are you flyink. Is it Mustanks?' and then offering us an escort because 'Lots of you fellows have had bullets in your tails'. This sounded like typical Kraut humour and it was greeted by the usual comments.

" 'D' Day plus five, Sunday 11 June. Weather u/s."

" 'D' Day plus six, Monday 12 June. Two trips today. *Ramillies'* shooting and r/t lousy. I don't think they could hear us as their shots went everywhere but on the target, just keeling over a few cows here and there. In the afternoon trip we went a bit further inland. We saw some Jerries digging themselves into a hillside, it must have been, with guns mounted on top of tanks and lorries, etc. But 'Spunyarn's' r/t sounded like intermittent Chinese down a coalmine shaft and she and we were quite useless. Bugger me, it's a small thing surely to get her r/t working I should have thought."

" 'D' Day plus seven to nine, 13 to 15 June. "Went home to Sherborne. Must have arrived unexpectedly as the house was full of Sub-Lieutenants from Yeovilton, some painting the house cream on the outside. Wish I could have joined them."

"16 to 20 June. Don and I did six more spotting trips. Only one was a roaring success as the guns were shooting at extreme range. Some of the older battleships' guns (rifling) must be smooth by now as their shells weren't even hitting the right field. Michael Scott said they must have been arriving sideways! Several failed to explode at all and some of the errors were about two miles."

The Germans were now beginning to let off a few of their buzzbombs in the Southampton — Portsmouth direction, as well as many more towards London. Back at Lee, we watched them coming from the windows of our 'four star hotel'. They appeared, first of all, fairly low down over Bembridge. They then came past Ryde pier at about 400 feet doing about 400 mph. There were about 20 guns firing at them by then, some from ships in the Solent, the ships fired at them as they went past. They shot down their own balloons but failed to hit any of the buzzbombs. They continued on to Southampton and we could hear them going off. One went over Stubbington and hit the village but didn't kill any boys at the school there or anyone else in the village.

On Wednesday 21 June I had two days more leave. This time I stayed at 'Greenroof'. That night while we were returning from a drink at the Swan, (where I met Jeffrey Quill who said that Supermarine were designing a jet-engined replacement to the Spitfire) we heard and saw one or two of the night-flying buzzbombs come over the house. So, we stayed outside and watched.

The buzzbomb had a jet athodyd engine. It had no compressor like a true jet engine has. The fuel/air mixture was crudely burnt in an open-ended pipe. As the mixture of air and paraffin ignited, the front of the pipe closed, by venetian-type blind steel shutters leaving the burnt mixture only one way to get out — backwards. This gave the 600 lb thrust forward. Then, as the mixture was blown out of the back and the pressure in the pipe was reduced, the 400 miles per hour wind opened the venetian-type blinds in the front of the jet pipe again, more air/fuel mixture went in, and the whole process was repeated, about 20 times a second. This gave the buzz to the buzzbomb. It was designed, with its 17 foot wingspan, by the manufacturers of the Fieseler Storch. The whole contrivance was only airborne for 15 — 30 minutes. There was no way that the venetian blind principle could last for much longer than that without shattering to pieces.

At night my father and I watched. We could see the flame through the front of the jet pipe as the bombs came over Bursledon Hill. If the flame moved to the left or to the right as we watched it, then the bomb would miss. If the flame did not move and was therefore on a constant bearing coming towards us, and if the motor cut out a few seconds before it reached us, the bomb would land on us. We had several exciting moments as the straight ones came towards us, passed the critical cut-out position without cutting out, and continued on to Southampton to murder someone else. (The Hawker Tempest was able to catch them — with the help of the ACI stations and the Royal Observer Corps. A sea-defence gun-line also shot down a great deal more. From 12 June 1944 to 29 March 1945, AA claimed 1878, fighters claimed 1846 and balloons 231. The V1 killed 6000, in all, mostly in its approach to the Greater London area.)

On 25 June our spotting activities were shifted to the Cherbourg area. A pocket of the German army was holding out in the hills behind the town and the Americans needed the port facilities badly, for storms had slowed their reinforcements. The bombardment was mostly an American affair as it was their army involved, but *Rodney* and *Nelson* came to help. The shoots were carried out under way and all these ships were cutting great furrows through the Channel off the harbour entrance when we arrived overhead. Shells from the German shore batteries were falling amongst them and, sure enough, one of the American cruisers had the bad luck to be hit while coming in close to flatten the guns to the west of the Cherbourg inner breakwater. She retired with smoke pouring from her. We felt lucky to be safe, over the top, in our Seafires.

Our two ships, *Rodney* and *Nelson*, seemed not to pay the slightest attention to anything that Don and I said by way of spotting corrections, so we just watched. Major Scott said that the hilly country plus the short range and flat trajectory of the shells probably accounted for this inaccuracy. We hoped that at least some of their shells fell amongst Germans on Fort du Roule — our target — and not amongst the French houses on the hillside behind.

When Don and I got back to Portsmouth that evening, the weather suddenly clamped down over the Portsdown Hills. Lee-on-Solent was reporting cloud down to 300 feet and telling everyone to go to Hurn. We had no fuel to do that. We broke cloud over Portsmouth and I saw the frightening sight of barrage balloons flash by, about 50 feet below us. Don and I quickly pulled up into the cloud again. Luckily I had caught sight of Pompey Harbour and Southsea Pier and knew where I was. I steered a course in cloud towards Lee-on-Solent. The radio was cluttered up with lost aviators asking for RDF homings. I decided on a DIY let-down as the best way of avoiding having to bale out, as we were down to our last ten minutes of fuel. I managed to break cloud again with Don in close formation right over the top of the airfield at 300 feet.

On landing, we heard that S/Lt Horstead, on our spotting sortie, had crashed into the New Forest while trying to get into Needs Oar Point. Two RAF pilots were also killed. The sudden onset of a clamped weather situation had caught everybody by surprise and Lee-on-Solent had no proper bad weather landing arrangements.

We returned from Cherbourg to the Normandy area on 29 June. The only area where *Nelson's* and *Rodney's* 16 inch guns could now reach was in the area around Caen. There was a British sector offensive there and the Germans were providing some tempting gun targets, perhaps thinking that they were out of range of the 'Naval Artillery'.

The Chief of Staff of 9th Panzer Division wrote about Montgomery's Caen and Falaise Gap offensive after the war. He said:

"Now, if the Luftwaffe had been able to deal with the Allied Navies, and also stop the air attack, particularly the heavy guns of the battleships, the British and Canadian offensive would have fallen back into the ditch. Why, when one of these shells dropped near a Panther (a 43 ton German tank,) it was blown over on its side, just from the blast. It was the broadsides from the warships more than the defensive fighting of the enemy troops which halted our Panzers."

In this fighting, from 25 to 29 June, Don and I had a marvellous target in an area south east of Caen. Several ships were firing at our shoot. As the cloud was about 3000 feet and the smoke hung around the area in almost windless conditions, it was necessary to come down low to see. Soon after we had started, Don noticed a bang in his aircraft and he had to leave, landing at B4 — an emergency airstrip on the beach-head. When my relief came — S/Lts Heath and Bowen of No 808 Squadron — I also landed at the same matting strip as Don, as I was short of fuel.

I was just looking at the hole in Don's tailplane when Heath came in with an even bigger hole in his wing. As I had burst a tyre on landing I stayed the night with them while it was repaired. We slept in a tent and listened to the sounds that soldiers hear all night. The straw palliasses, the Army tinned rations and the noise of transport and gunfire all night, reduced our sleep to almost zero. I flew back thankfully next day in my repaired Seafire. The other two came back in a Stinson Reliant, "driven by a mad RAF type," much to their dismay.

Morale was still very high in 3 Wing. This was in spite of about 14 pilots having been shot down and with six killed and four still missing. One was shot down by RAF Spitfires and at least one by our own AA. The RAF at Lee-on-Solent had nine shot down with three killed and the United States had nine shot down with two pilots killed. The total number of spotting sorties by each, respectively, were 1230, 969 and 209. The American losses per sortie, flying fighter aircraft for the first time in their lives, were rather high.

The Jerry air force had tried its best to help its army, as it always did. However, from what I saw of their fighters, I felt that they were a crowd of 'sprogs'. Their leaders seemed to do all the firing and the rest just followed, firing straight ahead on orders, and not at anything in particular. They attacked us, eight against two, and usually came off worst every time. Only when decoys were used did they seem to manage to hit any of us. Perhaps the ascendency which we obviously had over the Fw 190s at this time was responsible for our high morale. It could not have been the success of the spotting, as we were all fighter pilots at heart, not spotters.

So far we had done about 25 sorties of one kind or another over France in the short time of three weeks. There were few signs of fatigue or 'twitch' as there certainly would have been had we been operating from a carrier. Besides being grateful for having Buster Hallett, it was the sheer luxury of an airfield environment, with no need for split-second timings for decklandings, easy navigation, fairly good weather, better radio, proper briefing, good food and a comfortable bunk, space and time, and the possibility of relaxation, which made life so easy when operating from shore.

By the time the major part of the 12th US Army, 2nd British Army and 1st Canadian Army had advanced beyond the range of the battleships' guns, we were beginning to look for jobs to do. Buster asked for permission in accordance with Inskip — from the RAF, Group Captain Jamie Rankin, on B2 airstrip — for us to do several small 'private' fighter sweeps over the area south of Evreux. Then there were 'anti-goose' patrols. These were mini-submarine hunts, conducted to the east of the beach-head over the sea. The idea was to spot two-man German mini-subs on the surface. They were using the west-going tide to take them and their limpet explosives into the Allied anchorage, to blow up a few ships. Several of these were spotted and sunk during daylight, although all that Don and I could see were a few upturned ships' boats and other wreckage. One interesting feature of the anti-goose patrol was that the Germans opened fire on us with their still unsilenced coastal guns at Villerville, sending huge watery spouts up 100 feet into the air.

By 18 July we were spending much time on the grass outside our dispersal, listening as usual to Glenn Miller, Tommy Dorsey, the Andrews Sisters and Artie Shaw, and tinkering with our cars. We were waiting around, hoping to find out what was going on and how long Number 3 Wing would be required at Lee-on-Solent. Buster came out and told us that the RAF heavy bombers — which had done nothing up to that time — were taking over our job and that the Wing would no longer be needed. He told us that the bomb line to the south-east of Caen was so confused that it would be unsafe for any more Naval bombardment for fear of hitting our own troops, and, to the west of Caen, both the Canadian and British Armies had now advanced beyond our range.

In those days we had faith in the accuracy of the heavy bombers, so we totally accepted that it was probably safer for the troops for the RAF to take over around Caen in place of the Naval guns. However, having cleared a three mile bomb line for Harris' bombers, the results "had no observable effect other than to alert the Germans to an impending attack". On this day we also heard that Rommel's car had been attacked on 17 July, the day before — and that he was seriously wounded. We discounted it as our own propaganda, but after the war a Typhoon squadron claimed the success.

A month previously, on 20 June, my name had been in the *London Gazette* for a Mention in Dispatches. Then during the first week in July and in the period of bad weather, Buster had asked me what I would like to do next. This was an extraordinary question to ask a young and rather immature fighter pilot who, at 24 was not yet old enough to be a Lieutenant in the peacetime RN. However, I think that my boss was merely trying to find out whether I wanted to go on with operational flying or whether I would like a quieter sort of job. I opted for operational flying, of course, and also suggested to him that as I had already done a stint as Senior Pilot, I might possibly be included on the list of future

Squadron Commanders if there was such a list. There was nothing like aiming for the top.

But Buster must have taken me seriously, for I got the job, and a good one too, of Commanding 880 Squadron. I received my "repair on board" on 25 July, took two weeks leave and was at Hatston in the Orkneys by 6 August 1944, wondering what had hit me.

Cdr. N. 'Buster' Hallett, DSC, RN. Wing Leader, No. 3 Naval Air Fighter Wing, Lee-on-Solent. 'D'-day, 1944. Note the blitzed hangar in the background.

Barracuda II. *(FAA Museum)*

Furious. *(FAA Museum)*

Corsair F4U. *(FAA Museum)*

Chapter 17
880 Naval Air Squadron

In the few days before going to the Orkneys, my immobile Wren and I had to get used to the new facts of life, that we were to be separated yet again, possibly until the end of the war.

During the five months I had lived — on and off — at our house in Sherborne, we had tried to secure our moorings, but we had found it impossible to plan more than a few days ahead. Neither of us yet had the emotional security we needed and which we had hoped might have come with marriage.

I found that a Seafire LIII needed to be delivered to Donibristle near Edinburgh and I flew up in that, refuelling at Ouston. Thence I sat, terrified, in the back of a de Havilland Rapide with a Lt France driving it.

The flight from Doni/B took two and half hours at an average height of 250 feet above the ground, in heavy rain and a cloud base of 500 feet. The only level part of the journey was across the water of the Pentland Firth. At all other times, a look out of the various windows revealed a series of rushing rivers, steep mountains and shaggy sheep, all at a seeming distance of 50 feet. Meanwhile, Lt France, in his French naval uniform, could be seen clasping the 'spectacles' with one hand and eating his sandwiches with the other, his 'St Christopher' turning and twisting on a string round his neck as if the Saint was trying to hide his eyes from what lay ahead.

On arrival at Hatston I was met by the outgoing CO of 880 — Lt/Cdr (A) 'Moose' Martyn, DSC, RCNVR. Needless to say, with a name like that, he was a Western Canadian; a relaxed six-footer, well known as one of the successful Hurricane COs in *Indomitable*. His most recent major operation had been to provide CAP — with 801 Squadron from *Furious* — on the raid against *Tirpitz*. On this highly successful operation, planning and preparation had been superb, the weather had been kind for high level dive bombing and *Tirpitz* had been caught out of her usual smoke-filled habitat by means of *Ultra* intelligence. She had suffered irreparable damage and she never went to sea offensively again. The new fighters — Corsairs from *Victorious* and Hellcats of 804 and 800 Squadrons from *Emperor* — a new escort carrier — had actually outnumbered the strike aircraft on this raid. This was an entirely new departure in FAA strike history. Moose said that although there were many Me 109s on the adjoining airfields, none had taken off to defend *Tirpitz*. This was odd because the Germans must have had adequate radar warning of the Barracudas' approach. When asked about AA effectiveness from the multitude of guns which we had seen from photographs of *Tirpitz*, he said there were supposed to have been about 80 guns of 40 mm and 20 mm calibre firing at them, mostly from the shore, where they had been landed from the ship. He said that the Germans had probably worked it out that they could not elevate their guns high enough when aiming at a steeply diving bomber, and they had moved their guns ashore for that reason. He also said that the Barras had "got away with it" because they had made a co-ordinated attack and it was all over in about three minutes.

I asked whether Seafires took part and he said that Seafires had been confined to CAP, over the Fleet. The reason was their lack of endurance, even with the 45-gallon slipper tank. I asked 'Moose' about Jerry aircraft opposition. He said that there had been no interceptions on the last three Norway strikes but one of his pilots had been shot down and killed by our own AA.

There had been no serious Seafire decklanding accidents in 880 or 801 Squadrons in *Furious*. This was because the old ship did not have an arrester barrier. If pilots missed the wires they just went round again for another try, as in *Eagle*. The Captain, Captain Phillips, and Commander Flying, 'Ben' Bryant were great characters. *Furious* was obviously a happy ship and the crew knew their squadrons well and *vice versa*.

"But what's the future ploy for our lot in *Furious?*" I asked Moose.

"That's in the crystal ball, old son. They don't tell you a thing until a day before it happens here."

"Who's your, or my, Senior 'P'?"

"Shorty Dennison, (Lt (A) George 'Shorty' Dennison, RNVR), but he'll be leaving and you'll have to get your own replacement. George Whitehead and 'Cherry' Westwood will also be leaving. That will leave you with nine. There's talk of you expanding to 24 and going aboard *Implacable* when she gets out of the builder's yard."

"I've asked for Norman Goodfellow as Senior 'P'," I said. "It looks like 'all change' to me. I suppose it was bound to happen. Most of your chaps are much older than me anyway."

"Well, 'Crusty' Pye's the daddy of the squadron. He's 30. He drove dirt-track bikes for Wembley. He's a very good Seafire driver, too."

Norman Goodfellow arrived next day. I could not have been more thankful and happy. We knew each other well.

Then Norman, Moose and I went aboard *Furious* in an MFV (Motor Fishing Vessel) to meet the Captain and Commander Flying. She was at anchor in Scapa Flow with the rest of the Home Fleet. Norman and I were given a repaired Seafire III each to fly off her deck, back to 880's base at the RAF Station at Skeabrae. The Mark FIII Seafire which we flew was a heavier version of the LIII in 3 Wing. It had heavy catapult spools added and (manually) folding wings. Nevertheless, it leapt into the air from *Furious'* deck at anchor and with only 15 knots of wind.

Moose had arranged for me, and now Norman, to fly to *Ravager* to do some decklandings. Neither of us had done any in Seafires before. She was in the Clyde off Greenock on the other side of Scotland.

After doing six landings each we flew back to the Orkneys on 10 August. Moose then said goodbye to the squadron at Skeabrae and we put him aboard the ferry for Scotland with a spare bottle of Scotch and a carved squadron crest as going-away presents.

Three days later I embarked with my ten pilots aboard *Furious*. There I met the eight pilots of 801 Squadron, and the boss of 827.

The boss of 801, Stuart Jewers, showed me my cabin. My Gieves tin trunk had miraculously arrived on board with one or two spare pairs of pants and things were beginning to settle.

That night, the Captain was 'dined' in the wardroom. He told us that all leave was now stopped and he would be "lighting the candle" again on 14 August. We should be going for a few days ops, 200 miles north of the Arctic Circle. "We shall all be back at Scapa by the end of the month," he said, "our boilers won't stand it for any longer."

Before I turned in that night, Norman and I talked to the men maintaining our aircraft in the hangar. By now, I could just about remember the names of the pilots and the Chief Petty Officer in charge. Norman Goodfellow, Bob Simpson and 'DC' Richardson (ex-21 Course at *St. Vincent)*, Claude Leighton (RNZNVR), Neville Turnbull, Dicky Dankaster, Ken Boardman, Doug Patullo, George Whitehead, Harry Westwood, I. I. Fraser (RNZNVR) and Edwin ('Crusty') Pye.

I took the squadron 'Line Book' to my cabin. The squadron had formed in early July 1941. 'Butch' Judd had been the CO until his death in 'Pedestal' in August 1942 when Dicky Cork took over. After 880 'A' Flight had done the Petsamo/Kirkenes operation on 31 July 1941, the squadron was given eight more Hurricanes (which were just becoming available) embarked in the new carrier *Indomitable,* with Captain Dennis Boyd in command. After taking part in the desperate attempt to defend Ceylon and Colombo from Admiral Nagumo's carrier group, the squadron accompanied *Indomitable* to the Indian Ocean and assisted in the capture of Diego Suarez, Madagascar. The ship and her squadrons returned round the Cape of Good Hope to the Mediterranean in August 1942 for 'Pedestal' with Captain Troubridge in command. In November and while *Indomitable* was under repair in the USA, 880 re-formed in Britain on Seafire Llls and embarked in *Argus* for 'Torch'. After Operation 'Husky' in the repaired *Indomitable,* she having been again damaged, the squadron embarked in an escort carrier — *Stalker* — for Operation 'Avalanche' — the landings at Salerno, in September 1943.

Although the line book made much of the prangs sustained aboard *Stalker* at Salerno — with remarkable photographs of Seafires hanging by their tails with their props dragging in the water and the pilot climbing back aboard over the tail — the squadron did quite well, having enough aircraft left over to supply half the 20 Seafires disembarked to Paestum, a few miles inland from Salerno.

Since 'Avalanche', 880 had embarked again in *Furious* and, with 801 had taken part in several Arctic operations against iron ore shipping and shore installations in the 'leads', off the north and west coasts of Norway. Since the April raid it had also supplied CAP on three further raids on *Tirpitz.* However, none of these subsequent strikes had caught *Tirpitz* with her drawers down, as she was well defended by smoke generators by the time the Barracudas arrived.

When we arrived aboard *Furious,* the name *Tirpitz* was still on everyone's lips. She still represented to the Admiralty the greatest threat since naval warfare began. She kept a fleet of up to four battleships, six cruisers and at least one fleet carrier permanently at Scapa for 18 months of the war and she kept Admirals pacing their cabins throughout the length and breadth of Britain, thinking up new ways of getting rid of her. The most brilliant and successful of these was her total disablement for six months by Godfrey Place's mini-subs in September 1943. Admiral Tovey, C-in-C Home Fleet, ate, slept and drank *Tirpitz,* 24 hours a day. Naturally, we in 880 also became equally paranoid at the sound of her name and were itching to have a go at her ourselves, somehow or other. All this was in spite of the fact that Hitler had announced over two years previously that *Tirpitz* would "never again carry out prolonged operations at sea". In fact she would never fire her guns at ship targets in her life and was now about to become a floating battery, with half her guns and her crew taken ashore and her bottom filled with concrete to keep her afloat. The Admiralty knew most of her movements from 1942 onwards, through *Ultra*. Why they disregarded this priceless information and allowed everyone to get so steamed up over her remains a mystery to this day. Perhaps one of the reasons for their obsession was that *Tirpitz*, unwittingly and without menace on her part, had been directly responsible for the First Sea Lord's tragically wrong order for the entire Russian-bound convoy — PQ17 — to scatter, resulting in the loss of 14 ships to German air attack and U-boats. This order was given by Admiral Pound because he considered that *Tirpitz* was at sea, although *Ultra* told him clearly that she was returning to harbour (because the German Admiral learned that *Victorious* had put to sea after her). Pound, placing himself in the shoes of the German Admiral, could not believe that such a ship could fear an aircraft carrier and could not see why *Tirpitz* should return to harbour.

So that, to be at Scapa in August 1944 was to re-enter the old-fashioned world of the battleship. Who were we to say that our senior officers were all wrong? Yet, had we known it, 40 more aircrew on 200 more bombing sorties by RAF and Russian crews, were to lose their lives driving this wreck of a useless ship deeper into the mud, before the Admiralty and the C-in-C Home Fleet accepted that *Tirpitz* no longer held any menace. Finally, in November 1944, she was capsized in Tromso harbour by Barnes-Wallis' 12,000 lb blockbusters, and the Admirals slept, exhausted, but happy, at last.

My new ship *Furious* was an interesting ship. She had started life in 1917 as one of Admiral Fisher's fast battlecruisers which, with her four 18-inch guns could hurl 1½-ton shells for 30 miles — farther than anyone else. She, and two others, were intended to win the next battle of Jutland. Beatty however, convinced by a greater need for aerial reconnaissance to find the targets for such guns, converted her two forward guns to an aircraft take-off platform for Sopwith Pups. When the pilots subsequently objected to the wasteful ditching of such beautiful aircraft after each flight, a landing platform was erected over the aft guns. By the early thirties she had been fully converted.

When we arrived on board we were introduced to the Officer-in-Charge of the flight deck machinery — Lt/Cdr (E) John Lefaux, RN. He introduced us to his favourite bit of machinery. This worked the aeroplane-shaped lifts, the aerials and arrester wires by driving a hydraulic pump. It was a double-expansion, double/acting, horizontal steam engine. It was fascinating to watch this latter-day piece of high quality British workmanship as it turned two huge flywheels almost silently, at 60 times a minute at full throttle, with its mahogany-lagged cylinders, drip-feed lubrication and its brightly polished gunmetal pistons and connecting rods turning majestically in the bright, carbon-filament lighting — which it also supplied. John Lefaux said that it had originally worked the aft pair of guns in *Furious,* and was second-hand even then.

The "few days ops" mentioned by our Captain, turned out to be yet another go at *Tirpitz*. We were to be joined by *Indefatigable*, newly arrived at Scapa, and by her 36 Seafires, 12 Fireflys and 24 Barracudas. She had two hangars and could carry double the number of aircraft of any British carrier launched so far. She completely swamped our contribution in *Furious*, so that when we sailed, we were very small fry indeed.

This, had we known it, was to be the start of a new method of carrier use — by a combined strike with several carriers, remaining at sea for a considerable period, refuelling the smaller ships at sea, as necessary — a dress rehearsal for the Pacific.

We were all anxious in 880 that our Seafires should be allowed to see some of the action over Norway and not be confined entirely to CAP over the Fleet.

However, as I was a new boy I had to proceed cautiously. Too often, enthusiastic new COs of squadrons had led their boys to their doom. After one day at sea and making good speed, we arrived off St. Kilda, a rocky islet in the Atlantic. We used it for a practice strike with real ammunition and bombs. There was nothing like flying with 880 Squadron to get to know them. We wondered what the St. Kilda fulmar colony must have thought of us.

After this we journeyed north until we were about 350 miles inside the Arctic Circle. As it was summer, the hours of daylight got longer and longer and we spent much time on deck, strapped in our cold cockpits, waiting to hear from *Indefatigable's* radar whether a Ju 88 or two had taken off from Norway to come and search for us.

I also spent some time on *Furious'* bridge in the starboard 'catwalk'. I had noticed some blocks of wood lying around on the gratings. These had come from our Seafires. We used 15 degrees of flap on take-off. The early Seafire IIIs only had a two-position pneumatic selector, fully up or fully down. The intermediate position was only obtainable by using wooden blocks to jam the flaps open for take-off purposes. After take-off the blocks were freed by selection to the down position momentarily. The propeller slipstream and the slight crosswind from port always used for carrier operation (to prevent turbulence in the lee of the Island when landing) deposited them on the bridge. There was a competition between 801 and 880 to see who could get most blocks to hit the Officer of the Watch.

Deck operation and flying from *Furious* was relaxed and easy. The only need for urgency was to make sure that each Seafire, Barra or Firefly approached in pairs, so that if the first aircraft had to go round again for some reason, there was always another one to land immediately behind him. On landing, he would cut his engine and be pushed back to a carefully marked position athwart the aft lift. The lift would then descend with the Seafire, with about two inches clearance, to the hangar. It took about two and a half minutes.

At dawn (0300) on 22 August, eight of us took off for CAP. I had got permission for us to carry out our patrol over Nord Cap, a point of land about 40 miles north of Alten Fiord, where the *Tirpitz* lay. At 2000 feet altitude, *Indefatigable's* radar could still keep us on her plot and vector us onto any Jerries that might make the journey towards the Fleet while the strike was in progress. At the same time we could also cover the withdrawal of the strike as it made its way back to the ship. We were to take off after the strike had set course, so that surprise would not be lost and the Germans would not 'see' us on their 'Würzburg' coastal radar.

Twenty-two Barracudas, armed with 500 pound SAP and 1600 pound A/P bombs formed the main strike. Our four, of 827 Squadron, although they alone had had the experience of making the April strike on *Tirpitz,* were not senior enough and were not leading the strike, neither did they — nor anyone from *Furious* — attend the main briefing in *Indefatigable.*

When we landed after our CAP, having seen nothing except the distant mainland of Norway enshrouded with cloud, we learned that the main strike had turned back when eight miles off the coast due to bad weather. The leader had been told not to go near the coast if the weather looked bad, so that surprise would not be lost for any subsequent attempts. However, we were unaware that the German hill-top radar had already 'seen' the Barracudas, as they had to start their climb 20 miles before they reached the coast. Subsequent strikes were therefore unsuccessful, for *Tirpitz* was by then completely covered with smoke from the smoke generators around her, and bombing was a lottery.

Once the Germans had radar, they could never be surprised by the Barras or similar slow-climbing, low performance, strike aircraft. (See Appendix 2.) However, when the Corsairs and Hellcats later went in alone, surprise was achieved. Instead of staggering in at 100 knots and with a barely perceptible rate of climb they were able to zoom up from sea level at the last moment, giving insufficient time for radar warning of their approach. Thus it was that the only hit of the first day's strikes was made by a Corsair, as they arrived overhead before her smokescreen was properly formed. Furthermore, being fighters, they could manoeuvre easily and neatly round the rain storms, without ploughing straight through them in the headlong and insensitive way that Observer-led strikes seemed to do. Fighter-bombers could also remain in a cohesive group for far longer than the Barracudas when the weather was bad. Their leaders did not consult with each other before every alteration of course, their formations were manoeuvrable and they could see where they were going.

Before embarking on this trip, I had met Lt Geoffrey Russell-Jones, DSC, again, at Hatston. He was still in a high state of nerves from his dreadful Malta experiences and to heap the Barracuda upon him for the April raid afterwards must have tried his spirit beyond its defences, as he himself admits. So that all those who flew this dreadful aircraft anywhere near a hostile airfield in daylight in Norway were brave men, like the Skua pilots before them. We just thanked God for giving us the relative safety of our Seafires.

I had noticed that when I had flown with the RAF, that if other squadrons from other stations were taking part in the same operation, we had always managed to hear how they had got on, the moment we had landed ourselves. This was done to promote thought and discussion on future tactics and to learn fully from past experience. In operation 'Goodwood' we were also operating with other squadrons, but there was as yet no contact whatever with them, either before, during or after the operation. It was therefore impossible in the FAA to learn quickly from each other's experiences.

This state of affairs persisted until the last two days of the war in the Pacific, when the 'Air Group' system was at last begun. So that we only learned *after the war* what had happened to the others taking part in 'Goodwood'. For instance, we saw lots of Seafires landing aboard *Indefatigable* but we had no idea at the time what they had been doing. In fact they had done very well. First, they had taken part in a strike on an enemy seaplane base at Banak and had sunk seven seaplanes at their moorings. Next, their CAP had intercepted two Bv 138 float planes as the Germans took off from this same base to try to find out who'd done it. They intercepted them 30 miles from the Fleet at 700 feet above the sea in appalling weather, and without the help of *Indefatigable's* radar, of course, at that altitude; a superb feat by Lt H. Palmer (SANF) and S/Lt Dick Reynolds in Seafires of 894 Squadron. This would have been of the greatest interest to us in *Furious,* not least because it would have been very encouraging to know that, at last, the four 20mm cannon of the Seafire LIIcs could now outrange the guns and pierce the armour of the Bv 138 aircraft. All we heard was from our own Barras. They claimed three hits on their second strike. After the war, we found that they had had one hit, with a 1600 pound A/P bomb. The bomb had pierced two or three decks and landed on the top of one of the ship's magazines where it had failed to explode. Part of the reason might have been that it was half filled with sand. The 500 pound SAP hit from the Corsair had predictably failed to pierce the eight inch deck armour.

Next day, 23 August 1944, we prepared to get airborne on a repeat performance, but as 'seaweed' forecast a force 10, we went down to the hangar and lashed down our aircraft and prepared for the worst.

The day after, the Captain announced that *Furious* would be returning one day early because of the weather and lack of fuel. The same day we heard that *Nabob,* an escort carrier in company, had been all-but sunk by a torpedo. She and *Trumpeter* later returned in company, with *Nabob*'s quarters awash and making only seven knots.

While we were withdrawing with *Formidable, Devonshire* and a few destroyers, *Indefatigable* (we heard after the war) returned to the area and managed a few dozen more bombs in the general direction of the shrouded *Tirpitz,* though no further hits were claimed.

The Captain decided to use our spare day to make a call upon the Faeroes. These islands, north of the Shetlands, belonged to Denmark. They were fairly friendly to the British. We spent two hours walking ashore and bought some dried fish to put in Crusty Pye's bunk.

We continued back to Scapa, burning some ancient oil normally used for ballast. This caused serious complaints from our faithful destroyers astern. They flashed: "Bridge no longer tenable, steering from aft!" Our skipper made his usual biblical reply — some thoughts about Delilah "Opening a pitcher of rare oils and spices" in Samson's favour.

On 28 August we flew off before reaching Scapa and landed at Skeabrae. Here I found a note in the Mess letter rack inviting me aboard *Kent,* my brother-in-law's cruiser, where he was the Chief Engineer. It was the finest lunch I have ever had in a warship in peace or war. We also witnessed the exit from Scapa of the '*Royal Sovereignski*', an old 'R' Class battleship which Churchill had given to the Russians. When she steamed out, her Russian crew 'cheered ship' in the usual style. Their cheers sounded like the ruminations of a disappointed bull seal, and lacked conviction. I asked my host what possible use she might be to the Russians. He said he had not the slightest idea.

When I got back to Skeabrae, I could not help but notice the difference between life aboard a County Class cruiser and a Naval Air Station ashore. I helped myself to some water at the dinner table. A mosquito larva was swimming up from the bottom of the glass to take a breath of Twatt air at the surface.

There was very little time for social pleasantries for we were soon required to embark again. The trip had originally been planned to include *Implacable,* the sister-ship of *Indefatigable.* With 801 we were to be her two Seafire squadrons, of 24 Seafires each. But she was not ready and poor old *Furious* had to heave up her anchor again and we re-embarked in her.

On 10 September *Furious* and the repaired *Trumpeter,* with 18 of the new American TBM Avengers, set off from Scapa, bound again for the leads off the coast of Norway. The aim was to interdict the German/Norwegian ore-shipping and so encourage the Russians.

The 'M' in the TBM designation of the Grumman Avenger stood for 'mining'. Our task in 880 on 11 September was to provide 'top cover' for 18 mining Avengers in the leads near Statlandet. 801 Squadron was to supply 'close escort'. The operation was given the name 'Begonia'.

The weather was reasonable, only a few snow flurries here and there and with layers of stratus cloud from 1000 to 5000 feet and no sun. I had got permission to come down from top cover once the mining had been accomplished — if there were no Jerry fighters around — to do a bit of strafing with my lot. We found two small flak ships and a minesweeper. Together with 801, we emptied our magazines at these most satisfactory targets, and left them on fire and stopped.

Operation 'Begonia' was a great success, apart from one Seafire and pilot lost, S/Lt Glennie of 801 Squadron.

We returned to Scapa next day and flew off to Arbroath. From there, instead of returning to Skeabrae, we were told to go to Macrihanish instead. So we refuelled and flew across Scotland in good weather, and arrived by teatime on 12 September .

Recently, a new pilot — S/Lt Dennis Kirby — had joined the squadron. He was a large, intelligent-looking chap with a red beard and a ready wit. I had had no time or inclination to set about the task of organising the squadron's bumph (paperwork). Dennis looked just the man for it and was made squadron 'Adj'. His first job was to arrange leave from Macrihanish the moment we arrived. Work on *Implacable* in the Glasgow shipyards was two months late and we would not be required to embark for seven weeks. This would give time for me to get to know the squadron well and perhaps to try to improve the reliability of the Seafire's long range 'slipper' tank system. (See Appendix 11 (k).)

I do not remember much about the fortnight's leave that followed. I flew south from Donibristle by Seafire to Henstridge and back from Lee to Donibristle, so that I could spend most of the leave with my wife. This was a pleasant surprise for us both, for we had more or less written off the prospect of seeing each other again until the end of the Japanese war. On my return to Macrihanish, I found that we were due to get a trickle of new pilots to assimilate: S/Lts Peter Arkell, David Crabtree, CPO 'Chiefy' Watson, S/Lts Bob Armstrong, Alan Dent; Lts Dougy Yate, John Boak (RCNVR); Midshipman Mike Banyard and Ian ('Penny') Penfold. This made 20 in all. Lt Dougy Yate and Bob Simpson were in answer to my special request to the Admiralty, for we needed a stiffening of new flight leaders in place of those who had completed their time in 880. With Norman and Dougy as the nucleus, I now had to find a few more section leaders. Dennis Kirby writes of this period:

". . . You, a very young CO, were taking us all up one by one to see what we were made of in dummy dogfights."

During the winter at Macrihanish, we set about getting to know the squadron ratings. We wanted to show our appreciation of their hard work and their skill. Every pilot had his 'own' aircraft and crew. There were already 80 ratings in the squadron, 40 riggers/fitters, 20 armourers, ten electricians, five radio fitters and five senior ratings including one ex-pensioner Regulating Petty Officer.

So far as discipline was concerned, because we were always moving about between one station and another, I was allowed to 'weigh off' those who were AWOL or who had put up some 'black' or other. I had to use 'Scale' stoppage of leave and/or pay. If the squadron RPO[1], the 'buffer', thought a man needed punishing, he would always tell me first. Everyone knew in advance what the punishment would be and there were never any complaints. Perhaps it was because we got to know the men so well while we were in 'Manchers', through organised squadron dances and other parties with the men, that discipline never became a problem and almost no flying was lost through careless maintenance standards. Much was owed to the Senior Pilot, Norman Goodfellow. He is a solicitor in real life. It must have been his sensible and good humoured approach to the many human as well as the many technical problems, which made life easier for us all for the 12 months he and I were to be in the squadron.

At Macrihanish the squadron and 801 were given the usual small offices and a hangar each. We had a good view of all the 'occurrences' on the airfield. These mostly concerned Barracudas. Two squadrons of Barras were working-up for

[1] Regulating Petty Officer.

duty in the Indian Ocean at this time. There were terrible tales of them flying straight into the sea instead of pulling out from dive-bombing practices. We watched with ribald scepticism as they lined up on the runway for take-off. They looked like so many grey-painted Christmas trees, festooned with ASV aerials, struts, Forth-Bridge-type undercarriage legs, footrests, handholds, ventilation holes, other holes, bay windows, windscreen wipers, hooks, tailwheel guards, rear view mirrors, wing 'fences' and catapult hooks, bumps and sharp edges everywhere, and with faces peering out of every window. At the front, it was just possible to see the tips of the four-bladed propeller sticking out beyond the huge, wide fuselage, originally intended for an engine twice the size and power of the overboosted, short-life, Merlin 30. Altered to a high wing monoplane for the benefit of the Observer — a factor which contributed to tail ineffectiveness when dive brakes were used and many fatal accidents — it was exactly the aircraft one might expect to evolve from 'Group 3' adherents. (See Appendix 2 — Naval Air Power in 1940.)

While the Barra squadrons struggled, luckier Seafire pilots carried out low-level form-ups, stream landings, dogfights, 'splash' firing at a wreck off the Mull, dusk landings and formation aerobatics. Our formation loops and steep turns were quite safe. However, with the changes of yaw with power, and rpm and airspeed in the Seafire, we were unable to make safe formation rolls in fours, but several of us managed it in pairs.

We had several interesting dogfights with the much larger and more powerful F4U Corsair. In turning dogfights, the Corsairs were unable to get a bead on us if we saw them first. However, they could, like the Fw 190, out-dive us (both starting together) because of their much higher density (weight/frontal area). Also, above 15,000 feet, they were faster than Seafire LIIIs. However, the FIII with its two speed, uncropped supercharger, could easily keep up with the Corsair at 20,000 feet and above.

The Corsair could not out-turn a Seafire I, II or III as has been claimed. However, if the Corsair slowed down to about 90 knots and then the pilot selected half flap — provided it was down to its last 50 gallons of fuel — it could hold a Seafire LIII in a turning match at this speed and configuration at heights above 10,000 feet. Below this height, the Seafire, if it did not overheat (Seafire IIIs all had additional thermostatically controlled engine cooling radiators under the port wing), could outclimb the Corsair while making the turn and 'spin it off'. Each type and mark of fighter aircraft ever built has its 'best' height for various performance aspects and where it can out-perform most of the others over a narrow height band. For the Seafire LIII, this height band was 0 — 12,000 feet. During our work-up at 'Manchers', we had our first serious case of a Seafire 'self tightening' in the pullout of a dive which fatally overloaded the wings. This highly dangerous and insidious longitudinal instability characteristic only concerned the Seafire III series, and in particular the 80 or so FIIIs built by the Cunliffe-Owen Company and which had flush riveted fuselages. All pilots were, of course, warned about it and the fitters always inspected the wing-fold bolts after each flight for 'notches'. However, in the heat of action, there was no time to think about such things and there was no easy way of avoiding its consequences for we did not know the basic cause. When a wing came off in action we tended to put such losses down to enemy flak. The pilot never returned to tell us what happened. (See Appendix 11 (c) — Stability problems in the Seafire.)

Chapter 18
HMS Implacable

By September 1944 we were more than ready to embark in the huge *Implacable;* but first she was to have her baptism of Seafires from 24 Wing (Lt/Cdr Wiggington, DSC, RNVR) with 894 and 887 Squadrons. They, and 1771 Squadron of 14 Fireflies, raided the Norwegian leads near Bodo. They sank *U-1061* on the way. One Firefly was hacked down. (It was recently dug up and placed in a Norwegian museum.) During this operation, *Implacable*'s new flight deck party (the 50 ratings organised by Lt/Cdr (Flying) responsible for the movement of aircraft on the flight deck) had had their first Seafire 'incident'. It had made them nervous. One of 887 Squadron's Seafire LIIcs had leaped the barrier and had landed full toss into the forward deck park of 20 other aircraft. In the resulting fire, its 20 mm cannon ammunition had 'cooked off' and shot up several more aircraft. There were many casualties. Number 24 Wing flew south after this work-up operation and finally embarked in their own ship on 30 October, bound for the Indian Ocean, Palembang (January) and Okinawa (March 1945).

We ourselves embarked on *Implacable* (Captain Charles Hughes-Hallet, who had just relieved my old *Eagle* Captain, Mackintosh of Mackintosh) on 8 November, and received a superb welcome. My diary records: "Made a reasonable show except for the start-up at Skeabrae. We had to do this 'pilots only' as our crews had already gone aboard and the RAF were unable to help. We had to unlash and push out, of course. The main trouble was having only one 'trolley-acc' (a half-ton, twelve-volt accumulator on wheels) amongst 14 aircraft. However, Red (mine) and Blue (Simpson's) Flights landed on without fuss in three minutes and 20 seconds, which is very nearly a record. Norman followed with the six remaining aircraft, also without a hiccup. Unfortunately in their second practice sortie, 801 managed to prang our 'D' and their 'R'." This was very unpopular as squadrons did not like using each other's aircraft. Luckily, we again had no accidents and managed to land 12 aircraft in five minutes flat. The third range of the day was cancelled, as *Implac*'s windshield hydraulics 'went for a Burton' and also some of the arrester wires would not reset.

Commander Charles Evans, DSO, DSC, RN, our Commander (Flying) had recently returned from Quonset, USA, where he had been organising the work-up of new Fleet Air Arm F4U Corsair squadrons for the Pacific. He may have been a little disconcerted to find that his new ship, *Implacable,* was to have such a large number of Seafires. However, he soon made it clear to us that he thought we were the best in the world — or shortly would be, under his guidance. He always appeared to be in command even when the Captain was on the bridge and particularly when flying was in progress. He would brook no criticism by non-flying Admirals. He would reply to their signals (which were usually asking pointed questions such as "What is the delay?" or "What was that pilot's name?") in a cool choice of words, which would remind the Admiral that *Implacable* had twice their number of aircraft to land and was already doing so at half their accident rate and in half their time. As a result, we would do anything for Charles Evans.

He had arranged no flying for the next day. The ship was testing her 'degaussing'. This was an electromagnetic arrangement of wires round the ship carrying many thousands of amps in order to reduce the magnetic 'signature' of the entire ship to zero in case she passed over enemy magnetic mines. This meant that we could gather in the wardroom that night and have a few beers and get to know the ship's officers. There were 120 of us airmen and only 40 of them, so we managed to get many of them, including the padré, into a receptive state of mind by bar closing time. They were already learning the words of several of our filthy songs.

Several of us surfaced next morning early enough to finish reading several large tomes of 'Orders'. Charles Evans' Flying Orders started off:

"The difficult we will do at once. The impossible may take a little longer."

Thus *Implac* was called '*HMS Impossible*' from that time onwards. At sea, life aboard was like some overcrowded space ship. Everything in a state of crisis, but seldom falling apart. One of the first 'impossible' things that Charles Evans suggested that I and my squadron should do was to carry out some harbour decklanding practice. As he had not asked 801, we were proud to have a go. I had had the experience of harbour decklandings in *Biter* and thought I knew the snags. As we set off, there was a 40 knot wind whistling round the 'Island' on deck and squalls of rain were over the hills surrounding Scapa Flow. After take-off, the joy of flying over the Flagship at nought feet was cut short by a searchlight from *Implac,* giving us the 'F' for 'Land-on now'.

I had warned the pilots not to land if the ship was swinging out of wind. This annoyed the batsman. He was a 'personality batsman'. This was the new type of batsman who must have done a course of theatricals at RADA. He took it far too seriously, throwing himself all over the deck, his body contorted with signals, several at a time. If, in the midst of one of these extravagant and outgoing gestures, the pilot were to open the throttle smoothly and go round again, making a 'V' sign as he passed a few feet away, well, he could expect trouble when he landed. It was my fault. I should have warned the batsman Lt (A) Trevor David, RNVR — for he was really the most charming man and later became Flight Deck Officer. But there never seemed to be enough time for good manners in *Implacable.*

We had, as our Lt/Cdr (Flying) none other than Charles Lamb, DSO, DSC, RN. Of course, we realised that he must have done something to get the two gongs that he had, but we had to wait until after the war to read his book *War in a Stringbag,* to get the full, unbelievable story. He led his flight deck party with a mixture of terror, kindness, example and pugilistic prowess. They were a very tough crowd indeed, and as everything tended to be their fault when there was a 'balls up', which there usually was, they and Charles Lamb could often be seen giving each other 'the treatment'. If he had asked them, however, they would have knowingly followed him into hell. He was that sort of man.

Implacable had originally been designed to take only a little more than half the 78 aircraft that she would shortly have to accommodate in her two hangars. No guns or other impedimenta had been removed to compensate for the extra space now taken up to be the extra hangar. With 500 extra crew, she was grossly overcrowded. When 880 and 801, with 828 (18 Barracudas) and 1771 (12 Fireflies) arrived, the squadrons' ratings had to take pot luck with the left-over messdecks. The initial result was that most of our squadron were having to sling their hammocks in the passageways. These were in use day and night and our men were being bumped by people trying to get by and were losing their sleep. Many of the more junior officers in the ship had to 'treble up'. As all us (A) RNVR boys were most junior of all, we got a particularly poor choice. I had the deepest, noisiest and least ventilated cabin the builders could have devised. It was three decks down and over the starboard outer screw. Still, it was at least mine own and there was plenty of room to spread out.

On 21 November 1944, we set off for northern Norway again in company with two Woolworth carriers, *Trumpeter* and *Pursuer.* This, we thought, was in the nature of a working-up exercise for *Implac* before she and ourselves went out to the Far East to fight the Japs.

My diary reports:

"Implacable, with the two 'banana boats', stayed out of sight and sound of the Norwegian coast for the next three days, waiting for a 'window' in the weather. It has been blowing a 70 knot gale all day (23 November) and that was as good as saying goodbye to the two banana boats. One's flight deck began to bend in the middle and unpeel. The other, *Pursuer,* had trouble in her hangar, most of her aircraft breaking loose and ramming each other. We think there may be a shipping strike tomorrow. We and 801 might be allowed to shoot up Orlandet airfield, and if there's nothing there, to find some shipping near Trondheim."

"Monday 26. The weather has at last improved somewhat. Hanging about with everyone seasick was getting on everyone's nerves. We were able to carry out a strike involving about 40 aircraft today. We took off in a snow storm, not good for the nerves, and over the target area (south west of Alsten, round Vefsen Fiord) there were frequent rain storms. In a clear patch we saw four big ships and half a dozen flak boats in a convoy that the Firefly recce had reported. We were supposed to be top cover, but once again Charles Evans said we could come down and do a bit of strafing if there were no Jerries about. The first ship I came across in the fiord was a small flak ship. It started to fire as I dived on it. I opened fire at about 1000 feet — and using the gyro gunsight to correct drift — in half a second the whole ship disappeared in white spray as the 20 mm hit all round her. As I was pulling out below the cloud I could see a larger ship with smoke already coming from it, so I gave that a burst too, followed by all the rest. She was stopped or going slowly towards the rocks and seemed to be on fire." (She was the *SS Korsnes,* a Norwegian ship of about 3,000 tons, which later sank.) "I later saw her discharging grey-clad German troops over her bow, on to the rocks."

Implacable seemed satisfied with the day's strike. Two flak ships sunk, one stopped and on fire and our *Korsnes* on fire and sinking. After the war I sent a copy of my G45 camera-gun film to Knut Store, a Norwegian, and he told me that the *Korsnes* was being used for running military supplies and army replacements to the north from Germany at the time. The Norwegian skipper had taken the first opportunity to run his ship aground when she was hit. Armour piercing and high explosive cannon fire and 3" rockets seemed to be very effective. The 3" solid, rocket projectile, eight of which were carried by Fireflies, was a ship-sinking weapon and much more accurate than bombs, particularly when using the GGS.

On the way back we joined in with a couple of returning Fireflies from 1771 and strafed some oil tanks at Mojoen, near Sandnessjoen. We saw no results from our shell flashes as they hit the tanks and there were no results from theirs aimed at us. After this strafe, I looked down at my compass — the gyro compass — and found that it had toppled with the pullout having been over the vertical. I had to reset it from the magnetic compass. This was easier said than done, for we were so near the earth's magnetic North Pole that the angle of dip was nearly 80 degrees, allowing no proper horizontal component. With the slightest angle of bank, the needle would execute a complete 180 degrees towards the earth and stay there. Eventually I remembered what 'Buggy' Muir had taught me in the physics lab at school. I turned the aircraft — together with the seven others — towards what I hoped was a northerly course and waited patiently with wings level until the compass needle settled down. I was then able to reset the gyro compass and steer for the ship, using the ship's beacon.

"There is the usual talk of a gy-normous gale, Force 11, tomorrow, so we are going west at 25 knots to try to get out of its way. The millibars on the weather chart look like the cross-section of an oak tree. All 50 of our aircraft were recovered without a single accident, except our favourite New Zealander Claude Leighton, who burst a tyre. One of the Barras of 828 broke one of its immense undercarriage legs off. The wreckage was towed forward by the tractor, but the leg was left behind. A couple of sailors thereupon tried to shove it over the side to clear the deck for the next man to land on. They couldn't move it. Eventually eight were needed."

"It is marvellous seeing Charles Lamb's 'supporters' working on the flight deck. It's just like a Rangers v Celtic football match when the spectators get on the pitch, with Charles Evans adding his pithy comments from time to time over the Tannoy. There is never a dull moment and 'a seat in the goofers is worth 50 quid', cold though it is. Trouble is, I or Stuart Jewers have to get up on Charles' bridge during every land-on. It is a harrowing sight, sometimes. Today, when eight men were pushing my aircraft from one side of the deck to the other, *Implac* rolled badly. The man on the brakes was too late and they shoved some chocks under the wheels to stop her going over the side while she was doing five knots. She nosed over until the prop hit the deck and two bits broke off. It's either a prop change or a 'cropping' job, to make them all an equal diameter and weight."

It was a frightening sight watching up to 30 men pushing and heaving the three-ton machines in a 50 knot gale, controlled by a Petty Officer with a flag, a man on the brakes in the cockpit and two further men ready to place chocks in front or behind the wheels for an emergency stop. Yet there were very few cases of damage to our Seafires. In two cases of cockpit damage, Crusty Pye had his radio socket crushed by a boot and another had his long-range tank jettison lever half-pulled so that it dropped off on take-off and caught fire as it slid along the deck, plunging into the sea just ahead of the ship.

At the end of this period of flying in *Implacable*, 880 had done 127 decklandings with only two burst tyres. This was then a record for any continuous one-squadron effort with Seafires, but had we been at Salerno with 15 knots of wind over the deck, we should have had half a dozen by now. We flew off to Skeabrae on 5 December, having waited off Norway in vain for the weather to moderate again. While on the way back, I had asked Charles Evans whether there was any chance of my seeing the new, very 'clued-up' Fifth Sea

Lord, Dennis Boyd, to use his influence to get us some better Seafires, the Mark XVs. These had a Griffon engine of about 1800 horse power combat rating, more fuel, plus a stronger, 'long stroke' undercarriage, capable of withstanding heavier landings. It also had more external fuel in the form of a proper bullet-shaped tank of 60 gallons and had rocket launchers. It all seemed to be just what we wanted and there were several of them already flying. (See Appendix 11 (m).) Considering that we now know that the first low-level Griffon-engined version of the Spitfire — the Mark XII — had been in service since January 1943, my hopes were well justified that the FAA should have them a year later.

'Wings' allowed me to fly off from the ship. I was delayed on the way to North Weald by fog at Milltown and Crail, but I eventually arrived at the Fifth Sea Lord's Office in St. James's Square, and was shown in.

He removed the wraps from the future FAA models he had round his office walls. They all looked very formidable and complicated, especially the Blackburn Firebrand. Its nose seemed longer, by far, than the Corsair, and its size about the same as a heavy bomber. I asked what it was. Admiral Boyd said that it was the new torpedo/fighter/bomber — the new multi-role combat aircraft for the Fleet Air Arm. I also saw the new 'cut down' Centaurus-engined Typhoon (later the Sea Fury) which was on order at the time, and a Griffon-engined Barracuda and a Short Sturgeon. He could make no promises for the Seafire XV, the first 40 of which had not yet fully passed through the Storage Depots. (The first flight of a Spitfire with a Griffon had been by Jeffrey Quill in November 1941.) Neither would we get clearance to use the new 'Zero Length' rocket launchers for our existing Seafires. He said that their rocket motors were only cleared to fire safely in low air temperatures. I returned north, empty handed.

While I was away, *Implacable* had gone to sea again for another strike on Norway, but she was unable to embark either 801 or ourselves on the planned day, and by the time I returned, she had been so damaged in a storm that she had to retire into dock for two months at Rosyth. This effectively put an end to Admiral Sir Bruce Fraser's plan to use *Implacable* as well as *Indefatigable* in the Pacific for Operation 'Iceberg', March-May 1945.

We were now about to have an entire change of aircraft Marks, from IIs and FIIIs to FLIIIs. Apart from that, we had to train up 15 new pilots — each straight from Fighter School — in elementary interceptor fighter and decklanding skills and also in ground attack and escort fighter duties. An additional task was to instruct them in the use of the Gyro Gunsight (GGS) and, for eight out of the 20 pilots, to use the vertical and oblique reconnaissance F24 cameras, with which six of our new (PR) aircraft were fitted.

We also had to be allowed some time for Christmas leave. In order to make our unexpected arrival home more welcome, we decided that we would each take a turkey with us on the journey south. Dougy Yate, whose father ran a chain of London East End butcher shops, knew all about turkeys, and he came round on the squadron BSA motorbike and side-car to visit the crofters on the islands. The crofters would then parade their turkeys, either in the farmyard or in the kitchen, depending on the weather. Dougy would pick the ones he liked, diving on the poor birds before they knew what was coming. Our cabins at Skeabrae were full of feathers for the next few days as Dougy organised a squadron plucking party.

In the snow of January 1945, we set about collecting our new aircraft. Some had already arrived while we were on leave, by the ladies of the ATA. Dougy was wondering how they managed at five 'g'. He reckoned their bra straps would part. He invented a new type, with a cantilever system of weights and pulleys, which was self-compensating. The Mark II version used more sophistication still — solenoids and rheostats to arrange constant uplift at all 'g' loadings from minus two to plus eight.

We had to taxi our 'old' aircraft to a dispersal hangar. This was three miles from the airfield and up a country road with an incline of 1:5 in places. The road was covered in snow. This was badly rutted and it was necessary to have a person walking alongside to direct the pilot away from the ruts and the hidden ditches either side. Half way, with the radiator temperature over 120 degrees C and the brake pressure nearly zero, we would stop to replenish and cool down. It took several days, but it was accomplished without more than a single ditching.

Half way through January 1945, just as the snows had melted and we could guarantee that we would be able to stop in time on the runway (which had not been cleared of snow and had therefore become icy) we were told to take ourselves to RNAS Grimsetter — a new FAA-owned wartime airfield. It was on the opposite side of the island, north of Kirkwall. We were getting too big for RAF Skeabrae.

At Grimsetter, we were joined by Lt/Cdr Colin Campbell-Horsfall. Our two Seafire squadrons were now known collectively as 30 Wing — not 38 Wing as in some history books. 'C-H' was a magnificent choice as our Wing Leader.

Seafire L III. A sequence of three photographs showing a barrier crash. Note broken tailwheel and propeller.

Lt. (A) Norman Goodfellow, DSC, RNVR. Senior Pilot of 880 Squadron, August 1944 — October 1945.

Seafire II, a midday take-off from *Furious,* off Northern Norway, Winter 1944.

Chapter 19
Grimsetter

The domestic arrangements at Grimsetter left something to be desired. We were beset with failures in heating, fuel supply and transport. However, with a diet of baked beans and watery beer we would repair to the squadron dispersal, shut the doors and windows and build up a nice fug with the coal burning stoves.

Most of the squadron had read the famous inscription on a Northern Ireland tombstone. This read:

'Where e'er you be
Let your wind go free.
'Twas holding it in
What kilt me.'

So the atmosphere could have grown a lettuce by lunchtime. Something had to be done. Dougy Yate devised a system of fines. The price list was as follows:

880 Squadron, FART FUND Price List			
Type	Description	Price	Remarks
Peep	Short, musical note	1d	Very small effect
Fizzy Foo	Intermittent	Free	Highly Entertaining
Dandy Peep	Longer, with high steady note	2d	Small effect
Fandauzer	More noise, deeper note	3d	Routine
Royal Fandauzer	High pressure version of above, very noisy.	4d	Vulgar. Inclined to overshoot.
Scotch Mist[1]	Silent	6d	Insidious
'Harry' Clearers[2]	Dreadful	1/-	Mass evacuation of crew room[3]

Notes:
[1]Duty Boy to judge, if no one owns up to items starred.
[2]Credit is allowed. Please enter fines against your name on list alongside.
[3]Patrons are asked not to evacuate the crew room unnecessarily as it cools the place down too much.

Dougy found that 'Note (3)' was necessary, as those who thought that the fund needed a boost would suddenly get up in a mass evacuation for insufficient reason. An unsuspecting type would then be left behind to pay.

In February we had a charming visit from Major Michael Scott and his C-Balls assistants who were joining *Implacable*. They arrived at dispersal in a desert-camouflaged Austin tourer, with the hood down, still bronzed from last year's summer spent in the south of England.

Their Lordships had by now realised that they were losing their best surviving pilots for ever in making them continue to fly too long on operations. They therefore took 'DC' Richardson and Neville from us. However, 'Crusty' Pye and Bob Simpson (Willy's younger brother) became replacement Flight Leaders for Richardson. C-H became the sixth on occasions, when he flew with us. We were also joined by Doug Graham (a 26-year-old married New Zealander), Len Simpson, Brian Wager, 'Legs' Lathan, Peter Dixon (another New Zealander) and 'Paddy' Seigne. These made our numbers up to 23. Two or three others did not make the grade. It was most unusual to refuse the selections made by NA2SL — the appointments division in the Admiralty for Fleet Air Arm aircrew — but time was short. 'Below average' pilots were unable to make the grade in the time available. They would have been a danger to themselves and to the rest of us, had they remained, for 880 Squadron was now adopting some very 'dicey' ground attack methods and these took a month or two to assimilate.

During our stay at Grimsetter from 15 January to 15 March 1945, we heard stories of the trials and tribulations of the Seafires in 24 Wing now in the Dutch East Indies in *Indefatigable*. This was only hearsay on the grapevine but it reminded us of the Salerno business and rang true. The Seafires had long lost their original Wing Leader, Buster Hallett (to 3 Wing for the 'D' Day operations at Lee-on-Solent), and their recent training in the UK had tended to suffer. We heard, in disgust that the two Seafire squadrons (887 and 894, Lt/Cdr 'Shorty' Dennison (later Andrew Thompson) and Lt/Cdr Jimmy Crossman) had been confined either to CAP over the Fleet, or to anti-submarine low-level reconnaissance, or to making practice Kamikaze attacks on the Fleet for the benefit of their gunners. Their morale had suffered and, at one stage, because they had only 17 aircraft left out of the 33 after only seven hours flying per pilot — mostly due to decklanding accidents — they had been stopped from flying altogether. Something better would have to be offered by 30 Wing if Admiral Vian, the AC1 to the Far Eastern Fleet, was going to put up with us when we arrived there. So we practised our 'ground attack' exercises.

Norman, Dougy and I had had much experience in 804 in manoeuvring fighter formations easily in the air. All that was necessary now was for us to use this formation and method of manoeuvre to position our Seafires for a *simultaneous* dive on ground targets, so that the strafing attack could be completed within about 20 seconds and before the enemy gunners could 'remove their fingers'. Up to 16 of our Seafires would dive simultaneously from three different directions, and the enemy would not know which to aim at. After careful thought, we worked it out that 16 Seafires diving at once would have only one sixteenth of the gunners firing at each Seafire for one sixteenth of the time! In theory, we would therefore have about 60-100 times less chance of being shot down. Our formation dive, from at least three entirely different directions, would also reduce the time taken to re-form afterwards and so save fuel.

We practised these co-ordinated attacks — with radio silence — on every 'target' we could find. Islands in the middle of Scottish lochs, various ships —

with prior permission — and our own airfield and dispersals. At times our aircraft crossed over each other in the pullout of the dives. Of course there was bound to be danger from our own shells when we used our guns instead of the camera-guns. However, we reckoned that the risks from this were slight compared with the risk of coming down singly to zero feet on an airfield well alerted and defended by 200 guns or more. We naturally used a low level approach. This obvious precaution allowed us to approach unseen by the enemy radar or enemy lookouts. The climb up to the pushover height of 8,000 feet was left until the last possible moment to give no radar warning, so that the enemy gunners might still be asleep, be shaving, or be drinking Suki-Aki or whatever Japanese gunners do. It was matters such as this that made us in 880 feel special. Of course we were not special. We were just ordinary. But we thought we were special and that was half the battle. However, as far as I know, no one else used this form of attack. Our (actual) losses due to flak were one tenth of Corsair or Hellcat squadrons' per operational sortie.

With *Implacable* capable of flying off at least 50 aircraft in one strike — more than two (British) carriers-worth heretofore — constant decklanding practice was essential. Knowing the poor reserves of fuel which Seafires had, take-offs, form-ups, returns and land-ons had to be done in the minimum of time.

We knew that decklanding accidents in Seafires were inevitable, and were a certainty when landings were made into the sun, in heavy rain, on a pitching deck, with exhausted pilots or with defective aircraft. The slightest thing would put the pilot 'over the top' in his battle with his nerves. Everything, therefore, had to be done by constant practice, to make the difficult stuff appear easy. The brain would then be better able to cope with the landing itself, the 'impossible' bit. (See Appendix 11.) We aimed at 20-second decklanding intervals. Charles Evans was always delighted if we made it. However, in order to keep to an average of ten seconds, some had to be within ten seconds of each other, with the barrier still down while the next chap was over the round-down. As it was Charles' responsibility, he would always take a risk. It usually came off, but with half-a-second to spare sometimes.

Seafire Mark III take-offs were never a problem, for R. J. Mitchell had designed the Spitfire I for quick 'scrambles' and the Seafire LIII's power/weight ratio was even higher. With a 30 knot wind, it leapt off the deck in a distance of 130 feet, with a minimum unstick speed of 58 knots! Even with a 90 gallon overload tank, we could still get airborne safely with a run of 180 feet in that windspeed, half the distance of the catapult runs of today.

While we were at Grimsetter, we had all 48 Seafires in the air at once. This must have been a 'first' for the FAA from a single carrier. With C-H fighting our administrative battles for us, Stuart and I could concentrate on the flying and it seemed to be paying off. Morale was higher each day.

One day the Wing was practising its 'live' dinghy drill in Scapa Flow with an ASR (Air/Sea Rescue) Walrus. The exercise needed a 'baled-out' pilot to be rescued from his dinghy in his Mae West. The Walrus had to land alongside the pilot, who would be using his distress flares, dye marker and mirrors — if there was any sun — for all he was worth. The Walrus would taxi past with one wing over the top of the dinghy. The dinghy occupant would then catch hold of the wing and be hoisted aboard the Walrus wing and then through the hatchway in the hull and flown back to the ship. Midshipman Ian Penfold of 880 Squadron had volunteered for this task in spite of a water temperature of four degrees Centigrade and with no immersion suit. We watched from the rescue launch, cheering from time to time. That night we drank to Penny and we sang 'For he's a jolly good fellow'. The high-domed Nissen hut wardroom was just the place for singing, with John Boak, the Canadian, at the piano.

Next day we did another of our 32 aircraft 'Balbos'. This naturally involved formation take-offs in pairs, otherwise we would all have run out of fuel before we had time to form up and land.

I did not see the accident myself or even hear of it until I had landed, for we operated in r/t silence. Penny had 'gone in' on take-off. His aircraft had piled in at the end of the runway in flames. A vital piece of evidence showed us what had gone wrong.

A few days before his immersion, Penfold thought that he would go to Hatston and ask the stores department to renew his flying gloves. These were long, leather gauntlets with a zip fastener from the wrist to half way to the elbow. The zip had bust on his right glove and he wanted a new pair.

The Commander (S) at Hatston, having already refused us a *pair* of boots on occasion, had refused to give Penny a pair of gloves and had only offered him one in replacement. He would then have had a new glove on his right hand and a well worn soft and comfortable glove on his left, with a different pattern of 'feel' altogether. The stick forces in a Seafire were a matter of ounces, not pounds, and a gentle touch was essential for smooth flying. So Penny refused the new glove and continued with the old, the zip fastener of which would not zip up at all.

It was found that his right hand had jammed in the cockpit hood, held by the remains of his glove. While shutting the hood, sliding it forward from its leading edge with his right hand, the outflow of air through the gap between the windscreen and the forward part of the sliding hood had taken the unzipped part of his glove over the top of his hand and had jammed it in the hood as he closed it, imprisoning his hand and holding it in front of his face in the vital seconds after take-off. In formation, it was enough for Penny to lose control, and he hit the ground in the second or two when he could not see where he was going.

We all felt very angry and I felt particularly sad having to tell Penny's parents, who came up for the funeral. He was such a lovely fellow.

By February 1945, most of us in 30 Wing, in 1771 Firefly Squadron and 828 Avenger Squadron were quite certain that our next stop would be alongside the Americans in the Pacific. It was obvious that our Seafires would be required for low level CAP against the expected hoards of Kamikazes. However, C-H wanted to be sure that we were also capable of joining in strikes as well as 'ramrods' — provided we could get a suitable long range tank for our Seafires — so it was necessary to practice fighter support with the Avengers and Barracudas. In spite of the recommendation — following my NAFDU trial a year previously — that formation corkscrewing and close escort of Avengers with Seafires was out of the question and that '*area* defence', like the RAF, was the only feasible form of fighter defence for slow-moving, low altitude, strike aircraft, the Avengers still insisted on *close* escort. They wanted the reassurance of being able to look out of their aircraft and actually see us there. We could appreciate their viewpoint — with Zeros about — but we wanted to tell them of our difficulties too. We had all had experience of attempting to formate on 100 knot aircraft with our Seafires or Hurricanes — whose minimum safe flying speed was about 160-180 knots. It was very difficult indeed, even with very small numbers and in crystal clear weather. To attempt it in bad weather or through cloud with enemy fighters about, was madness.

Many of the strike squadrons were commanded by Observers. This was doubtless because the Observers had had a head start over the pilots in the FAA due to the Navy's 'foot in the door' policy in the early thirties, where RN Observers were much more numerous than RN pilots. We sympathised with their job, of course and realised they were extremely brave men — being flown by someone in the front and unable to see where they were going. However, we were sceptical about their ability to lead a formation from the back seat and found little in common with them when we tried to explain our difficulties to the very few from other carriers that we managed to meet. Our difficulties were compounded still further when we found that nearly all Operations Officers in carriers were also Observers (ours in *Implacable* was ex-*Dasher* of Oran fame) and had not the smallest appreciation of a single-seat fighter pilot's difficulties. However, if we were to be allowed to take part in any strikes at all in the Pacific, we were in honour bound to, at least, try a few practice strikes with the Avengers, before we left the UK.

All our practice strikes had so far taken place with Barracudas of 828 Squadron in *Implacable*. As usual, they led us into the nearest cloud — and that was that. However, we could at least meet the CO of 828 afterwards and apologise and give our reasons for our disappearance en route. In the case of much larger exercises involving other carriers' strike aircraft, we could not meet them afterwards (or before, for that matter) to tell them of our difficulties. There was no 'Air Group' organisation, as in the RAF, and therefore nothing was done to remedy matters. We found that other carriers' strike leaders were usually senior to our own, so that we could not meet them to tell them that we wished to give them 'area support' and 'top cover' and their ideas on close escort were a waste of time and effort. When we got to the Pacific and read the American equivalent of our *Flight Deck,* we learnt for the first time how they managed. They had such a large number of aircraft in each carrier — up to 110 each — that they could mount an entire strike, unsupported by any other carrier's aircraft. In this way, they could brief and debrief their strike and escort aircrews and learn from their experience as time went on. In the case of the BPF, with only half the aircraft per carrier, strikes had to be made up from two or more carriers' aircraft, with the 'junior' leaders totally ignorant of where their seniors might be going until they were on their way and had been briefed in the air, somehow.

We knew little of the command structure of the BPF, except that we knew that Admiral Vian was our AC1 and that he had been having a difficult time with his Seafires in *Indefatigable* in January 1945 when he had received his first baptism of fire from the Japanese in the East Indies. Nevertheless, during the next three months, his carrier fleet had greatly contributed to the downfall of the Japanese Army and Navy in that area. It had destroyed one third of the Japanese Southern Pacific oil supply, with strikes on Medan, Soeni Gerong and the docks and General Motors works at Batavia and the Palembang oil refinery. This series of strikes, together with Japan's lack of aircrew to replace their huge losses at the hands of the magnificent American carrier-borne fighters, contributed significantly to the Japanese retreat from their southern outlying island strongholds, one by one.

We heard of the Japanese new method of attack and how it had made our gunners even more trigger-happy and that life was getting even more difficult for the Seafires of 24 Wing in *Indefatigable.* If they chased Kamikazes to the bitter end, they got fired at. If they returned to the Fleet short of fuel — having chased a non-Kamikaze decoy out of sight to no purpose or perhaps even shot it down — they got fired at. Finally, if they stood by, strapped in their cockpits on the flightdeck, they got the personal attention of a complete Kamikaze in their cockpit.

From January - March 1945, 30 aircrew had been lost at Palembang and other operations in the East Indies. Nine of these losses of aircrew were left behind at Palembang and were subsequently beheaded by the Japanese. They had made their way to the rendezvous to be picked up, but fuel shortage dictated the Fleet's retirement and the rescue Walrus was told to leave them behind. We had no illusions in 30 Wing about our fate if we were taken prisoner, all we hoped for was, that if we baled out, someone in the tradition of Admiral Troubridge and Nelson would stay behind and rescue us.

So that, as we sailed out of Scapa on 15 March 1945, *Indefatigable* had completed her East Indies strikes and was on the way to her next operation with a reinforced BPF, operating from Sydney. The new BPF's task was to help the Americans in their onslaught on the fortress island of Okinawa. The operation was to be called 'Iceberg', and the BPF was under the seagoing command of Admiral Sir Bernard Rawlings in *King George V*, with Admiral Sir Bruce Fraser as overall, shore-bound C-in-C in Sydney and, of course, Admiral Vian as AC1 in command of the BPF carrier force.

The events leading up to Okinawa were these: in the preceding autumn, General MacArthur's wish to make 'a media' return through the surf of the Philippines had led to a sea battle near Leyte in which most of the remaining Japanese seagoing fleet had been sunk or put out of action. The Japanese could neither understand their own plan nor that of the Americans, but as the latter had a far greater and more flexible carrier force and better communications, they prevailed in the end, inflicting immense air losses on the Japanese as well.

After this victory off Leyte Gulf, the Third Fleet under Admiral Halsey cleared away for 'Iceberg' — the attack on Okinawa. This island had been a Japanese possession since 1880. It was a vital step across Japan's supply route to their possessions further south and east. It had to go. The secondary task given to the British in 'Iceberg' was to interdict the airfields on an island chain which also lay across the Japanese air reinforcement route from Japan to Okinawa itself — Sakashima Gunto. Each of the four main islands had an airfield which required to be flattened and kept that way throughout the expected short period that the American amphibious forces would take to capture the airfields on Okinawa. Once these airfields were in American hands they could be turned over to the USAAF and the new B29s, and some of the medium range bombers. All of these aircraft could reach the mainland of Japan from north to south and the way could be opened up for an Allied landing on the Japanese homelands in the autumn.

The BPF spent five weeks in Sydney harbour preparing for the new offensive in the Pacific, but when they left Sydney on 10 March for the north they still did not know exactly where they would be required. First they called in at Manus. This was an equatorial offshore island in the British Admiralty Group seized back from the Japanese by the Americans a year previously. By 15 March they had reached Ulithi, a further 2000 miles north. Here it was decided that the BPF should be under the command of Admiral Halsey rather than Admiral Kinkaid further south, as the British supply system could now cope with a 3500 mile supply line from Sydney far better than the Americans had first thought.

It was an enormous and unaccustomed task for the BPF to keep itself supplied at sea. Having been designed for Europe and without refrigeration or air-conditioning, and yet having promised Admiral King that it would not sponge upon the Americans — even for its supplies of aviation and fuel oil — Admiral Rawlings would be hard pressed to find a way. A British Fleet Train of 60 ships was therefore organised to carry out the task of supply. It was trundled north from Sydney in advance of the main force, the single journey itself taking a fortnight.

The southern end of this supply route ended in Sydney docks where the dockies were notoriously difficult. There were continuous go-slows and blackings and several ships had to sail half loaded. Mail, however, did not suffer, as it came via San Francisco, and morale was good even if general health among the BPF was not. The inevitable substitution of fresh food and vegetables with powdered (dehydrated) food and food in tins, took its toll early on in 'Iceberg' and the doctors could do little to stop dysentery. There was also an immense difference in the American aviator's life style. (Appendix 12.) Often they carried an overbearing of 50 aviators so that if ill health struck they could continue at full throttle with their flying programmes. All their carriers were superbly air-conditioned throughout. Thus, when the Kamikaze onslaught at Okinawa delayed the capture of Okinawa for an unexpected week of flying, the BPF began to suffer from lack of aircrew, replacement aircraft and poor health. Nevertheless, the four British carriers — *Indom, Vic, Indefat* and either *Illustrious* or *Formidable* — flew 2500 sorties between them in 28 days flying. They lost 41 aircrew and needed 173 replacement aircraft at the end, having started with 225. Twenty-six aircraft were lost to flak, none to air combat and another 43 wrecked on deck by four hits by Kamikazes. The armoured decks of the British carriers could easily withstand the gentle 300 knot arrival of a Kamikaze complete with bomb, but this same arrival went right through the Americans' decks, taking deck-parked and loaded aircraft down into the hangars with it. Explosions and fire amongst the Americans took their toll.

During 'Iceberg' the BPF claimed to have destroyed 100 aircraft on the ground in the target areas, but they were unable to interdict the airfields to prevent aircraft movements. Another lesson learned by the BPF — beside the near impossibility to close an airfield by spasmodic interdiction — was that the Japanese AA appeared to be aiming at the leaders of strafing and bombing attacks almost exclusively as they dived in steady lines, one after the other at their ground targets. Four out of the eight COs were killed as a result.

On 10 April we heard that the last of the giant Japanese battleships — *Yamato* — had been sunk, with only 170 survivors out of a crew of 3000. She had put to sea from Japan with a one-way supply of oil, intending to commit suicide like some mammoth and senseless Kamikaze. She failed to fire even one effective shot in the war, or against the 40 American aircraft which sank her. It appalled us to think we should soon be fighting such an enemy.

Such was the true picture of what we should find on our arrival in the Pacific, one tenth only of which we knew at the time.

880 Squadron before enlargement, September 1944.
Left to right: Yate, Leighton, Penfold, Richardson, Boardman, Simpson, Pye, Patullo, Frazer, Turnbull, Kirby, Author, Goodfellow.

Seafire F III. *(FAA Museum)*

Anti-shipping strike off Norway, 1944. *(Stuart Jewers)*

Chapter 20
'Sydney, here we come!'

Let us return to Scapa. When we repaired aboard *Implacable* with our 48 Seafires and 49 pilots of 30 Wing on 15 March 1945, we knew that many of us would be saying goodbye to our wives and sweethearts for ever. Nevertheless morale was high. The 880th 'persoot group' had now made a running total of 243 landings without a serious prang and bets were being made as to which pilot would break this record spell. Brian Wager obliged on 22 March, making a full toss into the barrier, never higher than six inches off the deck, with his hook bouncing between the wires, its damper u/s. We all, including Wager, said a rude word.

On our way into the Atlantic we carried out four days intensive flying while spare aircraft from the UK were still within flying distance. Lt/Cdr Alan Swanton, the CO of 828 Squadron — newly equipped with Avengers — was also glad of the practice. Although the Avenger was a very easy, strong and highly prized replacement for the Barracuda, the pilots only had about 20 hours flying experience in it and needed more. Lt/Cdr (A) Jock Ellis, DSC, DFC, RN, the CO of our 1771 Firefly Squadron, hit the round-down on a night decklanding approach and was not found in the icy waters. Lt/Cdr (A) Bill MacWhirter, RN took over the squadron in his place.

The Flight Deck party now seemed to have settled down, but the ADR team still had a lot to learn. They could not yet match Tricky's skill in spite of having a better radar.

On 4 April we passed through the Straits of Gibraltar. It was nice to think we almost 'owned' the Mediterranean now and that stand-bys on deck were not necessary.

We stopped for 24 hours at Port Said. This showed that the Commander and the Captain had great faith in the crew's discipline, for none missed the ship when we sailed, a very good sign. We were there long enough for some of us to have a walk through Simon Artz' bazaar and buy a few trinkets and a fez each. Dougy, Norman and I and a few others went ashore in the evening and went upstairs into a bar. The only drink available was 'oozoo'. It made you blind if you had too much, so we only had about three each. On the way back to the ship, Dougy was approached by a small boy, who said:

"Like my sister, Sah? All white inside like Mrs Captain?"

We had been warned about such things by the more experienced officers on board. Our Chief Engineer, Commander Holt-Wilson, told us how some friends of his in another ship had fared one night in Cairo, earlier in the war. They had been caught with their pants down in 'Mary's' — a house of evil repute in Cairo. The reason they had been caught was because Mary's suffered a direct hit with a bomb. They thought they had better submit 'Hurt Certificates' in case their visit had any long-lived consequences — from the bomb damage. When they came to the column in the Hurt Certificate which asked them to 'Name the place of duty where the injury occurred', they gave Mary's address. Their Lordships returned their certificates, demanding what duty they were performing there. Back went the reply to the Fleet Medical Officer at Alexandria, that they were blown in through the front door by the bomb blast as they happened to be walking past. So they received their certificates in due course.

During our run south through the canal, we exercised on the hot steel deck, melting the soles from our shoes and wondering why the British had imagined that the canal could ever have been much use to them — and worth 70 years of Egyptian subjection — in an air war. *Implacable* would have made a perfect bombing target, surrounded with sand, still air and a blue sky. As we walked up and down we began to notice that the slight breeze over the deck had fallen calm. The ship had stopped, slightly aslant, and with her bow nearer one bank of the narrow canal than the other. We had gone aground. *Implacable's* huge cross-section was such a large percentage of the canal's as she passed in between its narrow sides, that the 'hydraulic' effect had offset her to one side uncontrollably. Once off-centre, there was nothing that the Canal Company Pilot could do to correct her in time. There is a very small rise and fall of tide in the canal, so that later in the day we were able to get off with the help of a tug. One of these small Arab-owned tugs 'exceeded its limitations' in its efforts to help us, and had an engine room fire. The crew emptied buckets of water down the funnel to put it out. Some even used their fezs. Each fez-full produced a burst of steam from the funnel and we and they were beside ourselves with merriment.

By 16 April 1945 we were off Colombo (Sri Lanka). We and 801 Squadron took half our aircraft ashore to RNAS China Bay near Trincomalee on the north east side of the island. On the way, I heard Bob Simpson, leading Yellow Flight, shout:

"Pull out, pull out, pull out!"

"Yellow One. What's wrong? Over."

"Armstrong's gone in, straight down."

Bob Armstrong was one of the most able fliers in the squadron. His aircraft must have suffered a petrol leak, the vapour of which, pleasant to start with as it is, must have eventually made him pass out in the cockpit. There was little or no ventilation in the Seafire's cockpit. Like *Implacable* herself, it had not been designed for tropical use and everything about it made it almost as unsuitable to operate at low level in the tropics as the ill-fated Buffalo, especially in the very humid air of the Indian Ocean on the Equator. We found our seats wet with sweat when we climbed out under the palm trees on China Bay *(HMS Bambara)* landing strip, and we all-but passed out ourselves, without any help from 100 octane petrol.

I saw the tower from which a year ago the signal was sent to tell Dicky Cork to go round again. I realised what an impossible position it was in for a Corsair pilot to see, approaching as Dicky had done. (See Appendix 8 — Dicky Cork's Accident.)

The wind at China Bay only had two directions, there and back, according to the onshore and offshore breezes. It changed 180 degrees at about lunchtime. Care was needed to check which end was which every morning as "two aircraft had recently collided", head-on we heard.

When we flew ashore we had only managed to get a small bag with toothbrush and shaving gear into the wing-gun panels of our aircraft. Dennis Kirby therefore had to oblige once more with a marathon trip to the ship at Colombo to collect the men and the rest of our khaki tropical gear. He sent some tea home for us. This was done for five shillings for a pound of tea, but it never arrived.

We slept in straw huts. These were impervious to the huge rainstorms but entirely pervious to everything else, including lizards, snakes and cockroaches. We had to feel in our shoes before putting them on, and sleep under exceedingly hot mosquito netting. Everything you looked at either walked, hopped, flew or stung, sometimes all four together.

In the cool of the evenings, we visited 'Trinco'. I bought a Topaz for £1. It measured one inch by half an inch and was about three eighths of an inch deep, beautifully hand cut. We also bought various teak and ivory elephants, book-ends, and so on. It was an absolute paradise of a place. Wherever we went there were white sandy beaches, oysters growing on the rocks and crystal warm water to bathe in.

In the evening we would repair to one of the village cafes. We were told by the doctor to go to the ones which had waitresses-with-shoes-on. After a week at China Bay we took some of the new boys across the island to the west coast — RNAS Puttalam *(HMS Rajaliya)* — where we did some desultory GGS air-to-air firing. A couple of us also called in at Colombo and picked up some mail from the ship. It was odd, flying over miles and miles of forest, with hardly a road or river and then suddenly catching sight of the white stone western architecture of Colombo itself, sticking out of the greenery.

There were two replacement aircraft waiting for us when we got back to Trinco. They were unflyable. The perspex was yellow and full of bubbles. The panels did not fit. The arrester hooks would not drop. The radio did not work and the tyres were rotting. As for the brakes, they made no difference whatever, like the MG's.

When the day came on 23 April for us to fly back on board I volunteered to take one of these 'new' aircraft. It was an anxious time, for none of us — especially our own squadron riggers and fitters — had had time to check them beforehand. On the way, at about 5000 feet and 20 miles out to sea, I noticed that the normal slight, pleasant, smell of petrol was getting worse. I opened the hood, but the upward rush of air made matters much worse and neat petrol soon splashed up from under my feet in the region of the fuel gauges. I pulled down my goggles — as it was wetting my face and stung like mad — and turned the oxygen on to 100 per cent. Having no other option but to breathe the vapour, I began to feel a sense of mental detachment and my eyesight became blinker-vision. I lost touch sensation on the stick and throttle. I tried shutting the hood all-but a crack, and sticking the unplugged end of my oxygen tube out into the slipstream. The rush of fresh air into the pipe was a great improvement, but the damage was done and I wondered whether I had left it too late. I had pulled away from the rest and I told them I would return to China Bay alone and get the fuel leak fixed. I do not remember much about the flight back or joining the circuit, or even landing. I remember waiting in the cockpit until my legs would bear my weight, climbing down out of the cockpit, soaked with fuel, and telling the rating who had put the chocks in position that the aircraft was a time bomb and not to switch anything on or off in the cockpit as it might blow up.

Next morning, having evaporated the petrol from my flying overalls, I climbed up into the same cockpit again, hoping that the statement on the Form 700 'fuel union tightened and locked' meant what it said. When I got back on board I found from the aircraft's Log Book — NN268 — that it had been repaired after Salerno and had travelled out east on the deck of *Chaser*. It had then spent six months out in the sun on China Bay airfield. I also learned the bad news that Len Simpson and David Crabtree had each bent an aircraft while landing on. There had also been two in 801 Squadron. Everyone was feeling the heat.

The next point of land on our way to Perth in Western Australia was the British colony of the Cocos Islands — a beautiful series of coral islands about 2000 miles from Ceylon and about half way to Perth. The Cocos are noted in Naval history as supplying the grave for the German WW1 raiding cruiser *Emden,* run ashore by her Captain on its northern coast. Cocos was also not far, 300 miles that is, from Christmas Island. I asked 'Wings' whether we could use our photo-recce Seafires to take a 'vertical line overlap' of the Cocos Islands as we passed by. He agreed that it was a good idea. So we loaded up six of our 880 Seafires with vertical F24 cameras with eight inch lenses, and took off. Cocos was 150 miles off so we used our 45 gallon slipper tanks. Mine did not work and my r/t was u/s as well. I could not go with them, so my absence made a few 'holes' in the photography. However, it was the first time that an accurate map had been made of the Islands and the locals were grateful when the Captain sent an Avenger to drop them a copy.

I watched the land-on from Wings' bridge. It was awful. We had not flown for some days and two aircraft were bent, one by Peter Arkell. He told me that when he had tried to open his throttle on the landing approach, the engine had cut-out completely. He had to close it fully and 'pump' it before he could get his engine to pick up. His wheels all but touched the sea.

The fault — in the accelerator pump — was because the pump plungers had dried out in the hot sun and were not working properly. We had no spares, but we asked all pilots to beware. If they had a cut out, they were to pump the throttle furiously — like a garden syringe — to regain power. We kept our fingers crossed. But in vain, for the next day Ken Boardman, a future Flight Leader, our best decklander, spun-in on the final approach — for precisely the same reason. His aircraft remained afloat with just the tail sticking out for five or six seconds. We were shattered to hear that by the time the rescue destroyer arrived a minute later, there was no sign whatever of poor Ken, although several of us thought we saw him climbing out of the cockpit.

We tried to work out why he had suddenly disappeared. We dismissed the idea of sharks and concluded that he had landed-on with his dinghy pack still made fast to his Mae West by its long lanyard and had been pulled under when it and the aircraft sank. Yet another cause could have been the gunsight knocking him out. Yet another Squadron Flying Order was made. 'Pilots are to disconnect their dinghy packs from Mae Wests as well as parachutes when entering the landing circuit'.

The Avengers were also having engine trouble. It, too, was caused by high temperatures and the extreme humidity. They had salt in their sparking plug harnesses which earthed the spark in the humid air, causing both spark plugs to fail on two or three of the 14 cylinders.

They spluttered and banged whenever full power was demanded by the pilot. Three fell into the sea with immense splashes off the end of the catapult. Free take-offs were tried. As they took the whole of the flight deck, this was not popular. No one else could be ranged on deck at the same time. We had to sit, strapped in, in the 120 degree heat of the hangar. However, if we were not flying, it was exciting to watch them. They would stagger off the deck, radiator gills fully open, flaps down, the pilot willing it off like a jockey at the last fence. It would then settle down a few inches off the Indian Ocean and fly in the ground effect, leaving a trail of ruffled water and blue smoke behind with its slipstream.

The pilot would get the undercarriage up and hope for a little excess thrust-over-drag. No such luck. So he would not be able to raise the flaps for fear of sinking further and he could not close the gills for fear of overheating. He would then fire all manner of Very Lights, send a variety of radio messages and ask for instant land-on priority to save his aircraft, himself and his crew from the sharks. The spluttering and backfiring 'Pratt-and-Watney' engine would then make another exciting circuit at nought feet. The pilot would put the undercarriage down just in time, and the whole lot would subside onto the deck at its last gasp. Spares were eventually flown out from America and the fault was rectified, but not before we had lost a few more Avengers. We found out later that *Indefat's* Avengers had suffered from precisely the same fault three months before we arrived.

Next day, 28 April, when a few miles off Perth, we had planned a full day's flying with 200 sorties. There were no less than four decklanding accidents in 880 and three more in 801. Ours were by Hugh Smith, Alan Dent, 'Legs' Letham and CPO Pete Watson. S/Lt Keith Jelley of 880 flew slap into an Avenger in poor visibility. The Avenger pilot alone survived this accident.

On 30 April we steamed into Fremantle Harbour, near Perth, the capital of Western Australia. We were made exceedingly welcome by the Aussies. Then we lost the services of Claude Leighton owing to ill health. Much to our regret, he finally left the squadron a month later. He married a Wren in 1946 and was killed in a car accident in New Zealand in 1947. I asked for Tim Singleton as a replacement Flight Leader. He was at that time in 899 Squadron. This squadron had already been cut up into small pieces to make replacement Seafire pilots for No 24 Wing and we were in high hopes of getting him.

Twenty-four hours after entering Fremantle and after some of us had enjoyed a dinner as guests of the Royal Perth Yacht Club, we had completed our refuelling. We set off round the south of Australia for the last leg to Sydney. On the way we heard of Hitler's last days in Berlin and of the similar and satisfactory fate of Himmler and the rest. So ended their war against two thirds of the world to establish their vainglorious Thousand-year Reich.

We hoped that our loved ones at home would remember us on VE night, 15,000 miles away. But I had found only one letter from home when we got to Fremantle. Perhaps there might be some at Sydney.

Chapter 21
Truk

On our voyage round the arid southern coast of the Australian continent, we had time to read newspapers taken on board with the mail at Fremantle. They made no mention whatever of any British activities in the Pacific although the BPF had already been a month and a half at sea in Operation 'Iceberg'. In fact we wondered where the British carriers were, for they were not in Sydney Harbour when we eventually steamed through the Heads on 8 May. The reason for the news blackout had been that Admiral Rawlings wanted nothing to do with the Press aboard his Flagship, *King George V*. Although he eventually relented and allowed some very incomplete and inaccurate coverage so that Britain could read about it, few if any were allowed on board the carriers during 'Iceberg' and afterwards. These security considerations and the lack of space for journalists, contributed to the BPF becoming the 'Forgotten Fleet' in direct contrast to the Americans.

We flew off before entering harbour to a newly constructed Mobile Naval Air Base (MONAB) at Nowra. This airfield was carved out of the usual eucalyptus forest a few miles from the sea and about 60 miles south of Sydney. Morale of both squadrons could not have been higher while we were at Nowra. The beautiful city of Sydney welcomed us and the BPF with open arms. The hospitality of the Australian families, with their own sons still overseas or POWs and with a far higher percentage of their population in the forces than ourselves, had to be seen to be believed. There was only one minor incident during our stay at Nowra. Norman Goodfellow landed 'wheels-up' one day. It improved morale if anything, for if the Senior Pilot could do it, life wasn't quite so critical for the more junior boys.

One night in a Sydney nightspot, Romano's, Dougy Yate, Norman and I ran into Tim Singleton. We asked him why he had not yet joined our happy throng. He went straight back aboard *Chaser* and organised his immediate transfer. We were so glad to have him, with his wise good humour.

The VE Day party at Nowra went on until moonrise at 0100. We went outside the wardroom, a wooden hut with rafters and a tin roof, and we listened to the sound of revelry within. We could also hear the cicadas and the squabble of a few parrots, disturbed from their night quarters by the unaccustomed noise. Miles from home and with a sense of foreboding, we wondered what we were going to have to do now. We did not have to wait long. We were summoned aboard *Implacable* again on 24 May. All 22 aircraft which we had taken ashore landed-on in five minutes flat.

Our sister squadron, 801, has managed to preserve its Line Book. It is now in the Fleet Air Arm Museum at Yeovilton. Of this period, I read the following:
"We were told to be ready to be back on board by 0630. We are still

straining to go by 0800. A signal arrives, 'ship delayed'. We are used to these little setbacks, having been attached to the lady for nearly seven months. Jimmie Primrose leads a small choir to while away the time. The morning is hideous with negro spirituals, and my landing-on twitch comes out in peculiar forms."

"Around 0830, 880 leap into the air. The powers that be have ordered a rather significant delay of one hour before we are to follow. The ship was steaming along in perfect weather, for a change. We must have arrived early for she was just about in the rendezvous position so the usual square search wasn't necessary."

Later on, the Line Book continues:

"As we near New Guinea (on the way north), 801, 12 Flight, make history. With a loud fanfare by the ship's buglers and accompanied by the National Anthem, Lt Ray Saxe, S/Lt Squires, Lt McLean and S/Lt Temple walk out to their first Seafire 'readiness' in the Pacific. Or did they just shamble up, keeping out of the way of the deck hockey. Now you come to mention it, perhaps they did."

There was, of course, much rivalry between the two Seafire squadrons, and our sister squadron was keen to uphold its seniority. Reading its Line Book for the first time in nearly 40 years, the competition seems to have figured much in our thoughts and this was probably encouraged because it helped to keep us all on our toes.

The voyage north had been without incident, except that Lt/Cdr W. R. MacWhirter went over the side like his predecessor. He was picked up, but his Observer was not. The Firefly Mark II with its Griffon engine seemed to have a nasty power-on stall, with little or no warning to the pilot.

The first night in the small, deepwater anchorage of Manus was disturbed by an air raid. This was the first Japanese inspired 'red' warning we had had. It was a fitting reminder, after Sydney, that we were in hostile territory, with the Japs not very far away in the hills of Manus and New Guinea a few miles to the south.

On the second day at Manus, some of the BPF arrived from Operation 'Iceberg' — three rather shaggy carriers, with *Implacable's* 'high speed finish' standing out in the otherwise deserted anchorage.

Two days later, we all steamed out to sea. Although a huge exercise had been laid on, we spent the whole morning sitting in our cockpits on deck waiting for the fog to clear. At lunchtime the exercise was cancelled, but ten minutes later the fog cleared, so a new scheme was hatched up in Wings' sea cabin on the bridge. This was limited to a single, 880 low-level 'strike' on the Flagship, *Formidable,* 40 miles away. It was a brilliant opportunity to catch the Admiral with his head down after lunch. Of course we went in at nought feet. By a miracle there were no navigation mistakes, and we happened upon the 'enemy' dead ahead. Twelve Seafires made a simultaneous beeline for the Admiral's bridge in *Formidable.* We had terrific fun — according to my log book — and polished off *Formid* in ten seconds flat, before a gun had moved round to follow us.

In my diary I noted that we received a signal from Vian that day. It said:

"Proud to have you with us."

Our Captain's obsequious reply was no better. It said:

"Thank you. We hope to improve as we operate under your command."

This reply gave everyone else in the BPF and future historians the wrong impression, for it was *Implacable's* air group that led the way in combat and ground attack techniques and in carrier procedure in the forthcoming operations — albeit the ship, herself, had much to learn.

Next day we were back in harbour. At five o'clock we attended a 'Fair' on the flight deck, organised by the 'springer', the Physical Training Instructor. Coconut shies (with local coconuts), skittles, ballgames, Aunt Sallies and deck tennis. The ship's company were issued with one bottle of beer each, whether they were tee-total or not. The big attraction at sunset was the final of the tug o' war between the Stokers' and the Petty Officers' teams. The Stokers won.

More Seafires were obviously not going to be welcome in the BPF unless, first, we could operate for longer than the two hours maximum afforded by the existing slipper tank of 45 gallons. Secondly, we needed something else to offer besides CAP, for we would soon die of boredom if there were no Kamikazes and THAT was all we were allowed to do. We therefore determined (a) to find an alternative to the 45 or 90 gallon 'ferry' tank, and (b) to offer dive bombing as a subsidiary role.

The ship went to sea once more on 5 June and we practised strafing and making dummy dives at a splash target towed astern. No 801 Squadron's Senior Pilot, Lt Bill Brewer, RN, had already done some bombing practice at St. Merryn before he joined. He led eight of 801 and I took four of 880 with a 500 pound bomb apiece and we dived from about 6000 feet in a 45 degree dive. Needless to say we did not hit the target, but it was fun while it lasted, until we heard that S/Lt Dane (801) had pulled his wings off in full view of the ship. He had been in the squadron since June 1944 and his loss was felt very much by 801 Squadron (See Appendix 11.)

Later that day, a new Admiral, Rear Admiral E. Brind, CB, CBE, whose designation was CS4 (Flag Officer Fourth Cruiser Squadron), waffled over the round-down in an Avenger to pay us a visit. He was going to command us from his Flagship, *Newfoundland,* in a forthcoming operation. A Walrus also 'splashed' on board. It was to be our Air/Sea Rescue craft.

Our next ground attack training effort was made on the unsuspecting island of Towi, a very small, uninhabited — we hoped — coral island offshore and suitable for a bombing target for our Fireflies, Avengers and Seafires. This was obviously a dress rehearsal for something, and we wondered what. By the end of the day all that a photographic Seafire could find of the island was "a few floating palm trees and excited monkeys shaking their fists". Was it Churchill who said: "Nothing in life is so exhilarating as to be shot at, without result".

After two more days intensive flying, we returned to Manus on the evening of 7 June to store and replenish the ship. I see from 801's diary that we played them at water polo and beat both their teams. We also attended lectures and heard our C-Balls — Major Scott and his assistant, Captain Bob Hudson — giving us all a lecture on photo-recce and survival in the jungle.

In the extreme heat and humidity of Manus, the skipper allowed bathing for the whole ship's company. The ship's boats crew threw small depth charges to scare the sharks. Johnny Boak and another Canadian pilot, this time from 801, did a 60 foot swallow dive from the flight deck and won a bet of five shillings (25p) each.

During these three rest days, our search increased for a replacement for the 45 gallon tank. We needed a 90 gallon torpedo-shaped tank, as in US Navy aircraft. We did not want a 90 gallon slipper tank designed merely for ferry purposes as used by 24 Wing in *Indefatigable.*

I was allowed to fly off in harbour to Ponam airstrip, to ask the Americans for help. There I was given a seat in a Stinson Reliant which took me to the Naval Air Maintenance HQ on Pittilieu Island, which we shared with the Americans. I was shown into an American Colonel's office to talk about long range tanks. He told me to get my Commander (Air) to phone him on the TBS link or send a signal if we didn't have a linkline (which we didn't) and have a talk about it. He said that he knew of 60 or so Kittyhawk (P40) tanks in New Guinea. These were ex-Australian Lease-Lend torpedo-shaped, 90 gallon tanks and they would doubtless let us have them if we supplied the transport. He even gave me some rough drawings of them, which I took back on board.

It looked hopeful and C-H and Wings made the necessary arrangement for payment — two crates of Johnnie Walker — and gave the drawings of the tank to our Chief Air Engineer, Lt (E) Brian Hattemore, RNVR. He quickly produced some bomb-steadiers welded to our 500 pound bomb rack fitting and we were about to be in business. All we now needed was the supply of 90 gallon tanks to be sent from New Guinea.

On 12 June we steamed out of Manus once more and set course northwards. The ships in company were *Ruler* (escort carrier), the four cruisers *Achilles, Swiftsure, Newfoundland* and the Canadian *Uganda,* plus our faithful rescue destroyer, *Terpsicore,* and a few others.

Our target was to be Truk. The name Truk laid a cold finger of fear upon all of us when we first heard it announced. It was the Japanese Pearl Harbor, a possession of theirs since 1920 with 40,000 men in a 40 mile radius atoll, crowded with airfields and a deepwater anchorage sufficient for all the world's navies. Stuart and I studied some recent American photographs. After this, we gladly concluded that it was an empty shell of its former self, consisting mainly of bomb craters, burned out buildings, sunken ships and with scarcely a target in sight. But you never knew with the Japanese. They might all be dummies.

At dawn on 14 June we were about 80 miles off the atoll. We started on the largest flying programme the ship had attempted. A couple of recce Fireflies took off before us in pitch darkness. Eight Seafires of 801 then took off as CAP over *Ruler* — our 'spare deck' — and another eight of 880 for CAP over *Implacable* and the five cruisers. At 0545 another four of 880 and another eight of 801 took off for photo-recce and strafing. Our targets were to be anything reported as worthwhile by the Fireflies, on the main island of Dublon. C-H was leading the two flights from 801 and I was leading my own 21 Flight.

Although we took off in a rain squall we still managed to form up without delay and set course for the target. However, there was a solid wall of black cloud 'down-to-the-deck' in front — we were operating in the middle of an inter-tropical front — and C-H was heading right into it. We were at sea level when we entered this thunderhead and there was absolutely no point whatever in attempting to fly in formation through it. It went up to 20,000-30,000 feet and raining stair rods throughout which obliterated the windscreen, and sideways visibility to half a wing span. There was nothing for it but for me to take my four on a gentle climbing turn through 180 degrees in the cloud and return to the ship, hoping that the ship would now switch on her beacon for us to get her position.

Still on radio silence, I came out of the cloud without Arkell, my number three. (My number two was Mike Banyard; Arkell's number two was Scott.) Pete Arkell had lagged behind for the past mile before we entered the cloud and had not joined up close before we hit it. I flew the remaining two into a clear patch a few feet above the sea and climbed up into the cloud myself to listen for the ship's beacon.

Having joined the other two again, I luckily found the ship (without the aid of the beacon which had not been switched on) and was sent, by Aldis lamp signal, to *Ruler.* She was not on the course given so I had to carry out a square search, still with only two Seafires besides myself, and worrying about Arkell. As wireless silence was still in force in spite of the ship being outside VHF enemy wireless range of Truk, I could not even tell them that Arkell was probably lost.

I and my two then landed on *Ruler* with our last five gallons. Just as I taxied forward, last on, I saw Pete appear out of a black cloud about two miles off. He just made it before the ship was engulfed in almost solid water. His propeller stopped as he opened up to taxy forward of the barrier after he landed, his tanks barely damp with petrol. 'Bats' then climbed up on his wing and bawled at him for stopping where he had. Pete's reply was unprintable.

Then the squall of tropical wind and rain hit *Ruler.* In 20 yards visibility and in almost solid, stinging, stair rods hitting us at 50 mph, we helped the crews lash down our aircraft.

When it was over, our folded Walrus ASR aircraft parked forward of the barrier on the port bow had disappeared. The Captain reversed course to find it and we saw it just about to go down by the stern. That was the end of our Air/Sea Rescue arrangements. It had blown over the side, unseen by anyone.

I found out what had happened to Pete. After our take-off we had set course so quickly that no one noticed that he could not get his starboard undercarriage fully up. This had made his engine boil (the undercarriage leg obstructs the cooling air to the radiator unless it is fully locked up) and he had to reduce power. Whilst searching for the ship he had come across a Japanese aircraft. His story, told 40 years later, is as follows:

"It was a radial-engined job, perhaps a Myrt, and going very fast. It didn't take any notice of me at all. I was boiling and couldn't catch it, although I gave it a long distance burst, probably too far away to have any effect. When I went up to the bridge of *Ruler* to report, the Captain told me not to judge it so fine next time, presumably referring to my shortage of fuel. He wasn't trying to be funny, either."

The reason for the near loss of Pete and the probable reason for the actual loss of S/Lt Mervin Payne of 801 on this, his first operational trip, was doubtless due to his becoming lost on the formation entering rain and cloud at zero feet, and the ship's insistence on radio silence. The forward view in heavy rain in a Seafire was nil. Even sideways view in tropical rain was only ten yards. Wireless silence also prevented a leader's necessary tight control of the aircraft in such weather. The heavy rain, mixed with salt on our aircraft radio aerials, also caused r/t failure in most of our aircraft. Payne did not appear at the far end of the cloud with the two others from 801 Squadron in C-H's Flight who made it to the target area. He was neither seen nor heard, after entering the cloud. In future operations, 'r/t tell-offs' were allowed on deck before take-off, even in conditions of wireless silence. This enabled pilots to check that their radio would work if they had to use it in an emergency.

On the subsequent land-on in *Implacable,* 801's diary reports:

"Merv Payne did not turn up at the r/v and after waiting five minutes C-H turned once more into the murk and we made our way on instruments back to the steamer. There, the situation was nearly as fraught. Ben Tillet had to do an emergency (landing). The rest of us, still airborne, then had to watch an Avenger go into the drink before Gunson hit the barrier, causing still more delay . . . So with this inauspicious start for 801, we continue the day's work, parking down in *Ruler* for a spell while *Implacable* sorted herself out."

My diary reports:

"On our second trip we had a go at some oil tanks at Dublon with 500 pound bombs. (C-H was leading again, this time in better weather. Radio silence had at last been lifted, so everyone knew what was happening,) One of 801 Squadron's eight Seafires said he read the gauges (on the oil tanks) as he went by and they were empty. We may possibly have cracked one of the tanks, but there was obviously nothing in them to catch fire. All our bombs were close together, downwind, as Seaweed had given us the wrong aim-off direction."

"Next day, with the Avengers playing 'intruders' all night and keeping us awake, we were briefed to do some bombardment spotting. I obviously had to lead this, being an old hand at the game. I was given a complicated code and told that the four cruisers would each fire different-coloured smoke shells, so there would be no chance of the aircraft spotter pilots muddling up whose shells were which. There were six of us, operating in pairs."

When I reported to the bridge after the spotting trip I was not particularly surprised to see long faces. It had been ghastly. The shoot had been a complete waste of time, as the ships' r/ts had not been working properly. Furthermore, one of the ships reported that her 'gunnery table' aiming system was u/s and she was shooting independently. This she did all over the place, and confused the rest

However, shore bombardment was important to the Navy for it was the only independent contribution which the non-carrier fleet was capable of making in the Pacific. It therefore figured large in their reports to their Admirals and to the Press, and thus the history books, in spite of its insignificant accomplishments and vast consumption of valuable stores. The *Daily Telegraph* said, under a heading: "Japan's Gibraltar a battered wreck":

"Truk Atoll has been heavily attacked by elements of the British Pacific Fleet. Aircraft carriers, with a strong escort (sic) of cruisers and destroyers, directed a 48 hour battering of the Japanese garrison on the islands."

"On the morning of the second day, closing in on the outer reef to some 8000 yards range, cruisers supported by destroyers, pounded the seaplane base, airstrips and oil installations. Over the targets, Seafire spotting planes led by Lt/Cdr R. M. Crosley of Sherborne, Dorset, observed the fall of shots. Fireflies led by Lt/Cdr W MacWhirter of Keyhaven, Hampshire, circled the outer coastal defences to neutralise any resistance. Large shell bursts could be seen on the seaplane base and airstrip and runways. . . ." etc., etc.

The results claimed were rubbish of course and must have made the Americans smile as it did us when we saw it several weeks later, repeated in our overseas mail.

When I arrived on the bridge afterwards — having seen no hits on anything — it was obvious that I was in the rattle. The Captain said:

"What actually did you say on the r/t Crosley?"

"Well, sir,' I answered in my best manner, 'we had very poor r/t from the ships. We missed a lot of their transmissions and they must have missed a lot of ours. They carried on shooting on their own and without any help from us. My target was already being covered with shots before I got there, by someone or other."

"Yes, but what did you actually say?"

"Well, I think I said something like, 'There's only one bit of sea round here and all the shots are falling into it'."

"It's certainly offended the gunners. They are saying you were unhelpful."

"Yes, sir, but we couldn't help them. Their r/t was useless and I think their targets must have been too close to each other as their shooting overlapped."

The Captain was determined to get to the bottom of it if he could.

"But they used different-coloured bursts, didn't they? Couldn't you see which was which?"

What the Captain did not know — or anyone else — was that the colours could only be seen if they burst in water. They could not be seen over the land, as coral dust made it impossible to see any colours.

"All right Crosley. I know you did your best and you've had a bit of spotting experience, I hear. Let's hope we don't hear any more of it."

There was no debriefing, so no one learned a thing from it. Ships with intermittent and fading radio (probably caused by poor siting of the radio aerials) could never be expected to realise that it was their own radio at fault. Later, it became clear that, unable to communicate with the spotters, the ships had turned to 'visual control' from their bridges. They could see in the clear weather what they assumed were their own shell bursts. They had therefore made their own corrections, not realising that it was the coloured water misses they could see and not the lesser (uncoloured) explosions on the coral on land and which remained below their horizon. No wonder all their shells landed in the 'oggin because that is where they were directing their own fire. Later, when I read of this, I learned that three of the four ships were new to shore bombardment and none had done it with aircraft before.

The lack of heavy flak and any effective air or sea opposition at Truk could have made us overconfident. Nevertheless much was learned by *Implacable,* and not without its tragedies. Charles Lamb was gravely injured by a Firefly propeller. It happened in the first range of the day, in darkness. The trolly which was used for catapulting Fireflies was being reset for the second Firefly. The tubular steel arms of the trolly had not sufficiently collapsed as they should have done, and, as they passed back through the undercarriage legs of the second Firefly, unseen in the darkness, they were struck by its whirling propeller. One of the hard 'Jablo' blades was flung off and all but severed Charles's legs. He tells the fantastic story of being found on the flight deck in the darkness by a rating. He asked the rating to get a stretcher. 'What for?' was his reply. He was taken ashore at Manus, protesting in case Surgeon Commander Keevil, DSO, the PMO in *Implacable,* might amputate the remains of his legs. He recovered after a year, his life saved by American penicillin and his indomitable will. He finally returned home at the end of the war in *Indomitable,* a brave and unselfish man.

Lt Trevor David stepped into Charles's shoes on the flight deck and life was able to continue.

Later, on the same day as this accident, an Avenger was catapulted off with only one strop. The aircraft went off the catapult ramp sideways and hit the sea. It was at night and the pilot was not picked up. The Observer and TAG (Telegraphist Air Gunner), however, got clear of the aircraft before it sank and both were picked up by *Terpsicore.* The third loss was, of course, Mervin Payne of 801 Squadron.

Two days later we were all back at Manus again. The ship was melting under a vertical, midday sun, bang on the Equator, on Midsummer's Day. Even the fish in the lagoon had passed out and with their beautiful colours bleached white, were floating on their sides on the surface.

These were to be our last five days at Manus. We flew ashore with six Seafires from each squadron to Ponam. The airfield was in sight of the ship lying offshore. We had to say goodbye to Tim Singleton as well as Claude Leighton, and to Crabtree. All were suffering with the heat. David Crabtree eventually rejoined, but Tim and Claude were grounded by the doctors and could take no further part. Dougy Yate also had ear trouble and was temporarily in the sickbay.

Several new pilots joined the squadron at this time, all 20-year-old Sub-Lieutenants. John Marshall, John Joly and Roy Gilmore. I knew Marshall from Henstridge days where he had been my pupil with Lowden and Reynolds. He became my Number 2. John Joly made a good impression immediately and was able to take part in the forthcoming operations, but Gilmore and a few others lacked experience and could not cope with our attack methods. It would have been unfair to have asked them to join in immediately.

As the sun beat down upon *Implacable* in the tropical harbour of Manus and as sickness became a serious factor in the ship's forthcoming usefulness, the ship's officers waived their seniority rights to the better cabins, and the ship's company ratings waived their 'first come first served' rights to the better mess decks and sleeping arrangements on board. The air department on board was then better placed to withstand the humidity and the high temperatures between decks. But the fans continued to blow hot, wet air through miles of steel trunking to no purpose. By the time it reached E deck and my cabin it consisted merely of a loud noise, the air itself having been waylaid *en-route* by many thieving devices. Showers were possible twice in the 24 hours, but no water had been brought up from Sydney and the ship had to make use of distilled water from her own evaporators, at a cost, so said 'Chiefy' of £2,000 per ton at today's prices. The ship used 40 tons a day when at sea, and about 20 tons when in harbour, half due to steam leakages.

While at Ponam I arranged to fly a Corsair. In WW II, few strictures applied to flying each other's aircraft and no questions were asked. The version I flew for a couple of hours was the F4U-2. I compared its responsiveness to that of a Lagonda to my much lighter MG, for it was half as heavy again as the Seafire. However, as it had geared tabs on the ailerons — being a much later design than the Spitfire — the aileron stick forces were half those of the Seafire at speeds above 300 knots. When the throttle was closed in the landing configuration it had the gliding angle of a brick and when it hit the runway with a thud, it stayed there, keeping itself straight with its lockable tailwheel. The view over the nose was far better than the Seafire's, as its engine cowling was rounder and subtended a narrower angle, but the sideways view over the edges of the cockpit was not as good. The cockpit layout was immaculate compared with the hotchpotch of the Seafire, but the multitude of chromium-plated switches needed long arms to reach. The general comfort, cockpit air-conditioning, and lack of noise, was superb.

The Royal Navy's social comforts ashore were in stark contrast to those of the Americans; but directly the Americans realised how we lived, our men were allowed to visit the American canteen on the island of Ponam. In fact, had it not been for the overall feeling that we were about to face further privations and death in the forthcoming operations against a fanatical enemy, we would have enjoyed our last five days on this island paradise.

Ashore, I had a reed hut to myself. It was beneath the palms, against a blue lagoon and with a snow white beach strewn with coconuts. Flying foxes with their prehistoric eight-foot wing spans crashed around overhead. Lizards scuttled to and fro in the brilliant sunlight. But sandflies and the humidity reduced our sleep, for it was too hot for mosquito nets until just before dawn.

There was often time for bathing. This was at a little bay along the side of the lagoon where either the Japanese, or the Americans after them, had scooped a deep pool out of the coral with explosives. We found it only slightly cooler in the lagoon than ashore in the shade. The temperature of the water was about 90 degrees F, like a warm bath, and, to cool down it was necessary to stand wet in the slight on-shore breeze which occasionally wafted the palm trees in the early afternoon.

Some of us put on shoes and walked out into the shallow expanse of the lagoon. Through the crystal clear water amongst the sea urchins and multi-coloured fish we could see all manner of marine life. Huge clams, with two-foot, wide-open jaws, would suddenly snap shut and send sand and water six feet into the air.

Then there was the joy of a cool, early-morning flight over the outlying islands. We would open the cockpit hood for a clearer view of those below — the beautiful smiling native girls with their arms raised to us as we sped overhead. What could they be thinking? Then we would circle over more mundane things such as the Officers' Heads. These consisted of a line of stalls at the end of a 'T' jetty over the lagoon. We flew as low as we could past them. We wondered what interesting arrangements the French would have designed for their Navy, had *Richelieu* or *Dunkerque* been around.

The RN wardroom ashore had the longest bar in the Pacific. American wardrooms were 'dry'. Although we did not drink 12 hours before flying, we often had a night free. On one of these, Dennis Kirby won the jackpot on the fruit machine in the mess just before closing time. He was therefore late getting back aboard ship that night and he missed the liberty boat. He, Dankaster and Griffiths of 801, decided to swim back aboard, in deep water, regardless of sharks. Luckily the Officer of the Watch saw them in time and sent a boat to pick them up.

In spite of these diversions, we still had our troubles. We were doing ADDLs with the new boys one afternoon. Stuart's boys were performing. S/Lt Peter Record was making the usual curved Seafire approach. As at Trinco, the station had been incorrectly laid out for curved-approach decklanders, so that the approach path of the Seafires lay straight over a wireless aerial post 150 feet high. We therefore had to move the touchdown position for our ADDLs further down the runway in order that the Seafires would miss the wireless pole by a safe distance, and near-miss a few palm trees instead. When Record had done his six ADDLs, he was told, over the radio, to land. However, forgetting about the aerial and not warned by the control tower, he moved his final touchdown position back to the unsafe position to get the maximum landing run. He hit the wireless mast. The Seafire overturned as it hit the runway, pinning Record in the cockpit. We rushed up and lifted the tail high in the air, and, had he been conscious, he might have been able to scramble out, helped by many others who had come running up. But he had hit the gunsight and had been knocked out. Suddenly there was a roar, and the whole aircraft went up in flames, engulfing us nearby and causing us to drop the tail back on the runway. Seconds only had elapsed and the fire tender arrived. But its crew were dressed in bathing shorts rather than their proper, fireproof, asbestos suits — because life would have been impossible in them — and they could not enter the flames at once. Neither would the CO_2 extinguishers douse the flames sufficiently for Record to be immediately dragged clear.

After a full two minutes of this torture a crane arrived. It slid a strop under the tail to lift it. Record's poor body was removed and taken to the sickbay. He lived for six hours. There was no escape from the war, for a day later, someone found a dead Japanese soldier trapped between rocks close by our bathing beach, where he had been for the past six months.

When we got back on board we found that 100 rusty Kittyhawk tanks had arrived. The Americans and Australians had delivered them just before wardroom bar-opening time, in a dishevelled-looking picket boat. The tanks obliterated the picket boat and crew up to a height of ten feet. We hoisted them and the crew aboard and stowed them everywhere, even in our cabins. The two American officers were entertained to lunch in the wardroom. We managed to make it a memorable occasion, for us, for they could not have remembered a thing about it themselves. Every time they asked for their gins to be diluted with water, they got water-laced-with-gin. It was a self-defeating process. They were mostly horizontal by the time they got back to the picket boat. Their crew wasn't any better. The 'gasoline gig' picket boat took a very dangerous and un-seamanlike course back to the jetty.

Two days later C-H and I were flown off in harbour to check out the tanks. We both complained about the tail buffet at speeds above 180 knots. It would have made their use impossible. I suggested dropping the tanks a further four inches to allow more air to pass between the fuselage and the tanks. This cured the buffet, but only allowed a mere four inches of clearance between this half-ton of petrol and the ground; not very much when the main oleos were compressed for a decklanding. However, the benefits were so great, the fuel flow so easily checked (we fitted a transparent feed pipe as well), and Admiral Vian would be so pleased, that we modified all 48 of our Seafires with the necessary 'claw' type fitting to hold the tank under its belly. We could then stay in the air for about three and a half hours and, except for bombs or rockets, take part in all the strikes and all operations on a par with the Corsairs and Hellcats in the other carriers.

Formidable, 1943. Sea Hurricane Ib's on outriggers and Albacores. *(FAA Museum)*

Cdr Charles Evans in working 'rig', *Implacable*, July 1945.

Hellcat with 100 gallon LRT. *(FAA Museum)*

Implacable and *Indefatigable*, Sydney, 1945. *(Mike Banyard)*

Chapter 22
The Final Onslaught

During the next few days at Manus we collected eight new pilots. Only two of these new pilots could be trained up and made use of in time for the forthcoming operations. They were S/Lts Jimmy Sheeran and 'Isaac' Newton. They had already been acclimatised at Puttalam in Ceylon.

On 25 June we steamed out of Manus yet again and, taking on a few replacement Seafires and Fireflies from Ponam, we set course for the south. We were making our second rendezvous with Admiral Vian who was coming up from Sydney in *Formidable*. We planned to give *Formidable* and *Victorious* *(Indefatigable* was delayed in Sydney) a shake-up which they would long remember.

For the second time, we arrived over the Flagship, *Formidable*, before a single gun had moved. We had gone ahead of the Avengers and Fireflies for the last 20 miles, coming down to nought feet, as usual. We arrived and disappeared again before they knew that they had been under attack. It now seems extraordinary, but our method of attack must have been entirely new to the BPF. They were obviously not expecting it and their CAP did nothing whatever to stop it. It was not mentioned in their report at all. When we got back to the ship, our morale was very high indeed. Not only had our strike been a success and without CAP interceptions, but theirs had been a failure. 801 Squadron had intercepted all the Avenger aircraft as they came bumbling over at the usual obvious height of 3000 feet for their bombing runs. The Corsairs from *Formidable* were no better, as they made copybook bombing runs at us too, all in straight lines and all from the same height and direction, one after the other.

We saw 801's and our own G45 films afterwards and cheered ourselves up immensely by seeing how many we had 'shot down'. John Snow (Eton housemaster) and John Forsyth, our ADR team leaders who had done the interceptions on our radar, were very pleased with us as well.

That evening, 3 July 1945, the ship 'did a *Dasher*' and began to bounce up and down in time with one of the ship's propellers. We soon came to a dead stop. After an hour we began to move once more, but this time the rhythmic bouncing changed to a harsh vibration. This was so severe that the paint on my cabin deckhead flaked off and, in spite of its spring attachment, the bulb filament disintegrated.

At dinner that evening, 'Chiefy' Holt-Wilson told us that one of the main thrust blocks had melted and the vibration was because his engine room staff had locked the offending propeller shaft. As we were trying to make a speed of 20 knots to keep up with the rest of the BPF, the cavitation effects of a 20 foot diameter stationary prop dragged sideways through the water at that speed could be heard by a Japanese submarine for 20 miles. It was also vibrating our soup plates off the table. Things were getting serious. Without ourselves and *Indefatigable,* the other two carriers — *Formidable* and *Victorious* — of the BPF would hardly impress the Americans with their 13 carriers. Chiefy said that he would have to try to fix it at sea. Failing that, it was back to Wooloomaloo docks in Sydney.

On 10 July we at last caught sight of the US Fleet — part of Task Force 37 — through the gloom. After a week's work round-the-clock, in hellish conditions, Chiefy's men had now only one more three-foot bolt to bore out and refit and we should have four propellers again and be able to make our proper speed of 30 knots.

On 16 July we flew purposefully over the three American carrier fleets and their 100 or so cruisers and destroyers, so that they would recognise a Seafire and a Firefly as a friendly aircraft when the time came. We admired their carriers, 100 barrels following us round with 100 aircraft on each deck, their white wakes shining in the sunlight.

The Americans were polite enough, but they must have wondered what we would be able to contribute without *Indefatigable* and with only 175 aircraft compared with their 1200. The three American and one British carrier groups were spread over 300 square miles of ocean, out of sight of each other. They used an imaginary position on the chart as their navigational reference point. This point, called 'Option', moved steadily throughout the day and night on a pre-conceived course and speed. The BPF was to be north of the American line. The American Admiral, McCane, had his carrier Flagship at the southern end so that orders from him to Vian had to be passed a distance of 60 miles. The Americans used VHF r/t, not the old-fashioned w/t for inter-ship communication. VHF was entirely new to the British and they were consequently inexperienced in its use as a means of TBS or 'talk-between-ships'. Orders to Vian from J. S. McCane's Flagship therefore took a considerable time to arrive. This was not only because of the poor standard of British r/t but because the maximum distance that VHF, UHF or radar can cover at sea level is 20 miles owing to the masking effects of the earth's curvature. Relays were required, with consequent further delays. Briefing for our targets in the forthcoming operations was therefore often late, inaccurate and incomplete.

The Americans had already carried out a few days of operations off the northern coasts of Japan before we joined them. We learned this from reading a copy of their printed-on-the-spot aviation journal, similiar to our own Fleet Air Arm's *Flight Deck*. The American journal contained all manner of additional, up-to-date, operational information. Its information on ASR, accidents and operational results, and verbatim reports by pilots, was invaluable. We were particularly impressed with the immense efforts they made to effect rescues of airmen shot down. They used 20 or more submarines, 50 ASR flying boats and a huge back-up organisation to make sure that every aviator was rescued before he could fall into the hands of the Japanese. Every rescue submarine, aircraft or detached destroyer had its own CAP overhead, wherever it went. The rescue submarine would come close inshore, submerged, inviting the downed airman in his dinghy to catch hold of the periscope as it passed him. The submarine would then tow him offshore out of gun range, come to the surface and take the airman on board. He would then be flown back to his carrier the same day, suitably refreshed with rum from the sub's medicine chest.

TF 37 was ready for trouble in the forthcoming operations against Japan, for during the landings in 'Iceberg', the Japanese had launched a thousand Kamikazes in 30 days. The huge losses to the Americans had all the makings of a disaster and emergency defence methods had had to be adopted to try to prevent the low-flying Kamikazes from getting through. The Japanese were very clever. They knew all about radar defences and how the cover provided by masthead radar was useless beyond 20 miles with a zero height approach. Therefore not only did the Kamikazes approach at zero feet, but they adopted the cleverest of ruses to further foil the defence. The suicide pilots were inexperienced young airmen, and they needed to be accompanied by more experienced pilots flying alongside to help them to navigate to their targets. At a distance of 20 miles from the Fleet, the experienced pilots would wave goodbye to the suiciders, who would then flog on alone to their deaths. The leaders, who alone had fuel enough for the return journey, would then climb up and 'expose' themselves on the radar and tempt the American and British fighter pilots to come after them. They would then hare back to base, hoping to decoy our fighters away from the Kamikazes who would continue unseen at zero feet until they saw their targets. These radar ruses were nothing new to the Navy in the Mediterranean or ourselves in 30 Wing at the time, and, after 'Iceberg', they were not new to the Americans either. (However, it is worth mentioning here and now that the Royal Navy had apparently forgotten about this obvious low-level method of attack some 40 years later. In the Falklands in 1982, they had no effective defence against it at all.)

The US Naval losses at Okinawa were of the same severity as those suffered by Admiral Cunningham in the Greek campaign, and they also delayed the conquest of Okinawa by a fortnight. But they would have been even greater had they not taken urgent steps to increase the radius of their radar cover for fleet defence against the Kamikazes. The only possible method of doing this was by providing radar picket destroyers at all four corners of their fleet at a distance of 20 miles from its centre. These 'Tomcat' destroyers, as they were codenamed, then conducted their own fighter interceptions with their own 'stop-me-and-buy-one' crews against the approaching Kamikazes and their escorts, shooting many of them down before they could get to the carriers at the Fleet's centre. The BPF immediately adopted this method of defence. However, because none of our 30 destroyers was yet fitted with an ADR system (although many had gunnery radar fitted), Admiral Rawlings and Admiral Vian had to make use of valuable ADR/AA cruisers for this purpose.

Privately, we considered that Operation 'Iceberg' was a mere rehearsal compared with what we in TF 37 could now expect off Japan. We expected that the Japanese would concentrate their Kamikaze fighters, new 450 mph 'George' and 'Jack' fighters, on their airfields near the coast, with their reconnaissance aircraft further inland. Each day might then begin with a series of reconnaissance flights by the Japanese to establish our position before launching 200-300 Kamikazes in our direction, and end with another series to establish our losses. The Seafires of 30 Wing and 24 Wing would therefore be of the utmost use in providing a high performance, low level, defence. Nevertheless, we still hoped that Vian would now recognise that we could also strike at a distance of 180 miles or more with our long range Kittyhawk tanks and that we would be useful for 'ramrod' attacks on Japan itself. On the night before 'Day One', we all attended a series of briefings in the wardroom and went to bed wondering what the next day would bring. A copy of the flying programme for 30 Wing is placed opposite.

30 Wing Flying Programme — 17 July 1945.

Time	Serial	Duty	A/C	Allocation		
H	1	CAP	12	**22** (880) Pye Smith Kirby Wager	**24** (880) Lt Simpson Gilmore Boak Graham	**26** (880) Dancaster Wheeldon Marshall Seigne
H+2.30	2	Ramrod	16	**13** Wingleader Cowley Green Steel **12** Saxe Squires McLean Tillet	**16** Luing Stock Sheeran Losee	**11** CO 801 Primrose Griffith Glazebrook
H+2.30	3	CAP	12	**21** (880) CO 880 Dixon Arkell Scott	**23** (880) Goodfellow S/Lt Simpson Patullo Tucker	**25** (880) Yate Banyard Dent Lethem
H+5	4	CAP	16	**14** Brewer Geary Jervis Holway **26** (880) Dancaster Wheeldon Seigne	**15** Gunson Clark Thomson Bedore	**24** (880) Lt Simpson Gilmore Boak Graham
H+7	6	Ramrod	12	**21** (880) CO 880 Dixon Arkell Scott	**23** (880) Goodfellow S/Lt Simpson Patullo Tucker	**25** (880) Yate Banyard Dent Lethem
H+10	8	CAP	16	**11** CO 801 Primrose Griffith Glazebrook **17** Green Steel Losee Culling	**12** Saxe Squires McLean Tillet	**16** Luing Stock Cowley Wright
H+13	10	CAP	20	**13** (880) Wing Leader Marshall Dancaster Wheeldon	**15** Gunson Clark Thomson Bedore	**22** (880) Pye Smith Kirby Wager

880 and 801 Squadrons Flying Programme 18 July 1945.

Time	Serial	Duty	A/C	Allocation		
H	1	CAP	12	**12**	**16**	**17**
				Saxe	Luing	Green
				Squires	Stock	Steel
				McLean	Cowley	Sheeran
				Tillet	Wright	Losee
+2.30	2	Ramrod	12	**21 (880)**	**23 (880)**	**25 (880)**
				CO 880	Goodfellow	Yate
				Dixon	Simpson	Banyard
				Arkell	Patullo	Dent
				Scott	Tucker	Lethem
H+5	4	CAP	16	**22 (880)**	**26 (880)**	**25 (880)**
				Pye	Dancaster	Saxe
				Smith	Wheeldon	Squires
				Arkell	Boak	Thomson
				Scott	Snell	Bedore
H+7.30	6	Ramrod	8	**11**	**14**	
				CO 801	Brewer	
				Primrose	Geary	
				Griffith	Jervis	
				Glazebrook	Holway	
	7	CAP	12	**21 (880)**	**24 (880)**	**15 (880)**
				CO880	Simpson	Gunson
				Dixon	Gilmore	Clark
				Arkell	Boak	Thomson
				Scott	Snell	Bedore
H+10	8	CAP	16	**22 (880)**	**23 (880)**	**25 (880)**
				Pye	Goodfellow	Yate
				Smith	Simpson	Banyard
				Kirby	Patullo	Dent
				Wager	Tucker	Lethem
				26 (880)		
				Dancaster		
				Wheeldon		
				Marshall		
				Seigne		
H+13	10	CAP	20	**11**	**14**	**16**
				CO 801	Brewer	Luing
				Primrose	Geary	Stock
				Griffith	Jervis	Cowley
				Glazebrook	Holway	Wright
				21 (880)	**24 (880)**	
				CO 880	Simpson	
				Dixon	Gilmore	
				Arkell	Boak	
				Snell	Graham	

Squadrons — 801 and 880

				14	**24 (880)**	
				Brewer	Lt Simpson	
				Geary	Gilmore	
				Jervis	Boak	
				Holway	Graham	

(Those **not** marked 880 are 801).

Day One. 17 July. 801, the 'senior' of the two Seafire squadrons on board, had first pick, and took off at 0630 with 16 Seafires — on a ramrod. The fleets were steaming into wind at a distance of about 160 miles from the Japanese coast. The first strikes were to be against a part of the coast of Honshu just south of Sendai, north of Tokyo. I had taken off at the same time with 12 Seafires of 880 for CAP. We immediately realised that the weather on this day was to be the main enemy. The cloud was down to 500 feet and we circled for half an hour before finding a hole through which to climb, to carry out our CAP. We flew for three and a half hours without seeing the sea once, positioning ourselves some 20 miles to the west of the BPF by means of our radio beacons.

When we landed we learned with surprise that C-H and Stuart Jewers had been sent off for their 'ramrod'. It was obvious that they were not going to be able to see a thing. They returned three hours later, just before flying was cancelled, to say that they had been over Japan. This was a bit of a line shoot. They, too, had not seen the coast or the sea throughout their entire trip. Meanwhile, we were not surprised that the Japanese had not attempted to find Task Force 37 for their weather would have been as unflyable as ours. The experienced Americans made no strike effort whatsoever. The only success of the day was by 1834 Squadron in *Victorious*. The CO, Lt/Cdr George Baldwin, DSC, RNVR, had found that the weather over Japan was clear on the far westerly coast. He had flown with great skill and determination clean over Japan and the weather and had attacked Niigarta airfield on the other side. Three of his Corsairs had been hit by flak, however, and these ditched alongside the Fleet. All three pilots were picked up by *Terpsicore,* our attendant ASR destroyer. After our 0830 CAP landed, Charles Evans told us that the Admiral had at last called it a day.

Day Two. 18 July. The weather seemed to be the same as the day before. A glance at a fair copy of the flying programme for this day will reveal that 21 Flight was due to carry out three flights, some nine hours flying. As Stuart had had first pick the day before, I was allowed to choose on the second day and chose the first 'ramrod'. My target, with Goodfellow's and Yate's Flights, was Kanoike airfield, in the same area as the day before and about 150 miles distant. Our take-off time was 0530. We all managed to get off and form up in the drizzle and we set course for our first attack on Japan.

We could not keep low, for the cloud merged with fog down to sea level in places. We dodged about on the way in and eventually found a hole to climb through. We were then able to fly between two layers of cloud, hoping that we would catch sight of the coast so that we could fix our position and find our target. Five miles from the coast there was a small clear patch and we came down through the cloud over the sea. We crept up on our target's estimated position at nought feet. This was exactly as we had practised so often in the Orkneys and in much the same sort of weather.

During the dive on the target I was so busy looking at the ground for a Jap aircraft to shoot at that I did not see any flak. We made the usual single strafing run from three different directions and immediately retired to our rendezvous out to sea. Peter Arkell, my number three for this and many other strikes at this time, describes the scene:

> "You could often see the tracers coming up as you dived and you got shaken around by their 40mm too as you approached sometimes. But with our newly invented scheme it was all over in 30 seconds. We fired everything at them and never came back. We made a fair bit of mincemeat of them and there was no need for another one. As we came in from so

many different directions, the Jap gunners didn't know which way to look and they were running all over the place. Some of the aircraft that we shot up were marvellous dummies and I can't remember seeing many of them burn. I think the real ones must have had no fuel in them, for they never seemed to catch fire properly."

During the dive, I pulled out much lower than I should have done. While only a few feet above the airfield, I caught sight of one of these dummies. It had greenery growing out of it and it looked a very crude shape indeed. However, from 8000 feet, our pushover height, it would have been difficult to distinguish from the real thing. Only stereo photography would have done so from that height and this was not in use yet in the RN.

After we re-formed out to sea, we flew south along the coast for a while. The leader of any formation has a much better opportunity than the others to have a look round. The others have to watch out for enemy aircraft or changes in course, height or speed and to maintain formation. While I was looking round for another target, I saw a line of fishing boats moored to a long quay in the harbour of Chosi. They were neatly bow-on to the quay and they made perfect targets, for if we missed one we were bound to hit another, they were so close together. The Japanese must have been warned by telephone from Kanoike, for they had plenty of guns ready and started to fire at us well before we started our dives. At this we made a turn out to sea and came back fast from three directions. This divided their fire at each aircraft by a factor of 12 and their flak was not so worrying. We emptied our magazines in a single dive at these 30 ships. Dougy turned on his F24 camera as well.

After the strafing run at Chosi, we turned for home. I changed to our 'Tomcat's' homing frequency, hoping that we would see her in the thick weather. The returning instructions were complicated. The Kamikazes, never sure of the exact position of their targets, had adopted another clever ruse. They sometimes followed astern of returning strikes, hoping that their radar blips would then merge with ours and so escape detection. The Tomcats' CAP of about 16 Corsairs, circling astern, above and below us, would 'delouse' any possible Kamikaze from us. This was the procedure and it took a great deal of extra time, particularly in bad weather in an 'alert'. If a mistake was made, the Tomcat might fire at us. The American Corsairs might not have seen Seafires and they, too, might be trigger happy. However, we passed unscathed through their net and joined *Implacable*'s waiting position with about 50 others, dropping our hooks ready for landing.

Admiral Vian was quite right keeping most of our Seafires in reserve until the Japanese showed their hands over their Kamikazes, and until *Indefatigable* arrived. Ours had therefore been the only Seafire 'ramrod' on Day Two, and the first offensive strike by Seafires on Japan. That night, as the BPF and the Americans withdrew to replenish, we were able to relax. The Captain of Marines ran the ship's internal 'radio' entertainment. I was asked to describe the first trip over Japan. I should have realised that 801 would be listening, for they claimed to be the first over Japan. *Implacable*'s Fireflies were first of any British aircraft over Japan, and the Seafires of 801 probably the second, but as neither saw the land, or a target, their claim is meaningless. George Baldwin's Corsairs were obviously the first BPF aircraft to *strike* Japan.

By the afternoon of 23 July, we had finished our replenishment and had also been joined by *Indefatigable,* hot-foot from Sydney. We now had 250 aircraft in the BPF, 90 of them Seafires.

Day Three. 24 July. As usual, we were briefed the night before. We learned that the Japanese had started to reinforce their airfields with new aircraft. There were now supposed to be nearly 60 at some airfields. Susuka, Akenogahara and Tokushima and the seaplane base at Komatsushima were reported as having 350 aircraft between them.

We were also told to expect to see Superforts (B29s) in our area. The American carriers themselves would be attacking Japanese Naval shipping almost exclusively for the next two or three days. The US Navy wanted to complete their revenge for Pearl Harbor, and they wanted no help from us.

Norman had put my lot down for the first 'ramrod'. This had a take-off time of 0345 in darkness. I was given a 'shake' at 0230 after about two hours sleep. My and Bob Simpson's Flight's target was Tokushima, a distance of 150 miles, well into the northern entrance of the Inland Sea. We formed up in the darkness and set course.

Our target was easy to find on the coast. It was also in a clear patch. I aimed at a twin engined aircraft. None of us stayed long enough to find out how we had got on. On the way back we dived at Komatsushima. Here the flak was very easy to see. They had obviously had warning from our attack further up the coast and were ready for us. There were several twin float-planes drawn up on the sloping concrete slipways and we hit many of them. It was rewarding to see our cannon shells exploding in bright flashes in the dawn light as they hit the slipways round the targets. Once again the attack was all over in ten seconds or so and none of us were hit by flak. Now, in the lightening early morning, we set course for home and began to feel less lonely and afraid once we were over the sea.

On the way home, my Flight — 21 — was below the cloud at about 4000 feet. Bob — 24 Flight — had climbed up in visual contact as usual, to get a bearing on the Tomcat's beacon. We had no sooner set course when David Graham, Bob's Number 4, came up on the r/t and said that his engine had stopped. He said it was not picking up on the main tanks. Pete Arkell followed him all the way. Graham was gliding with his hood open. Pete kept telling him to bale out. Graham left it until he was no higher than 200 feet over the sea hoping his engine would re-start. He did not get clear of the aircraft. I summoned the ASR 'Dumbo'. It landed by the splash mark within about ten minutes and reported over the distress frequency that Graham's Mae West was not inflated and he was still attached to his parachute. He was lifted from the sea, but was found to have been injured and had drowned. David Graham was a fine Kiwi with a wife and family and we missed him badly.

At 1100 it was 801's turn for a 'ramrod'. Their target was the seaplane base at Suta, on Shikoku. Stuart Jewers, leading, flew blind over the 6000 foot mountains in the island's interior, coming down over the Inland Sea in clear weather on the far side in a very successful strike. His ramrod shot-up several 'Mavis' aircraft. While pulling out of his dive, S/Lt Glen Bedore's wings came off and he went in. He was a Canadian and one of the new boys who always flew with enthusiasm and skill.

At 1700 it was 880's turn once more. Our target was Takamatsu airfield, supposedly crammed with 50 aircraft. Our briefing photographs showed that it also had 120 guns surrounding it and we were told to expect fighters too. The weather was much better than we had expected and we were able to make our usual attack system. We hardly saw any flak. I aimed at a 'Myrt'. Norman Goodfellow also chased a train into a tunnel. He said that he could not resist it as it steamed its way peacefully along the coastal railway by the airfield. We flew back, using the seaward route round the Inland Sea. If any of our engines stopped on the way back, we would rather bale out over water than over

Japanese territory, for we had heard what the locals might do to us if they caught us. Some Fireflies from 1772 Squadron on *Indefatigable,* later made a second strike on this worthwhile target. (This attack is depicted in a painting in the Fleet Air Arm Museum. From the picture, it appears 1772 encountered a great deal more flak than we did.)

According to my log book I landed from the Takamatsu strike at 1950, when it was almost dark. I had just returned to my cabin on E deck when the Action Stations bugle sounded. I went up to the Ops room and found the usual chaos, with two Seafires running up on the flight deck in the last of the twilight. The Flagship had ordered them off, it seemed. The two 880 pilots were John Boak, the Canadian pianist swallow-diver, and his Number 2, the new boy — John Joly. They carried no tanks so they could climb quickly if required. Their target was a series of incoming enemy 'plots' which *Formidable's* skilful ADR had disentangled from the 'friendlies' returning with us from our evening strikes. The BPF's chief 'stop-me-and-buy-one' was Commander Lewin[1]. He also alerted the Americans and they scrambled eight of their AI-equipped Hellcat nightfighters. These were in addition to our two Seafires and a flight of four 'specialist' Hellcats from *Formidable.*

Our two Seafires, being low-level aircraft, were useless for high level interceptions, but the Flagship, apparently unaware of this, vectored John Boak out on a course of 050 degrees and told him to climb to a height of about 15,000 feet. At this height he and Joly could hardly make 250 knots flat out. They saw nothing, and after explaining over the radio that the contacts were probably radar decoys dropped by the overhead Japs, he asked permission to return to land on. It was getting darker by the minute — even at 15,000 feet — and Joly had about 15 minutes fuel left.

Meanwhile, the Americans had succeeded in intercepting all the Japanese aircraft with their AI-equipped Hellcats and had shot six down. In addition, the flight of Hellcats from *Formidable* had found there was still enough light to see at 20,000 feet — the Japanese approach height — and S/Lt Atkinson of 1884 Squadron had destroyed another — a 'Betty'.

A late evening attack on his Fleet was not an entirely new set of circumstances for Admiral Vian, but in order to operate a single aircraft from one of the carriers in BPF that evening, the Admiral had to turn his entire 25 ships through 180 degrees and head westwards into the westerly wind, back towards Japan, and burn considerable quantities of valuable fuel oil while doing it. (Not so the Americans, who operated their light Fleet carrier *Bonhomme Richard* exclusively for their night fighters, well away from the main fleet; and, whereas the British were loath to use any sort of landing lights to assist land on, the American carriers, out of range of the Japanese strikes, could do as they wished.) Therefore, when John Boak made his plea to be allowed to land on, he got short shrift from the Flagship, who told him to 'ditch astern'.

Charles Evans knew, as everyone else in *Implacable,* that ditching astern in the ten foot swell left by the passage of 25 ships at high speed, would be suicide, even for a Sunderland flying boat in daytime, let alone for a Seafire at night. Baling out would be just as hazardous.

I heard from Charles that the Flagship was still unwilling to turn into wind to land them on — before the Hellcats — but I was able to get them to change to the *Implacable's* private land-on frequency and join the ship's landing circuit. In this way, they would be talking to friends, at least, during their last moments,

[1]Captain E. D. G. Lewin, CB, CBE, DSO, DSC, RN, later commanded *Eagle* and after retirement, became Managing Director of Hawker-Siddeley Dynamics.

and not to the Flagship, who had no idea of their difficulties and seemed to care less. At last, the Hellcats were ordered to return. The fleet turned into wind and John Joly made his first night decklanding. Had he missed or crashed, there would have been no fuel left for Boak to go round again. That would have been the end of him. Having unselfishly allowed Joly to land first, he just made it, bursting both tyres.

I cannot imagine anything more frightening for the 'new boy', John Joly, than a night decklanding in a Seafire, short of fuel. With no reference marks whatever on the ground, dropping the hook, opening the hood, even changing radio frequencies, a few hundred feet from the blackness of the sea below him, is asking a great deal when flying a day fighter unequipped for night flying. The batsman's illuminated wands were all the deck lighting these pilots were allowed. John Joly said that he could hardly see a thing, either in the cockpit or outside. The sparks from the exhaust kept blinding him, the red hot exhaust stubs too. The only reason, he said, why he managed to keep straight, was that the ship had her mast head light on and he aimed at that, keeping it in line with the reflection in her white wake, "until he saw Trevor David frantically waving his bats about".

Day Four. 25 July. This was another chaotic day. I tried to describe it in my diary:

"Today's targets were in the same area as yesterday. My (21) Flight and seven others did a CAP at dawn. C-H led the first 'ramrod' by Seafires. He had a Flight of 801 and one of ours, Norman Goodfellow's. He led the strike literally into the coast, seeing it at the last moment before breaking away. Norman just saw the cliff ahead in time, but Len Simpson, his Number 2 managed to hit it. He arrived back on board with a piece of Japanese tree sticking out of his starboard radiator intake. To make matters worse for Len, his engine failed to pick up on the approach. He pumped furiously with his throttle, and it managed to cough into life just as he was about to ditch. As he had his wheels down — like Ken Boardman — it is doubtful whether he would have got out had he hit the sea. Len was still smiling. His mum would have been proud of him."

"Twenty-one Flight had originally been put down for a 'ramrod', but when I got to the briefing, Ops had changed it to a (close) escort for an Avenger strike. The leader was from another carrier and there was no opportunity to find out where and at what height he might be going. I had already made up my mind before take-off that unless the weather was superb, there would be no future whatever in forging on over Japan at 5000 feet, straight into cloud, not knowing where the target was or anything about it. So that when this very thing actually happened and the Avenger leader forged off straight into the nearest flak and into a wall of cloud, I pulled off to one side and had a look for my own target with 21 and 23 Flights. We set a small coaster on fire and hit two tug-sized ships in the Inland Sea."

"On returning I heard that Doug Patullo was missing. He was returning with his Number 2, Tucker, when his engine had stopped. He was above cloud and his aircraft turned over on its back while he was baling out but he did not seem to get clear before it disappeared into the cloud, upside down."

"The correct drill was followed but the Dumbo[1] and the rest of the formation found nothing whatever under the cloud, having searched for

[1] American ASR Flying Boat.

an hour. Poor Doug. He was a good pilot. That's two from 880 and one from 801. The only consolation is that we have heard that the Corsairs are losing a lot more in their bombing runs."

"Dennis Kirby led a CAP today. He was briefed to carry out his patrol at 27,000 feet. As we only had LIIIs, it was rather a stupid requirement. He managed to get there all right, but only just. He had about 95 knots on the clock, maximum IAS. If any Japs had come along he would have been unable to do anything about it. They need a copy of Pilot's Notes in *Formidable's* Ops, I should think. I will ask Wings whether I can drop them a copy."

Day Five. 28 July. "Dougy (Yate) is OK again. We go back to the same area. There's a typhoon warning."

"Stuart did a 'ramrod' to Sato, and, later, another to Minato. Sato is on the western shore of Shikoku in the Inland Sea. Minato is a small island in the Inland Sea, west of Wakayama."

"Our three Flights — 21 and Dougy's and Crusty's — go to Minato, taking off at 1130. Alan Dent and Dougy do an F24 camera run and the rest of us do the usual 'surprise' strafing. Dougy chased the occupants of a junk round the far side of their deckhouse and they fell into the sea. The Inland Sea looks so peaceful — until we arrive. Then it erupts in all manner of corruption from all directions, and the scene is changed entirely."

"Almost immediately after landing and with no lunch, the target was again Minato. Armed with the photographic results from our earlier 'ramrod', we each had our private targets to aim at. Norman went a little further west afterwards with his four towards Sato. He told me that he had not fired at his shipping target as he had seen women and children on board. But as he pulled away he had caught sight of a 'grey device' poking out of the cliffside, 'obviously a heavily camouflaged Jap destroyer'."

Alan Swanton's Avengers of 828 Squadron bombed it next day. They missed.

Day Six. 30 July. "Stuart did the first 'ramrod' but returns having seen nothing in thick fog over the coast. By 0830 it seems to have cleared, so 21, 25 and 22, with Dennis as Number 3, set off. Our target is Susuka. This is a very heavily populated airfield in the Mitsubishi factory area south of Nagoya. It is supposed to have had 80 fighter aircraft on it and 200 guns. I could not work out any suitable approaches to it on the photograph at the briefing, for guns seemed to be everywhere."

"We made our usual low approach, in clear weather. When we got past Akenogahara, low cloud had come over the land as far as the beach, right where our target was supposed to be. We obviously could not attack it by going under the cloud, and it would be too risky diving through the cloud without first checking its height above the ground. I asked Dougy to take his Flight low down over the sea, to have a look *under* the cloud to assess its height. He did so and piped up that it was about 2000 feet. I did a 'tell-off' so that everyone could hear the plan of action, to go *through* the cloud in our strafing run."

"We had lost surprise by hanging about making up our minds. As we climbed to 10,000 feet for our usual attack, I, and it seems many of the others, were bumped clean out of our seats by the flak. We turned back and went away for ten minutes. We came in faster from a new direction, from Nagoya, and this time it seemed to surprise them. I saw no flak on my dive. The dive through the cloud was very dicey indeed — watching the altimeter unwind — and I was relieved to see the target as I came out of it in the middle of the airfield, heading towards the hangars. I shot at a black-painted twin-engined job (probably a 'Betty'), I flew on between the hangars, which seemed to go by above me. I could see people staring up as I passed and I also began to notice a bit of flak."

"Above the clouds and the airfield, once more I turned round to see what was happening to the others and I could hear some voices on the r/t warning someone about flak. I could see a mass of 40 mm bursting over the clouds over the airfield and Seafires turning and twisting to get away from it."

"Out to sea and safety once more, I heard Dougy's voice shout, 'I've been hit'. Then after a pause, 'I'm in trouble'. Pain was in his voice. Then again, 'I'm in trouble'. I told him he must fly over the sea and bale out. We would look after him."

"I thought I could see his aircraft, but it probably was not him. I told the others to watch for the splash if he ditched and went over to the Dumbo radio channel. I searched on my knee pad for the codeword for the rescue position. 'One downed Circus Chicken, 15, 'Mother's Monthly', 260, over.' The reply came immediately. They were on their way. I changed back to the squadron strike frequency to hear how things were getting on. Had Dougy baled out yet? Pete Arkell came up and said that Dougy had turned over on his back and had gone straight in. 'I was right behind him when it happened,' he said."

"We searched the sea along the coast, right by the airfield. I could see a white splash mark on the sea and I wondered whether it was Dougy's."

After landing-on, none of us could believe that we had lost Dougy. But as the day wore on and we had heard that the Dumbo had found nothing except dye marker in the water we began to believe that he really must have gone in with his aircraft. It was indeed a terrible tragedy to us all. There was no one who could replace him. However, we had done some damage to Susuka, and there would be several less Kamikaze pilots and their death machines.

Our next 'ramrod', for 21, 24 and 26 Flights was scheduled to take off at 1430. None of us felt like lunch except 'Iron-swede' Mike Banyard, who seemed, as usual, remarkably unruffled by the morning's experience. Just before take-off, the 'ramrod' was again changed into a close escort. There were to be about 46 planes in our strike and my 12 Seafires were to be close escort for about 20 Avengers. No one could tell me the name of the target. I was told to "get briefed in the air".

The leader of the Avengers circled the entire BPF three times before eventually setting course — for I knew not where. I took three sheets of foolscap out of my knee pocket. In between flying the aeroplane, looking at a few instruments and watching where I was leading the others, I thumbed over the pages headed 'Not to be Taken into the Air'.

I was trying to find out what the call-sign of my leader might be. His name, I afterwards discovered, was Lt/Cdr J. C. Shrubsole, RN. He was the senior aviator in the party and therefore was the leader. The fact that he was an Observer and couldn't even see where he was going in the back of an Avenger, did not alter things. The three sheets of foolscap had been written by another Observer of impeccable background, one of the bravest men in the Fleet Air Arm. But he naturally knew nothing whatever of what went on in a fighter cockpit approaching the Japanese coastline at 5000 feet, any more than did Lt/Cdr Griffith.

Reading the 'crib', I worked out that assuming we were taking part in the fifth strike of the day and we were the squadron in the right hand, forward close escort, there would be a chance that our call-sign would be Five Network, Forward, Right, 21 Leader. My number two would be called the same amount with '2' at the end of it in place of the word 'Leader'.

I managed to wait patiently until there was a gap in the gossip on our strike frequency. As there was no 'Mr Speaker' keeping order, I finally butted in and asked the leader where the hell we were going? Apart from a tactical interest, I also wanted to know so that I could arrange for the Dumbo. Without my knowing where I was, I could not give the Dumbo a reference point, neither could anyone else in my lot. When the leader replied, I could not understand a word he said, I think that he was trying to give me the information in latitude and longitude, with the code word for the reference point 'shackled' in an MI5-type code system. By the time I had decoded his message — that we were going to the western coast of Honshu in the direction of Maizuru Naval Base — we were there. So much for 'airborne briefing'.

Through the haze I could just see the outline of a small fiord-like inlet. It was half hidden by flecks of cloud, or perhaps by smoke from the burning nearby town — which the B29s had just 'worked over', I have learned since.

Before I had time to think, we had arrived over the top of a destroyer. It was under way, leaving a white curved wake behind it as it sped for the entrance of the fiord. I told my lot to fan out for a quick dive and down we all went, very steeply.

The angle was extremely steep, at least 65-75 degrees. My speed at the bottom must have been about 400 knots. I found myself having to push hard on the stick during the pullout to prevent too much 'g'. (See Appendix 11 (c), Stability problems.) My shells had scarcely had time to hit the water round the destroyer target before it was time to start the pull-out. I hoped that the others had managed to get a better bead on the target than I had. At 7000 feet once more and having 'come to' from the usual blackout, I caught sight of a few flying boats at their moorings in an inlet on the northern shore of the fiord. We had come a long way and I had not much ammunition left. I called the rest down to have another go. We had the satisfaction of seeing one of them keel over and another two catch fire.

Feeling cut off from our friends and lonely on the far side of Japan, we formed up clear of the flak and set course to the east once more. The heavy calibre flak followed us as we climbed furiously. It was accurate for line and deflection. However, because we were fighters and could climb far faster than the average bomber, we were able to keep one jump ahead of its height computing system, for the shells burst a few hundred feet below us all the time. Nevertheless, we could see their angry red centres as they did so, and we could hear them too. It was a bumpy ride back.

The ship had moved well to the north of our take-off position so we headed nearer to the immense and sacred mountain of Fuji Yama, visible above the 10,000 foot haze layer, as our beacons told us to head in that direction. We had been 200 miles to the target, and back a further 220, so that the Tomcat's delousing procedure seemed particularly ponderous that evening. The 'Not to be taken into the air' foolscap sheets said:

"Aircraft will return via Tomcat on prescribed sector in enemy direction, thence transferring to own carrier YE beacon sector on disengaged side. After visual 'delousing' by CAP and by visual and radar identification (IFF) on Tomcat's radar, CAP will then look for the trailing enemy. Returning formation leader, now at 5000 feet or below overcast, will then call Tomcat, using coded callsign of the correct day/time group as necessary. This will be on Channel D, for reporting IN and OUT."

There was no sign of the Tomcat in the haze. We expected its CAP to come whirling out of the mist at us any moment. We could hardly have cared had they done so. The radio was totally cluttered up and we were feeling knackered.

When we eventually landed-on with a few gallons to spare, I went up to see Wings, as usual. I was greeted with Charles Evans'welcoming smile and, "How d'you get on Mike?" But the Captain was looking a little worried and I could feel that there was considerable tension on the bridge.

Later I found out from C-H that Charles had doubtless saved many of our lives again. He had 'done a Troubridge' and had refused to answer the Flagship's order to turn 180 degrees away from the Japanese coast during the latter part of our land-on. He knew that, having just emerged from the fog, he would have to head back into it once more. By the time *Implacable* could have got clear once more and into wind, her Seafires — all our eight — would have run out of fuel and would have had to have ditched. As there was a ten foot swell running, we should have killed ourselves if we had tried to ditch — as was the usual suggestion from the Flagship — and attempting to bale out would have been equally fatal. Perhaps the Flagship's attitude might have been understandable had the Seafire been an ordinary, ditchable, bale-outable Naval aircraft, for the Fleet was heading into Tokyo Bay, almost in sight of land. But we resented the inference that we were expendable in *Implacable*. *Indefatigable* had stopped operating Seafires owing to the swell and the pitching deck, so perhaps *Implacable* deserved to be taught a lesson. The Flagship obviously thought so.

Charles Evans, later Vice-Admiral Sir Charles Evans, KCB, DSO, DSC, RN, wrote later of this episode. He said "he (Vian) never forgave me" for turning a blind eye to his signal. Admiral Vian, on his part, was additionally peeved because the Americans later described his action as that of an "inexperienced carrier Admiral", knowing that he already had three years experience.

That evening we were to retire for refuelling once more. This time we had several days rest. Our sister squadron's Line Book reads like this:

"**3 August.** Kamikaze TOSX Exercise with 880."

" **6 August.** Oiling with Fleet Train. Stores taken on board by jackstay. Lt Luing, S/Lt Primrose and S/Lt Green ferry aircraft from *Chaser.*"

"**7 August.** Another day of rest. Maintenance on aircraft, we are to strike again on 8th, but weather does not look too promising. Briefing on targets."

"**8 August.** Everyone had early shakes. The first strike was cancelled by AC1. Reverted to 'condition 12'. In the afternoon, condition 11 was piped but nothing happened. It was a long, hot, boring and frustrating hang about. We hope for better weather tomorrow. The Americans 'splashed' one 'Dinah' and one 'Nick'. They had to chase the latter a long way. S/Lt (A) D. G. Anderson, RNZNVR, joined from the Seafire Pool."

During this 'rest' period, during which Hiroshima received the first atom bomb, it might be a suitable point in the narrative to record progress, for the BPF had already carried out more 'ramrod' strike sorties in six days than in the whole of the 24 days of Operation 'Iceberg'. The highest number of sorties-per-day, so far, in the BPF, had been 416 on 24 July, of which 261 had been over Japan. On 30 July the Fleet had done 216 offensives, 30 Wing's share having been 46 plus 42 CAP sorties. This was 34% of all sorties with but 18% of the BPF's aircraft.

Our reward in *Implacable* for this hard work was to receive no special congratulation from the Flagship but a 'round robin' exhortation to do better:

"To: 1st AC (All Carriers) From: AC1 (Admiral Vian)

The richness of the opportunity offered our squadrons in the past few days and in those few which lie ahead must be unparalleled in our sea/air history. Nor does it seem that such golden chances are ever likely to be offered us again in the same degree.

2.   Thus in the estimations of the future much may depend on the results which are achieved against enemy aircraft and shipping in the present operation.

3.   Having in mind that the shipping targets have often been combative vessels at anchor, that airborne opposition has been non-existent and flak not unduly severe, the hits so far obtained from TBRs (the Avengers) have been less than might have been expected.

4.   All attacks however simple must be properly planned and carefully and deliberately executed.

5.   Formation leaders must brief subordinates either on the ground or in the air of their general intentions and special instructions.

6.   When flak is light press low to bomb, to hit, and sink."

Although this signal apparently referred mostly to the Avengers, the most "subordinate" aircrew could see that it was written by someone who was used to controlling battleships rather than aircraft and that it was full of the most frightful blunders. To imagine that after four years of war that airborne briefing was an alternative to proper ground briefing was absurd. To suggest that "if flak is light" — and if such could be assessed beforehand — that hits could be better obtained by "pressing low", with the highly unsuitable level bombing techniques used by the Avengers, was equally absurd. Bombing release heights are strictly controlled to match the type of target — hard or soft — the weather, terrain, fuze settings and cloud height. The Avenger was totally unsuitable as a 'ramrod-type' strike aircraft. It approached at medium height giving warning of its approach. It had none of the sophisticated sighting apparatus of a high level bomber nor the speed and manoeuvrability of a dive bomber. The Corsairs and Hellcats were, on the other hand, ideal. They could carry 2x500 lb bombs plus a full load of .5 inch ammunition from six guns; but even they could not improve their chance by paying the slightest heed to AC1's signal. It destroyed what little faith remained in our hearts for our leader.

Had we been given the opportunity to criticise our Admiral we would have taken him to task for sending us out in impossible flying weather. We had the suspicion that he had done this on several occasions to get one over on the Yanks.

Following this signal, we were delighted to get a congratulatory message from Admiral Brind, CS4, who had been our Admiral at Truk. He said:

"I have been watching *Implacable* and her airmen with special interest and admiration. Congratulations."

This was very bold of Admiral Brind, for he repeated his signal to the Flagship. He probably knew of the problems and the prejudices concerning the *Implacable* and the Seafire.

We replied "Very many thanks for your nice signal".

Although the rest period after 30 July extended to seven days, there was almost as much nervous energy expended for several of these days as if we had been operating. The 'TOSX' (Throw Off Shoot Exercise) on 3 August was an American idea. We dived steeply like Kamikazes to give a realistic approach speed and angle of dive to the gunners. They fired live shells offset by ten degrees. We hoped that they would always 'throw off' by the correct amount.

When we landed from this exercise, the ship was rolling in a cross-swell. It was coming in from a typhoon to the south-west, at right angles to the wind. This made it necessary to lash each aircraft down on deck immediately after landing for fear it might roll over the side with us still aboard.

During this period I was told that 880 Squadron would be merged with 801. Stuart Jewers would be going ashore at Nowra to take over the Seafire Pool and train up new pilots. C-H would shortly be going back to the UK to take over St. Merryn Fighter Leaders Course on Seafire XVs and 47s, and I would take over the combined squadrons. A new post was created — that of Air Group Commander. Lt/Col Peter Nelson-Gracie, Royal Marines, would be filling this post. The idea was that instead of a 'Douglas Bader' — leading 'fighters only' into air battles — it was now felt more appropriate that we should have a Strike Leader to take over the briefing and the leading of the entire carrier's aircraft. Our complaints about lack of effective briefing and poor strike leading must have borne fruit.

Peter Nelson-Gracie was a super chap with a very relaxed manner and with sufficient humility and skill to fall into place in *Implacable* without fuss or bother. At the same time as these changes in the command arrangements, I learned that I had been given an immediate award of a Bar to the DSC.

The chaos and indecision of the last few days and the dearth of information about our movements had come about — apart from the diversions caused by atom bombs on Hiroshima and Nagasaki on 6 and 8 August — because of the BPF's dire shortage of oil and the need to get clear of any possible nuclear fall-out. Apparently, much of the oil supply destined for carriers had been needed for yet another bombardment of the Japanese mainland. But as *KGV* now had technical trouble, the urgent arrangements made to refuel her had been cancelled at the last moment. This resulted in many ex-bombardment ships not having enough fuel to close with the tankers. AC1 was determined not to cancel flying operations, even if "we had to tow a few destroyers back to Sydney," but the consequent refuelling chaos had separated the BPF from the Americans by 120 miles. As the RN had no r/t relay aircraft, a string of ships was required to relay the air operational briefing for the strikes scheduled for 9 August. The information arrived late and garbled. By the time I had 'turned in' on the evening of 8 August, we still had no idea of the details of our targets on the morrow. As we were due to 'man our ships' at 0345 for the first 'ramrod', we got little sleep.

Day Seven, 9 August. We arrived for briefing at 0300, feeling sick and having had no breakfast. I discovered that our land-on time was only two hours after take-off. The target — Matsushima — was 170 miles away. Those in the Flagship must have looked at the Pilot's Notes which I had dropped on their flight deck from my aircraft and discovered that the Seafire's max cruise speed, without overload tanks of course, was 275 knots, which indeed it was. What they would not have known — because not one of them had ever flown a fighter, let alone a Seafire — was that it used treble the amount of fuel at the full throttle power necessary to achieve this speed with a long range tank, and that we would run out of fuel after 1½ hours. Having made my complaint to Ops (C-H had said that we should go straight to the 'Dud Circle' and not go at all) I went up to the flight deck and climbed into my aircraft. Then I was handed a note. The messenger had appeared suddenly and disappeared as quickly — a grey fleeting figure in the dawn light. By the lights in the cockpit I read: "OK to take 2½ hours". Even at that we should have to motor.

The ship was already heeling, turning into wind. My rigger waggled an aileron to get my attention to start up. When the ship had righted a little, I pressed the starter and booster coil buttons. I had no time to test tank transfer or magnetos and barely time to warm up before I was tearing down the deck into a dark, grey and featureless sky. Once airborne, and away from the total chaos of a carrier's flight deck, the mind had time to settle down and fright vanished. The boys did a marvellous join-up and we set course without wasting a drop of fuel.

We arrived within sight of the grey coastline in about 80 minutes of fast going, at plus four boost and 2400 rpm. The coastline changed from distant grey to nearer green, then to individual terraced fields and buildings, looking down at us. We had not spoken a word on the r/t. The boys were so used to the drill by now that talk over the r/t was unnecessary. We made our usual climb and descent onto our target, Matsushima airfield, sending up clouds of earth and fire as our 20 mm explosive shells hit the shapeless, camouflaged humps of aircraft parked out on the airfield. In the lightening sky, Len Simpson took pictures overhead. He used a single oblique F24 camera loaded with '400' panchromatic film. It had an eight inch focal length lens, iris at F 4.5 — fully open — and the 'interval-ometer' at two frames per second, shutter speed at one five-hundredth of a second. We set course home.

Expecting delays at the Tomcat — enemy action had been reported over the r/t — and not sure of the ship's position, we climbed for a beacon course home and changed to internal tanks. We used maximum weak mixture cruise, plus two boost and 2000 rpm. As we carried the same fuel capacity in our jet tanks as in our internal tanks, the fact that I had had to transfer to internal tanks half way through the trip meant that there would be no fuel left for waiting at the far end.

We made *Implacable's* circuit after three hours and 20 minutes — nearly an hour late. The ship was 50 miles further south than briefed. Once again we had to thank Charles Evans and the Captain for keeping the flight deck open for us. At least *they* knew what the problems were.

When I got to the bridge, Charles Evans did not mention my late arrival from the 'ramrod'. However, he smiled as he showed me a signal from Vian, which said:

"What is the delay?" — the third from the Flagship during these operations.

While we had been airborne on our first 'ramrod', Lt Ray Saxe had to lead C-H's first trip, as C-H and his Number 2 had collided on the flight deck and neither got off. Their target was Matsushima, their time of arrival was an hour after we had left. Saxe's and Tucker's engines stopped after their attack and they both ditched in the shallow water at the side of the airfield. They were reported to the Dumbo by Squires and Tillet of the same strike, but the latter had to leave before the Dumbo arrived, owing to shortage of fuel. (They too, had had to try to get back in 2½ hours.) Although the Dumbo found both aviators in their dinghies and brought them back, Squires and Tillet were not so lucky. Not finding the ship in her briefed position they flew past her without realising it. They climbed to try to find her by homing beacon but failed to hear it. They then transferred to the American rescue frequency, to ask them for a homing. The Americans heard then but could not identify them from the clutter of other aircraft on their radar. Although Squires and Tillet could be heard by everyone at this stage, they could not hear any of the ships answering them. The Americans eventually sorted out their the BPF's IFF code from the multitude of other aircraft on their plots and sent the CAP after them to intercept them and bring them home. However, the Seafires ran out of fuel before this plan could succeed. They were transmitting a running commentary. Tillet's last transmission was to say that his engine had stopped, so, to keep together they both baled out. Then there was silence. They were never found. Knowing, as we do now, the immense dangers in trying to bale out inverted from a Seafire III (See Appendix 11 (d)), it is not surprising. In spite of searches lasting for two days during all the daylight hours, only an airman's dinghy was found and that was empty.

Continuing the narrative for the remaining sorties on 9 August, C-H's second attempt to get off the deck was successful. He had been briefed to go to Matsushima but chose Onagawa Wan because the targets were likely to be more fruitful. His attack must have arrived half an hour or so after one made by 'Hammy' Gray with his nine Corsairs from *Formidable*. C-H found a most inviting target. He had John Joly as his Number 2, three from Dancaster's Flight and another three from 15 Flight. The targets in the Wan were well-defended by shore flak. The Japanese fired down on the aircraft from the fiordlike hills on either side of the inlet. John Joly describes some aspects of this trip, told to me 40 years later:

"I was wingman to C-H whom I remember as being a Commander. You will appreciate that it was rare to see a straight-striper amongst aircrew in the Fleet Air Arm. At my age (21) it was extremely tough and frightening to follow this man on the dives we did from different directions to split up the Japanese defence fire. You can imagine that no one looked forward to the high speed encounter with the rest of the squadron over the target."

"C-H, followed by me and the others, proceeded at 8000 feet to the landward or western end of the Wan. He then signalled to me that he was going into the attack and informed the others by radio, and we both rolled over and dived vertically towards the creek which ran into the Wan. He was 400 — 500 yards ahead of me and I saw him pouring cannon and machine gun fire into the destroyer. In my inexperience I had trouble controlling my Seafire because of the tremendous speed, so I only got a quick shot at the ship and then, just as I was passing over it, it blew up. Subsequently on return to the Fleet, the bottom of my aircraft was full of bits of the destroyer."

"At debriefing I told of the destroyer that blew up, and the others said that one other in the Wan had been beached and a third escaped, damaged. I remember C-H being interviewed when we got back to Sydney by the Press, and we thought that we were the first on the scene at the Wan, before the Avengers and Corsairs from *Formidable*."

I had missed the drama of C-H's debriefing. I was doing a CAP at the time with my lot as we had hoped for a Kamikaze bonanza at dusk as we had been promised. After we landed-on at dusk I went to the Ops room as usual and found Norman preparing next day's programme. He told me that five of *Formidable*'s Corsairs were missing including 'Hammy' Grey, who was shot down just before or after C-H's strike on his destroyer at Onagawa. It had been a busy day for 30 Wing for we had managed 95 Seafire sorties, 50 being over Japan. This was 27% of the sorties with but 17% of BPF's aircraft.

Day Eight, 10 August. Up again at 0330, our first trip for 21, 22 and 23 Flights was escorting our own Avengers and Fireflys to Onagawa Wan again, taking off at 0500. The strike was led by Peter Nelson-Gracie, our new Air Group

Commander. No other ships' aircraft were involved so that briefing was properly arranged and everyone knew what was required as a result. The weather was perfect and the trip was entirely uneventful. We close-escorted our Avengers there. They near-missed all their targets and we close-escorted them back. In between, we took a dive at one or two smaller targets in the Wan, with Dent, Arkell and Banyard taking a few photographs — including one of 'Iron Swede' upside down over Japan for a 'line shoot'. The atmosphere was remarkably relaxed. I had also told the boys not to do anything heroic at this late stage of the war.

C-H did the second trip — a 'ramrod'-recce — to Harago and Awaki. He confirmed over the radio that there were no targets there. Stuart Jewers then led five Seafires to strafe Koryama, an important target some 40 miles inland and crowded with 45 aircraft, all making very tempting targets on the briefing photographs.

He made a single pass and with his five Seafires destroyed five aircraft. Later that day, four other strikes — 55 aircraft in all — visited the same airfield, completing the destruction of all 45 enemy aircraft. However, as they made repeated passes, they suffered five casualties including one Avenger and one Firefly from *Implacable*.

My second 'ramrod' at 1415 was also without incident. Dennis Kirby led 25 Flight. All eight of us were told to strike at Onagawa Wan once more. All we saw at this time were a few small vessels close inshore, trying to pretend they were not there. We dived at a larger one which was firing at us and left it going round in circles and smoking. We returned to *Implacable* at about 1730, 3½ hours after take-off. This time the ship was well to the north of her proper position and we had to fly over three American Fleets of four carriers each, before we could get to her. We had further delay while we asked for permission to do this and we had to come down low to be visually identified each time, so losing our own ship's beacon. At this moment, Mike Banyard and his Number 2 — Newton — suddenly reported only seven gallons left. As this was only enough for seven minutes aviation, I asked the Yanks for a quick pancake. They replied:

"Limey chickens, join Eagle 1 *(Essex)* traffic now. You will be number one to land. Over."

"Eagle 1, Limey Seafire Leader. We have only two. Over."

"Limey chicken leader, we'll take any number you have in mind. Come straight in. Out."

So Mike ('Iron Swede') Banyard and 'Isaac' Newton landed aboard *Essex*. (His story of life aboard an American carrier is at Appendix 12.)

I turned out early next morning 11 August and consulted the oracle in the Ops room. Two hours later at 0530, it became clear that we should have to supply two Seafires all day as 'strapped-in' deck standby.

We longed for some definite sign of peace or war. Indecision was beginning to get on our nerves. We went to bed early every night ready for an 0330 turn-out the next morning — just in case we might be needed. Would the Japs settle? Would we have to face another period of operations? We heard that the Russians had declared war against Japan. We heard that *Indefatigable* and *King George V* were to be refuelled and continue operations in the area with the Americans while we went south with the remainder "to replenish" — for what? Apparently the Japanese were still attacking the Americans' cruiser screen and four Kamikazes had been shot down, so war was still a possibility.

It was now five days after the first atom bomb had been dropped on Hiroshima and three days after the second at Nagasaki. We heard afterwards, that the Japanese home defence organisation had kept the news of these catastrophes from their people so that they would not insist upon an early armistice. The result was that no help was sent from the surrounding cities and casualties from burns were ten times as great as they need have been. Meanwhile, as we turned south in *Implacable,* committed suiciders continued to try to find the American Task Force with *Indefatigable* in company. The Seafires of 24 Wing with Jimmy Crossman and Andrew Thompson as the two COs, and the Wing Leader Buster Hallet once more, were having a busy time. Many suiciders failed to find the fleet at all. *Indefatigable's* radar watched them as they circled. It was a macabre ritual. One by one they dived into the sea as they ran out of petrol, the radar plot slowly disappearing as they did so.

In the middle of this indecision, the Admiral paid us his second visit in *Implacable.* His first had been at Manus and is worthy of mention, for it warned us of what to expect for his second.

At his Manus visit — months ago it seemd to us — we were at anchor and it was unbearably hot in the wardroom. One hundred and fifty of us RNVR airmen waited for his entrance. We were dressed in white shirts, shorts, buckskin shoes and long white stockings. The fans were full on, blowing irritable, water-laden air from one streaming brow to the next in their futile way. The Admiral, Captain and a few others entered at last, and we stood up. Our visitors were wearing 'Number Tens' — white duck trousers with knife-edge creases and tunics buttoned to the neck.

"Why aren't they wearing their wings?" asked the Admiral. There was a long, awkward silence and we sat down. There could be no meeting of minds on this occasion, no warm handshake, no charming expression, no twinkle in the eye. The Admiral and ourselves, thrown together by the exigences of war, came from two different worlds. We came from the fun and the fright of aeroplanes and from school; he came from a world of destroyers and from Dartmouth. Neither had the smallest technical knowledge of the other's task. As if to confirm this state of affairs, the Admiral had now made his demand: "Why aren't they wearing their wings?" when everyone knew that wings were never worn by aviators dressed in working tropical rig. If he had spent the last three years in close contact with his aviators as a carrier Admiral should, how could he not have known of this? He had made a bad start with the aviators in *Implacable.*

The memory of the Admiral's first visit tended to set the scene for his second. In addition, before his visit, there had been another most unfortunate signal from the Flagship which implied that we were cowards. The signal was as follows:

"To 1st AC — From AC1

Board of Admiralty have signalled that high percentage of strikes and good results achieved reflect great credit on all concerned.

2. I doubt Their Lordships can have known how high in some cases has been our percentage of abortive sorties which we must and will reduce.

3. Let us be judged both as to sortie output and damage inflicted on the enemy by the two strike days immediately before us."

Well, we had just had these two strike days and all our casualties had been doubled. Poor Hammy Grey had indeed done his best to satisfy para 3 and had paid unnecessarily with his young life — together with 11 others. *Implacable* had been singled out for a visit, for our casualties had been light by comparison. Even if Yate, Graham, Patullo, Saxe, Bedore, Tucker, Tillet and Squires had all been shot down by flak and had not mostly been lost by failures and dangers in the aircraft itself (See Appendix 11 (e)) the losses were small by comparison with the Corsairs of *Victorious* or *Formidable*. He may have considered that there was a simple correlation between high casualties and bravery.

So that, as the Admiral stepped from the back seat of his Firefly ferry onto *Implacable's* flight deck that sunny morning, some of us could perhaps have discerned the ghost of Admiral Byng, with quill and parchment ready to write down what was said.

The Seafires did not have long to wait before one of them was accused. The incident which follows is told by John Joly.

"We had the usual three Seafires on deck, two warmed up and one spare with folded wings. Our Chief AA — CPO Ferrier — didn't like the sound of my engine, so I dismounted to get into the spare. While I was doing this the tannoy told me to report to the bridge. The Admiral advanced and said:

'Are you afraid of flying young man?'

'No sir'.

'Well, get back into your aeroplane.' "

Had I heard of this, and that Joly had been accused of cowardice in this way, I should have been able to tell the Admiral that there was no one in the entire ship who could have got "closer to the enemy" than John Joly. Mechanics were still picking bits of Japanese destroyer out of the fuselage of his Seafire from his action two days before in Onaga Wan.

None of us bothered too much at the time, for that night we heard that peace was indeed imminent and we had a party in the wardroom. We forgot about the Admiral. Neither were we concerned about casualty rates in 30 Wing. We knew we had done more than our duty and that our low casualty rate followed from our attack method. We did not know by how much we had done our duty until after the war and the official figures on sortie rates per aircraft/aircrew were made known.

Taking the entire 86 Seafires in both large carriers, they constituted 35% of BPF's embarked aircraft. Yet these 86 Seafires had done 51% (1280) of the total offensive sorties. For three of the nine days of flying operations, *Indefatigable* had been absent, or not operated her Seafires at all, so that 30 Wing's percentage (now 801 Squadron) was even higher. In retrospect, for we hardly gave it a thought at the time, the only reason for the Admiral's attitude to the Seafire in particular — if not the whole ship *Implacable* in general — was that she and Charles Evans had made the Seafire work, something which he had found impossible. Was this why Charles Evans said: "He never forgave me," and why he and *Implacable* had had to field one rude signal after another?

We wondered how *Indefatigable* was getting on with the Americans. We saw a signal from the American C-in-C, Admiral Bill Halsey. He was a rugged leader. He drove from the front seat and knew what went on under the bonnet. He warned his men of Japanese treachery following their peace overtures. In spite of the ceasefire, the Allies were to "shoot them down in a friendly manner" if they made an appearance. As the Japanese had still not made up their minds, the Americans authorised *Indefatigable* to strike at Odaki Bay. As the last of the Seafires, Avengers and Fireflies turned for home after this brilliant strike, orders went out for the ceasefire. In this last action of the war, although the Seafires of 894 Squadron had shot down almost all the A6Ms sent to intercept them, one of the Seafires — S/Lt F. Hockley — was bounced while he was slowing down to drop his tank. He force-landed in Japan.

S/Lt Hockley could not be found later amongst the prisoners of war in Japan by our peace commission. The local army commander had apparently taken him out and shot him where he landed. Such was the sort of enemy that we should have had to fight if 'Olympic II' had gone through and the bomb had not saved us.

After we had heard from Churchill himself on 13-14 August that Japan had surrendered, we could at last relax. We went to a thanksgiving service on the quarterdeck with our excellent padre — the Reverend Knight — and thanked God for the atom bomb that had saved countless Allied lives. No doubt it would have saved half a million more civilian Japanese lives too — from the B29s — but we cared not about them at the time.

Charles Evans told me to recommend two of 880 Squadron for DSCs. They were bound to be Norman Goodfellow and Edwin 'Crusty' Pye, the two longest serving officers in the squadron. Norman had been flying continuously on operations — with but one break — since the war started. Otherwise, there was no act which stood out from the rest, for all were identical in their determination to give of their best. Our only regret was that so many of the new boys were unable, due to inexperience of our methods, to take their place in the front line at once on joining. Measures were of course already in hand to remedy this by Stuart Jewers, who now left for the Fighter Training Pool at Nowra.

The suddenness of the onset of peace made major changes in war plans impossible. We in *Implacable,* therefore continued on our planned journey south to Sydney as if we were still preparing for 'Olympic II'. Only at the very top could the plan be altered, so that our C-in-C, Bruce Fraser, could now leave Sydney in his Flagship — *Duke of York* — to add his presence to the proposed peace-signing ceremony in Tokyo Bay.

The *Duke* was an extraordinary choice of Flagship. Whereas the Americans in the Pacific had heard of *Formidable, Victorious, Indefatigable,* and perhaps, *King George V,* they had never heard of the *Duke of York.* She had had the signal honour of catching the *Scharnhorst* on a dark night in the Arctic winter of January 1944. She had taken advantage of 'Ultra', her possession of radar and an inexplicable error by the Germans, to sink her with her guns and with 50 or so torpedoes from her accompanying cruisers. This irrelevant feat was not appreciated in the Pacific either by the Americans or by the Fleet Air Arm. It was not therefore in the least surprising for us to hear that 'the *Duke*' had been pelted with potatoes by the carriers as she had steamed into Guam on her way north to the peace-signing with Admiral Fraser on board.

In his address to his troops in the *Duke*'s sister battleship, *King George V,* the Admiral had been extremely courteous and at pains to excuse his choice of ship for the peace-signing ceremony. He had mistaken the potatoes for the Carrier Fleet's wish to have the *King George V.* Little did he ever know that the BPF wanted neither battleship but only an aircraft carrier to represent the Royal Navy at Tokyo. So once again the Press unwittingly, and the Navy wittingly, beguiled the public into thinking that battleships were still the core of the Royal Navy.

Four days after the potato episode and a few days before we entered Sydney Harbour in *Implacable,* a small British contingent of Royal Marines went ashore on the Japanese island of Azuma on 24 August in a symbolic landing. They found an arsenal of weapons. Further foot-reconnaissance on the mainland in the course of the next six months revealed that Japan had prepared to defend herself from a landing on the Tokyo Plain — the area chosen for the main landing in Febuary 1946 — and had secreted in the surrounding countryside no less than 4,000 apparently serviceable fighter aircraft suitable for conventional defence and Kamikaze attack. Many of these were new types, the 'Jack' and 'George', similar to the Typhoon fighter-bomber with 2000 horsepower radial engines and level speeds of 400 mph. However, at one airfield, no less than 25 'George' fighters — otherwise fully operational — had their port undercarriage legs buckled, implying that they suffered from directional instability on take-off or landing, and that there was a serious lack of spares.

On 13 September, off Sydney Heads, we finally flew off the remaining 37 Seafires of our 48. We landed in fine style at Schofields, a MONAB[1] a few miles west of Sydney. Refusing, in *Implacable,* to adopt the fashionable 'centralised maintenance', we took with us our 160 marvellous ratings who had so faithfully transformed our hot, worn out, leaky and misfiring aircraft into serviceable flying machines for the next day's flying. We had formed up in a Balbo as we left to pay our respects to our fine ship, to Charles Evans and to our Captain. We then split up and shot past the bridge at zero feet.

Formidable, Speaker and *Glory,* the latter a new Light Fleet carrier, had also entered Sydney Harbour with us. They soon emptied most of the American Lease-Lend aircraft, Corsairs, Hellcats and Avengers, into the Pacific, and filled up with as many Allied Prisoners of War that the overworked 'peacetime' Services staff in Sydney could find alive. They took them back to Australasia, Canada, India and the UK. *Implacable* herself took almost 2000 POWs back to Esquimault in western Canada. It was one of many mercy missions. Some 14,000 British POWs had already died in captivity and were still dying in the ships on their way home.

While *Implacable* had formed part of the US Fast Carrier Force TF 37, her aircraft had destroyed 46 enemy aircraft on Japanese airfields and damaged another 67. Some 10,000 tons of small shipping was sunk and another 130,000 tons probably sunk.

Losses in 30 Wing from all causes since leaving the UK and while working up in the Orkneys and over Norway, totalled 15 pilots killed. Seven pilots failed to return from raids against the Japanese mainland and Truk. Of these, only one or two could have been shot down by Japanese flak, the others having died when attempting to bale out following fuel supply failure or by other causes connected with enemy action but not directly caused by it. Two pilots had structural failure on the pullouts of dives, one collided with an aerial due to a poorly sited runway, one was killed taking off due to his glove having caught in the hood, one collided in mid-air in cloud, another from suffocation from a mid-air fuel leak, another from engine stalling on the approach. The poor state of development — due to lack of time and appropriate test flying — of the Seafire III was probably responsible for the major part of these losses, thus the aircraft itself was, perhaps, many times more dangerous to us than the enemy. There is little doubt that had 30 Wing followed the current practice of diving in succession on targets, its casualties would have been far higher. As it was, one or perhaps two casualties due to flak in some 600 hours flying on offensive sorties, compare with five times that rate amongst the other squadrons in the BPF who did not use 30 Wing's technique. Perhaps the most extraordinary aspect of these losses is that none were caused by pilot error.

Vice-Admiral Sir Charles Hughes-Hallett opened a display at the Fleet Air Arm Museum on 30 July 1984. This featured the work of the BPF during the war with the Japanese Kamikaze. While there I happened to read a short account of TF37 in an illustrated book entitled *Fleet Air Arm at War,* published in 1982. In it a paragraph caught my eye; it said: "At the end of May 1945, *Implacable* was

[1]Mobile Naval Airbase.

despatched to Manus to gain experience in modern combat techniques before participation in a major operation". Some of us 'Implacables' wondered whether this referred to her Air Group or to the ship herself, and whether it was the opinion of the rest of the BPF when we arrived on the scene. So far as her Air Group's combat techniques were concerned, the answer to whether they were modern or not was answered in 1959, when 30 Wing's attack system for 'ramrods' was adopted by the Navy and written into Naval Air Fighting Instructions. It was 14 years ahead of its time! So far as the ship's fighting efficiency was concerned, *Implacable*'s sortie rate per aircraft was by far the highest of any of the four Fleet carriers in the Pacific.

Implacable entering Sydney, 1945. *(Mike Banyard)*

A few of 880/801 Squadron, Launceston, Tasmania, 1945.

Seafire XV. *(FAA Museum)*

Seafire XVII with clear rearward view and 'tear-drop' hood. Note that the curved wingscreen has been removed. *(FAA Museum)*

Chapter 23
Peacetime at Schofields

We were still unable to believe our good fortune in having the atom bomb to give us our sudden deliverance. Schofields was barely ready for our arrival so we were allowed a fortnight's leave. Once again the generous Australians welcomed us, their own sons still absent abroad or as POWs.

When we returned to Schofields each night after our visits to the welcome laid on for us in Sydney, we began to sleep soundly once more and to wake each morning without the thought of decklanding or of engine failure over Japan. I was determined to make life at Schofields like it had been for 804 Squadron at Charlton Horethorne, a holiday camp.

We shared the airfield with a newly formed AI-equipped Firefly night-fighter squadron commanded by Lt/Cdr (A) Derek Empson, RNVR. It was a good outfit, but of course, not now required, like ourselves. For us, the first two months at Schofields was 'all change'. The four Canadians, Boak, Stock, Geary and Losee, left almost immediately for home. Pye, Dancaster, Kirby and the New Zealanders Sheeran, Glazebrook and Anderson also left. Bill Brewer and Gunson became instructors nearby. Five time-expired members of the original 801 — Saxe, Luing, Thompson, Jervis and Green also left. We then had ten replacement pilots to absorb. These were straight from UK training, or had come through the training school at Puttalam or from *Chaser*'s 899 Squadron. Only one, Lt (A) Pete Phillips, RNVR, had sufficient experience of flying and the Pacific to be useful immediately.

It is interesting to note that had the war continued, we should have had an impossible task to maintain safe flying standards and to keep up our fighting ability. Most of the latest batch of new boys were the first to agree that they would have been a liability to the squadron and a danger to themselves. We had still not used many of the replacements who had arrived since we had left the UK. Some of them had returned at once. It was obvious to all in *Implacable* and other BPF carriers that in any future conflict, replacements would require to be trained to a much higher standard and by those experienced at the battle front. There would be no time for training during or between operations.

Eventually the planners caught up with events and they 'unwound' Olympic. Stuart, Brewer and several others therefore went home and the special training of new boys was disbanded.

When Their Lordships had called for volunteers from the RAAF to help the Fleet Air Arm during the latter stages of the Pacific War, the response had been overwhelming. To try to reduce the numbers, Their Lordships insisted upon a drop in rank and "only those with more than 500 hours flying need apply". Almost exactly the same number applied again. The result was that two of the Australians now appointed to 801 at Schofields had been Wing Commanders, three had been Squadron Leaders, and there were four DFCs and one DSO among them. It was clear to me and Norman Goodfellow, who had mercifully not left yet, that we were dealing with a race apart. I asked them whether they would mind forming their own Flight and organising their own flying training programme while at Schofields. They were to ask me only in case they got stuck. This worked very well indeed.

These Aussies were full of brilliant suggestions to make life at Schofields even more entertaining. We arranged flights — up to 24 aircraft at a time — supposedly for official reasons, to places all over eastern Australia. To Mildura — a new wine growing area in the southern outback — to Launceston in Tasmania for Spencer Brown's wedding, to Point Cook at Melbourne for the Melbourne Cup, and also to places such as Archer's Field and other airfields round Brisbane near the now famous beaches of Surfers' Paradise and Ewing Head, to collect more Seafires.

Each afternoon, in the heat of the Australian midsummer, we climbed into three or four Dodge trucks and took the whole squadron bathing to Palm Beach on the Hawkesbury River estuary north of Sydney.

If we wanted a change of scenery, we could take a few Jeeps to any of the other beautiful Sydney beaches, Googee, Avalon and so on. Then there was Bondi. The procedure for getting to Bondi was slightly different. After a tub of oysters for half-a-crown (12½p), washed down by Foster's 'Cascade' Lager, we would get on a tram to Bondi. This in itself was a challenge, for once the green flag let these trams out of their terminus at one end of the track, they made a beeline for the other. The very last thing that they had in mind was to stop en route for passengers. This was because once they did so, the supply of cooling air blowing through the tram diminished to a damp trickle. This was bad for the driver's and the clippy's health.

If you had been lucky to get on a tram in Sydney, it would eventually arrive at the terminus at Bondi, opposite the beach. The clippy and the driver would then disappear into their air conditioned caboose. We would then undress on the beach and would have our bathe. We would watch the de Havilland 'Dragon' overhead watching for sharks, and we would watch all the other beautiful sights around us too, for there were many. We also watched the caboose, for to miss the emergence of the clippy and the driver was to miss the tram home. They would leap into their tram, select full speed immediately and with sparks from the wheels and more from the overhead pickup they would disappear in the direction of Sydney empty of all passengers. The whole scene still lives in Australian memory and is immortalised by the expression "Off like a Bondi Tram". There was even an Australian offshore racer at Cowes in 1982 named 'Bondi Tram'.

After the bathe at Bondi and the '6.30 swill', those with any money left could go to Romano's Club. At Romano's there was a band, cheap oysters, rich mums and pretty daughters. There were no dads in sight. They were all making money on their sheep stations 400 miles away.

When Christmas leave came up, I stayed a fortnight with the Kater family. They had a smallholding of about 8000 acres 250 miles west of Sydney called 'Swatchfield'. It was near a small town called Oberon over the Blue Mountains and "half way down the other side".

John Kater was the middle son of a famous Australian family who owned vast farms in the outback, millions of acres. His beautiful house had a swimming pool, a tennis court and air conditioning. It was surrounded by a 500-yard-wide ploughed firebreak. His nearest neighbour was about 20 miles away — quite close. One neighbour — a Pole — heated up eucalyptus leaves in a ten-ton steel cauldron and condensed the vapour in a pipe running under the local stream. He sold the eucalyptus oil in five gallon drums in Sydney for £50 each at the rate of one per month. It was hard work.

I tried to help John Kater and his men in their task of branding. His land was 'improved' pasture. It would keep about 0.25 cattle per acre in food. The cattle had to be driven into the stockade for branding. Without fences and with only rudimentary skill at riding, I was not much use in the rounding-up process. It was a mass of flies, sweat and new swearwords.

John Joly and Pete Arkell often elected to collect our new Seafire XVs and Joly also played much cricket while on leave. He came to fetch me back, two days before I was due to take the squadron 600 miles down to Point Cook for a Balbo for Melbourne's 'War Loan' Pageant.

On the way back to Schofields we had a front tyre blow-out. We carried no spare, for it would surely be stolen. We had to force on to Katoomba, the next town, on the rim. We were down to the brake drum by the time we arrived in the town.

On the way, John told me all the news. Norman Goodfellow had left for the UK to resume law studies. Bill Griffith had taken over as Senior Pilot as planned, and 'Nat' Gould had taken over the Aussies as Flight Leader.

Back at Schofields, I and Joly set off to catch up with the squadron on their Balbo to Point Cook. I got as far as Malacoota and both hydraulic pumps went u/s on my Seafire, I had to use 'emergencies' to land and I was a day late arriving at Melbourne. Refuelling at Malacoota was from 50 gallon drums parked round the airfield. Australians at Melbourne were, if anything, even more hospitable than those at Sydney. It was a beautiful, clean, Victorian city.

Our new Seafires were Mark XVs. They had an extra 450 horsepower and an auto-change, two-speed supercharger, which maintained this extra power up to 30,000 feet. It also had a properly designed 60 gallon torpedo-shaped belly tank. It had 100 gallons of internal fuel, with proper electric immersion fuel pumps in each tank to prevent vapour locks. It also had provision for small, droppable wing tanks of 35 gallons each. It was fitted for firing six rockets from zero length launchers, and from number 51 onwards, would have 'sting' arrester hooks. The propeller was fitted with an extra fine pitch stop. This was set at an angle of two degrees finer than normal It allowed the propeller to fine off to an angle more 'flat-on' to the airflow, thus greatly increasing the drag after the pilot cut the throttle when decklanding, and so reducing the length of the float. Later versions had extra-long-stroke oleos on the main undercarriage. This further absorbed the bounce and made three point landings easier. Later versions also had a beautiful 'teardrop', fully transparent, sliding hood, with a streamlined windscreen fairing. The latter acted as a rain clearance device, making blower windscreen wipers unnecessary.

On the face of it, it all seemed to be just what we wanted, but in fact, had 'Olympic II' gone ahead and had we flown these Seafire XVs, we should have suffered even more losses than with the Seafire III. This was for the reasons which follow.

Although the fuel supply system and the instability had been cured — the latter by the heavier engine in front, effecting a better fore and aft balance — there were other characteristics in the early Seafire XV which made it just as dangerous to fly from a carrier on the tasks that we expected.

The Seafire XV's Griffon produced almost 2000 horsepower in 'overide'. It still had to be absorbed by a propeller of similar diameter and blade area to that of the Merlin, and at lesser engine rpm. This greatly increased the torque imparted to the propeller's slipstream, and also greatly increased the tendency for the aircraft to turn in the opposite direction to that of its propeller. As the fin and tailplane effectiveness had remained as before, it was hardly surprising that directional control was extremely poor during take-off in the Seafire XV. Futhermore, the new aircraft suffered from aileron reversal, a serious defect which killed one of our new Australian pilots, S/Lt (A) J. Norton. RANVR.

The effects of torque on the Seafire XV's lateral and directional handling characteristics were to have many fatal consequences and the increased weight of its propeller made air gunnery difficult due to gyroscopic effects. There would have been no time to change the aircraft back to the Seafire III in any operation such as 'Olympic II' and the results, together with the new pilots, would have been catastrophic. (See Appendix 11(m) The Seafire XV.)

By the end of 1945 it had seemed to me that I should do my best to get back to the UK as soon as possible. I had a growing feeling that things were not all right at home. My immobile Wren and I had spent so little time together during our marriage that we had become strangers. I began to think that she might imagine that I was not bothering about her in Australia and that I was not wanting to return. I asked the Captain at Schofields what my chances might be. He told me that the Admiralty plan was now for two and a half year 'peacetime' overseas appointments for all those who had volunteered for Extended Service Commissions. As I was one of these — it was all that I had been offered — I would probably not be relieved until early 1947 after *Implacable's* return to the UK. I realised that I and my immobile Wren could not possibly last out until then so I requested a 'compassionate' appointment back to the UK. These were — and still are — greatly frowned upon in the peacetime Navy, for it was tantamount to tearing up a Naval Officer's unwritten employment agreement to go wherever he might be sent. It did me no good at all, but I saw no alternative. I pointed out that there were many of my contemporaries in *Formidable, Victorious* and *Indefatigable* who had done far less foreign service than I, and had yet returned to the UK a year before. So my relief was appointed. He was Lt/Cdr (A) Jack Routley, RNVR. Jack needed a little time to get used to the Seafire XV, for he had been flying a desk. However, by February 1946 the turnover was complete.

Before I left for the UK, he and I attended the Sydney Opera House one night. Although we were all much thinner from our wartime rations, the ballet in Australia had put on weight during their wartime rest and were only just beginning to get into trim again. We saw "Les Sylphides" — or as the Aussies said: "Lez Silfides". The ballerina Sylphide was very large indeed.

Every time the principal man lifted her, there were shouts of "two-six" and "eeeeve" from the stalls. When she landed, her points collapsed and the boards creaked. Clouds of dust rose in the footlights. Even the orchestra — wheezing away — could not keep a straight face.

After I had left the squadron, I heard that 801 had lost one of our original 880 pilots, S/Lt Hugh Smith. The accident had occurred when flying from *Implacable* on the way to New Zealand. The entire 24 Seafires had made a co-ordinated attack on a rock off the coast of Tasmania using 20mm 'ball' ammunition. Smith's aircraft had been hit by a ricochet from the cannon shells off the rocks. So it had happened at last.

Following on my 'passionate request', I was appointed to command 894 Squadron for the journey home in *Indefatigable*. The other squadron, from the original 24 Wing, was 887 Squadron — Andrew Thompson's old squadron. We had about 20 Seafires. In our Carrier Air Group, there were four squadrons.

Buster Hallett was our CAG boss. Dennis Holmes — ex-21 *St. Vincent* course —
was 1772 Firefly CO, and 'Shorty' Dennison had taken over 887 Squadron from
Andrew. There were many ex-880 Squadron pilots in 894 with me, so that I felt
amongst friends.

Before we left Sydney for the journey home in *Indefatigable* we attended a
memorable victory celebration ball aboard *Glory* in Sydney Harbour. There
were 3,000 guests and I met Murdoch Tait on board, the Senior Pilot of 831
Corsairs. The flight deck was a fun fair and the hangar a ballroom and
restaurant. Access to the hangar from the flight deck was by gangways through
the lift openings. The lifts were lowered to the half way position to allow this to
be done. The aft liftwell was a nightclub and the forward lift had grottoes and
caves under it, with a fountain and pond with real live ducks in it. The ducks had
been washed in soap before the event, as the Subby i/c ducks had considered
them too dirty when he borrowed them from the Sydney Park pond. As a result
they floated below their Plimsoll marks, and unless they maintained a speed of
about five knots, they heeled over and capsized. They eventually took to the
dance floor, where they followed each other in close line-ahead, quacking in
time with the music of the Royal Marine Band. We fed them caviar canapes and
duck sandwiches. At the close of the ball, the Royal Marines played Elgar's
moving version of the Last Post for all those who could not be with us. Even the
ducks stood silent, thoughtful and sad.

It was a fast and uneventful voyage back to Portsmouth. We stopped to refuel
at Port Elizabeth and did a Balbo over Cape Town. We also photographed
Ascension Island on the way past. At the land-on from this last trip, S/Lt
Hatton of 887 Squadron made three attempts to touchdown, but each time
drifted over to the port side of the deck, and lost sight of Jimmy Hancock the
batsman. On his last attempt he stalled his port wing, hit the batsman's position
with it and went over the side. His aircraft, with its hood open of course, sank
immediately and he was not recovered, probably having hit his head on the
gunsight. This was the very last landing of all by 7CAG in *Indefatigable* and it
was a sad ending.

We landed at Lee-on-Solent at 1000 on the morning of 15 March 1946. We
taxied our Seafire LIIIs to the hangars, left them there, and never saw them
again. Before we finally left the airfield on the way back to Portsmouth to collect
our belongings and clear customs from the carrier after she had docked, we
shook hands with Admiral Sir Dennis Boyd, the Fifth Sea Lord. He had come
all the way from London to do so. He was the only Naval Officer to say hallo to
any of us. The Mayor of Portsmouth was not even told of our arrival.

Peter Arkell, who returned to his family farm at Butler's Court and to the
Berkley Hunt near Cheltenham, said of this homecoming: "That's the last we
saw of anyone in 880 or 801 until a Fleet Air Arm anniversary 25 years
afterwards. I wish I could have flown my aircraft back to our farm. It would be
worth a quarter of a million quid by now."

On my return I was appointed to St. Merryn. The CO of the Course was C-H.
The two squadrons at St. Merryn produced Flight Leaders! They instructed us
how to carry out and lead ground attacks! Some of the instructors were my ex-
pupils. The two Flights — air and ground attack — were commanded by Dicky
Law (ex-886 Squadron, 3 Wing,) and by Dick Turnbull. Both were now
Lt/Cdrs, RN, but I had now lost my acting half stripe and was a Lieutenant once
more, along with everyone else on the course. One of these 'pupils' was also an
ex-Pacific CO — Lt Doug (Chauncy) Parker, DSO, DSC, and one of
Formidable's Corsair squadron commanders. Needless to say we both enjoyed

flying Seafire 17s and 47s and I was given the top grade of 'exceptional' as a present from C-H for my passing-out assessment. It was obvious that some of us had been given the course to 'Mark time' between appointments.

I then relieved 'Shorty' Dennison as CO of a training squadron, 718 at Eglinton in Northern Ireland. There was a Firefly training squadron there as well, commanded by Lt (A) Cedric Coxon, DSC, RN. My Senior Pilot was Lt (A) Don Cameron, DSC, RN, a New Zealander. He had been shot down and taken prisoner twice during the war, once by the Germans and once by the Japanese. He had escaped from the Germans in Sicily by climbing over Mount Etna. He had tried to escape from the Japanese at Okinawa and had found them a different proposition. They beat him senseless every time he was rude to them — which was often — and he came back from the Pacific a pathetic wreck of his former self. However, the RN does not forget its heroes and everything was done to try and get Don back on an even keel after his dreadful war experiences.

On 20 January 1947, Cedric and I took our pupils aboard *Implacable* just back from Australia. We were flying Seafire IIIs once more. The later versions were required for the RNVR and the very few 'first line' squadrons. We accompanied King George VI and Queen Elizabeth and other members of the Royal Family in *Vanguard* to South Africa. The King and the rest of his family came aboard *Implacable* and he sat in the Captain's chair. He asked to see Cedric and me to thank us and our boys for, as he put it in his signal, "your magnificent flypast". We were very pleased about that.

While calling in at Freetown on the way, who should come aboard to see us but Dennis Kirby, complete with pith helmet and fly swot. He was then an Assistant District Commissioner. He is now an international banker.

On the way back, I was a trifle ill. As I was not allowed to fly, I organised a small regatta at Dakar. The Commander helped by allowing sailing practice in the ship's dinghies, cutters and whalers. One morning, while at anchor in Dakar harbour, it was the Royal Marine's turn for a little sailing practice. I watched the cutter, with about 20 men on board, set off from the port gangway. The Petty Officer Seaman at the tiller knew even less about sailing than the Royal Marines. As he steered across the harbour, close-hauled on the starboard tack, he ruined the chances of success by setting the jib in the hove-to position each time he went about. The cutter accordingly sailed sideways at about half a knot, and the 20 Marines were beginning to wonder why the cutter came back with a crash each time to the same place it had started from, after a quarter of an hour's hard sailing. To make matters worse, the boat was getting lower and lower in the water. None of this seemed to be worrying the Petty Officer Seaman who continued to shout orders, such as "avast" and "belay" and "what the fuckin 'ell" from his position of advantage in the stern.

I leapt aboard when the next crash alongside came and tried to sort things out. I found that each man was holding at least one rope. Some were holding two. Others had ropes round the bottoms of their boots and tied up over their shoulders. They all seemed to be bearing immense loads. Nothing was made fast, so had I given the order "How" — like Chief Petty Officer Willmott at *St. Vincent* — the sails, masts and everything would have come down with a run and the boat would have stopped.

As each Royal Marine was now standing in two feet of clear bilge water, his boots submerged but still glistening, it was first necessary to bale out the boat. The dry planks had obviously not felt water since *Implacable* had left Scapa with us in 1945.

In spite of such vicissitudes, the French only just won the regatta. The

Captain's gig happened to have a fair turn of speed and took them and us by surprise. Cedric also performed well in one of the 14 foot sailing dinghies. The French had, however, caught us napping on a number of items. They had lightened their boats by removing all floor boards and buoyancy tanks, oars, water billycans, sea rations, lifebelts, spare crew and bilge water. They had also painted their boats with enamel and all had racing-smooth bottoms. Their sails were of a light material straight from the boards of an expert colonial sailmaker. They also knew the course. We had taken on board a fair measure of *entente cordiale* at lunch and few of us knew the course. However, we cemented a few friendships back into place at Dakar. It was not before time, considering what the two Navies had done to each other during the war. However, the RN had to learn how to be a peacetime Navy all over again — unlike the French — and we RNVR types had to begin again from the bottom rung of the ladder, and learn how to be sailors.

The Royal Navy has now learned to sail. Up to 1953 it had considered that it was unnecessary for a Naval officer to learn such things. However, after several near collisions between 'Windfall' (ex-German) yachts at Cowes and 'Cowslip' — the Duke of Edinburgh's Flying Fifteen — which were well publicised in the daily papers, the CO of Dartmouth was ordered to procure some proper yachts. Standards improved and by 1963 it was safe to invite RN officers aboard a yacht, something that had never been possible before.

On the way back to Gibraltar, a signal came from the Admiralty to summon me to an interview for selection for the Empire Test Pilots School (ETPS). This is what I had requested. It would teach me a bit about flying and it would open up a whole new career. It would give me a chance to help the RN find out what it wanted, before abortions such as the Skua, Barracuda or Firebrand were unloaded on its unsuspecting squadrons. It was certain that no Naval prototype of the future would ever be right first time and that I and others like me would be kept busy for many years to come. It would also give me a better chance of a permanent commission in the Navy or, if not, a chance of a good civilian test-flying job if I wanted one.

Trying to discover peace after six years of war is a turbulent and insecure business. I found that there was much jostling for position in the new, peacetime Navy, and also in my domestic position at home. I found that I had returned from Australia too late, on both counts, to secure my position. Although I could do little to remedy either, I could at least preserve my second love — flying. After 600 hours in the Seafire I still loved it — for all its faults. It still remains the most beautiful of all aircraft and I wanted nothing more than to be able to continue to fly it.

I was left £50 in my grandmother's will. I spent it on a skiing holiday with Boris Morris. A few weeks after, I joined the Empire Test Pilots School at RAF Cranfield in Bedfordshire, and life became an adventure again.

Seafire 45. Note 'sting' hook. *(FAA Museum)*

Seafire 47. Note ram air intake. *(FAA Museum)*

Mike Banyard's arrival in USS *Essex*. Note the huge expanse of wooden deck. *(Mike Banyard)*

880 and 801 Squadrons, forming No. 30 Naval Air Fighter Wing, before embarking in *Implacable*, 15 March, 1944.

Epilogue
High Flight

High Flight

Oh! I have slipped the surly bonds of Earth
And danced the skies
        on laughter-silvered wings;
Sunward I've climbed,
        and joined the tumbling mirth
of sun-split clouds,
        — and done a hundred things
You have not dreamed of —
        wheeled and soared and swung
High in the sunlit silence.
        Hov'ring there,
I've chased the shouting wind along,
        and flung
My eager craft through
        footless halls of air . . .

Up, up the long, delirious, burning blue
I've topped the wind-swept heights
        with easy grace,
Where never lark
        or even eagle flew —
And, while with silent, lifting mind
        I've trod
The high untrespassed sanctity of space,
Put out my hand and touched the face of God.

Pilot Officer John Gillespie Magee, Jr.,
Royal Canadian Air Force.

Pilot Officer Magee composed this beautiful poem on 3 September 1941 after his first trip
in a Spitfire. Aged 19, he was killed in a mid-air collision on 11 December 1941.

Appendix 1
Asdics

'Active Sonar' as it is now called, makes use of the sound echo principle. Just as a person hears the echo of his hand clap in an empty hall, and some of the sound returns to his stereo-hearing system — his ears — so the same system is used in Asdics. Not only the direction from which the echo returns, but the distance it has travelled can be computed, for we know the speed of sound in water just as we know it in air. In addition the relative speed of approach can be assessed from its doppler effect.

As water is a very good conductor of high frequency sound, echoes from small objects in water can be heard for 20 miles or more in the right conditions, as every whale knows. However, there are snags. Just as light is 'bent' or refracted as it passes through glass to air or from air to glass, so sound is refracted as it passes from water at one density to water of a different density. Water in the oceans and ponds varies very much in density due to changes in salinity, temperature and pressure (depth). It remains for long periods in these separate density layers which are very clearly defined when the water is calm and tideless.

The path of a sound beam, therefore, seldom travels in straight lines in water, and, like a stick is 'bent' when it is half in and half out of the water, sound appears to come back to the listener from an entirely wrong direction. So that if the sound from an Asdic transmitter under the hull of a destroyer strikes a very well defined layer or interface between waters of different densities, the sound will be refracted or reflected, depending on its angle of incidence to the interface. If it is refracted, it may eventually come back to the Asdic 'transducer'. If it is reflected — as if from some giant mirror under the surface — it may never return. In both cases the sound will appear to 'come back' from the wrong direction.

The cold waters of the North Sea and Atlantic are usually mixed by tides and wind, and are not particularly well warmed on top by the sun. In the Mediterranean, however, the situation is entirely different as the Captain of *U-73* knew perfectly well when he sank *Eagle*. The Mediterranean waters are full of well defined layers at different densities, with the warmest at the top of course — for there is little or no tide and in summer there are no continuous strong winds nor surface drift. There is also one further important difference — just where Rosenbaum was hunting, a few hundred miles east off the Straits of Gibraltar. For here, the cold water from the Atlantic, which flows in through the Straits to compensate for heavy evaporation during the summer, undercuts the warmer water already in the Mediterranean 'pond', and stays in its well defined layers for huge areas of the western Mediterranean. The Navy knew of the effects of changes in density in 1939-41, but had no idea just how marked their effects were in the Mediterranean compared with the Atlantic or North Sea, because they had not carried out hunting exercises in the Mediterranean between the wars. After the war, they carried out extensive bathythermograph 'dips', to establish the extent of these marked changes in density.

The problem is not now so great, for we have 'dunking sonar' to get below such layers. But in WW II, the layering effect in the Mediterranean gave the Germans an advantage which they exploited to good effect. The only answer possessed by the Royal Navy at that time was to provide more and more A/S destroyers and manufacture variable-depth depthcharges. In the case of 'Pedestal', even 24 destroyers and 12 A/S Swordfish of 813 and 824 Squadrons were not enough.

Appendix 2

Naval Air Power in 1940 and Naval Aircraft: How they were used 1939-42

In 1940 I was crystal clear on what I should be asked to do as a pilot in the Fleet Air Arm. Provided I was selected as a fighter pilot and not for the far more dangerous job of flying a 'Stringbag' or, worse still, as an Observer in the back seat, I would do exactly the same as any fighter pilot in the Battle of Britain. The only difference would be that I would operate from an aircraft carrier instead of an airfield and have to learn the additional job of decklanding. If an incoming raid was spotted on the carrier's radar, I would take-off with the others and be vectored out to intercept the enemy bombers and shoot them down in the normal way. The destroyers and cruisers and battleships would then be free once more to 'command the sea' as in days gone by before the aeroplane, without fear of being constantly blown out of the water by German Stukas. Carrier-borne aircraft would also allow our own torpedo-bombers to attack enemy ships, harbours, submarines and airfields. We fighters would also escort the slower Swordfish to their targets and fight off the enemy opposition en route. This seemed to me to be the likely position, exactly the same as the Germans had been doing over England for the past six months in the Battle of Britain. As neither the Germans nor the Italians seemed to have a Fleet Air Arm of their own, our job would be that much easier over the sea. I thought that the Navy would be in an excellent position to win any sea battle that cropped up from time to time.

Unfortunately, my new bosses, Their Lordships of the Admiralty, had no such clear picture at that time. Their minds had gradually clouded over on the subject of naval air warfare, ever since they had handed over the Royal Naval Air Service to the Royal Air Force in 1918. The RAF had then taken over a Service with a complete command structure, ten times the size of the 1940 Fleet Air Arm, with 55,000 sailors, 100 shore stations and 2375 aircraft, balloons and airships. In the past 20 years the Naval Air garden had become a mass of weeds, with but a few patches of Naval brilliance here and there, growing wherever they could. The RAF had taken almost everything and, when they finally left again in 1938 with the Inskip Report as their bible, they left a hole of immense size.

I and the general public had no knowledge whatever of this state of affairs. The Navy was "the Silent Service", with scarcely an office boy running its Public Relations Department. However, it was the general opinion amongst all those who I knew at this time that our Navy would naturally see to it that it now got the best of everything, as it always had in the past. That was good enough for me. However, it was to be three murderous years before the task given to the Fleet Air Arm resembled my imaginary plan, and another year still before it could carry it out with any degree of success.

Most of the Senior Naval aviators had left *en bloc* in 1918. They did this because, if they had stayed in the Navy as professional airmen, they would have been little more than a 'branch', an auxiliary force; whereas if they formed a new Service — the Royal Air Force — they would become the *root* of a new Service — not a 'Branch' or an 'Arm'. Their promotion would be secure, their fight for money from the Exchequer would be straightforward and they would not have to compete with an entrenched line of Admirals wanting to build more battleships with bigger and bigger guns. The RAF became single-minded and skilful in this task — particularly in building up Fighter Command with radar interception — and deserved the admiration they later received for their victory in the Battle of Britain. The man responsible for this feat of dedication and endurance was AVM Sir Hugh Dowding. No such person existed in the Royal Navy at this time.

The 'established' Navy had not taken much interest in Naval aviation since 1918. None of its schools or weapons' training establishments had airmen on their staffs and none were near airfields where the interchange between 'specialisations' — gunnery, communications, submarines and airmen — could easily take place. Between four and seven years of the formative training for permanent peacetime officers was carried out 100 miles from the nearest Naval airfield. Embryo officers then continued their 'specialisation' training, their minds closed to other matters — including air matters — from that time forward. Whether they wanted it or not, non-airmen could not hope to learn anything about air warfare, command of the air, or air weapons, unless they volunteered to become pilots or observers themselves. Until 1935, they would not even be able to do that in significant numbers.

Meanwhile, at the top, few if any at the Board of Admiralty knew one end of an aircraft from another and none had commanded an aircraft carrier of any sort. Their minds were set in casements of steel. Their plans were limited to the range of a 16 inch gun and proceeded at the speed of the Grand Fleet at Jutland. Of course, I and my fellow volunteers in 1940 had no idea we were about to be employed by such a management. We naturally assumed that the Royal Navy, with its fine history and its traditional good sense, would now turn the new weapon which it had just re-acquired into its main striking force, and that they would obtain the very best aircraft, including fighter aircraft, against all other competition to defend it for this purpose.

Having handed over the Royal Naval Air Service to the RAF in 1918, by 1921 the Navy realised that they would soon lose operational control as well as administrative and material control of the RAF's "Fleet Air Arm". To keep a foot in the door they recruited Observers — a new RN 'specialisation'. The Naval Observers would fly in the back seats — and they would purposely be made senior to the RAF pilot in front so that the Navy would then command the aircraft. By 1936, Observers were being attracted into the Navy with the recruiting slogan "Become a Naval Observer and command your own aircraft". As these Naval aircrew rose in rank they would command the new aircraft carriers, would advise on air matters in the Admiralty and take their place as senior officers on Admirals' Staffs.

However, time was too short for this idea to begin to operate before war came in 1939. The 'short service' 1936 intake had scarcely reached the rank of Lieutenant when they were needed to fight in such aircraft as the Skua and for their numbers to be decimated for little result.

Besides the Navy's lack of senior officers to advise on air operational matters and how aircraft and aircraft carriers could best be used, it also lacked those with the vital experience and technical knowledge necessary to write specifications for new aircraft and weapons. Two such specifications resulted in the production of the Blackburn Skua/Roc and, three or four years later, the Fairey Barracuda. The Skua was designed as a torpedo/bomber/recce/fighter. It was, and still is, impossible to design such a dream of an all-purpose aircraft, any more than it is possible to produce a lorry which, once it has dropped its load, turns miraculously into a racing car. Two or three fundamentally different roles — such as strike/fighter, cannot be combined into the same basic structure and remain effective in either. The Skua was consequently a ghastly failure, both in its basic flying characteristics and in its performance. When a version of the Skua — the Roc — was fitted with floats for the Norwegian campaign, it could only just remain airborne at full take-off power!

The Barracuda was designed and built as a replacement to the Swordfish/Albacore just as the Grumman Avenger of the US Navy was designed and built as a replacement to the Douglas Devastator at about the same period. The Grumman Company was given only the barest outline to work on. They had already started to produce the Hellcat single-seat US Naval fighter to replace their Wildcat and they had the US Navy's full confidence. Although the RN's counterpart to the Avenger was, in time, cost, and task, almost to the same specification, the 'Barra' was a travesty of an aircraft. Their Lordships had altered its original logical design concept to a high wing design. This was decided upon without regard to the damaging effect it would have on the aerodynamic problems. Apparently, the high wing design was required so that the Observer, sitting on his throne at the back, could take bearings from two enormous compasses sited in bay windows on the mezzanine floor behind the pilot and have an unobstructed view of the earth and sea below. Besides the obvious structural problems of supporting a large tailplane at the uppermost extremity of the tail fin, the designers had to make sure that the tailplane itself was high enough to clear the expected turbulent downwash from the mainplane itself when airbrakes were in use.

In fact, they never succeeded, as the hangar height of the *Illustrious* Class carriers was too low to allow this. The Barra therefore suffered from a fatal design flaw, an unpredictable change of trim in the pitching plane when dive brakes were used. The wingfolding arrangements were also thrown off course and the undercarriage was so long and heavy that when a leg broke after a heavy decklanding it required eight men to lift it and throw it into the sea. The equivalent Seafire undercarriage needed only two. It was so overweight and underpowered that its rate of climb was too slow for any hope of surprise in its approach to the target, and barely perceptible at all in tropical temperatures — if a useful load was carried. It was little wonder that the Barracuda was soon declared unfit for use in the Far East, almost the moment it arrived there in any quantity. Of course it is easy to blame Their Lordships for the various iniquitous flying abortions which they caused to be produced, but the firms of Fairey and Blackburn — the main contributors to this sorry line of lethal failures for the FAA before and during the war — should have used their wisdon to warn their customers of the consequences of their impossible demands, as, no doubt, designers such as Sydney Camm, Folland and R. J. Mitchell would have done before money and time were spent on them.

Naval Aircraft: How they were used 1939-42

The Inskip Report

When, in 1938, the Navy eventually re-acquired a measure of control of the air over its Fleet, it only possessed about 150 obsolescent aircraft in first-line duty. This compared with 1300 in the US Navy, 550 in the Japanese Navy and 350 of Goering's Luftwaffe permanently assigned to the Kriegsmarine. Under the terms of the Inskip Report, its most impracticable and illogical measure of all was to allow the RAF to retain not only ownership, but operational control of Coastal Command. The Navy was therefore mainly dependent upon its rival service for A/S and surface surveillance and, as we shall see, for the major defence of the air over its Fleet.

The Inskip 'agreement' was a management document of a semi-political nature, first written in 1936, mostly by Winston Churchill. Its ideas on air defence of the Fleet were entirely out of date by 1939 yet it was religiously used by the two Services as a day-to-day job specification in all its unworkable aspects through the first, vital, three years of the war before the Americans joined in.

At the outbreak of the war, Churchill became First Lord of the Admiralty and Chairman of the Military Co-ordinating Committee soon after. On becoming Prime Minister on 2 May 1940 he was in charge of Defence. He, together with the First Sea Lord, Admiral Pound, and his Deputy, Admiral Tom Phillips, perpetuated these unworkable arrangements. For instance, when dealing with air defence of the surface Fleet, the Inskip Report announced:

"The Navy could never be required to maintain air strength sufficient to cope with a concentrated attack upon it . . . by a large air force of great power. When the hostile air force, or any considerable detachment from it, is encountered, it must be by the RAF."

This beautiful, archaic language described the writer's dream of an air defence requirement for a large Fleet setting off for another Jutland. The Navy would supply the AA gunfire — with its dual purpose guns in which it had the utmost confidence — and the RAF would supply the fighter defence overhead. Let us suppose that just such an attack on the Fleet took place — as indeed it did in miniature in the first few days of the war — and that warning was somehow received by the Admiral that it was a "considerable detachment" of enemy aircraft that was approaching. The Admiral would then contact, somehow, his RAF Group Commander ashore and ask for fighter support overhead. With no communications, with no Air Defence Radar (ADR) in HM Ships and with no agreed priority in the usage of the RAF fighters, the arrangements could not possibly work. Neither did they. Pre-planning, where the Navy and RAF could sit down beforehand, was the only workable method of making use of the available RAF fighter support. Even this was quite plainly uneconomical in the use of aircraft. Additionally, the RAF fighter pilots would be entirely untrained in flying over the sea, and the Navy itself had no means of communicating with the fighter pilots, nor of directing them by radar. The RAF quite rightly rebelled in such misuse of its slender resources and was unwilling to provide alternative uneconomical 'standing patrols' over the Fleet except on a low priority basis and where the Navy was within easy reach of its few well defended airfields. The Biggin Hill experiment in 1936 had already proved that ADR-directed interceptors were five times as efficient as 'standing patrols' of fighters patrolling on the likely approach path of the enemy and using visual interception techniques only.

Such was the position in home waters and in the Mediterranean in the opening stages of the war, until the end of 1942. From 1939-1942 Their Lordships' minds were still 'encountering' the enemy at speeds of 40 knots, instead of 400 knots, the approach speed of fighters sent to intercept the oncoming Stukas. For it was the Stukas which had brought the enemy's hitting power half way across the North Sea and half way across the Mediterranean, in the same time that it took the Fleet to raise its anchors from Scapa, Gibraltar or Alexandria.

The average Dartmouth-trained Naval officer not only had little knowledge of the air threat or how to deal with it but was also saddled with an impossibly slow and archaic flags and morse communications and warning system for air-age warfare which could not react in time. Naval Gunnery officers shut their minds to the threat from the air believing that their AA gunnery was the best in the world and that no aircraft could live for long in its grasp. They could think of no case in any preceding war where an aircraft had sunk a capital ship. They considered that their air defence over their surface Fleet was 'well balanced' and able to do without the RAF in all cases except where there was a 'large' and hostile air force of great power about to descend on it. They also preferred Churchill's maxim: "Airforce versus Airforce, Navy versus Navy", when it came to a decision on a demarkation dispute.

The Navy therefore considered that they had no need for large numbers of Naval interceptor fighters, such as the Gladiator or Hurricane. Radar direction was not in any case available aboard ships, only to the RAF for the Battle of Britain, and Naval ADR crews had not been trained for the task of fighter direction in significant numbers before late 1941. The space in the carrier's hangars would be filled with 'strike' aircraft to cripple the enemy battle-fleet. One or two Gladiator and Hurricane fighters might, however, be carried for the sole purpose of shooting down enemy 'snooper' reconnaissance planes outside AA range in conditions of w/t silence. Silence and secrecy were of paramount importance in surface warfare when two fleets were looking for each other. Chattering fighter pilots were an anathema, as their aircraft transmitters, high over the top of the Fleet, could be received by the enemy 100 miles away. The Navy had a hatred of noise, in all its forms. Radar had double the 'noise' range of r/t and was particularly unpopular afloat. The Navy eventually allowed GDR (Gunnery Direction Radar) afloat at Churchill's insistence, in time for its use at the beginning of the war in so-called 'AA Cruisers'. But ADR (Air Direction Radar) was not much in use — or very effective — until the first of the armoured carriers of the *Illustrious* Class was in service in 1941.

The Royal Navy's faith in its gunnery as a means of defence against air attack was even more optimistic than its faith in its ability to hit warships. In 1916, for instance, the actual effectiveness of the battlefleets' main armament at Jutland was 2.2 per cent hits (light damage) and 0.3 per cent hits (heavy damage). (These are German figures obtained after the Great War.) The same guns were in use in the 1939-45 war. They were designed to shoot against slow-moving and very large targets, in a single plane and within their sight more often than not. In 1939, the same design of firing piece — with its surface accuracy of 0.3 per cent hits — was then pointed at targets of ten times the speed, one twentieth the size and manoeuvring in three planes with great rapidity, and it was still expected to hit!

So the position the day war was declared, founded no doubt on unrealistic peacetime practice, was that AA gunnery would suffice for all normal occasions, and in case a large enemy formation was encountered, this would somehow be dealt with by the RAF ashore, 200 or 300 miles away! Had I known this, I should have doubtless waited for the RAF, like Ralph Kirker. I had never bothered to consider the unlikely situation that Naval fighters were to be numbered in their ones and twos, biplanes at that, and that they would be used only for visual interceptions of 'snoopers' in conditions of r/t silence.

The first mini-encounter on the lines envisaged by Inskip occurred a few days after the war started. Naval AA gunnery was therefore almost the first weapon in the Naval armoury to be put to the test. In it, *Ark Royal* was attacked by a formation of Dornier 17s and Ju 88s. The *Courageous* had already been sunk and the subject of vulnerability of aircraft carriers, roaming the sea in so-called 'hunter-killer' groups and unprotected as they were allowed to be, was a tricky one, particularly in the House of Commons. So that when the Fleet returned to Scapa from its first trip into the North Sea, the "first brush with the enemy" (as Churchill described it) was a subject of great interest.

The Fleet had been at sea on 26 September 1939, hoping to tempt the German Navy out of harbour in just the same manner as Jellicoe, a quarter of a century earlier. This time, however, German Zeppelins had been replaced by the far more effective reconnaissance Do 17, and our Fleet was spotted almost immediately. The appropriate number of bombers was then sent by Goering to deal with the *Ark Royal.* She was a priority target, because, even at that stage in the war, the Germans considered her to be the main threat. They almost ignored the battleships with her.

A hit was claimed with a 1000 pound bomb on her bow. In the next two hours the Fleet was reported again while plodding its way back to Scapa. However, on this recce, the German pilot could not see the *Ark* in company (she was 20 miles off) and he claimed her as "missing, believed sunk". The final aircraft sent over confirmed she was still missing and the pilot of the Dornier 17 who had scored the (near) miss was decorated and promoted for having sunk the *Ark Royal.* Lord Haw-Haw repeated this every evening for a fortnight on the German radio.

When Churchill in the Admiralty heard of this incident, he sent the first of many War Memos to Admiral Sir Dudley Pound:

"The first brush with the enemy against the Fleet passed off very well and useful data was obtained, but we do not want to run unnecessary risks with our important vessels until our anti-aircraft fire has been worked up to the required standard against aircraft flying at 250 miles an hour."

Churchill's faith in Naval AA gunnery had not yet been shaken sufficiently for him to start to insist on more interceptors aboard the carriers. However, he was sufficiently worried to ask the Navy to ensure that its training methods were more realistic. Unfortunately, the Naval Gunnery Department was entirely fact-proof where criticism of their gunnery was concerned and did very little to improve the realism of their AA gunnery practices. The only action taken by the Navy to implement Churchill's answer to the problem, was to buy two US Navy Maryland bombers and convert them to towing targets at speeds above 160 knots — the speed in universal use throughout the country.

It was not until late 1943 when the American VT-fuzed 40 mm and the gyro-sighted 20 mm guns came into service in very large numbers in the Navy surface fleets, and their TOSXs (Throw-off shooting exercises) allowed realistic practice, that an effective form of *short* range AA gunnery came into being. The gyro gunsight was particularly useful, for it showed the inexperienced gunners by how much they would have missed their real-life targets (flying at double the speed of their practice targets) had they been shooting in a real-life situation. Long range AA gunnery — 3.7" and larger — remained entirely ineffective throughout the war. It was no more than a frightening nuisance to us aviators.

In his delightfully worded Memo to Pound, Churchill made no mention that the Skua fighters on *Ark*'s deck had not been used at all in the engagement. This was not only because of the wording of the Inskip Report, which made it an RAF task to protect the Navy in its foray over the North Sea, but because there was no radar to give *Ark* warning of the position of the German bombers. They were taken by surprise. The Skua was almost entirely useless as a fighter against the Ju 88 and this may have influenced the Captain of the *Ark* against maintaining a 'standing patrol'.

Following this episode and perhaps in a further effort by Churchill to disentangle the job specification in the Inskip Report, he wrote the following:
"Naval aircraft should be confined to three main duties: (i) air reconnaissance over the open spaces of the ocean, (ii) spotting for Naval gunfire, (iii) launching torpedo attacks upon the enemy."

This confirmed that the carrier-borne aircraft were to be confined to finding and disabling the enemy fleet, so that it could be "brought under the guns of the Fleet" for its *coup de grace*. There was never any question that the aircraft themselves might be capable of inflicting this *coup de grace* or that Naval interceptor fighters might be required as air defence.

There was, however, ample evidence that aircraft bombs could sink capital ships. Tests in America had convinced "all except wilful men" that they could, with ease. The Navy's answer was, predictably, to provide more 'AA cruisers' and more deck armour. The fact that the Americans themselves had a 1000 pound bomb which could, when dropped from 7000 feet, pierce no less than 12 inches of deck armour, was ignored.

Conceived in 1934, the *Illustrious* Class of carriers had been coated with 1500 tons of armour plate specially imported from foreign sources. Designed for another Jutland, they were crowded with guns in turrets, further limiting stowage space for aircraft, reducing their radius of action without refuelling and making living conditions for their full complement of men almost unbearable for periods longer than a few days. The three to five inches of deck and hangar sidewall armour was designed as a shelter from enemy shellfire in a cruiser action, so that they could still operate their aircraft in the reconnaissance and torpedo role while under fire. The 'high-angle' and time-fuzed, dual-purpose gunnery was intended to provide them with AA protection as well as anti-surface gunnery. Their close-range weapons — a few multi-barrelled, low velocity, 30 mm 'pom-poms' were also intended to provide AA support at ranges of 5000 yards or less. It was not until they signally failed in this — particularly in the *Repulse* and *Prince of Wales'* action — that they were replaced by the much more effective high velocity Oelikon 20 mm cannon, demanded in vain by Lord Mountbatten as early as 1934. The protection afforded by the armour on their flight decks was designed to withstand plunging fire from 8" armament, not bombs from aircraft. Such forward thinking had not occurred to their designers. The deck armour was not designed to withstand, nor could it, 1000 pound AP bombs. It could, however, withstand a 500 SAP bomb more or less 'placed' upon it and still attached to a diving Kamikaze. This fortuitous circumstance enabled the BPF to survive the Kamikazes better than the wooden-decked American carriers. The mere 300 knots of a Kamikaze — the first 'thinking' guided missile — was insufficient to pierce 3" of armour, although the German Stuka's 1000 AP bomb, released to strike the flight deck near its terminal velocity and at near 90 degrees penetration angle, was far too much for it. No practical amount of armour had a chance of stopping 1000 AP bombs dropped in this manner, as was repeatedly pointed out by the Naval Ship Construction Branch at Portland during the war. The Americans said that 12 inches of armour would be required, sufficient to capsize a battleship or carrier with ease.

In 1939, the Fleet Air Arm had its own dive bomber — the Skua. The Fleet Air Arm was keen to prove this new weapon both for its own and Their Lordships' benefit, to show what an aircraft could do against surface ships when used correctly and where there was no fighter opposition en route. They did not have long to wait.

On the morning of 10 April 1940, a total of 17 Skuas of 803 and 800 Naval Air Squadrons, operating from the Orkneys, sunk the German heavy cruiser *Königsberg* while she was alongside at Bergen. They sank her with several hits and near-misses from their 500 pound bombs, dropped in steep dives. Surprise was achieved in a dawn attack; only one Skua was lost on the way back. The leader of the Skuas in 800 Squadron, Major R. T. Partridge, DSO, RM, describes the action in his book *Operation Skua.* One of the main characteristics was the extreme accuracy achieved, an average error of 20 yards. These hits were the equivalent of a shell from a 15 inch battleship gun, but at a range of 300 miles and with an accuracy 2000 times greater. It also proved that whatever its other serious shortcomings, the Skua was a good dive bomber in terms of aiming ability.

Unfortunately, Their Lordships, though impressed with the bravery, ignored the technique and military significance of this novel form of attack. They did not even announce it as a Naval action and allowed the RAF to reap the media rewards. They were busy using the carrier *Furious,* the proper home for the two Skua squadrons, as an air transport ship for RAF Hurricanes and Gladiators for the Norwegian Campaign. The senior Admiralty officer responsible for such matters was Admiral Tom Phillips. He it was who was later sent from his Admiralty desk to take command of the *Prince of Wales* and *Repulse,* where they were immediately sunk by air attack off eastern Malaya. He was a convinced battleship man and there is no record that the manner of the sinking of the *Königsberg* made the slightest impression on him.

Not so the Luftwaffe. They immediately perceived its importance and trained up a complete Fliegerkorps, 200-300 aircraft, in dive-bombing and ship-sinking techniques. Sixty of Fliegerkorps X's pilots spent some time in Sicily to work up on ship-sinking techniques. The high cloud base and reliable weather made this a pleasurable business, and in all such environments, new ideas flourish. Their new idea — or so they thought — was to saturate the AA defences by, first, concentrating on a single target — the carrier, if any. The second was to make a co-ordinated attack with up to 30 Stukas, completing their attack from different directions within a few minutes, diving at the steep angle of 70 degrees to obtain maximum bomb penetration. Neither could any gun from their target elevate to that dive angle, so they would come under fire only on their approach and get-away. Simple arithmetic told them that by sharing the risk amongst all 30 aircraft for, say, three minutes at the most, it gave the individual Stuka pilot and his crew exactly 30 times fewer bullets aimed at him than if each Stuka came in separately on the same heading. They also realised that with the ability of the British radar to spot them a good distance off on their slow climb to push-over height of 8000 feet, they must fly to the target in a tight bunch, escaping at zero feet to return out of radar contact. They also practised using decoys. These pretended to be torpedo-carrying aircraft coming in at low level from a direction opposite to that of the dive-bombers. The fighter (Fulmar) defence would then be caught at low altitude when the high-flying Stukas approached.

The Norwegian campaign had shown the Germans that the British had very few 'naval' fighters to protect their ships and they thought that it might even be safer using the Stuka against shipping targets than against tanks on the battlefield. Once in the Mediterranean, the Luftwaffe were certain they could end the rout of the Italians in the North African campaign and if they could replace the ineffective high bombing techniques of the Italians, they could rout the British Fleet as well. They even began to train Heinkel IIIs to drop torpedoes in pairs. Nevertheless, as if to show the immensity of the mistake made by Their Lordships on not having sufficient fighters in the Mediterranean in 1940-41, the very few that there were in *Illustrious* — 806 Squadron of nine Fulmars commanded by Charles Evans — struck terror into the hearts of the Stukas and the Italian Air Force for the short time that the Fulmars survived, and the Stukas determined to remove *Illustrious* as soon as possible. This they did in two months, using their well rehearsed techniques, without much assistance from the Italians.

Air Power

When experts, unthreatened by outsiders, meet together, they tend to disagree. As technical disagreements concerning air defence in wartime could have fatal consequences, the subject of Naval air power became of interest to outsiders. One of these was a Naval historian called Douhet. He wrote a book about Naval Air Power. He divided the various options into four groups. These opinions are still of interest today, for the arguments between the missile and the manned aircraft continue unabated. In 1938, the various leaders — Pound, Tovey, Cunningham, Vian, Troubridge, Boyd, Fraser, Rawlings, Tedder, Harris, Dowding and others, all seemed to belong to one of the four Douhet Groups. These are outlined below.

Group 1. Entire wars could be won by aircraft. The relative importance between bombers and fighters would be determined by the composition of the likely opposition. Civilians and industry would be the main targets, as well as any fast moving enemy military units likely to give trouble. Lord Trenchard and AVM Sir Arthur Harris might have been supporters of this Group. For instance, the latter wrote to Churchill in June 1942: "We can knock Germany out of the war in a matter of months. The use of the 1000 bomber plan has proved beyond doubt in the minds of all but wilful men that we can dispose of a weight of attack which no country . . . can survive."

His assertion that a complete war could be won or greatly shortened by area-bombing, presupposed — amongst many suppositions — that there would be an almost unlimited supply of aircraft and aircrew. The bombing may have lengthened the war, in fact, for no thought seems to have been given to a more sensible utilisation of the available aircraft and crews. A quotation from *Brassey's Annual* makes this point: "It has been estimated that in its lifetime of 30 sorties, a Liberator used by Coastal Command over the Atlantic could save three merchant vessels from destruction by U-boat. The same Liberator used over Berlin could perhaps destroy a few houses and kill a couple of dozen enemy civilians. The difficulty was to get anyone to believe these figures at the time."

Group 2. This Group considered that in any surface encounter of Naval units, the air above and surrounding the airfields should first be cleansed of enemy aircraft. Command of the sea could only come after command of the air above it. This Group relegated the battleship to night or poor visibility actions (a prophetic assertion made possible, even then, only by the British invention of radar) and it was not popular with the Navy. The Americans and Hitler adopted this Group's thinking. The latter, it will be remembered, refused to risk his army to invade Britain before he took command of the air over the Channel. He also turned back *Tirpitz* from convoy PQ17 when *Victorious* put to sea. Admiral Iachino, the Italian C-in-C, supported the carrier and continually complained about the lack of support from Mussolini's Air Force. Doenitz also supported the use of carrier-borne fighters — not considering strike aircraft at all — but Goering put a stop to the completion of the *Graf Zeppelin* carrier.

A British example of this Group's thinking was their brilliant use of aircraft in arming the 'Harpoon' and 'Pedestal' convoys — the two 1942 convoys to Malta from the western end of the Mediterranean — with an effective complement of carrier-borne fighters and only a few A/S Swordfish in addition. Naval officers senior enough to make their voices heard at this time were Dennis Boyd and Tom Troubridge. They both considered that command of the air was not only part of the battle for command of the sea, but was a vital prerequisite.

Group 3. This Group considered that command of the sea could be obtained separately from command of the air. They considered that a Fleet carrier should be capable of taking her place alongside the light/heavy cruiser force (sent ahead as at Jutland) and capable of fighting off cruiser and destroyer opposition with her own guns and armour-plate. The carrier's complement — half that of contemporary US carriers — should be limited to TSR aircraft and a few fighters to escort them and to shoot down snoopers, using visual interception in radio and radar silence. The enemy fleet would then be "brought under the guns of the battlefleet" for the *coup de grace*. As for the surface Fleet itself, it was considered — until 1943 at least — that it could look after itself by AA gunfire and that the air battle could still be left to the RAF if "a considerable enemy air force were encountered."

There are numerous examples in WW II of this Group's misuse of carriers. One example occurred on 10 January 1941. This was when the new *Illustrious* was dive-bombed off Sicily and disabled for a year. Two months later, her replacement, *Formidable*, received the same treatment in the Aegean. In both actions neither carrier was carrying more than a few Fulmar fighters and their hangars were full of Swordfish or Albacores. The Swordfish from *Illustrious* were intended to cripple the Italian fleet and Cunningham had therefore refused the request of his carrier Captain to allow him to hold the carrier out of range of the Stukas as it passed Sicily. In the case of *Formidable,* the Albacores were intended to interdict Aegean airfields to try to halt the Luftwaffe's carnage of our Mediterranean Fleet in the withdrawal from Greece. She only had three serviceable Fulmars as fighter protection in an area where German airpower was supreme. So far as this Group's faith in RAF assistance was concerned, even if the RAF fighters were planned to be available as they were on two or three important occasions in 'Pedestal' and 'Harpoon', the RAF were unable to prevent the Luftwaffe sinking most of the remaining convoys as they approached Malta after the carriers had left due to the lack of Naval fighter direction ships. In the case of the 'Second Battle of Sirte', the Navy's ability to mentally separate the Naval battle from the air battle was well demonstrated. Admiral Vian was knighted for his "brilliant victory" when his westbound convoy to Malta, scattered and delayed though it was by a foray by the Italian fleet, managed to get within 200 miles of Malta unscathed, through the brilliant action of Vian's destroyer escort. This almost bloodless skirmish was not a victory in truth, for the entire convoy either turned back or was sunk before it reached its goal, in the last 200 miles of its journey. We heard about this "victory" while in *Eagle* at Gibraltar. Although we did not believe Vian's claims of having shot down 25 German aircraft with the destroyer's AA, we believed that most of the convoy had been sunk by the failure of the RAF to protect it, not realising how difficult their job was — having no ADR ships to control them and with the remnants of Vian's convoy spread over a thousand square miles of sea.

Group 4. By 1943, very few of this Group remained in the Navy. They had believed that the gun could deal entirely with the air threat — until the loss of the *Repulse* and the *Prince of Wales* proved otherwise. However, they have begun to resurrect themselves. They are beginning to put their trust in the missile and the anti-missile missile. Their claims are hard to shoot down for their views cannot hope to be tested properly except in war conditions. When these occur and show that the existing arsenal of Naval missiles is inadequate to cope on its own against an air attack, they either make immense claims for enemy losses which cannot be verified, or they say that there were unexpected disadvantages which made the situation "abnormal". They are indeed the original diehards but, because their missiles are cheaper to buy and operate in peacetime, their view prevails with the politicians. (See also Appendix 3.)

Appendix 3

Air-to-Air Firing from a Fighter Aircraft in World War II

Shooting at a bomber or at a practice drogue when it is flying straight and level, is all very well. But shooting at an evading target while manoeuvring a fighter aircraft to its limits, is obviously more difficult. The bullets from Brownings of a Hurricane or Spitfire travel at about 1800 mph, and shells from a 20 mm cannon travel at about 2000 mph. They have to arrive at exactly the same time and in the same place as the target — moving across the bullets' line of flight at an angular velocity of from 0-100 mph. The amount of aim ahead required is gauged by the fighter pilot looking through a gunsight fixed to the mean fore-and-aft flight path of his aircraft and pointing in the same direction as the eight guns. The judgement of how much lead to allow is now made electronically. In 1938 it was made by the pilot looking through a 'ring-and-bead' gunsight and judging his target's speed and its 'angle off'. By 1939, the ring-and-bead had been substituted by a reflector gunsight — the GM II. This was a great improvement as it allowed the pilot to see his target and surroundings at the same time as taking aim and made it unnecessary for him to alter the focus of his eyes to see all three once as the 'ring-and-bead' images were focused at infinity. Neither did he have any need to hold his head still, but could move it about a little and with both eyes open. It made aiming easier and much quicker and gave less time for an enemy fighter to 'jump' him from behind while he was trying to get into a firing position.

How much aim ahead is needed? Anyone who has practised skeet shooting will know that a clay pigeon travelling from its launcher at about 30 knots will require about two barrels width aim ahead when shooting at 30 degrees angle-off its flight line, and about four barrels deflection at 90 degrees. Apart from firing within range and assessing its line of flight accurately, the main secret lies in the amount of aim ahead to allow so that gun pellets and clay pigeon arrive at the same spot at the same time.

In the case of the Hurricane or Spitfire/Seafire pilot, he could only alter the direction of aim by altering the flight direction of his entire aircraft. Not only that, but he also had to position his guns-plus-fighter within range. The skeet shooter finds that this has already been done for him. The next thing for the fighter pilot to assess is his angle-off to his target, once again already done for the skeet shooter. Finally, he has to assess the target's speed. This, once again, is almost a standard 30 knots or so for the trap shooter. The fighter pilot's target may be doing anything from 90 knots in a turning fight to, say, 350 knots in a chase situation.

The difficulty of doing a job can be assessed by the amount of practice needed to accomplish it well. We would spend hours of flight time in the practising of range, line-of-sight and deflection estimation, using our G45 16 mm camera guns instead of live bullets, and using each other as targets.

We would then have the film developed, in ordinary black and white negative. By projecting this film on a screen, one frame at a time, the size of the image would give its range. By modelling a shadow image to that on the film, we could also assess its angle-off and line-of-flight accurately. Knowing our bullet speed and assuming a target speed, we could then calculate, in theory, whether our bullets, had we fired them, would have hit.

The angle-off of 30 degrees obviously reduces rapidly as the target continues to fly ahead, just as the clay pigeon flies ahead past the skeet shooter. The attacking fighter gradually falls into a line astern position — unless the target evades in a steep turn — and the amount of deflection that he allows consequently reduces second by second, until it is zero in the line-astern position.

The 'amount' can easily be converted to a number of degrees by solving a velocity triangle, ie a four degree aim ahead is required for a crossing speed of 100 mph. This was the angle which a radius of the '100 mph ring sight' subtended in the GM II.

In the case of the Seafire/Spitfire — the long nose prevented the pilot from seeing his target at greater deflection angles than four degrees — even with his seat fully raised and his shoulders clear of the armour plate behind him. A shot at 30 degrees angle-off was therefore the maximum he could attempt. However, if the target had been a Swordfish doing about 80 knots, a fighter pilot could open fire at an initial 90 degree angle-off and still hit, while keeping his target in view. His range would get too close too quickly to allow more than a couple of seconds firing. Those who describe 'beam attacks' on World War II targets could not have been firing in range, unless a Swordfish was encountered.

The ring-and-bead in the reflector sight was reflected back into the pilot's eyes by means of a small semi-silvered screen. It was the first 'Head-up display' in the cockpit of an aircraft. (The author invented the second in 1949. This was Patent Number 622987, dated 12 May 1950. It gave readings of several cockpit instruments while looking through the windscreen. It was allowed to lapse as no one at that time saw much use for it. It is now used in all pilot-operated attack systems and by speech-makers, sometimes pretending they are speaking without notes.)

Of course there was — and is — an immense difference between theory and practice. Although, in wartime, the problem of providing money for realistic training methods in a proper operational environment is not so difficult as in peacetime, there is usually insufficient time. 'Pipe-line' pilots therefore had only a bare chance of survival on appointment to their squadrons.

Both skeet shooting and cinegun attacks taught the principle of deflection shooting, but when cine results were assessed, they could not allow for skid errors, the effects of high 'g' or the variations in speed altering the flight attitude by ten degrees or more. Films were assessed by the Wren assuming a constant target speed of about 250 knots TAS in 1 'g' flight without yaw. Neither was practice firing ever carried out at high altitude, where target speed (TAS) estimation was even more difficult than at low altitudes. Neither was it carried out — as on operations — at full take-off power and high engine rpm, where yaw, due to gyroscopic effects, became serious.

With such built-in errors in the training process and where habit takes over in the stress of real-life combat, it was a wonder that any hits were obtained at all. However, many of the smaller errors were catered for by the 'spread pattern' of gun harmonisation, quite apart from their growing number. (The Hurricane IIb had 12 Brownings.) It was not until the GM II, '100 mph' reflector sight was replaced by the Gyro Gunsight Mark IID in fighter aircraft in 1944, that most of the yaw, pitch and target speed errors were automatically allowed for by the sight and the pilot could then see by just how much he had been missing with the GM II. A camera monitor, aimed through the light itself was also available, but it was very unpopular as it obstructed the forward view.

The most serious built-in error of all when assessing a weapon's effectiveness in the hands of a gunner is the total lack of realism in *peacetime* training exercises. Cost effectiveness by the gunner, by the CO of the detachment, by the manufacturer and by the Defence Minister himself has always to be demonstrated, regardless of realism, to the tax payer. It rules out any chance that any £100,000 missile fired on exercises should ever miss. The WW II drogue-towing speed of 160 mph — remarked upon by Churchill in 1939 as unrealistically slow — was half the likely target speeds of the day. When, in real-life situations, the target speeds of enemy aircraft were also found to be far greater, pilots, including the author, had the greatest difficulty in positioning for the attack and I and most others usually under-deflected when we opened fire and also failed to trim out the unaccustomed yaw experienced at the higher speeds. Over-confidence of the pilot in himself and in his weapon usually led to exaggerated claims in the number of enemy he shot down. Wartime claims can be divided by between two and four in the largest air battles, although these were made honestly at the time. Likewise, claims by AA gunnery were grossly exaggerated. True peacetime gunnery and missile firing results can bear no relation whatever to their true wartime effectiveness or reliability, unless money and time spent on realistic practice is unlimited.

Appendix 4

HMS Dasher and 804 Squadron's failure at Oran

Dasher was the last of the four *Archer* Class to leave the Hoboken Shipyard in USA. She was commissioned on 1 August 1943 and she sailed for Greenock almost immediately. When *Dasher* arrived in the Clyde, all was not well. Her Chief Engineer tells the following story:

"Directly after we arrived in the UK from Hoboken, we went into dock. The Clydesider's output (Messrs Scott-Lithgow) was a mere fraction of their American counterparts. The ship was therefore late for Operation 'Torch' and we had to sail for that operation at very short notice. Not only did we sail late, but we lost our original Captain and had a dashing destroyer type in his place. The Chief and Senior Engineer Officers on board were of course Naval officers, but the rest were not. The remainder of the engineer officers were ex-Merchant Navy engineers and lacked even the basic knowledge of a half-trained Engine Room Artificer, Fifth Class. These men were known as T124X men. They were civilians dressed in Naval uniform for the duration of the war. They were, however, paid the same rate and allowances as in the Merchant Navy. This was no less than three times that of their equivalent rank in the Royal Navy."

"The notice for the next operation, although very short, was not short enough and a surprising number of the T124X crew managed to miss the ship when she sailed. These men would then report back to their civilian depot at Liverpool, would be given 'scale' Naval punishment and would go to the bottom of the seagoing roster once more — where they wanted to be. Had this process continued we would, indeed, have eventually achieved a loyal remaining complement on board *Dasher*. However, it was not allowed to work for long, for the 'leave jumpers' were detailed for the Pioneer Corps. This had a salutary effect and few ever missed the ship afterwards."

"However, when we sailed for 'Torch', this weeding-out process was still in its very early stages in *Dasher* and we were far from a happy and efficient ship."

My 19 year-old steward in *Biter,* who made my bed and cleaned my cabin drew more pay than a Lieutenant, RN. Had it not been that we all found our living conditions infinitely better than anything that we had ever experienced before in the Navy, we might have had some serious complaints. As it was, the crew in *Biter* could not have done enough for us 'visitors', as 800 Squadron was, and we hardly gave the pay difference a thought. We were far too busy to have any time to worry about pay.

Nevertheless the junior engineers were no match for the 'Sun-Doxford' diesel engines which drove these ships. These 8000 horse power opposed-piston engines had eight cylinders, several feet in diameter. If for some reason they had to be started — they were seldom if ever stopped — there would sometimes be an explosion of some kind. This would blow some vital bits of the engine up through the exhaust pipe, such as a valve stem or two and would bring the engine to a grinding halt. The engine then had to be dismantled, the loose bits and pieces removed and the whole thing bolted together again, minus the offending connecting rod and pistons. the engine would then have to run — seriously out of balance — on six cylinders instead of eight until the next start up time, when it would probably have another explosion. Explosions occurred several times in *Archer* and, of course, in *Dasher*. The latter spent the whole of Operation 'Torch' with one of her engines firing on an odd number of cylinders and with the whole ship jumping up and down at 100 times a minute in time with the crankshaft. Her maximum speed was thus 13 knots, too slow for safe deck operation. Nothing else worked properly in *Dasher* either. The radar, the Ops room, the r/t, the water supply, the compressed air supply, the petrol supply (it was contaminated with water half the time) and even her aircraft.

The ships had hangar space for about eight non-folding aircraft such as the Sea Hurricane. Six more were carried permanently on deck, lashed to the wooden flight deck with ten or more spring-loaded lashings, tightened by rigging screws. Three Swordfish were also carried for A/S duties.

There were six arrester wires instead of *Eagle's* four. There were also two other new items. The wind brakes and the barriers. The latter were two hydraulically-raised-and-lowered wire mesh nets, strung across the deck at just above Hurricane spinner height. They aimed at collecting the aircraft that had missed the wires before they could crash into the deck park forward. Unlike the British equivalent, the American barriers were not designed to give way gently in a civilised and interesting manner. There were therefore several cases of Hurricanes which had impaled themselves semi-permanently amongst the wires in the American-type barrier and which could not easily be removed by the cranes or 'bumper cars' then in existence. In one case, a Hurricane refused to move forward. One of its wooden ('Jablo') prop blades had dug itself into the wooden deck and could not be broken off. To prevent a demarkation dispute, the ship's 'Chippy' was told to report with his tools on the flight deck. With dedication to his trade, he took a tenon saw from his polished tool box, sawed off the prop blade, and, disregarding all about him, preceded to plane off the rough edge of the prop blade still stuck in the deck, finally finishing off with sandpaper and grey paint.

In *Biter,* the six arrester wires were each 35 feet apart. They therefore covered about 170 feet of deck. The total take-off run of the deck was 450 feet, some 200 feet less than *Eagle.* With only 17 knots of wind over the deck (on days with no natural wind) this allowed only a period of two seconds for the landing Hurricane to get amongst the wires. During these two seconds the pilot had to get his aircraft within a few inches of the deck to be sure that his hook would catch a wire. If he did not catch a wire, the aircraft would of course carry on into the barrier, hitting it with an impact velocity of about 50 miles an hour and a deceleration of about 20 'g'. Even with a ten knot natural windspeed added, the pilot would only have three seconds to hook on, but, if he still failed to do so, he would at least hit the barrier with far less energy.

In 1940 the Hurricane was believed by the 'test pilots' to be "too tricky by far" to be decklanded on board a carrier, even on the vast 800 foot decks of the *Illustrious* Class. Now, this same feat was being performed regularly by wartime-trained pilots with only 200 hours in their log books, and on decks half the length and with windspeeds 50 per cent slower.

The Sea Hurricane's main decklanding advantage was its good view over the nose, an exceptional asset for any Naval single-engined fighter. It also had a crisp response to small control movements during the approach to land and good stall warning characteristics. However, it was not given folding wings like the Seafire, so that it took up too much room in the aircraft carriers' hangars and was unpopular with the gunners if stowed on deck.

Furthermore there were very few left for the FAA after Russia had been given 20 per cent of production during 1943-44, and they were in very short supply.

804 Squadron's failure at Oran

It is with this poor aircraft supply situation in mind that we should now judge 804's performance in *Dasher* at Oran. Jacky Sewell, the CO, was subsequently called to a Board of Enquiry to explain his squadron's failure.

He did not know the entire reason why *Dasher* and his squadron had failed. He only knew about his part in it. In the event, he managed to convince the Board that he would have been justified had he refused to fly at all.

The basic cause of the failure was the fact that Their Lordships had not allowed sufficient time following the ship's first Atlantic crossing after her commissioning on 1 August 1942. The change of Captain and the untrained and disloyal members of her crew further delayed her finishing date. At the time that we in *Biter* had already done a fortnight's flying on board (only just enough for ourselves to get used to the new aircraft and new ship), *Dasher's* two Hurricane squadrons had not yet embarked, they had only half their aircraft, there were no spares, no log books, the guns were unharmonised and only three out of the 14 aircraft were flyable.

It might have been considered by Their Lordships that the best part of three months was long enough to get the aircraft organised, just as *Biter* and *Avenger* had had. However, because *Dasher* was last in the queue she had suffered the most from the inadequacies of Scott-Lithgow. Several additional factors had slowed down the arrival of the Sea Hurricane Mark II into service, in addition to Beaverbrook's apparent wish to give Russia and the Far East and the desert priority over the Fleet Air Arm. The RAF had recently been blamed for taking too much of the Country's production potential for its Bomber Command build up. It had retaliated against the Navy — the Fleet Air Arm — by accusing it of precisely the same selfish behaviour, causing Churchill to say: "There can be no question of taking machines which will be used in action by the RAF (Hurricane IIs) in order to build up inordinate reserves for the Admiralty". (Churchill's Memo, dated 22 August, 1942.)

The Admiralty then pointed out to Churchill that Takoradi, the West African staging post, had 140 Hurricane IIs doing nothing there, apparently waiting for ferry pilots to fly them to the Middle East. So it went on. Both the Navy and the RAF had to keep vast numbers of aircraft in their 10,000 mile pipelines, from factory to front, but as the RAF ruled the aircraft allocation organisation, they won.

Thus it was that Jacky's Hurricane IIs arrived late and the entire ship, *Dasher*, late as she was herself, could do nothing useful at Oran as a result. Three-quarters of 804's Sea Hurricanes on the dawn operation in 'Torch' were doing their first flights, straight out of packing cases lifted aboard by cranes in the UK. Their Lordships should not have sought to blame Jacky. They should have blamed themselves, the go-slow Clydesiders, the T124X system, the inadequate machinery in the *Archer* Class, the RAF procurement system, and the political demands of Russia.

Appendix 5
Some reasons for the Seafire's poor showing at Salerno in 1943

After the Salerno landings, we heard at Henstridge that the commander of the inshore operations — Rear Admiral Vian — had severely criticised the Seafire on three points. The first was that it had a weak undercarriage and was also entirely unsuitable as a carrier-borne fighter. Secondly, it was not fast enough to catch the low-flying Fw 190 fighter-bombers over the beach-head — its main task. Third, it lacked endurance to remain on CAP for the necessary two hours in spite of the 45 gallon slipper tank.

It was true that out of 500 sorties there had been only two or three successful interceptions and out of this number of landings there had been 50 crashes on deck. However, most of these criticisms could have been avoided by better planning before the operation started. First, by arranging for the fighters to operate from faster carriers capable of a better speed that 15 knots, so giving them more wind speed for landing in the calm conditions prevailing in the Mediterranean at that time of year. Second, by operating the carriers further offshore, clear of the radar 'ground clutter'.

The accident rate of about ten per cent of landings was inevitable, for, with the maximum vertical touchdown velocity of 7ft/sec allowed in the Seafire, a mandatory $3\frac{1}{2}$ degree descent path and with only 15 knots of wind over the deck, an undercarriage failure was a mathematical certainty, even on a perfect landing. Many pilots knew this and tried to 'flare out' at touchdown. However, this resulted many times in the aircraft floating over the wires and making a full toss into the barrier. Others landed off-centre or stalled, with the same result.

The second criticism — that the Seafire LIIc was too slow — was very hard for us to believe for it was the fastest low-level version of the hooked Spitfire Vb in existence. The poor interception rate was entirely due to our radar suffering 'the robbing effect' of ground clutter, and the ships and thus the aircraft received little or no warning of the low-flying approaches of the Fw 190 fighter/bombers by radar. With but a couple of minutes warning at the most, the Seafires on CAP, at their maximum feasible 240 knots patrol speed to conserve fuel, found it impossible to accelerate to the 350 knots diving approach speed of the Fw 190s and in the poor visibility which prevailed, the enemy got away each time. The Germans, like ourselves, already knew — even at this stage in the war — that all they had to do was to keep a bit of high ground behind them, in-line with their sea-level approach, and they could not be detected at *any* range by the ships' radars. If the carriers had been ordered to keep further offshore and away from the ground clutter, the sea-level approach of the Fw 190s would have been detected at 20 miles, and this might have been sufficient for a powerful fighter like the Seafire LIIc to accelerate to the Fw's get-away speed of about 300 knots in good time.

The third criticism — that the Seafire's endurance of two hours was insufficient — was perhaps less unjustified. However, with the need to conserve fuel having to give second place to a high patrol speed, and the fact that the Admiral's positioning of the carriers made a careful and relaxed landing approach impossible in the short period of the carrier maintaining a straight course before hitting the shore and the crashes on deck further delaying matters, pilots would ask for a landing with plenty of fuel in hand. This considerably shortened their useful time on patrol.

The Naval Staff who planned the Naval task at Salerno should have learned from past history — two months previously — when radar clutter in operation 'Husky' caused a similar 'robbing effect'. (Readers will also remember that the Navy struck exactly similar troubles at San Carlos Bay in the Falklands in 1982 and officially blamed their heavy losses on the 'robbing effect' of ground clutter affecting the accuracy of their missiles, and the 'wave-top' approach height of the Argentinian Air Force planes allowing them to get in unobserved.)

When the decklanding trials unit in the UK got to hear of the Seafires' efforts at Salerno, it carried out its own trials in *Ravager*. However, the test pilots, keen to break new frontiers of science, used their own private techniques — not the curved approach but a 'crab' approach — so that their results were of no interest to the squadrons, who would not use such a dangerous method. So that, even if Admiral Vian had asked for advice on how to avoid Seafire troubles in the future, he would have received nothing useful in reply from the carrier trials unit.

Appendix 6
Inter-Service Rivalry, 1943-44 and Naval progress in the Far East

During the summer of 1943 Churchill was, as usual, trying to settle the demands of war fairly upon the three Services. In July he had issued a very interesting memo:
> "I think it rather a pregnant fact that out of 4,000 officers in the Fleet Air Arm, only 30 should have been killed, are missing or have been taken prisoner during the three months ending 20 April 1943."

It would indeed have been a pregnant fact if the figures had been anything like correct. The staff officer who made them up had failed to include the numbers lost at sea in *Avenger* and *Dasher* and had included all Fleet Air Arm officers as aircrew serving in first line squadrons, whether flying training or administrative. As no Naval Staff Officer would make such a basic error, it can only be assumed that the figures came from a non-Naval source. The figures should have been 200 casualties out of 1500 aircrew officers, not 30 out of 4,000.

Churchill had a difficult task to settle inter-Service rivalry. The misleading figures given to Churchill probably came from RAF sources. RAF casualties, particularly in Bomber Command, had recently been very serious. The Germans were using night fighters, against which the Lancasters, Halifaxes and Stirlings of AVM Harris' night offensive had little protection. Coupled with this, the FAA had recently complained about the lack of Sea Hurricanes. The RAF response was that the FAA made little use of the ones it had got, giving Churchill the 'pregnant' figures above. AVM Harris was also worried. He had promised Churchill that with his 1000 bomber offensive, he could shorten the war. He wanted to justify this assertion. He therefore wanted less German night fighters. The only way in which the number of German night fighters could be reduced was for an early start to be made in the American day bomber offensive and a large increase in Fighter Command activity over France, to tempt the Luftwaffe into the air and so inflict casualties. There were to be no spare fighters for the FAA.

The FAA had indeed not been particularly 'closely engaged' in the first three months of 1943, for they had been engaged in a massive regrouping programme. They had also been training and providing the entire air defence for the landings in Sicily scheduled for July and for the forming of squadrons for a further six carriers for the September landings at Salerno in Italy.

The latter involved retraining, on Seafires, of no less than 15 squadrons. Another ten squadrons were re-forming on American aircraft in the USA. *Victorious* had been loaned to the hard-hit American Pacific Fleet until September 1943. Although the Russian convoys had been suspended from March to September 1943 due to the shortage of suitable carriers and fighters, the Atlantic battle against the submarine was being reinforced. MAC ships

(Merchant ships modified to take Swordfish plus fighters in small numbers) were being manned from March 1943 onwards. Nineteen would be in service by the end of 1944. With the impending demise of Mussolini and his Navy, the Mediterranean and Malta would shortly be able to spare the *Illustrious, Formidable* and *Indomitable* for service in the Indian Ocean, the East Indies and the Pacific, using new American aircraft and American-trained pilots where possible.

Of course, Churchill was not intending to judge military success and activity by the length of a list of casualties. There could be no parallel between the carnage of the Western Front in World War I and that of the high technology air battles in World War II. Casualties in air battles have never been a sign of success, very much the reverse. Neither have they necessarily been a sign that fighting was taking place. Many of the most successful involvements of the Fleet Air Arm, at Taranto and at the attack by Barracudas and Corsairs against *Tirpitz* on 4 April 1944, were completed almost without casualties. Thus it was a shame that this great and busy man, Churchill, should have been used in this way to make a party point in the inter-Service rivalry. Churchill could easily be misled on technical matters and it was often the case that his first interventions did more harm than good as a consequence.

Whereas there was no just cause for the RAF to complain of Fleet Air Arm slackness in Europe, there might well have been cause for complaint by the Americans of our Naval efforts in the Indian Ocean and Pacific at this time. Our inactivity in that area was, in fact, part of a conscious policy of conservation on the part of Admiral Somerville. He knew, even if those in the Admiralty did not, that his four ancient, 18 knot battleships and his under-equipped carriers were no match for the Japanese Admiral Nagumo's 30 knot fleet — complete with a fleet of four fast carriers with six times the number of aircraft, with a proper fleet train in support. The Royal Navy in the Far East was therefore unable to make the slightest impression, either as a deterrent or as an attack force, with or without American naval assistance, during 1943 and the early part of 1944.

However, help was at hand. As far back as 1940, the MAP had sent a buying mission to the USA for more fighters. Although they mistakenly bought the Brewster Buffalo — which, in spite of Boscombe Down's damning opinion, the RAF consigned to the defence of Singapore — the Navy bought the Grumman Wildcat F4F-3. The order also included a redundant French order for a non-folding, Cyclone-engined version. All of this order was delivered by July 1941, 804 Squadron receiving the first of the 60 French aircraft by August 1940. Meanwhile the Buffalo predictably failed to perform in the Far East and Somerville was forced to use his depleted carriers to ferry more RAF replacement Hurricanes: too late, as it happened, for them to come into action. When Lease-Lend was well under way, Their Lordships were at last persuaded that there was a shortage of fighters in the FAA by Winston Churchill and by their own Director of Naval Air Production — Captain Caspar John. In 1943, they appointed him Assistant Naval Air Attaché, Washington, to supervise the introduction of new US Navy fighters — the Corsair, Hellcat and the strike aircraft, the Grumman Avenger, into the FAA. Assisted by two other officers taken from 'the remaining flashes of brilliance' who had stayed in the FAA — Commanders Richard Smeeton and Charles Evans — and a team of potential squadron commanders, eg Dicky Cork and Jacky Sewell, he was able to re-equip Somerville's carrier force by the beginning of 1944 so that he could resume the offensive in the Indian Ocean.

By the spring of 1944, the situation in the Far East began to improve and

Somerville, later relieved by Admiral Sir Bruce Fraser, could, by August 1944, prove to Admiral Ernest J. King, the highly sceptical Chief of Naval Staff, USN, in Washington, that the British could indeed look after themselves in that area and be very useful.

Of course we knew nothing of this in the spring of 1944 at Henstridge. All we knew was that we were beginning to win in the Mediterranean. Although the Atlantic battle against the U-boat had taken a brief turn for the worse following the German U-boat improvement in underwater range and speed, by the invention of the Schnorkel, our use of search radar from the air more than offset this advantage. We had also heard about the great American sea battles in the Pacific against the Japanese, of the Coral Sea and of Midway. Here, the Americans, with the inestimable advantage of ADR and the 'stop-me-and-buy-ones', now using up to four carriers in a single fleet and combined into Carrier Air Groups, had achieved a high casualty rate upon the Japanese aircrews which they could not replace quickly enough.

Nevertheless we were under no illusions that the war was won. We had read of the fanatical 'Kamikaze' bravery of the Japanese. The Kamikaze was a weird form of terrorism which seemed to us to deserve nothing but a painful death and eternal damnation. With their clever, decoy-led, low-level approach below the radar of the carrier air defence, it was worrying to think that 100 per cent kills would be necessary before a sure defence could be provided. Each one of these part-trained, one-way aviators could park a 500 pound bomb within a few feet of his aiming point if he was allowed to get within a few miles of the Fleet. However, we felt that the Seafire of all aircraft, would be the best possible defence in such circumstances, and we were not too frightened provided we could see them coming.

So far as RAF participation in the forthcoming Pacific War was concerned, it seems we neither saw nor heard anything of them and after late 1944, the FAA seemed to have achieved a remarkable degree of self-sufficiency of supply and training from America and Australia.

Appendix 7
The Gyro Gunsight Mark IID, 1944

The GGS IID began to replace the GM II in Naval and RAF aircraft in May 1944. The conversion in Seafire aircraft was complete by June. A simpler version was also in use in American-manufactured 20 mm AA guns by this time. The new sight had a 'moving' ring as well as a small fixed ring, side by side. Provided that the pilot kept the central blob of the moving ring on his target, the gyro mechanism in the sight made the blob lag behind the target as it appeared to cross the firing line, to lay off the correct aim ahead.

The aim ahead or deflection angle, would obviously vary according to the crossing speed of the target. However the gyro, spinning at constant rpm on its universal 'Hook's' joint, would take no account of target speed unless its 'tilt' could be altered to take account of range. A rangefinder was therefore incorporated into the sight. Nowadays this is done by radar, but in 1944 it had to be done by an input from the pilot, mechanically, by a twistgrip on the throttle lever. Range is difficult to judge by sight unless some size-comparison from known objects is available. Knowing his target's wingspan beforehand and setting this on a graduated dial, the pilot turned the twist grip so that eight, graticules forming the 'moving' ring in his sight 'nipped' the target's wings, while he kept the central blob steady on the cockpit — his aiming point. This movement simultaneously altered the tilt of the gyro, so altering the blob's lag to the correct angle. Needless to say, the gyro mechanism could not cope with large deflection angles and it toppled easily. The pilot's sight then went blank while it recovered, and recourse was hurriedly made to the fixed ringsight. This occurred to me in a dogfight situation when I was jumped by Fw 190s with my No 2 while bombardment spotting over Normandy. I was not able to spend enough time tracking the target for the gyro to settle down properly and I used the fixed ring. However, it was excellent for long ranges when smooth tracking was possible and when extreme accuracy was required, and for rocket firing and dive bombing. It also allowed for skid errors of all kinds — or wind errors for ground attack — in the firing and target aircraft, and it avoided line-of-flight errors. It computed the *actual* flight paths of the target and firing aircraft and not the apparent flight paths. It also had the advantage that it allowed for bullet (gravity) drop and it allowed for a reduction in bullet speed at longer ranges. By setting 'R/P' on the sight selector, it also allowed for the large gravity drop when firing rockets. It was very useful for training, for it showed us all — in a variety of conditions — by just how much we should have been missing had we trusted our own estimation of the amount of deflection required. Pilots consistently underdeflected in action because they seldom had a training target capable of a realistic combat speed on the few occasions when live bullets were used. Drogue speeds were never more than half the speed of most real-life targets, as Churchill remarked upon in 1939. No doubt the same lack of realism applies today in practice missile firing. By the time we used the GGS in the Seafire XV and XVII with its heavier five bladed propeller, the sight was essential to allow for the huge gyroscopic yaw effects in a turning fight at full engine rpm.

The GGS sight occupied four times the volume of the GMII which it replaced. In the Spitfire/Seafire cockpit — and in the Firefly and Beaufighter cockpit too — the sight was eight inches from the pilot's forehead. It represented a serious crash hazard when arresting into a barrier, or when ditching or making a forced landing ashore. Seldom if ever, did the pilot escape head injury and on occasion was knocked out and thus stood no chance of getting out from a fire or a ditching. As the space between the sight and the cockpit exit was narrower by several inches than a parachute plus dinghy, baling out snags were always reported by those lucky enough to make it. With a heavy Franks' suit as well, the chances were minimal. (See Appendix 11 (d) — Baling out of Seafire III.)

Appendix 8

Dicky Cork's Accident

Lt/Cdr (A) R. Cork, DSO, DSC, RN left Henstridge as our Chief Flying Instructor on 31 October 1943. He was appointed to command No 15 Naval Fighter Wing in the USA where he spent the next two months training his new pilots on the very formidable Corsair fighter. Fifteen Wing was then embarked in *Illustrious* for further working up, before taking part in strikes on the Japanese-held East Indies.

Before dawn on 14 April 1944, Dicky and 19 more Corsairs of No 15 Wing were about to be launched from the flight deck of *Illustrious*. The ship was about 100 miles off the eastern coast of Ceylon and engaged in working-up her squadrons before making their first strike on the Japanese-held stronghold of Penang in northern Sumatra on 19 April 1944. The sea was a flat calm and *Illustrious* — with no effective catapults and with such a large range of aircaft on deck — could not provide enough windspeed for a safe take-off in the distance available.

After much searching for wind, Dicky eventually agreed to try to take-off himself and, he said, if he found that he had enough room, it would be safe for the 19 others.

In complete darkness, he only just made it. He asked, on the r/t, for the ship to cancel the take-off until it got light for the others. He was told to land ashore at China Bay, the nearest Air Station.

He flew the 100 miles to China Bay and, in the early morning and still in semi-darkness, he found the place asleep. No radio, no nothing. He circled the landing strip twice. It was a single strip, carved out of the jungle. Nothing moved and there were no lights. A small shed on a 40 foot wooden structure did duty as an air watch tower. The tower was close to the runway on its east side and at its mid point.

Dicky began the usual carrier-type approach to land, flaps and wheels down, navigation lights still showing in the half light. He had no radio contact, either with China Bay or the ship. The latter was, of course, below the VHF radio horizon now that Dicky was below 1000 feet. As there was no natural wind which would signal a proper landing direction, he followed the landing instructions in the 'landing square' by the tower. The arrow in this square pointed to a normal left hand circuit and the white 'T' pointed in a northerly landing direction.

The Corsair had fuel for four hours flying. It would therefore be landing at its maximum permitted landing weight. Dicky would also realise that in zero wind conditions he would have to use every inch of the runway and would have to have excellent braking in his Corsair to pull up in time, before running off the end. Early Corsairs' brakes had a tendency to oil-up when unused, as on board a carrier, and Dicky would have known about this possible snag.

He made a normal ADDL approach, with the Corsair's tail down and in a steady, lefthand curve. The Corsair, like the Seafire, had a poor view forward. It was impossible to see the runway when landing unless the usual carrier approach was made, in a steady left hand turn. While in this turn, he could see the whole length of the runway, as in a Seafire, on his approach, until the final moment just before straightening up before touchdown. After touchdown and with the tailwheel locked and on the runway, and travelling at 70 knots, he would then be entirely blind to his forward view until he unlocked the tailwheel and turned off the end of the runway at the far end, to taxi back to the maintenance area. It was not possible to turn the aircraft more than a few degrees at a time while the tailwheel was in the locked position and with the weight of the aircraft on it.

The report says that Dicky was warned, by light signal, not to land on his first approach. This would have been by a red Aldis Light directed at him from the watch tower as he approached to land. However, Dicky would not have been expecting any signals nor have been able to see the watch tower on his left handed approach from the south, as the Corsair's nose and wing would have masked that side of the airfield entirely from his view. He would never have been in a position to see the tower or its warning signals on his final approach, unless he was making a normal, RAF, straight-in approach. Even then, the view would have been very restricted in a Corsair. However, if the light had been shone at his aircraft while it was in the downwind part of the landing circuit, provided it had been well directed, he might have seen it. He would not, however, have been expecting any signals for he had seen no activity on the airfield and, in any case, a landing aircraft universally had priority over an aircraft taking off, even if the latter was an Admiral and Dicky had been a Midshipman. This was before the days of universal r/t circuit and taxying controls at airfields, and much depended upon the directions given to the pilot in the 'landing square' and the fact that he would expect to have complete priority when making a landing.

Nevertheless, it is true that he went round again for some reason. This might have been because he was not happy with his approach, being over-weight and in zero wind.

He then made a second identical approach. The RAF report said: "He again ignored the warning, landed, and ran head-on into a second Corsair". The collision was stated to have occurred towards the end of Dicky's landing run. The other Corsair was apparently about to take-off in the reverse direction to Dicky's landing.

The pilot of the other Corsair had been ordered to carry out decklanding training on *Illustrious*. He was probably late for his rendezvous with the ship. It is possible that the normal, inviolate rule giving priority for landings over take-offs, might have been waived. The tower might therefore have exceptionally given Dicky a red Aldis warning light and the other pilot a green. The latter would then line up on the runway, lock his tailwheel and run up to full power for take-off. Once his tailwheel was locked, he would not be able to turn his aircraft until the lock was removed. This was done by a cable and lever in the cockpit. All Corsairs had had recent modifications to their tailwheel assembly and the cable Frelease arrangements were known to be unreliable. It is possible that this might have been the reason for what now happened.

The young pilot in the Corsair, about to take-off, may well have seen the signals from the tower now telling him not to take-off as Dicky was now on finals for the second time and apparently ignoring all signals. But the young pilot would not have been able to make a 180 degree turn to taxi off the runway until he could unlock his tailwheel. These factors and that the Corsair's forward view was almost nil, would not have been generally known to the RAF staff in the tower. They would normally have been dealing with twin-engined Beauforts, Beaufighters or Blenheims. These aircraft had a perfect view for the pilot to see the oddly positioned control tower when landing or taking-off. Decklanding, tail-down approaches from Naval aircraft would probably have been strange to them and they would not have known about the visibility problems in Naval aircraft and in landing and take-off procedures.

As it was, all the young pilot in the Corsair could do was to flash his navigation lights on and off — which he did — hoping perhaps to warn Dicky, now on the last part of his finals of his presence. But Dicky would not have been able to see them. The tower occupants did, for they mentioned this in their report.

Far from the fault lying with the pilots, the fault must surely have been inadequate communications and the bad siting of the control tower for Naval landing requirements. It was not for another two years that r/t control was fully installed in some airfields in Britain.

Dicky Cork and the young Corsair pilot were buried in the cemetery at Trincomalee. The ceremony was attended by their many friends in the United States Navy's No 200 Carrier Air Group from *Saratoga,* as well as by their own Air Group from aboard *Illustrious.* The two pilots lie there still, guarded during the day and night by the crocodiles in the nearby Mahaweili River.

Appendix 9
The Franks' Flying Suit

In 1938, Sir Frederick Banting, head of Medical Research at Toronto University, began a physiological research programme designed to protect aircrew "who were about to wage War in the tremendous air battles in the skies over Europe". Besides starting research on a new oxygen 'demand' system (in use by late 1942) his team also studied new flying problems associated with fatigue, noise, vision, nutrition, coldness, high altitude and the effects of high 'g'. Both Banting and RAE Farnborough knew that future fighter and bomber aircraft would make demands far exceeding the physical capabilities of those who were about to fly them. Something also had to be done to catch up with the Germans who had learned so much from their experience in the Spanish Civil War.

In spite of the lack of funds for military purposes in Canada and in Britain which followed from the pacifist governments of the early thirties, Banting was able to use his prestige, as the discoverer of insulin, to extract sufficient funds for his military research at Toronto University at a time when such research was not allowed in Britain. One of his staff at Toronto was Dr. Wilbur Franks. Although Franks had never flown, he understood the effects on animals and humans of high 'g' in tight turns. During a cancer research problem, he had invented a 'g' suit for some mice so that they could withstand the high 'g' of a centrifuge. This he did by kitting out each mouse with a condom, immersing the condom-coated mouse in water up to its neck in a test tube — also immersed in water for protection — and by placing the test tube in his centrifuge. Both tube and mouse withstood the strain of 150 'g'. In spite of this huge centripetal force, its heart and all its bodily functions continued to work perfectly, and the mouse walked away unharmed. Without such protection, it, and the test tube, would have been crushed to a pulp.

Franks perceived that by surrounding the human body with a similar rigid water jacket, the water in the jacket would then apply a pressure to the outside of the body exactly equal and opposite to that of the blood inside the body as 'g' was applied, and so prevent blood from collecting in the lower parts of the body. Blood starvation to the upper parts of the body could not then occur. The retina, the brain, the lungs and the heart could continue to function normally. The advantage of being able to see and to remain fully conscious in very steep, high speed turns of six to eight 'g' would give British and her allies' pilots a huge advantage over the Germans and allow them to turn inside them in a dogfight.

How does 'g' — or centripetal force — occur? The 'g' in an aircraft increases as its TAS squared divided by its radius of turn. It follows therefore, that provided the aircraft can cope, for a given rate of turn, the 'g' suffered by the aircraft and pilot depends very much on its speed. The first limitation on the 'g' a pilot can pull in an aircraft obviously depends upon the aircraft's ability to give the extra lift required without it reaching stalling incidence. If there is sufficient speed, the next limitation is upon the ability of the pilot himself to withstand the extra 'g'. Finally, there is the strength of the aircraft itself. Aircrew 'grey out' between four to six 'g' — depending on their fitness and sitting posture. They 'blackout' from five to seven 'g'. If 'g' between five to seven is prolonged — perhaps more than a few seconds — aircrew become unconscious. They quickly become unconscious — perhaps in a couple of seconds — if the 'g' is imposed suddenly and is more than seven 'g'.

Most fighter aircraft in WW II had sufficiently low wing-loadings for them to be able to deliver about seven to eight 'g' maximum without stalling at an IAS of 300 knots and above. Stall warning in the turn was given by 'judder' on the stick, caused by a wing-root breakaway in. the airflow hitting the tail surfaces. The pilot then relaxed back pressure on the stick. In a prolonged turning fight where the enemy aircraft maintained a fairly constant height in the turn, the engine powers of WW II fighters were insufficient to maintain speeds much above 240 knots IAS — usually they were far less — particularly at high altitude. The maximum 'g' a Spitfire could pull at this IAS at any altitude without stalling would be about five 'g'. With the extra thrust (to overcome the increased drag of a high 'g' turn) not available from the engine, the Spitfire lost speed still further in the turn. There was therefore no need for a 'g' suit unless diving turns were made in a prolonged turning combat. Pilots would always pull the steepest (ie, the smallest radius) turn possible without the 'judder', to draw a bead on the enemy. The target, if he had kept his eyes open and had spotted his attacker, would hope that he could turn tighter still and prevent a deflection shot on him, and gradually turn inside his attacker so that he finished up astern of him within a few gyrations. During such prolonged fights, the only recourse open to an aircraft about to be fired at was a quick roll into the turning direction, a dive and a quick pullout at the bottom of the dive. It was here that the 'g' suit was a life-saver. The dive away and pull-out would not blind the 'g' suited pilot, but would black out the enemy on his tail for a sufficient time for him to lose his bearings and lose sight of his quarry. The pilot with a 'g' suit could turn his aircraft with up to 7½ 'g' applied for longish periods.

However, the commonest set of circumstances where the 'g' suit was very useful was in the positioning phase of a fighter v fighter or fighter v bomber combat. The approaching attacker might need to have a 50-75 knot excess speed during this phase and so be much more vulnerable to 'g' effects. If the target was to see his enemy diving down on him, say, from his port quarter, he would immediately turn left towards his attacker as steeply as possible at the moment just before he came into firing range, to prevent a deflection shot. If he did not choose exactly the right moment to do this, the attacker with a 'g' suit might still be able to turn inside his quarry and get on his tail. Without a suit, it would not be worthwhile to do this.

The suit was made 'top secret' by 1940, for, if discovered early by the enemy, it would obviously lose all advantage. Nevertheless, Wing Commander D'Arcy Greig, of Schneider Trophy fame, could not resist carrying out the brief trials on the second prototype suit in a Spitfire, in full view of his relatives and friends. The brief tests showed that this early version of the suit could protect the pilot up to eight 'g' — for the short periods that such a high 'g' could be applied and maintained.

In February 1941, Doctors Franks and Banting determined to come to Britain to continue their work, where the prospects for aircraft tests were far better. Tragically, Banting — and his aircraft crew — died in their Lockheed Hudson Atlantic ferry plane. It failed to maintain height on one engine out of Gander and crashed at night in a field a few miles away. Dr Franks wisely followed by sea, a few months later.

With these delays, it was not until November 1942 that AVM Sholto Douglas — who had relieved Dowding as C-in-C Fighter Command — was able to say "I favour the adoption of the Franks suit for operational use".

By this time, the FAA had already carried out their in-service trials. They used 807, 801 and 885 Seafire Squadrons taking part in Operation 'Torch'. Afterwards, in December 1942, the pilots reported favourably. Lt (A) A. C. Powell, RNVR, said: "Had it not been for the suit I should have blacked out, for the aircraft was shuddering (180-200 knots) at the time". Another said that he was able to pull round so sharply in a steep turn at Oran that the Dewoitine 520 on his tail 'spun off'. Although an IAS of only 180-200 knots could not have given enough lift to black out any pilot — with or without a suit — it was obvious from the pilots' reports that the suit gave them confidence. But how much this was due to the suit at Oran — or the superior fighting qualities of the Seafire — it would be hard to say.

Nevertheless, their reports showed that in spite of all the extra trouble of fitting, filling, emptying and removing the suits in the chaos of a carrier's flight deck, the FAA pilots liked it.

It was therefore disappointing that for Operation 'Husky', the four squadrons of Seafires in *Indomitable* were not allowed to use it, for secrecy reasons. It was to be kept for the invasion of Normandy. Both Lt/Cdr W. H. 'Moose' Martyn of 880 Squadron and Lt/Cdr R. B. Haworth of 899 Squadron complained of this officially, but to no purpose.

By January 1944, with the assistance of Messrs Dunlop, some 8,000 suits were made in 17 different sizes, nearly half of them being for the FAA. Each of the 17 sizes was capable of a myriad contortions in addition — by means of lacing, adjustable webbing, zippers and braces, all pulling in appropriate directions upon the equally myriad shapes and sizes of the fighter pilots. A gallon of water gave the calves, thighs and the lower abdomen full 'g' protection. A small airspace was left to retain buoyancy in case of a baleout over the sea. The suit could be worn on the ground without too much discomfort for about six hours — over a pair of pyjamas. However, those who force-landed in Normandy'from 3 Wing found that a couple of hundred yards was all they could manage while the suit was still full of water, even when running away from the Germans.

Although by November 1942 it was already Fighter Command's policy to issue their pilots with the suit by May 1944 in time for 'D' Day, they made such a poor job of 'selling' it to the RAF that very few of the RAF pilots took up the offer. The FAA were the only serious takers. Those who were flying desks, not aeroplanes, in the Air Ministries of Canada and Britain, had to find a reason for the pilots' seeming ingratitude. Canadian HQ quickly found one.

The 'sellers' had made the stupid mistake, they said, of asking the fighter pilot himself what he thought of the suit. No wonder he had turned it down for: "this untouchable hero of all heroes . . . felt that the suit complicated his life style and detracted from his macho image". To explain the FAA's acceptance of the suit, they said that, instead of living like the RAF "On an airbase, close to pubs and young ladies and all the amenities civilisation has to offer," the FAA lived in a much harsher climate and were therefore "more survival orientated". They therefore welcomed the suit. The letter — to the Canadian Defense Ministry in Ottawa — then described this environment in such stark terms that it would not have been believed even by a Hollywood script writer. Such was the poor state of communications between the scientists, the Air Staff and those chosen to test the suit, in 1942/3/4. The real reasons for the RAF's lukewarm welcome were entirely different, for Fighter Command had asked the wrong people to evaluate the suit. They had asked two squadrons engaged in fighter escort duties *at high altitude*. There is a world of difference between the 'g' protection needed in the high altitude, close escort, of slow American bombers flying in straight lines for four to six hours on end at 25,000 feet, and those engaged in the cut and thrust of medium or low level interceptions and in the business of strafing and rocketting, where high IAS and high 'g's are possible for much of the time.

We were far luckier in our contacts with the 'medical airmen' in the FAA. We were a fairly close-knit lot and our internal communications were therefore better — even if our test flying was as inept as that of the RAF on occasion. We, in 3 Wing, also had our CO 'Buster' Hallet. He talked to the 'Flying Doc' at Farnborough and between them they arranged for the suit to be given to us for a job for which it was admirably suited — bombardment spotting. With up to six hours flying a day for a week or more, at high IAS and in continuous steep turns, we should need its protection if we were to last the course. There was never any likelihood that it would be required to prevent blacking out in these turns, of course, for it was not possible to maintain enough 'g' in a turn — without diving — in the Seafire/Spitfire (or any other fighter of that time) for more than a few seconds. It would, however, relieve the body from muscular and heart fatigue and it would nullify the effects of up to four 'g' for two or three hours a day. It would also enable us to dive and pull away at maximum 'g' if we were jumped by Fws or Me 109s, which many of us were, and still see our enemy when he could not see us. The suit must have saved several nasty moments if not complete lives in 3 Wing.

The Americans, whose standard of flying gear was superior to anything which we or the RAF had in WW II, had chosen the air-operated 'g' suit. In 1940/41, they used Franks' Canadian experience and their own results from their full-sized centrifuge, to develop an 'on demand' air suit. This used variable pressure air bags instead of water, the pressure of the air supplied being dependent upon the 'g' pulled by the pilot. It was much lighter and cooler than the water suit. Franks did not change to an air suit because of the lack of a sufficient supply of air from the small 'Heywood' air compressor in the Merlin engine. This compressor supplied the Spitfire/Seafires' guns and brakes with relatively small quantities of air pumped into a bottle at 600 lbs/sq.in, and it would have been quickly exhausted by a continual requirement for an air suit. However, once jet power was available, with high 'g's', in the Meteor, Vampire, Sea Hawk, etc, the air suit became standard issue for all operational pilots and Observers. Franks' vision was 20 years into the future.

Appendix 10
The improved chances for FAA aircrew, 1943

By the start of 1943, many new factors had begun to emerge to improve the chances of FAA aircrew in the struggle for survival. There were more senior officers who understood air matters and who now avoided the more obvious Balaclavas. There was more ADR in ships, homing aids, better Air Sea Rescue, more fighter aircraft to stop the ravages of the Stukas and Ju 88s, better A/S cover in the Atlantic, better aircraft — from America — and better flight instruments and VHF radio. Although only 18 out of 40 Sea Hurricane pilots had remained alive from those who had originally taken part in Operation 'Torch' — the *Avenger* and the *Dasher* explosions accounting for most of these losses — nothing could have compared with the murderous days when *Glorious*, *Courageous* and *Illustrious* were so badly misused. Almost from the day I had joined *Eagle*, things had started to improve, and survival in the FAA ceased to be such a lottery. I had been allowed to acclimatize gradually. I was not thrown in at the deep end and allowed to drown through inexperience like so many others before.

The main factor in our improved longevity was that the carriers themselves — always the priority targets of any surface fleet (and therefore singled out by the media as 'highly vulnerable' compared with battleships and cruisers) — were now better protected by our own fighters. Following Churchill's Memo of September 1942, more and more fighters were gradually displacing Swordfish and Albacores in the carriers' hangars. The carriers themselves were now operating together in twos and threes, something unheard of before June 1942, even in the US Navy in the Pacific. All this provided a better system of Fleet protection against the Stuka and torpedo aircraft, and allowed the convoys to get through.

Their Lordships had, moreover, begun to realise that young airmen not only had to face the normal sailors' anxieties of operating at sea from a primary enemy target but that they had the added task of flying over the wastes of the ocean with small chance of rescue if anything went wrong, and were operating dangerous and complicated weapons, with the minimum of training and experience in their use. They 'wore out' quicker.

The RAF had long-since adopted a system of 'tours' to ensure that the bravest of all, those who refused to allow 'twitch' to show, were taken off operations for a rest, before they became gibbering wrecks of humanity for the rest of their lives. There were at least half a dozen of such potential wrecks of FAA aircrew, little more than hospital cases, wandering about our Naval Air Stations by the early months of 1943. They were unfit for any duty. Had they been rested in time and then brought back to work, their operational experience could have been brought to good use in Staff appointments, displacing those who had held their jobs for the normal 2½ years appointments and whose personal knowledge of the war and its changing weapons and tactics was nil. Constantly repeated mistakes would have been avoided by such an interchange. Shortages there were, but the FAA appointers in NA2SL in the Admiralty had been operating like some thoughtless sausage machine where its junior aviators were concerned.

Aboard the carriers, the FAA knew that it was wielding weapons which were hundreds of times more effective and therefore more powerful than a battleship's guns. Although the FAA was never at great pains to belabour its importance, its rivals, the Gunnery hierarchy, were well aware that their future was threatened. Us young and mostly irresponsible RNVR 20-year-olds were not to be encouraged to usurp the rights of the professional, having spent only a few months training and knowing nothing of ships and the sea.

It was hard to imagine a greater contrast — a died-in-the-wool senior gunnery officer sitting opposite a FAA 'Subby' at breakfast. The former, with 30 years training, only just able to hit a battleship with one shot in 300 at 20 miles. The Subby, with a year's training, able to hit a battleship with one shot out of eight, of equal weight, at 200 miles range. All the gunnery Admirals could say in their memoirs of this point after the war was that no modern British battleship was sunk by an aircraft's bombs at sea in war — forgetting about the *Prince of Wales* and *Repulse* and, of course, the 50,000 ton Japanese *Yamato*. The reason why only two or three were sunk — which they failed to point out — was that battleships scarcely ever went to sea, and when they did, they were very low priority targets if carriers were about.

March 1943 therefore marked the beginning of the end of the heavy AA gun, much greater co-operation and dependence upon RAF fighter defence of the Fleet, and the emergence of the Naval interceptor fighter used, as in the Battle of Britain, with ADR control. Later in the year, the FAA also adopted many of the RAF's new ideas — adapting fighters to interdict airfields and destroy other surface targets rather than by using vulnerable 'strike' aircraft. By the end of 1943, Naval fighters, organised on a 'Wing' basis, outnumbered Naval strike aircraft by three to one. Until the arrival of the Kamikaze in 1944, the Navy's surface fleet was relatively safe from conventional air attack, provided that command of the air over the fleet was attained first in any operation attempted.

Appendix 11

Seafire – some of the problems

(a) Some Seafire flying characteristics

Take-off on a narrow runway was difficult. There were one or two characteristics to bear in mind. The propeller went round in a clockwise direction viewed from the cockpit. The resultant twist imparted to its slipstream also imparted a sidethrust to the upper part of the fin and rudder which turned the aircraft strongly to port — needing full and early right rudder to hold the aircraft straight. However, because of the poor view over the nose, the pilot would often be late in detecting a swing to port and would be unable to correct it once it had started, as anyone who has done a tail skid in a car will know.

However, the tail could be raised by the pilot if he shoved the stick fully forward (nose down), and he could then see over the nose and where he was going. The rudder then became effective in a straighter, faster, part of the slipstream.

The Seafire flew off the ground at about 70 knots, or it could be pulled off the ground at about 58 knots if ham use were made of the elevator.

The undercarriage was raised hydraulically. The lever which selected the position of the hydraulic valve to 'up' also rotated a mechanical lock to each undercarriage leg. The lock itself could not easily be rotated in its machined socket unless the weight of the undercarriage legs was held off by a momentary 'up' selection. This was applied automatically when selecting undercarriage 'up', but when selecting 'down' pilots would often forget. The 'down' selection could not then be made because the mechanical lock could not be rotated one way or the other. The leg stuck fast, with the pilot unable to move the lever. After a few aerobatics it might move, but when it did not do so, a wheels-up landing ensued. Other difficulties could also occur with the 'up' locks in the wheel-well fairings failing to catch. The undercarriage could then droop in flight and restrict airflow into the radiators. The engine would then overheat, necessitating a forced landing in some circumstances. One trip in ten was usually carried out with the pilot's undercarriage warning lights on in the cockpit, denoting some fault with the adjustment of the mechanism.

Landing a Spitfire/Seafire on runways as narrow as those at Henstridge was very tricky in crosswinds. On grass airfields, the landing direction could be made so that it was, like a bird landing on a lake, dead into wind. The longest runways at Henstridge were laid in the prevailing wind direction and would usually allow a pilot sufficient stopping distance for a faster than normal crosswind landing. However, when the crosswinds came from an unaccustomed wind direction and a short runway had to be used, the skid or offset approach was necessarily made at a much slower airspeed than Pilot Officer Jack would have allowed. This often resulted in heavy landings with drift, landings on one wheel or crash landings in the undershoot area. In such cases the Seafire's undercarriage was neither wide enough apart nor strong enough to take the sideloads which occurred. The aircraft would then drift off to one side and tip on its nose in the soft clay either side of the runway, or groundloop. With the Hurricane, the wheels were sufficiently wide apart to correct the skid by differential use of wheel brakes. Provided that they did not fade due to overheating, the aircraft could then be kept straight. With the Seafire, the brakes were insufficiently strong (designed thus to prevent the aircraft nosing over) and the wheels insufficiently wide apart, to allow differential braking effect.

Finally, there was the problem of the lack of view over the nose on the approach to land and during the completion of the landing run. This, and decklanding, was by far the most difficult part of flying the Seafire. To see the runway, it was necessary to come in on a steady, curved, approach path. Any further distractions, such as crosswind, even a dirty windscreen or a rough running engine, could so overload the human computer, that a pilot would make late corrections, and over-corrections. With the RAF's far longer and wider runways, its pilots came in fast so that they could easily see over the nose. They made 'wheelers', holding the tail up high until the aircraft was running straight and true and safely on the runway. This was commonsense and to be applauded. However, the RN needed to train its pilots for the decklanding approach. This was at 1.05 x Vse, or at a speed only five per cent above the 'engine on' stall speed. The aircraft was then in virtually the three point attitude and the view over the nose was nil. Fleet Air Arm pilots accepted this as a normal challenge.

(b) Pilot Gunnery Instruction in the Seafire

My PGI's course with the RAF at Sutton Bridge started on 1 October 1943 and lasted for a month and 30 flying hours. The RAF turned the art of deflection shooting into a theoretical science. Our cameragun results were confirmed — or not — by using specially point-harmonised guns, in fours and eights. No expense was spared. Towards the end of the shooting period, I managed to get 1600 hits on a 20 foot drogue target. This was 20% of the bullets fired. Most fighters in WW II — with wing-mounted guns — used pattern harmonisation for their guns. That is, if each barrel was looked through in turn, the eight or so, guns would hit a screen about 250 yards ahead in the form of a pattern and not at a single point. The pattern was arranged to allow for wing flexing, 'G' drop, gun chatter and variations in incidence and yaw, so that the bullets had a maximum chance of hitting the target with 10% of the bullets fired, at ranges from 50 to 250 yards range for 0.303 ammunition, and up to 400 yards with 20mm cannon shells.

In some German and Italian fighters, the guns fired through the propeller or through the centre of the propeller shaft and along the pilot's sight line. Point harmonisation was then a feasible proposition, less guns were needed to secure a given percentage of hits and the wings being much lighter would allow a crisper rate of roll. However, the problem of shooting through the propeller tended to slow down the firing rate, once this became a factor of high speed combat where 'snapshooting' was necessary to achieve a kill, and most single-engined fighters eventually used guns firing from the wings.

The RAF Course was for instructors at RAF Fighter Schools, so that I was lucky. They even allowed us pupils to take one of their Spitfire Vs back to our normal bases for each weekend. The RAF's Mark of Spitfire used for training, the hooked version of the Spitfire Vb, was only just in front-line Fleet Air Arm squadrons.

Although the object of the Course was to give confidence to us instructors in the theory of air-to-air gunnery, one of the attractive and practically useful features of the PGI Course was that we were taught to make attacks from all angles, from above and below, as well as from each side. The 'above and below' attacks were called 'Upward and Downward Jesus' attacks. The one from below involved a loop and a roll-off-the-top while firing. The one from vertically above was, however, much easier, just a rolling pullout from a vertical dive.

Back at Henstridge I became the Station PGI. I fixed up a 'private' Miles Master II with all manner of cameras and gunsights, and took petrified pupils in the back to show them how upward and downward 'Jesi' should be done. Not only that, I was sent all over the place in England and Scotland as a travelling salesman, seeing very little of my immobile Wren as a result.

Many of the pupils joining the FAA at this time in the war found it difficult to make quarter attacks. It over-loaded the human computer to have to judge distances, angles, approach speeds, convergences, line of target flight and deflection when shooting — and flying at the same time. The first problem to solve was how to position the fighter in the right part of the sky before starting an attack. Unless a pupil pilot could do this, it was a waste of flying hours and highly dangerous to allow him to continue. It was frightening to act as a target for those who did not possess this form of judgement. For those who have not tried it, it is somewhat similar to driving a car at high speed into a crowded traffic roundabout and judging it so that no collisions occur. The difference being, that in an aircraft, the meeting takes place in three dimensions and at ten times the speed.

There were, however, two or three pupil pilots at Henstridge who were 'naturals'. Among them were Sub-Lieutenant R. H. (Dick) Reynolds and Sub-Lieutenant Victor Lowden, both of whom met and entirely vanquished the 'Zero' in the Pacific war, using the 'attacks from all angles' techniques. (See Appendix 11 (j) — The Seafire in Combat.)

One of the PGI's 'perks' at Henstridge was being first in the queue for 'special' aircraft. The storage section possessed a beautiful hybrid Seafire Ib — NX910 — which they had fitted with the new Merlin 55M engine. It was flush-riveted throughout and the storage section polished it so that it shone like a Greek Admiral. The engine developed 1650 horsepower at take-off and only had to cope with a very light fuselage and a cropped supercharger. It could maintain the full supercharger pressure of 16 pounds per square inch manifold pressure up to 8000 feet and shot up to this height in less than two minutes at a climb angle of 45 degrees and could maintain a true airspeed of 370 mph. I looked after it better than I did the Wolsey Hornet and there was a queue to fly it. What a pity that Tim Singleton hit a crash tender with it a few days before his wedding. He was thinking of other things, he said.

(c) Stability problems in the Seafire

Luckily, the laws of physics dictate that lift on an aerofoil, at constant incidence and 'efficiency', is proportional to the *square* of the windspeed flowing past it — otherwise we might have swans taking off at 400 mph instead of 20 mph.

The speed range of a swan is from about 20-30 mph. His — or her — 'centre of lift' can be kept over his small changes in CG by sweeping his wings back a few inches at the wing tips when his CG is aft, and forward a few inches when he had just eaten and his CG is forward. He can even alter the thickness/chord ratio of his wings to suit high speed or low speed flight, and so retain a much higher degree of 'wing efficiency' than is possible with man-made wings. He can use his tail to correct temporary changes in fore-and-aft trim during flight, and use assymetric wing twist instead of ailerons.

The swan's changes in maximum lift between 20 mph and 30 mph would roughly be in the ratio of 1:2. The swan merely changes his wing incidence to give a smaller incidence at the higher speed if he does not want to climb.

In the case of a Seafire, its speed changes from 60-360 knots IAS. This would give a very large theoretical lift-increase ratio of 1:36. Assuming that a mere man-made wing can only maintain a 'wing efficiency' of some 33% at the high speed end of the range, this would still mean that the Seafire could lift 12 times its own weight, or suffer that amount of 'g' without stalling on a sudden pullout of a dive, if it was strong enough to stay in one piece. In fact, the Seafire began to 'notch' its wingfold bolts well before 12 'g'. It was more like eight 'g' that the structure began to fail. As this loading can easily be imposed at any TAS above 300 knots without stalling, and as the stick force per 'g' in the Seafire was only two to three pounds per 'g', the pilot could easily break the aircraft. In practice, the onset of 'g' blindness — 'greying out' — usually warned him, and he would relax his pull force. Nevertheless, as we will see, the Seafire pilot was sometimes unable to react quickly enough and when the Franks 'anti-g' suit was worn, even this 'seat-of-the-pants' warning was not available. (Stick force per 'g' in bombers and passenger aircraft was between 10-15 pounds per 'g', so that very heavy pull forces usually prevented excessive 'g' being applied by the pilot.)

During the acceleration process after take-off from, say 60 knots - 250 knots, wing incidence has to be 'wound off' by rotating the whole aircraft through about ten degrees nose-down, by pushing forward on the stick. Retrimming the small tab on the trailing edge of the elevator by a handwheel in the cockpit is necessary, so that the pushforce is 'trimmed out'. (Elevators, ailerons and rudders, plus their control circuits are, of course, mass balanced, so that 'g' applied to the aircraft does not affect them much.) Retrimming cannot be carried out easily in the heat of combat so that the designer of a fighter — as opposed to a bomber or passenger aircraft — designs his fighter so that elevator trim changes are very small or non-existent. This calls for careful balance between the centre of lift of the mainplane and the CG of the aircraft — like some very sensitive see-saw. Larger movements of the CG than, say, a couple of inches on a 3½ ton aircraft, cannot be allowed either way. Besides these small permitted movements of the CG itself made necessary by the carriage of stores, consumption of fuel in flight etc, the centre-of-*lift* position also alters during flight as IAS alters. Mitchell knew this and designed the lift characteristics of his tailplane to compensate automatically, not just during speed changes, but with 'g' changes, with flaps or undercarriage up or down and with engine power on or off. The original Spitfire pilot hardly had to touch his trimmer wheel from take-off to landing and his elevator stick forces were never more than a few pounds. In spite of this almost neutral 'stick-free' stability and because it also had almost frictionless, well-rigged controls, the aircraft would recover on its own to straight and level flight if for any reason the pilot blacked-out or became unconscious temporarily and let go the stick.

However, such perfection did not last long. Changes in propeller weight, supercharger weight, extra fuel tanks, and various other weights added aft of the CG in the fuselage, plus the doubling of the engine power, soon upset this careful balance. When the Navy finally completed the job by adding an arrester hook some 15 feet aft of the CG and were unable to compensate for it by sufficient (more than 28 pounds) lead weight added to the engine bearers, the balance was seriously upset. The balance had to be restored by 'fudging'. This was done by altering the original Spitfire elevator to include a device known as an 'unshielded horn balance', and a further clever device to the elevator control circuit which held the stick forward permanently to compensate for the tail heaviness. (Photographs of Seafires in flight will show this.)

How did they do this? Not by elastic, for the push force from this would not increase as necessary when 'g' was applied, and the aircraft would tighten in a steep turn or pullout of a dive in a very dangerous way. The designers therefore added a 'positive weight' to the elevator control so that, as 'g' was applied, it would help push the control column more and more *forward*. In the Seafire, they added a three pound lead weight to the bottom of the pilots' control column. The weight was at the end of a six inch steel shaft, the other end of which was butt-welded at right angles to the lower end of the control column just above its bottom hinge. If any of us had cared to look down to see what the stick was actually doing as we pulled back on it out of a dive, we should have seen it move *forward* as 'g' was applied.

The designers thought they had cured the problem of the Seafire's 'stick-free' instability. However, Mitchell's original balance required such meticulous airframe manufacturing weight tolerances that some turned out to be heavier than others in the aft fuselage, and this put the CG outside the authority of the 'positive weight'. Many of the flight conditions regularly used by 30 Wing in the Pacific and elsewhere could not have been test flown and the fatal effects were not discovered and remedied before the squadrons received these dangerous aircraft.

In 30 and 3 Wings, alone, there were four instances of wings shearing off — all put down to pilot carelessness or flak — and at least four near-misses with Seafires returning with 'notched' wingfold bolts, just about to shear off. Cunliffe-Owen manufactured 80 Seafires with flush-riveting in the aft fuselage, ten per cent of the total number built. All had CGs dangerously aft of the design position due to the use of thicker gauge skinning, and were prone to 'self-tighten' in pullouts or steep turns. Some Seafires carried F24 cameras weighing 40 pounds each. We were forbidden to pull tight turns when these were carried, a most inconvenient restriction for a fighter over an enemy airfield. However, even the bracing for the cameras made the aircraft dangerously tail heavy.

The steel shaft holding the positive weight was insufficiently strong. My rigger discovered the weight lying loose in my aircraft after the Maizuru raid. We had no idea how important it was, but luckily the workshop welded it back before the next flight, "otherwise the PO would not sign for it". The onset of 'g' from self-tightening was very sudden and it had to be anticipated if there was to be much chance of avoiding its consequences. In the heat of action, pilots often forgot.

I discovered the reason for this sudden and catastrophic onset of 'g' after the war while I was at the Empire Test Pilots' School. We had found in 880 and 801 Squadrons that the onset of 'g' was particularly sudden when we pulled out of steep dives — as against shipping. (The steeper the dive, the better the anti-flak protection.) I also remembered that the positive weight was welded at right angles to the stick, so that, during a 'vertical dive' — usually called 'vertical', but never more than 75 degrees — it would have little or no effect. However, the thought also struck me that with the aircraft approaching the earth at about 1g acceleration between 300-400 knots IAS, it would be 'weightless' in any case, so that with no 'g' in any direction, the positive weight could not function and its stabilising effects would be zero. This would only be transitory, but long enough to cause an initial snatch of very high 'g' at the moment of the commencement of pull out, sufficient to break the aircraft before the weight reimposed its stabilising effects and pushed the stick forward.

To make matters even worse, the makers had included in the elevator circuit another well known device. To restore the tendency for the stick to 'droop' forward under the influence of the weight, they had fitted a 'negative spring' to compensate. This amounted to a pull force of about three pounds, high by Spitfire standards, which, under 'weightless' conditions, would have still exerted itself. Unless the pilot made a conscious effort to trim this force out in the dive — and there was no time to do it — it would superimpose its three pounds on the pilot's, and unexpectedly add this force to his.

Once in the dive, — which because of the cocked-up sightline, would be in a slight 'bunt' — concentrating on aim, the shattering vibration from the guns, the airspeed rising to 360 knots and more, the ground coming up fast with the shells yet to strike the ground to give the pilot aim correction — he would leave the pull out to the last moment and tend to grab the stick at pull out. There would be a sudden nose-up pitch from the 'unstable' aircraft — the spring-overload added — and the wing bolts would shear before the 'positive weight' could reassert its authority, and before it could help the now semi-concious pilot to reverse his pull force.

Why was this not discovered? The reason was probably because the test pilots of the day used to 'trim into the dive' when checking 'stick force per 'g' ', and, when carrying out their dives, they would seldom check 'out-of-trim' stick forces in very steep dives or carry out 'stick-free' pull-outs from these dives.

Later Marks of Firefly also had a 'positive weight'. The makers did not make the same mistake as in the Seafire III, for they cocked the weight up on its shaft through about 45 degrees, so that, providing there was any positive 'g' in the dive, it would continue to help. Neither did they use a 'negative spring'. They accepted the inconvenience of the stick falling forward when the aircraft was at rest on the ground.

(d) Baling out of Seafire III — effect of instability

Another fatal consequence of the Seafire's instability (not in the early Spitfire of course, which was perfect) was the effect it had on the pilot's ability to bale out from the recommended inverted position. In the case of the Seafire, the 'positive weight' acted in the *reverse* sense (assisted by the 'negative spring') when flying the aircraft with negative 'g' and with the pilot 'hanging on his straps'. This aspect could only be partially discovered in our 'practice' bale-outs which we carried out — without actually releasing our straps of course. We found that the Seafire's nose had to be trimmed *fully nose heavy* before inverting the aircraft, to overcome the negative spring (now 'assisted' by the positive weight which had become 'negative'). This was essential to prevent the aircraft from completing the second half of a loop and so trapping the pilot in the aircraft with centripetal force — as in a roller coaster — and diving into the ground.

However, when Seafire pilots wanted to bale out in the Pacific, in most cases their engines had already stopped. In any case, in a real-life situation, they would have throttled back to reduce airspeed, so making it easier to fall out without risk of blowing back into the tail in the propeller slipstream. At this low speed and with the engine failed and 'windmilling', the nose trimmer was nowhere near powerful enough to hold the aircraft in level, inverted flight. Directly the pilot had pulled back or jettisoned the hood, trimmed fully forward, inverted the aircraft and then released his harness, he could no longer reach the stick. Whereupon, the aircraft nosed down in the second half of a loop, with the pilot half in and half out of the cockpit, and held there by 'g' and increasing wind pressure, until he crashed. In 30 Wing, this certainly happened to Dougy Yate, Patullo and Graham, and may also have happened to Squires and Tillet and many others.

We did not discover this for ourselves, for no one in his right mind would practice baling out near the inverted flight stall speed of about 120 knots with engine power off. No pilot ever managed to get out from the 'engine-failed' bale-out situation to tell us of these dangers. We put this down to bad luck or flak damage at the time. None of us had the time or the technical knowledge to hit upon any other reason.

(e) Deck Landings – effect of instability

A third important consequence of the Seafire III's instability was its natural tendency to 'float' over the arrester wires. Not only do all aircraft tend to gain drag-free lift — like birds — from flying near the ground, but the Seafire 'floated' so serenely and for so long, that 'Wings' would admonish the pilots for "pulling back on the stick", when nothing of the kind had happened. Besides the beautiful clean lines of the Seafire and the ground effect, there was another reason for the 'Float-float-float-prang' sequence — as in the FAA 'A25' song.

When the pilot cut the power and the slipstream speed reduced, the extra lift given by the positive angle on the elevator also reduced. The tail then lost a great deal of its lift and it, too, fell — without the pilot doing a thing. As this was equivalent to the pilot pulling back on the stick, in that it increased mainplane incidence and lift, and thus 'float', he always got the blame. It was a case of the 'V Squared' law making a much larger reduction to the lift on the tailplane than on the mainplane, when the slipstream over the tail surface fell from perhaps 100 mph during a power-on approach, to about 50 mph after the 'cut'. The reason why this did not occur to other aircraft was that there is 'negative lift' on a stable aircraft's tail surfaces — particularly when they are in the landing configuration — so that the 'cut' merely produces a nose *down* pitch, if any.

(f) American Aircraft decklanding compared

Although the American Naval fighters were equally light and almost neutrally balanced fore and aft, their handling characteristics were not altered dangerously by the subsequent additions of weight placed in awkward places. However, the early Mark of Corsair was well known as a 'bouncer' when it decklanded. The bounce occurred because, even when fully stalled and with the stick held back, a three-point landing was almost impossible. This was because the elevator power after the 'cut' was so reduced in the propeller 'blanket' effect that the pilot could not hold the tail *down* or the nose up. The first wheels to touch the deck were therefore the main landing wheels. The oleo design had considerable elasticity and bounced the nose up (the wheels were forward of the aircraft's CG, so, being first to touch, they rotated the aircraft nose up), and the aircraft became airborne again in the ground effect. The problem was neatly overcome by Chance-Vought, the designers and builders of the Corsair. They lengthened the tail wheel assembly by 12 inches. This effectively allowed the pilot to do a three pointer each time he decklanded, and with new, non-rebound shock-absorber oleos on the main undercarriage, the Corsair became a very good decklander. Not only were American Naval aircraft designed for decklanding to withstand a 12 feet per second rate of descent without undercarriage failure but their greater strength and their large margin of positive stability in the landing configuration allowed a very much larger tolerance in approach airspeed and angle of descent. The batsman gave 'advisory' signals only — not mandatory signals as in British batting — and gave the pilot immense latitude in his approach airspeed, from 1.2 Vse instead of the Seafires' 1.05 Vse. Lt (A) Mike Banyard describes some of the American techniques in Appendix 12.

(g) Tricycle undercarriages compared

The longer tail wheel assembly gave the Corsair much of the landing characteristics of a nosewheel aircraft. In the case of nosewheel aircraft, or aircraft with the tricycle undercarriage layout, the first wheels to touch are always the main wheels. These are *aft* of the aircraft's CG. Incidence at touchdown is therefore automatically 'wound off' and lift is automatically 'dumped' — unless the pilot purposely holds the nose wheel off the ground. The nosewheel aircraft will not bounce at touchdown, unless it has a poor undercarriage design or 'bouncy' tyres. In fact nosewheel-designed aircraft — Vampire, Venom, Buccaneer, etc — were and are remarkably easy to deckland for they not only had a good view over the nose, but they could be approached at speeds well above the stall — up to perhaps 1.25 Vse — and still sit down immediately on coming into contact with the deck. The only limitation then, for a Phantom or Buccaneer, is a structural one, for there are usually no aircraft handling problems at such speeds so comfortably above the stall speed. Engine handling is made equally easy by maintaining high power on the approach, made possible by extending air brakes in the case of the Buccaneer.

(h) Decklanding trials of the Seafire

In 1941, some preliminary trials were carried out by Lt/Cdr Peter Bramwell, RN, and others, to show that a hooked Spitfire could be landed on the deck of a carrier in just the same way as the Hurricane. Suitable or not, the Spitfire was, by 1943, the only available British single seat fighter for Fleet Air Arm use. Hawker had already transferred production from the Hurricane to the Typhoon and Tempest and the Blackburn Firebrand had another three years of testing to do before it would be safe to fly. The Fairey Firefly was a two seater and lacked the necessary performance. Folland's intercepter fighter was not proceeded with. Neither the *Implacable* nor the *Indefatigable* had the necessary deckhead clearance for American Corsair fighters. It was the Seafire for them, or nothing.

R. J. Mitchell had designed the Spitfire purely for grass airfield operation. In these landing conditions, crosswinds need seldom be experienced and low vertical velocities at touchdown, with 'wheeler' landings for a good view over the nose, allowed a light, narrow-track undercarriage. Why have a heavy undercarriage when it was only used for a second or two each flight and was useless baggage at all others? The Spitfire therefore had a vertical velocity of only seven feet per second. If the vertical velocity at touchdown was a trifle greater than this the undercarriage would bust.

The liquid-cooled Merlin engine allowed the frontal area of the Spitfire to be extremely small. But, by placing the pilot behind it in a low 'anti-g' sitting posture, the view over the nose was restricted to four degrees below the flight line. On the airfield or flight deck, the view forward therefore consisted of treetops or ships' masts. The RAF pilots resolved this difficulty by approaching to land in a semi-glide, at speeds well above the stall. They retained their forward view in the early part of the landing by doing 'wheeler' landings. This not only allowed them good forward view and good directional control after landing, but placed the loads vertically up the undercarriage legs, where Mitchell intended them to be. In the case of three-point, stalled, landings, there was a bending component, tending to wrench the attachment point free from the main spar. Naval decklandings were, perforce, always made in the three point touchdown posture, at which attitude it was at stalling incidence, about 15 degrees.

The touchdown speed for a Seafire was only three knots above the engine-on stall speed and below the engine-off stall speed — that is to say, 1.05Vse. Owing to the clean lines of the Seafire, the pilot could only lose speed, if he approached too fast, at the rate of about two knots per second if he were to close the throttle fully on a decklanding approach. As the distance over all the wires was less than 200 feet — a mere two or three seconds flying time — he had to make certain that he was at 1.05Vse by the time that he was over the round-down of the carrier. In practice, this obliged him to make a constant 1.05Vse approach all the way in. However, as it was five times easier to accelerate than to decelerate in a Seafire, speed control on the Seafire was very lopsided and pilots tended to come in too fast, particularly in gusty conditions.

The aircraft would not then be in the three point attitude when it hit the deck at its 3½ degree descent angle. The first wheels to touch the deck, the main landing wheels, being forward of the CG, pushed the nose up, while the tail was still descending. This and the 'instability effect' increased the aircraft's nose up attitude, increasing wing incidence and thus, lift — even more in the 'ground effect' — just at the moment it was not required. The aircraft would then remain airborne after the initial bounce and float in the ground effect into the barrier two or three seconds later. A bounce would also result in the same 'ballooning' sequence. A pitching deck might wreck the pilot's judgement entirely.

The Naval pilot's solution to the poor view over the nose was to approach in a steady, left-hand turn, all the way down to the deck. With hood open, locked in position by half unlatching the small side door, with goggles on, with the head to one side and the seat raised, it was then possible to see part of the flight deck and the batsman through the haze of the port engine exhaust. If the sun was low and the carrier had been thoughtlessly pointed into sun, the sun's reflection on the sea or on a saltladen windscreen would prevent a proper sighting of the deck or batsman. There was no windscreen wiper so that if it was raining — heavy rain completely obscured all view forward — the only way of seeing was to poke the head sideways out into the stinging rain and trust to luck your goggles stayed on and remained reasonably transparent. If the turn-in had been made too tightly or too easy, last-minute corrections could easily lose sight of the deck altogether, leading to a heavy arrival, an off-centre, or one-wheel, yawed, arrival, or a hasty 'go round again'.

In the 'yaw' or 'crabbed' approach, the nose was ruddered crudely to starboard to allow the pilot to see to port. It might then engage the wire while still moving sideways. This would damage the hook up-lock, the hook would not lock up into its catch, and this could lead to further damage on arrestment, resulting in a 'write-off', as described below. This method, making use of 'in-spin' crossed controls so near the stall, was abominable airmanship and was forbidden in all squadrons accordingly.

The Seafire's controls were uniformly light and responsive on the landing approach, befitting R. J. Mitchell's masterpiece. However, because of its light wingloading — especially when landing with nearly empty tanks — the slightest gust over the round-down would balloon it into the air and above the proper descent path. If this occurred very late in the approach, the only recourse for height adjustment would be to use the elevator. With only a few ounces of push or pull required, overcorrection would produce large errors in height. If, then, the pilot hit the deck harder than usual and the aircraft bounced on its 'grass-compatible' undercart so that its hook missed the wires, the pilot might try to remedy this state of affairs by pushing forward on the stick to try to regain deck contact. This would raise the tailplane plus hook once more. If, then, the hook caught a wire, even if there was no yaw, the retardation force would be applied from below, initially, and the hook would not rise to lock up into its proper locked position in the fuselage. The direction of pull might distort the hook, now only hinged from its forward hinges, and the position of retardation being so near the aircraft's CG it would not prevent the nose from 'pecking', the prop hitting the deck and the whole aircraft from crashing back onto its tailwheel, wrinkling the fuselage, driving the tailwheel up into the fin, shockloading the engine and breaking the propeller blades. Neither Boscombe Down, the decklanding trials unit, nor Farnborough knew how to cure any of these defects in the time available, neither had they made an extensive study of its basic causes. One of the test pilots — Lt (A). E. 'Winkle' Brown, DSC, RNVR — even used the 'crab' approach — until the inevitable result brought his efforts to a halt.

An added difficulty in speed control of the Seafire was the poor positioning and the unsuitable scale of the ASI (Air Speed Indicator). The indicator was at 90 degrees to the pilot's forward vision as he looked at the flight deck. The needle vibrated over a scale where one eighth of an inch represented about ten knots of airspeed. Pilots tended, therefore, to fly by attitude or 'by the seat of their pants,' trusting in the tail-buffet stall warning to tell them when they were about to fall out of the sky. Most Seafires had loose or poorly-fitted engine cowlings or camera gun hatches near the upper surfaces of the wing roots. As this was a very critical area and where the slightest excrescence would provoke an early stall of the entire wing, the resultant rough air flow would cause an early tail-buffet, making the pilot add a few knots 'for the sake of the wife and kids.' In addition, following Ken Boardman's death, pilots also feared poor throttle response, or even an engine cut following a throttle opening on the approach. This all tended to make a pilot add to his approach speed.

(i) Decklanding modern jet aircraft

It is interesting to note that by 1963, the Buccaneer and Phantom were carrying out decklandings with 99.2% safety records, although their approach speeds were twice that of the Seafire. There were about 12 good reasons for this:

(i) The view, forward, was perfect, even in heavy rain. All jet aircraft have 'blower' rain clearance.

(ii) The aircraft had a nosewheel configuration, three point touchdown attitudes were not essential, approach speeds some 15 knots above the stall were therefore allowed. This was a safe margin.

(iii) Engine acceleration response was perfect, as was the airframe deceleration response with the use of very large airbrakes on the approach. Speed control was therefore easy.

(iv) Aircraft *wing incidence indicators* took the place of ASIs and they even 'talked' to the pilot through his earphones, giving rate-of-change sound data to tell him if his speed was correct or how it was changing. The purpose of using wing incidence is that it automatically allows for changes in stall speeds due to changes in landing weight.

(v) There was no risk of hitting the barrier or wrecking an expensive aircraft that way, because the deck was angled-off to port, allowing the pilot to go round again on a missed approach. There was no need for a barrier.

(vi) Batsman's errors were a thing of the past because the correct descent and approach paths were monitored by a gyro-stabilised mirror landing sight, visible to the pilot in the worst weather conditions, against sunglare and at night, and steady on a pitching deck.

(vii) If the pilot's instruments failed, his approach speed could be relayed to him from radar information in the carrier.

(viii) If that failed, he had enough fuel, always, to divert ashore.

(ix) If that was not possible, he could ditch, knowing his aircraft had been tank tested.

(x) Or he and his observer could bale out, at any altitude, including take-off, using their hood-breaker ejector seats with or without auto hood-jettison. They would then have their seat automatically released and their dinghies inflated for them, right way up.

(xi) If, when they ditched they found they could not get out of the cockpit in time before the aircraft sank, they could select 'wet launch' on their ejector seats. This gently eased their seats out of the sinking aircraft under water, by air pressure rams, through the hood if necessary.

(xii) Finally, if the pilot or observer got a little hot under the collar thinking about it, they could select a little more ice in the cockpit fresh air supply and tune in to Radio One.

(j) The Seafire in combat – some comparisons

The issue of RAF Specification Number F5/34 for an interceptor fighter in 1934, sparked off three major contributions. First, the Gladiator by H. P. Folland (F7/30), next the Hurricane by Sydney Camm and finally the Spitfire by R. J. Mitchell, which ousted all others.

The first of these was the last of the biplane fighters. I flew a Sea Gladiator at Henstridge for nearly an hour, so that I know very little about it. However, it was obvious that its main attribute was its high rate of roll (through its short wing span) its tight turning circle (through its low wingloading) and its high power to weight ratio, giving it a high rate of climb compared with its contemporaries. However, it had to make do with a Bristol Mercury VI, of 600 horsepower, not enough for future requirements and without much development potential. The Gladiator first saw service in the Chinese Air Force in 1937. The Japanese Air Force, who were trying to shoot it down, were so impressed with it, that they designed one like it for themselves, believing in the same philosophy as H. P. Folland.

The next two fighters, which went into mass production for the RAF, the Hurricane and Spitfire, made use of an in-line power plant of much greater power and development potential, the Merlin. Although the Merlin/Griffon series never produced anything like the 'short life' 3000 horsepower of the racing engine in the Supermarine S6B of 1934, it eventually produced more than double its original 900 horsepower by 1944 in the Merlin 55M, a much larger percentage increase in power than in its German counterpart.

Single-seat fighter designers, like racing car designers, were all after one thing, a high power/weight ratio. Folland also wanted very good turning manoeuvrability. This meant large wing areas. He also wanted a high rate of roll. This meant small wing spans. The two could then only be combined by using two wings, one above the other. He also wanted thin wings, to cut down the 'V Squared' frontal drag. Fabric-covered thin wings could not support themselves, so once again his choice fell upon a biplane, which could provide mutual wing support by struts and wires. As his aircraft was by now a thin-winged biplane, he could find no space in which to stow a light, retracting, undercarriage, so that he gave it a fixed one. In spite of his efforts, the Italians had a better fighter than the Gladiator in the CR 42. The latter out-climbed and out-turned the Gladiator in combat at Yeovilton in 1941 on each occasion they engaged in mock combat. The problem for Folland was the lack of power in its Mercury engine. He had hoped for the 800 hp Bristol Taurus, sleeve-valve engine, but this was given to the Bristol Beaufort and the Fairey Albacore instead.

Sydney Camm provided sufficient wing area, sufficient lift and a sufficiently small wing span from a *mono*plane, the Hurricane. Strength in a single unsupported metal wing was obtained by its thickness, ie the depth of the main spar, and by internal bracing. The thick wing also gave a higher lift coefficient for its small area. Although its turning circle in combat was wider than the Gladiator, it could, with its cleaner design and its much higher power, continue to climb while turning, and it always ended up above the Gladiator in a dogfight. It could then break off the fight if it wished by pointing its nose down for home. High altitude performance was also assured by the Merlin engine's greater power at heights above 20,000 feet, due to its superior engine supercharging and its 'constant speed', variable pitch, three bladed airscrew.

R. J. Mitchell's Spitfire was, however, a thing apart. He managed to produce a thin-winged fighter weighing half a ton less than the Hurricane, with superior top speed and climb, and with the same turning and roll performance. This improvement, with virtually the same engine as the Hurricane, was made possible by his invaluable experience with the S6B Schneider Trophy winner. He was able to retain his original Schneider design team, from 1931 to 1936 — when he submitted his first Spitfire design — through the gift of money by Lady Houston, O.B.E.

The huge floats of the S6B, containing fuel and oil cooling, made use of the 'eggshell' principle. They obtained their strength from their outside skin. Mitchell used his experience with the S6B to manufacture the wings of the Spit in a similar manner, the 'stressed skin' construction method, which used no internal bracing nor heavy ribs nor stringers. Spitfire wings were therefore far lighter and thinner than the Hurricane's, but had equal strength.

The Hurricane virtually stopped in a dive at about 320 knots IAS. The

Spitfire, with a third less frontal area and with its 'ten per cent' wing — no thinner wing was in service until the appearance of the DH Venom in the 1950s — and its semi-retracted radiators and flush-riveted wings and fuselage, could out-dive the Hurricane by about 80 knots IAS. It would also go further — and 30 knots faster — on the same fuel. It seemed as if at last an aircraft designer had got something for nothing.

Meanwhile, the Japanese, having accepted the tight turning-circle philosophy as a very important requirement in a fighter, had produced the extremely lightly constructed 'Zero' Zeke, or A6M single-seat monoplane fighter. They had built this fighter's airframe half-a-ton lighter, still, than the Spitfire, for the same power and much greater internal fuel capacity. The metal skinning on its wings was so thin that the pilot could put his foot through it when stepping up to the cockpit. It had no armour plate and no self-sealing tanks. If hit, even by a few .303 inch Browning shells — to say nothing of the far more powerful American fighters' 0.5 inch guns — it would, like the Skua, become a fire death trap to the pilot. Its early success, such as it had without radar/ADR interception aids, was entirely due to high piloting skills in combat, using its very low wing loading to out-turn its quarry — should the quarry be inexperienced enough to indulge in a normal turning-circle dogfight.

It was possible to overcome the turning deficiency of the Seafire LIII in a turning fight with the A6M, by using the 'yo-yo' principle, taught originally at Sutton Bridge Fighter Combat School in 1943. In this form of fight, the heavier fighter avoids a circling combat situation and uses his superior speed and perhaps climb. He attacks vertically from above or below his circling enemy. He uses aileron turns in the dive and climb to rotate his aircraft and thus his guns, in the enemy's direction. The aspect then presented to the enemy, as he circles, would be a beam attack from vertically above or below him. The period of shooting would be extremely short, or course, as the range would close rapidly at the 90 degree angle-off. However, because the A6M would only be doing about 90 knots in the turn, the four degree deflection allowance of the gunsight — and over-nose visibility — was sufficent to hit. Very few hits would soon set it on fire.

Jet v jet (Phantom v MiG) combat in Vietnam was often similar. The MiG could out-turn the Phantom, but the latter, when light, had a better power/weight ratio and could climb vertically at lowish altitude. The combat was reduced to 'energy conservation', converting altitude to speed, kinetic to potential energy, and *vice versa*. Airspeeds varying from zero to supersonic, distances apart varying from ten miles (using radar to retain contact) to a few hundred feet, each avoiding the other's fire in a fantastic death struggle, until one or the other made a mistake.

(k) A note on some disadvantages of the slipper tank in Seafires, 1944 – 1945

R. J. Mitchell's team had designed the Spitfire 'overload' or 'long range' tanks to fit in close contour with the underbelly. The half inch gap between the 'slipper' tank and the underside of the fuselage was insufficient for a visual or any sort of check to be made that there was a fuel-tight fit in the pipe leading from the tank to the engine. A sliding fit was essential to allow it to be jettisoned easily, but the necessary suction-tight joint could not be guaranteed. The only check which could be made after fitting and filling up a new tank after the last one had been jettisoned, was to run the engine on the flight deck. This was not only inconvenient, it was no guarantee that the tank would still work once it got into the air. We had had three pilots unable to get their tanks to work in the air after take-off in operation 'Goodwood'. This made it almost impossible for the squadron to operate unless there was a spare deck on which to make emergency landings, before anyone else. It once again brought the Seafire into disrepute with the Admirals. The problem was not overcome until 880 Squadron reached the Pacific in the following year and 'invented' the Kittyhawk 'torpedo' tank carried on a modified bomb pylon.

The 90-gallon version of the slipper tank was intended for ferry purposes only. In the absence of anything better, 24 Wing in *Indefatigable* used this on operations. Besides its unreliability, and although the Seafire was able to withstand the half-ton of extra weight in a combat situation, the use of full power for long periods overheated its fuel lines and caused serious fuel 'aeration' (boiling) and consequent engine failure. This engine failure also occurred to the Seafires of 30 Wing when using the Kittyhawk tank, for it used identical fuel supply lines.

(l) Cause of Seafire engine failures believed at the time to have been due to enemy flak

In the last period of the Pacific operation, 30 Wing's 14 casualties had been caused as follows:

Two pilots, Bedore and Dane had been killed when their wings came off following pullouts from dives (Bedore's may have been by flak). Five had had engine failure after strafing and three of these pilots had failed to bale out or ditch satisfactorily. Seven others had crashed fatally for various reasons. Of these, one hit an Avenger in cloud; one had his engine cut out on the approach to deck land and failed to get out; one flew into the sea, got lost or got shot down in the Truk operation, having u/s r/t; one hit a radio mast when landing at Ponam; two became lost on the return to the ship and could not be found after saying they were about to bale out; one dived into the ground from probable fuel asphyxiation in Ceylon.

Of these 14 fatalities in 360 operational sorties and some 3,000 flying hours, only one pilot had certainly been shot down or had been killed by enemy action. All the remainder, except two, were probably attributable to the Seafire III itself and its unsuitable modification state to meet safety requirements for the job it was trying to do in the Pacific. The Seafire III was therefore at least six times as dangerous as the enemy. To have had but one certain enemy-action casualty (Dougy Yate) in 30 Wing instead of the assumed seven flak casualties, would have further convinced Vian that we were "failing to do our utmost".

The cause of engine failure, certainly to Graham and Patullo (who were killed) and probably Saxe and Tucker (who ditched and were rescued), was undoubtedly due to a peculiar fuel supply problem. The Seafire/Spitfire's main supply fuel pipe from the main tank lay close to the hot supercharger casing. With the huge overload tank in use, the fuel in this pipe would have been stationary for an hour or more while fuel was being sucked up from the Kittyhawk tank. During this long period, the main supply pipe itself would get very hot, uncooled by a flow of cool petrol from the insulated main tank further aft, and very near the over-boosted supercharger casing. During this time it was drawing fuel from a long-range tank, designed to be used only for ferry flights at economical cruise power settings, in *temperate climates at high altitude*. The temperature of the main delivery pipe from the main tank would be well above the boiling point of petrol (which at normal pressure is about 75 degrees Centigrade). It would boil the moment the vapour pressure in the pipe was reduced by the operation of the supply cock to 'On', when changing tanks from the 'jett' tank to partly-used main tank. Because we carried half our total fuel in the 'jett' tank, the change-over to main tank would always have to occur when more than half the flight had been completed and usually when the engine was very hot after the use of combat power, just after the final strafing run. Once the fuel had vaporised in the empty line the centrifugal pump would run dry and overheat and cause the engine to catch fire — as in Saxe's case. The failure in the Seafire III's fuel supply is, in fact, analogous to the fuel vapour lock sometimes experienced by some old cars when they are left in the sun after a hard, summer's drive.

(m) The Seafire XV. Some early problems

The first Spitfire to be flown with the new Griffon engine was flown by Jeffrey Quill in November 1941. In October 1944, he carried out the decklanding trials of the Seafire 46 and 47 in *Pretoria Castle,* and happened to be joined by Buster Hallett who was doing a few in the Seafire XV at the time. When I visited the Fifth Sea Lord on 8 December 1944 to ask whether we could take some Mark XVs with us to the Pacific, they were still not ready.

Thus, when we eventually received our first three XVs in Australia in November 1945, we were very proud of them. Three weeks afterwards, on 27 November, we were paid a visit at Schofields by the Australian Naval C-in-C. Not suspecting the Seafire's XV's potential dangers, we arranged a small flying display.

After an impressive balbo of all 36 Seafires, it was S/Lt Norton's turn. He was to do a solo demonstration in one of our Seafire XVs. In his display he was to carry out a slow roll on take-off followed by an immediate loop, to a fast run over the airfield at about 425 knots, then another loop and a roll-off-the-top to finish with. Like all Aussies, he was an experienced Spitfire pilot and knew exactly what he was doing. Lieutenant George Willcocks, DSC, RNVR, writing from Australia in 1984 writes of this incident:

"He went in just beyond the Wardroom. The aircraft broke up in mid-air and the starboard wing fell off. The engine travelled on for a mile with its prop still spinning, and set fire to some trees off the airfield. It was a tragedy, for Norton's parents were watching and so was his fiancée. He was due to marry next day with a large squadron party laid on."

The Board of Enquiry found that it was "Pilot Error". They said he was exceeding the limit of 425 knots IAS.

I was not at all happy about this, neither was Nat Gould or Ian Lowden of the Aussie's Flight. Norton would not have done anything so stupid. My own experiments for the next two days revealed that both of our remaining Seafire XVs became left-wing-low at speeds above 400 knots. By 450 knots, all the aircraft had become so left-wing-low that strong aileron forces were required to keep laterally level. I looked across to the starboard wing, the one which had first come off Norton's aircraft, and saw that the up-going aileron angle was much greater than usual, yet the down-going aileron on the port wing had barely moved at all. It was obvious that the control wires were stretching and that the aileron on the starboard wing was 'upfloating' a great deal. I thought that this might be a very dangerous state of affairs at high IAS, as I had not seen it happen before. Application of even harder aileron to raise the left wing had no effect and, if the speed was increased further in the dive, it showed signs of having the reverse effect. (The wing itself was twisting, the aileron acting as a tab, reversing the lift. No wonder Norton's wing came off, for the aileron would eventually tear off due to excessive 'upfloat' and this, and wing twist, would precipitate wing spar failure.)

I reported my findings to the ship's Senior Engineer Officer and he grounded all our new Seafires and those in the delivery pipeline at Brisbane. I had explained that I had thought that the large aileron forces to hold the right wing down were required at these very high speeds to offset the anti-torque twist built-in to the Griffon-powered version of the Spitfire. As 425 knots — the limit set in the Pilot's Notes — could easily be exceeded even in a shallow dive, we should be losing wings and pilots all the time in 801, unless something was done to improve things. The technical fault — well-known to aircraft designers — is correctly described as 'aileron reversal'.

Within two months, a party of aircraft technicians from the UK arrived. They stripped off the skin behind the main spar on the top surface of each wing root and replaced it with skin of a far thicker gauge. To be able to remedy this defect so quickly, it was obvious that the manufacturers had recently struck the snag themselves — 'aileron reversal' — but hoped that we in 801 would manage until they could get round to the remedy in Australia. After the modifications, we had no further trouble with wing twist, even when we exceeded 425 knots 'accidentally' by a further 50 knots or so.

The second lethal shortcoming of the Seafire XV was a supercharger fault. The 'self-change' mechanism from one blower speed to the higher speed was similar in action to the automatic clutch and gearbox of a car. When changing blower speeds on the climb, the blower speed of about 15,000 rpm had to be speeded up to about 20,000 rpm in a matter of seconds. If the clutch gripped too tightly it would strip the gears. If it gripped too loosely it would burn out. In both failures the engine would lose its supercharger and it would stop, catch fire, misfire or overheat. The only method of avoiding such failures was to engage the gear manually at reduced rpm. This was not always possible, neither did it always work, for there were several fatal engine failures.

There was a third shortcoming, much more involved and difficult for us to understand. One of the most welcome characteristics of the Seafire III had been its rapid acceleration, allowing it to take-off from the flight deck in 180-200 feet without the aid of a catapult for which it had been unnecessarily adapted. When the Australians in 801 took their first, halting, steps in our carrier training programme in January 1946, they tried to practice short take-offs — as on a flight deck — at Schofields. One just missed our flight huts as it swooped off the runway in a semi-stalled turn to the right, totally out of control. Pilots found that the extra 1000 horsepower of the Griffon VI, turning the other way to a Merlin, gave far more torque reaction. This was because of several factors, not just because of the increased engine power. First, the propeller was twisting the slipstream far more than in the Merlin engined version, for it had to absorb nearly twice the power in a propeller of the same diameter and at the same rpm. Second, the 'three point' unstick incidence of the Seafire XV was greater and nearer the stall, owing to the longer stroke oleos. Third, the aircraft weighed a ton-and-a-half more than the Seafire III, and therefore needed to unstick at a higher airspeed than the Seafire III. The static torque from the engine attempting to turn the aircraft in the opposite direction to the propeller was not the main reason for the trouble at take-off, for the torque on its own could be easily corrected by upfloating the port aileron a couple of degrees. It was only equivalent to a 200 lb weight on the port wing abreast the outer gun, and was not serious. The main cause of the 'right-wing-low' at take-off, or 'torque stall' as it was wrongly called, was a partial stall of the entire starboard wing. With two tons of lift on the port wing and very little indeed on the starboard, it was small wonder that the aircraft carried out a full half turn of a spin to the right, at unstick, on occasion.

At the moment of unstick, if the aircraft were 'wrenched off' at maximum incidence, both wings would be very near stalling incidence. The slightest dissimilarity in their airflow would upset the balance of lift between the port wing and the starboard — too great to correct by aileron. In the case of the Seafire XV, the starboard wing root stalled first as it was subjected to greater slipstream incidence. This stall then spread outboard, until the wing started to lose lift. The starboard wing then started to drop and in doing so, increased its incidence yet more, and fully stalled. Attempting to raise it with aileron would make matters worse.

In the case of a 'minimum distance' take-off on the flight deck when the pilot was pulling back on the stick to get off as soon as possible, the starboard wing might not establish a proper airflow, and therefore lift, at all.

Once the starboard wheel's lateral steadying effect was gone as the aircraft left the deck and flew over the ship's bow, it was inevitable that it spun to the right, into the sea, right in the path of the carrier. Further causes of this trouble might have been due to a gyroscopic 'kick' to the right if the pilot pulled the nose up too sharply at unstick, or it might have been that 'Woolworth' carriers, such as those used by 801 in their carrier work-up, had particularly bluff bows, and the upward airflow over the bow might have aggravated the situation. With insufficient left rudder available, and perhaps with too much aileron to raise the starboard wing, the aircraft would be 'pro-spin' at a speed at or near the stall. It was almost inevitable that the Seafire XV spun under these circumstances. It is interesting to note that the port wing root of the Blackburn Skua aircraft had a lift spoiler fixed to its leading edge — on its *down*-going propeller side, to equalise the stall characteristics between port and starboard wing when power was on.

Happily, a later Mark of Seafire — the 47 — was fitted with a six-bladed contra-rotating propeller. This entirely cured the aileron reversal (which killed Norton) and, of course, cured the swing and wingstalling on take-off and on going round again. It also made the Seafire 47 a beautiful ground attack and air-to-air combat aircraft, requiring no rudder trimming in the dive, and with no gunnery or rocket aiming errors due to skid caused by propeller gyroscopic effects (as in the five-bladed Seafire 17), and with slipstream yaw effects a thing of the past. In addition, the heavier engine in all Griffon-engined Seafires forward of the CG, had cancelled the need for the 'positive weight' and other dangerous palliatives intended to cure instability. Its extra weight forward also allowed a bigger tailplane, fin and rudder plus a sting hook and retractable tailwheel. The sting hook prevented 'pecking' and hung much lower than the original 'A' frame hook. The Griffon engine was also fitted with a Coffman starter which allowed a flight deck free of starter trollies.

Later versions of the Griffon in the Seafire developed over 2000 hp up to heights of 20,000 feet, using a two-speed, two-stage supercharger with an intercooler between each stage and a 'ram' air intake immediately behind the propeller. The Seafire 47 could reach 10,000 feet in $2\frac{1}{2}$ minutes from a standing start carrying 200 gallons of fuel. It had geared aileron tabs which allowed a crisper rate of roll at speeds above 350 knots IAS. It had improved engine cowlings and a 'teardrop' fully transparent hood and a cut-away rear fuselage to allow rearward vision. The streamlined windscreen allowed full forward view in heavy rain without the need for a windscreen clearance scheme. Many of these improvements might have made it in time for the final landings in Japan scheduled for February/March 1946, but none would have made it for FAA use in 'Olympic II'. The Seafire/Spitfire had come a long way in ten years. It had nearly trebled its engine power and rate of climb and nearly doubled its speed. The German equivalent — the Me 109 — came nowhere near doing this in its equally long life span.

Appendix 12

Mike Banyard's unofficial report after landing aboard USS Essex, 10 August 1946

"Both Ken Newton and myself were getting short of petrol by the time we were given our 'steer' from the Tomcat and I was pretty darned glad to see what I thought was *Implacable* after about five minutes flying. However, when we got there it turned out to be one of the American carrier groups and as I had only eight gallons left and Ken had six, the boss sent us down to land on."

"Ken went down first and was allowed on after a couple of dirty darts at the deck. It got me worried to see him float into the barrier. It seemed a hell of a long time before they got his cab untangled (it was wrapped round the barrier like a couple of rattlesnakes in the mating season) and were ready to land me on."

"There was a gi-normous bang when my hook broke and as the Americans' wires are not self-centreing, I was swung to port, but luckily the starboard oleo gave way with that expensive noise — 'ge-doink' — otherwise I would have been slap in the oggin. By the way, I had expected, and got, the 'cut', about 20 feet above the round down, so the last bit was 'solo'. I had hardly stopped moving before there was a bloody great rush for bits of my prop blades. I saw at least six bods grab a large piece each and set about them with pocket knives and other tools to share them out. Meanwhile the thought of our two lovely Seafires — of all aircraft — pranging in smart succession on a famous Yankee carrier of all places, kept me swearing and thumping the sides of the fuselage in rage. Eventually some Joe came along and said: 'What's biting yer, bud?' "

"After getting out I was taken up to the Island where I had to fill in some bumph about how I was and where I came from. After this Ken and I were taken down to view the wreckage of our cabs, show them how to fold the wings and to answer a whole lot of questions, which went something like this:

Q. What kind of engine is it?
A. It's a Merlin 55 M.
Q. What horse is it?
A. About 1650 on take-off.
Q. Say, that's an awful lot for such a cute little aircraft — what speed will she do?
A. About 370 mph at rated altitude.
Q. How much smaller is this than the Spitfire?
A. It isn't. Its exactly the same size.
Q. Well goddam'. Do you mean to tell me that a cute little ship like this shot down all those flying bombs back in England? etc, etc."

"Their fighter Ready Room was made our headquarters and we were asked to keep the duty officer informed of our whereabouts. When I say Ready Room, I mean Ready Room — not a poky little hole like ours. To start with it's air conditioned. Hot coffee, fruit and sandwiches etc, are always available throughout strike days. There is a talk-back radio connected up with all places of importance — such as the Ops Room and Flying Control. There is a teletype machine giving all the latest gen on met reports from pilots still out on a strike, what is happening on various targets, what damage has been done, what targets are left and everything that is necessary for a really comprehensive and efficient briefing. All telephones work on the dial system — and there is one in every cabin as well — so there is no waiting while the operator finishes the page of his book before answering. The Strike Leader doesn't have to shout to make himself heard at a briefing as he has a microphone and amplifier that will penetrate even the loudest background. The chairs are comfortable and there is a drawer under each for goggles, helmet and other gash stuff."

"Pilots leave their flying gear hanging up along the walls. I had a look at some of it. It was of superb quality and much more comprehensive. I was glad I was not wearing my 'issue' jungle flying suit as it would have been laughed at. Their suits contain everything that one could possibly desire for a really Ritzy picnic with some luscious Pacific Island babe."

"I stayed in the Ready Room for about an hour talking to some of the pilots just back from strikes, listening to the gramophone and to their briefing. Their arrangements were very flexible and communication between strike and fighter escort was excellent. Spare pilots were provided for all sorties in case anyone went u/s on deck. Their CO or 'Skip', as he was called, came up to us after he had completed his briefing and said: 'Mighty glad to have you fellows. Just make yourselves at home. If there's anything you want, why, tell our dooty officer here and he'll fix it for you.' "

"I watched one of their land-ons . . . I got a good view from the batsman's position right aft on the roundown. They do their circuits at a steady 100 foot altitude and they are much tighter than ours. Their speeds vary between 85 and 100 knots and they are accordingly given their 'cut' at an appropriate distance from the roundown compatible with their speed. As soon as the pilot was given the 'cut', he chopped his throttle right back and one could definitely see him push the stick right forward to dive for a wire, and then yank it back, hitting the deck on three points in a 'g' stall, without bouncing."

"It looked pretty fraught at first but personally I think it's better for them for their aircraft were designed to do it that way. There was only one barrier crash and one broken tail-wheel during two days I was watching — about 350 sorties in all."

"The Flight Deck is about 100 feet longer and 20 or so feet wider than *Implacable*'s and it has a catwalk all round it and none of those blasted bits of gunnery equipment sticking up all over the place. The flight deck is not armoured. All the 'merchants' I came across were very envious of our four inches of armour. When one of those goddam Kamikaze sons of bitches hits us, boy, how we burn . . ."

"As soon as I got into the bunk room people started lashing me up with cigarettes and chewing gum and asked all the gen about Seafires, Spitfires, Typhoons and Tempests."

"The liaison between the ship's officers and the air group was excellent and their is precious little red tape between the various branches. The stores people are a complete revelation and offered to supply us with any flying kit if we needed it — so long as we only wanted one of everything. I don't think I have ever met such sincere hospitality and no-one could do enough for us. Neither was there any of the expected line-shooting and other bulsh. Exactly the opposite. There was no personal trumpet-blowing whatever, in spite of *Essex*'s history having been one of continuous battle honours since her launch."

"Ken's Seafire was ditched on the second day but mine was still on board when we left, under guard in the hangar. I think that they were going to keep it as a souvenir until they got back to a museum in the States. I heard that we were sending them a replacement prop, too. While we were on board the Jap peace proposals started. If peace arrives, they will have a hell of a job getting me airborne again."

Appendix 13

The Falklands' losses – or how Naval history repeats itself

At the very start of the Second World War, the Navy, as always, was the first to come into action. This was when the *Ark Royal* accompanied the Home Fleet into the North Sea and was near-missed by the Luftwaffe. Churchill, as First Lord, thereupon complained to Admiral Sir Dudley Pound in his Memo about the ineffectiveness of the heavy AA gunnery, which, Their Lordships had assured him, could cope on its own with any but the heaviest air attacks. It was too late for Churchill to 'walk back' on the 'Inskip' policy or attempt to alter the composition of the Fleet Air Arm immediately and to provide interceptor fighters for Fleet Defence against air attack. All he could suggest to Pound was that he should provide his gunners with more realistic practice targets — ones which travelled through the air at 250 knots instead of the unrealistic speed of 150 knots. By about 1943, all forms of AA gunnery had largely been consigned to a 'last resort' defence against skilful air attacks and there was total agreement — even amongst some of the Naval gunnery experts from Whale Island — that interceptor fighters operated from carriers with radar direction, plus strikes against adjacent enemy airfields, was the *only* sure defence. The Pacific War provided eternal proof of this.

Forty years later, these lessons had been forgotten by the Royal Navy, but by no other. As a consequence, the Battle of the Falklands in 1982 — a true Naval battle if ever there was one — was nearly lost. The technical cause of the sinking of the *Sheffield, Coventry, Ardent* and *Antelope,* at the hand of a very few, beautifully flown, but 25-year-old subsonic jets, mostly loaded with ex-World War II SAP bombs, and operating at 400 miles radius of action, was not only because the Navy retreated before Healey in 1964 and hoped it could do without its fixed-wing FAA, but that it had also entirely forgotten every lesson learned in the Pacific War and at Salerno about the threat from low-flying aircraft. They had also forgotten that this method of low level attack against surface shipping and ground targets was *exclusively* used from 1944 onwards, not only by 801 and 880 Squadrons, but by all fighter/bomber-type aircraft and by Kamikazes. It was the only feasible method of getting under the radar and airborne air defences and to arrive at the target in one piece, with the enemy un-alerted and with its finger not poised on every trigger.

It is therefore beyond reason why the Royal Navy had failed in the Falklands to provide itself with an effective low-level air defence for its convoy and its surface fleet. Furthermore, before a defence system against low flying attack can begin to operate effectively beyond the range of 20 miles — or have warning of enemy airborne approach for longer than two minutes — the fleet would have to have provided itself with 'look down' or Airborne Early Warning (AEW) radar, complete with an airborne ADR set-up with airborne 'stop-me-and-buy-ones'.

The Royal Navy issued its first Staff Requirement for AEW in December 1943. This followed the experiences they had had with the low-flying Fw 190s and the 'ground clutter' on their ships' radar from the high ground ashore at Salerno. American ANAPS-20 radar — a result of US and RN initiative — appeared, eventually, in time for the Korean war. On 7 July 1951, Acting Lt/Cdr John Treacher formed 849 (AEW) Squadron, using Skyraiders. 'Tomcat' cruisers and destroyers were a thing of the past. The Skyraiders were replaced later by Gannets, which continued to supply AEW for the Navy from February 1960 until *Ark Royal* sailed for the breaker's yard in December 1978.

The AEW AN-APS20F in the Gannet AEW gave low flying approach warning for a distance of 200 miles from the Fleet centre in all directions. Without it, the fleet was blind and, with or without fighters, they were nearly defenceless too.

The American version of the Gannet — the Grumman Hawkeye — had a complete ADR crew 'in shirt sleeves' working in its pressurised rear fuselage. I flew it in 1963 and it was marvellous to see four 'stop-me-and-buy-ones', using 'potted' radar and huge 'TV' screens, controlling the fighter contents of two US carriers 16,000 feet below us and plotting the courses, speeds, altitudes and types of aircraft of all the traffic movements in and out of Kennedy airport 100 miles away — 500 separate plots in all.

The lack of AEW in the Falklands caused even the man-in-the-street to remark on it. I, too, wrote to the *Telegraph* in early May 1982 — on reading that a retired Admiral was suggesting that what the Navy needed in the Falklands was *more guns!* I wrote:

"When a task force is outside the range of its own airfields and within the range of enemy airfields, no amount of gunnery or missile magic, or anti-missile magic, can defend it on its own."

"The second layer of defence, by guns, suggested by Rear-Admiral A. F. Casewell are insufficient. Rear-Admiral Woodward (the Naval Commander in the Falklands) would be less worried if he had three more layers in the Falklands."

"The most important of these three layers is the provision of AEW radar of the type available to the US Navy but not available to us since the demise of the large carrier."

"The next two layers not available to Rear-Admiral Woodward are those giving strike and fighter protection of the type afforded by the Buccaneer and the Phantom."

"The first of these aircraft would prevent most of the enemy aircraft from getting airborne, let alone getting within missile firing range of our forces. The second of these types of aircraft would stop a large number of the enemy aircraft from getting within firing range."

"Then if all this fails, as experience has shown it will on occasion, the ship's missiles take over *as a last resort.*"

The NATO Atlantic Commander, when speaking of the cause of the Falklands War, ie the failure of the Naval Deterrent, said:

"If the UK had had one carrier of the *Kennedy's* (or *Ark Royal's*) capability, she would not have had a Falklands, as there would have been no way a Super-Etendard or an A4D Skyhawk would have got near such a force."

The Chief of the Air Staff (CAS) in Britain at that time, Air Vice-Marshal Sir Keith Williamson, had no illusions about the effectiveness of missiles for air defence against moving targets. He said:

"While long-range stand-off missiles (although costing £100,000 each) show prospects of becoming fairly effective against fixed targets, moving targets provide a problem of quite a different order."

"We are nowhere near the stage when weapons can effectively discriminate between friendly and enemy targets in the battle area or between high and low value targets further back."

"At the present time the human brain (in a fighter) remains the first and most flexible computer available to us."

Even small mistakes in high technological warfare — often made because of lack of training realism in peacetime — can be fatal. But the size of the mistake made by the Royal Navy in not having AEW radar in the Falklands to defend its surface Fleet and to provide cover for the amphibious landings, has probably never been exceeded by a reputable Navy in contemporary history.

But what does the Royal Navy itself think of its Falklands' performance? Does it see the Falklands as a success? How does it account for its huge losses against a small airforce, operating from its bases 400 miles away and using, with one exception, World War II bombs and 25-year-old subsonic aircraft?

The following is an excerpt from a 1982 Naval publication sent to certain retired Senior Naval Officers, to keep them in touch. It is issued by a Department of the Ministry of Defence and carries with it the signature and approval of the First Sea Lord.

The First Sea Lord begins by congratulating the Merchant Navy for their fine co-operation with the Royal Navy and praises the dedication and courage of its officers and men. The Royal Fleet Auxiliaries and the dockyards also share his congratulations. He then goes on to say, on the subject of Maritime Power:

"The low level of conflict (since World War II) has probably been due to an amalgam of deterrence and respect for international law. The effect of international law as a stabilising factor is, however, less and less certain. Scarcely any aspect of the Law of the Sea has been free of contention. The Falklands Operation demonstrated yet again the value of maritime power with its inherent flexibility *derived from a balanced fleet to deal with the unforeseen."* (Sic.)

How balanced? How unforeseen? Later in the Naval publication, a Royal Navy weapons officer accounts for the failures. This is what he said:

"Vulnerability of Surface Ships."

"Vulnerability cannot be measured in terms of losses alone, but in what was achieved."

"The Argentinians chose to attack at *wavetop height* in an effort to avoid our air defence. *Coventry* (and *Sheffield*) in exposed positions well forward from the main task group, were *overwhelmed* by several waves of attacking aircraft. *Ardent* and *Antelope* were employed along the gunline of San Carlos to protect the amphibious landing and were *robbed of the main effect of their sensors and weapons by the (high) terrain."*

Whoever wrote this could not have been aware of the world around him — neither can those in the Admiralty have been aware — to allow such excuses to go out to the public. "Wave top" approach and attacks have been current practice since Salerno in 1943. It was and is the *only* feasible method of attack, whether by missile or by aircraft. The Japanese and Americans and ourselves used it almost exclusively as a means of avoiding radar detection. This "wave-top approach", together with 30 Wing's co-ordinated methods, were written into Naval Air Fighting Instructions as standard drill, 30 years ago. Likewise the author of the excuses mentions that the two cruisers — used 'Iceberg' as radar 'Tomcat' pickets — were "overwhelmed", implying that it was not because of the ineffectiveness of the Navy's defence but by the large number of enemy aircraft. The result would have been identical had they been underwhelmed. In any case, those present saw but a couple of aircraft at any one time within 20 miles of their ships. The "robbing effect" of high ground was, of course, fully experienced by Admiral Vian at the landings at Sicily and Salerno in 1943 when the Fw 190s did as they pleased on the landing beaches even with ten Seafire CAP overhead. There was nothing new about that. The Argentine A4D Air Force and Etendard Navy pilots knew, as every airman knows, that masthead radar cannot see further than 20 miles, owing to the earth's screening curvature. *Coventry* — sunk by two bombs dropped by Captain M. Velasco — armed with the Sea Dart, Sea Cat and 114 mm gun, can only shoot at targets she can 'see', that is to say, high-flying targets. This fact was known and accepted in 1963 when this class of ships were designed, for in 1963 there was still a FAA with sufficient fighters and AEW in being to take care of the main low-flying threat.

The Sea Harrier defence had had to withdraw from the Islands at the time of the actions mentioned above. This was because the carrier *Hermes* could no longer operate within range of the Argentinian airbases safely without, at least, the small improvement in radar warning that the 'Tomcats' *Sheffield* and *Coventry* had, up to the time they were sunk, given her. The Sea Harriers therefore had insufficient range to provide CAP over San Carlos. This also left *Antelope* and *Ardent* without fighter cover, for the Sea Harriers had but 45 minutes endurance and carried but a third of the weaponload of say, a Phantom for a third of the distance and for a third of the time. Furthermore even if the Sea Harriers could have reached San Carlos, the absence of AEW and ADR radar there would have limited their effectiveness in the interception role, even though they had their own AI. *Ardent* and *Antelope* were therefore being "employed along the gunline" at San Carlos much as they might have been at Suda Bay, 70 years before: and with the same tragic results.

The Argentinians admitted a grand total of airborne losses of 35 (55 airmen killed) not 72, out of their 80-90 'attack' planes — Mirage IIIs and Vs and A4D Skyhawks, plus a few Etendards. According to Spanish-American on-the-spot investigation, the discrepancy between the two figures can be traced almost entirely to the San Carlos battles of 21-27 May. Here, the gun and missile crews claimed 31, whereas the Argentinians and the investigators claim that the loss was six, three only of which were at the Bay itself. So far as the Sea Harriers' claim of a total of 24 is concerned — or 'about half' the RN's official claim of 51 — it would seem that the Royal Navy, the investigators and the Argentinians all agree. In fact, the Argentinians give the Sea Harriers three more than the 24 they claim. This means that the Sea Harriers shot down 27 aircraft out of the grand total of airborne losses admitted of 35, in 1435 sorties from *Invincible* and *Hermes,* an extraordinary achievement in the conditions at that time. The Sea Harriers' official losses were six aircraft. Two were lost to ground fire (one pilot killed) and four in accidents of various kinds (three aircrew killed). It is interesting to note the words of Captain Uneta, one of the A4D pilots escorting a Super Etendard to attack a target they supposed was *Invincible:* "It was noticeable that there were very few CAP after the attack".

The claim by the gunners for 31 kills instead of the actual three or six they achieved, is exactly in accord with the exaggeration of wartime claims for AA fire from RN ships under intense air attack. They actually believed their claims and probably still do. When an enemy plane is seen to go down — whether it is just diving below the skyline or is actually shot down — and up to half a dozen guns and missile systems are, and have been, shooting at it from positions miles apart, it is beyond the wit of man to cut their separate claims to one or zero. The sad part of it seems to be that the myth of missile and anti-missile effectiveness (to say nothing of the current hopes for 'SDI') will doubtless be allowed to persist, nourished by the powerful weapons establishments and manufacturers, unquestioned by a sufficient number of airmen in the Admiralty and propped up by the optimistic results achieved in unrealistic peacetime firing exercises.

The First Sea Lord in 1982 officially referred to the Royal Navy and its surface forces as "well balanced and able to deter". When operating on its own outside the air protection of the US carrier fleets, it is obviously neither of these things; and for the senior Admiral of such a fine Service to have said this, merely emphasises the general ignorance of air matters amongst his staff, far greater than existed in 1939 when Churchill complained of AA ineffectiveness.

The RN College of Dartmouth teaches its young men, for the first four years, to be Naval officers in one of the finest courses for leadership that any Navy could devise. It is surely a privilege to be selected for such. However, the input on air matters consists of about two lectures per month by a visiting officer from Yeovilton — a hundred miles away. Then, after these four years at Dartmouth, they become locked up in their 'specialisations' and, unless they are the two RN permanent commissioned officers per year who elect to fly Sea Harriers, they will hardly touch the subject of aircraft and airborne defence against air attack for the remainder of their career. How else would it be possible for this great Service to be so complacent, so self-satisfied and seemingly so ignorant of air matters as to allow its First Sea Lord to write such excuses for the Argentine losses in a Naval publication?

Small remedies have now been applied to improve Naval air defence, just as in 1939, following Churchill's complaint, small remedies were made to the Navy's effectiveness in AA training. In 1984, the Navy's remedy was to re-form 849 Squadron with eight AEW-equipped Sea Kings.

All eight cannot do the work of a single Hawkeye, neither can these extremely vulnerable, slow moving, low altitude, short endurance aircraft give more than five minutes warning compared with the 20 minutes warning of a Hawkeye/Phantom combination.

Of the three Services, the Navy is the least likely to survive the next non-NATO-assisted confrontation, for it is the least likely to agree with its latter-day wartime Admirals that *it is first necessary to command the air* before commanding the sea, and that large numbers of men in the air are still necessary to do this.

Appendix 14

List of Squadrons and Names

(i) 813F Squadron, HMS Eagle – Malta Convoys

King-Joyce	'Spike' J	Lt	RN
Crosley	Mike	S/Lt	RNVR
Spedding	Bob	S/Lt	RNVR
Bullivant	Bernard	S/Lt	RNVR

(ii) 800 Squadron, HMS Biter (for 'Torch')

Bruen	Bill	Lt/Cdr	DSO, DSC, RN
Muir-Mackensie	Hamish	Lt	RN
King-Joyce	'Spike'	Lt	RN
Roberts	Bill	S/Lt (A)	DSC, RN
Roncoroni	Chris	S/Lt	RNR
Ritchie	Bill	S/Lt	RNVR
Bannister	Maurice	S/Lt	RNVR
Outwin	Bill	S/Lt	RNVR
Thompson	Andrew	S/Lt	RNVR
Thompson	'Greyhound'	S/Lt	RNVR
Crosley	Mike	S/Lt	DSC, RNVR
Hooker	John	S/Lt	RNZNVR
Hastings	John	S/Lt	RNVR
Yate	Dougy	S/Lt	RNVR
Young	'Junior'	S/Lt	RNVR
Hoare	'Sammy'	S/Lt	RNVR

(iii) 804 Squadron, HMS Dasher (after 'Torch')

Sewel	Jackie	Lt/Cdr	DSC, RNVR
Crossman	Jimmy	Lt	DSC, RNVR
Crosley	Mike	S/Lt	DSC, RNVR
McLennan	'Piggy'	S/Lt	RNZNVR
Goodfellow	Norman	S/Lt	RNVR
Burgham	Al	S/Lt	RNVR
Tait	Murdoch	S/Lt	RNVR
Barker	John	S/Lt	RNVR
Bullen	'Snottie' J.	Mid	RNVR
Mearns	Sam	S/Lt	RNVR
Yate	Dougy	S/Lt	RNVR
Oaks	'Titus'	Capt	RM
Cranwell	Bob	S/Lt	RNVR

List of Pilots' Names

30 Wing Leader – Cdr Colin Campbell-Horsfall, DSC, RN

(iv)   880 Squadron

Crosley	Mike	Lt/Cdr	DSC, RNVR
††Goodfellow	Norman	Lt	DSC, RNVR
SP			
††Simpson	Bob	Lt	RNVR
Boardman	Ken	S/Lt	RNVR
††Pye	'Crusty' J.	S/Lt	DSC, RNVR
Banyard	Mike	Mid	RNVR
Smith	Hugh	S/Lt	RNVR
Crabtree	Nigel	S/Lt	RNVR
Dixon	Peter	S/Lt	RNVR
††Arkell	Pete	S/Lt	RNVR
Watson	'Chiefy' P.	CPO	
Simpson	Len	S/Lt	RNVR
Bethem	'Legs'	S/Lt	RNVR
††Leighton	Claude	S/Lt	RNZNVR
Boak	John	Lt	RCNVR
††Kirby	Dennis	S/Lt	RNVR
Wager	Brian	S/Lt	RNVR
Graham	David N.	S/Lt	RNVR
Armstrong	Bob	S/Lt	RNVR
††Dancaster	Dicky	S/Lt	RNVR
Dent	Alan	S/Lt	RNVR
Snell	Alan	S/Lt	RNVR
Penfold	Ian	Mid	RNVR
††Yate	Dougy	Lt	RNVR
Gilmore	Ray	S/Lt	RNVR
Marshall	John	S/Lt	RNVR
Newton	'Isaac' K.	S/Lt	RNVR
††Singleton	Tim	Lt	RNVR
Wheeldon	Tim	S/Lt	RNVR
Tucker	Alan	S/Lt	RNVR
Patullo	Doug	S/Lt	RNVR
Smith	Hugh	S/Lt	RNVR
Scott	Jack	S/Lt	RNVR

801 Squadron

SP			
††Jewers	Stuart	Lt/Cdr	RNVR
Brewer	Bill	Lt	RN
Record	Pete	S/Lt	RNVR
Dane	Frank	S/Lt	RNVR
††Sax	Ray	S/Lt	RNVR
Thompson	Graham	S/Lt	RNVR
Watson	'Tinto'	S/Lt	RNVR

Cowley	Dennis	S/Lt	RNVR
Payne	Mervin	S/Lt	RNVR
Geary	Monk	S/Lt	RNVR
Holway	'Scratch'	S/Lt	RNVR
Steel	Alec	S/Lt	RNVR
††Luing	Peter	Lt	RNVR
Seigne	Paddy P.	S/Lt	RNVR
Coates	'Eric'	S/Lt	RNVR
Davies	'Dai'	S/Lt	RNVR
††Primrose	Jim	S/Lt	RNVR
Stock	Paul	S/Lt	RNVR
Temple	Gerry	S/Lt	RNVR
††Gunson	Dave	S/Lt	RNVR
††Griffith	Bill	Lt	RNVR
Lossee	Bill	S/Lt	RNVR
Miller	Eric	S/Lt	RNVR
Clarke	Mark	S/Lt	RNVR
††Green	Chris	S/Lt	RNVR
Glazebrook	Garry	S/Lt	RNZNVR
Sheeran	Jimmy	S/Lt	RNZNVR
Squires	'Bill'	S/Lt	RNZNVR
Tillet	'Ben'	S/Lt	RNZNVR
Joly	John	S/Lt	RNVR
Clayton	'Phil'	S/Lt	RNVR
Bedore	Glen	S/Lt	RCNVR
††McLean	Nigel	Lt	RNVR
Jervis	Joe	S/Lt	RNVR
Anderson	Dig	S/Lt	RNZNVR

(After amalgamation of 880 and 801, into 801 Squadron, 21 August 1945)

††Gould	'Nat'	Lt	DFC, RANVR
††Lowden	Ian	Lt	DSC, DFC, RANVR
Norton	Jim	S/Lt	RANVR
Willcocks	George	Lt	DSC, RANVR
Foulkes	'Junior'	S/Lt	RANVR
Armstrong	Kay	Lt	RANVR
††Phillips	P. H.	Lt	RNVR
Fraser	Ian	S/Lt	RANVR
O'Connor		Lt	RANVR
Miller		Lt	RANVR
Laser		S/Lt	RANVR
Spencer-Brown		Lt	RANVR
Culling	Nev	S/Lt	RNVR
Dowle	'Bernie'	S/Lt	RNVR
Montgomery		S/Lt	RNVR
Anderson	'Andy'	S/Lt	RNZNVR
Hamblet	'Hammy'	S/Lt	RNVR

Note:
†† = Flight Leaders
SP = Senior Pilot

Wing Leader Cdr Colin Campbell-Horsfall, DSC, RN
880 Squadron

Crosley	Mike (CO),	Lt/Cdr	DSC
†Goodfellow	Norman (SP)	Lt	DSC
†Simpson	Bob	Lt	
†Pye	'Crusty' E.	S/Lt	DSC
†Leighton	Claude	S/Lt	
† *Yate	Dougy	Lt	
†Dancaster	Dicky	S/Lt	
† **Richardson	D. C.	Lt	
† **Turnbull	Neville	Lt	
**Fraser	Ian (NZ)	S/Lt	
Boak	John (Can)	Lt	
†Kirby	Dennis	S/Lt	
†Arkell	Peter	S/Lt	
***Marshall	John	S/Lt	
Dent	Alan	S/Lt	
*Graham	David N. (NZ)	S/Lt	
Banyard	Mike	Mid	
*Patullo	J.	S/Lt	
*Penfold	Ian	Mid	
*Boardman	Ken	S/Lt	
*Armstrong	Bob	S/Lt	
Dixon	Peter (NZ)	S/Lt	
Simpson	Len	S/Lt	
Seigne	'Paddy'	S/Lt	
Snell	Alan	S/Lt	
Letham	'Legs'	S/Lt	
Wheeldon	Tim	S/Lt	
† ***Singleton	Tim	S/Lt	
Watson	'Chiefy'	CPO	
Crabtree	David	S/Lt	
***Newton	'Isaac'	S/Lt	
***Joly	John	S/Lt	
***Gilmore	Ray	S/Lt	
Smith	Hugh	S/Lt	
Wager	Brian	S/Lt	
Tucker	Alan	S/Lt	
***Scott	Jack	S/Lt	

801 Squadron

Jewers	Stuart (CO)	Lt/Cdr	DSC
†Brewer	Bill (SP)	Lt	DSC
†Saxe	Ray	Lt	
†Luing	Peter	Lt	
†Gunson	Dave	S/Lt	
†Green	Chris	S/Lt	
†Griffith	Bill	S/Lt	

†McLean	Nigel	Lt
Sheeran	Jimmy (NZ)	S/Lt
Jervis	Bill	S/Lt
Losee	Bill (Can)	S/Lt
Thomson	Graham	S/Lt
Cowley	Dennis	S/Lt
*Dane	Frank	S/Lt
Primrose	Jim	S/Lt
Stock	Paul (Can)	S/Lt
Geary	Monk (Can)	S/Lt
Glazebrook	Garry (NZ)	S/Lt
*Glennie	J.	S/Lt
*Payne	Mervin	S/Lt
Temple	Gerry	S/Lt
Steel	Alec	S/Lt
Holway	'Scratch'	S/Lt
***Wright	J.	S/Lt
Clark	'Mark'	S/Lt
***Clayton	Phillip	S/Lt
Watson	'Tinto'	S/Lt
*Squires	'Bill'	S/Lt
* ***Tillet	'Ben'	S/Lt
Davies	'Dai'	S/Lt
* ***Bedore	Glen (Can)	S/Lt
Coates	'Eric'	S/Lt
***Miller	Eric	S/Lt
***Anderson	'Dig' (NZ)	S/Lt
***Culling	J.	S/Lt
*Record	Peter	S/Lt

On 11 August 1945, just before the Japanese cease fire, 880 and 801 were amalgamated into 801 Squadron with CO of 880 as CO of both squadrons. On arrival at Schofields near Sydney, the following joined 801 Squadron from the Fighter Pool and from the Royal Australian Air Force. The squadron finally returned to UK in *Implacable* in February 1947, Lt/Cdr Jack Routley having taken over from Lt/Cdr Mike Crosley in January 1946.

† *Lowden	Ian	Lt	DSO, DFC*, RANVR
†Gould	'Nat'	Lt	DFC, RANVR
Armstrong	Kay	Lt	DFC, RANVR
O'Connor	Jim	Lt	RANVR
Miller	'Dusty'	Lt	RANVR
Willcocks	George	Lt	DSC, RANVR
Spencer-Brown	David	S/Lt	RANVR
Norton	Jim	S/Lt	RANVR
Foulkes	'Junior'	S/Lt	RANVR
†Phillips	P. H.	S/Lt	RNVR
Culling	'Nev'	S/Lt	RNVR
Hamblet	E. W.	S/Lt	RNVR
Montgomery	P.	S/Lt	RNVR

Notes:
†	=	Flight Leaders
*	=	Killed on operations
**	=	Left before *Implacable* sailed for Pacific
***	=	Joined in Pacific
(NZ)	=	RNZNVR
(Can)	=	Canadian
(SP)	=	Senior Pilot
(CO)	=	Squadron Commanding Officer

Index